A Guide to

Theses and Dissertations

A Guide to
Theses and Dissertations

An Annotated, International
Bibliography of Bibliographies

by

Michael M. Reynolds

Gale Research Company
Detroit, Michigan 48226

Copyright © 1975 by Michael M. Reynolds

**Library of Congress
Cataloging in Publication Data**

Reynolds, Michael M
  A guide to theses and dissertations.

  Includes indexes.
  1. Bibliography--Bibliography--Dissertations, Academic. I. Title.
Z5053.R49   016.013'379   74-11184
ISBN 0-8103-0976-9

Printed in the United States of America

Contents*

*Only a few subdivisions are indicated in some sections. Specific subjects can be located in the index.

Contents

Introduction

Purpose

This bibliography attempts to call attention to and thereby make available to the researcher a form of study, theses and dissertations, which is most difficult to identify and which is, consequently, under utilized. Theses and dissertations, undertaken in partial fulfillment of the academic degree beyond the bachelor, are a significant segment of the literature of all fields as they record concentrated research--frequently original-- on special topics, represent an initiative in research which may contribute to work already in progress or point the direction for future areas of study, and review previous research on the subject.

The requirements for making the information in a dissertation public vary among countries and institutions. With the notable exception of Great Britain, up to World War II it was frequently the responsibility of the candidate to have a small number (100-200 copies) of his dissertation printed. However, the increase in printing costs, as well as the greater number of students involved in doctoral work, has resulted in a withering away of this requirement. Theses are rarely printed.

Although there has been an increasing concern for bringing dissertations to the attention of prospective users[1]--in some countries and in some fields there has been an ongoing attempt to furnish a record of the work at the doctoral level--and both professional associations and individuals have been responsible for compiling extensive bibliographies covering dissertations, the total of the bibliographic control in this area is fragmentary, with little international coverage. And on the level of the masters' theses and work-in-progress, for all practical purposes, bibliographic control does not exist.

[1]In the United States a commercial firm has developed an extensive bibliographic and distribution system.

Introduction

In those instances when printing or publication took place (in actuality, theses and dissertations receive little attention from commercial publishers) it follows that the combination of copyright deposit or legal deposit and a bibliography on the order of a national bibliography, such as the <u>Bibliographie de la France</u>, the Library of Congress <u>Catalog of Books Represented by Library of Congress Printed Cards</u>, and the <u>National Union Catalog</u> represents a most valuable source of identification. In addition, while many academic institutions issue annual listings of their dissertations and/or theses--a diminishing practice--these receive only limited acceptance and unless the researcher is familiar with those institutions which are especially strong in a distinct discipline or employ a particular faculty member, these have limited scanning value. Theses and dissertations are for the most part in typescript and remain unknown, unless among that small percentage which is carried in part or as abstracts in professional journals (they are very rarely printed in full), in which case they may be indexed in standard bibliographies.

While it was originally intended that this be a subject bibliography, since researchers using this type of material are more concerned with works on a subject than with the works by an individual, sections covering universal, national, and special/racial group bibliographies were included in order to provide the possibility of identifying the work of individuals known to the searcher and an additional option for systematically assessing relevant materials.

Background Information

The origins of today's theses and dissertations lie in the Middle Ages, when the lecture and the disputation complemented each other in the educational milieu. The lecture was in the form of systematic and critical commentaries on previous work, disquisitions wherein a subject was presented and analyzed, and <u>summae</u> that comprehensively synthesized a subject field. The disputation took place between protagonists of differing doctrinal positions or between an individual who maintained a thesis and opponents (examiners). The lecture provided the arguments for the debate and the debate an opportunity for displaying competence as a teacher. By the time of the 14th century the Thomastian format had been established in academia. This began with (1) a question (problem statement); (2) a review of authorities which had previously dealt with the question; (3) an answer to the question; and (4) a presentation of evidence against positions which were contrary to the proposed solution to the question.

University teaching was controlled by the teachers' guild

and, as a member, the teacher carried the title of master, while students were considered as apprentice teachers engaged in attaining membership in the guild. Students, accordingly, practiced giving lectures and arguing theses. Master teachers, on the other hand, sought to protect their reputations by requiring their students first to engage them in a public disputation and, subsequently, to defend their theses against a group of examiners. If successful, the student became a bachelor or assistant teacher.

The titles accompanying levels of academic achievement, like the format of the academic exercise, retain features which were developed in the Middle Ages. As master teachers, teachers were entitled to be called masters or doctors, and regardless of faculty both terms designated teachers of higher learning. By the 13th century the use of the term doctor began to be limited only to theology and medicine, while master continued to be the designation for professors in the faculty of arts. However, as it gradually became necessary for theological students to complete a Master of Arts prior to going on to the faculty of theology, the doctor's degree developed into the higher degree. Generally, in European universities degrees are granted in the five traditional faculties of law, medicine, theology, arts, and philosophy, and the largest number of students take the degree in the faculty of philosophy. Different countries have developed differing practices of higher education. At variance, for example, are the number of years of study for the doctor's degree, the level of performance in the academic paper in undergraduate studies, and the requirement for candidates for the doctor's degree to take a preliminary master's or licentiate degree. Yet, whereas a first graduate or master's degree is not awarded in many European institutions and frequently institutions that award this degree do not require a written exercise, the doctorate (or highest) degree nearly always requires a dissertation. In this bibliography an attempt is made not to evaluate practices or quality but rather to include lists which carry items of graduate programs.

Scope

This bibliography is a retrospective international listing of bibliographies of theses and dissertations produced through 1973, which appear as separate listings. Theses are defined as work for the first graduate degree, such as the master's, diplôme, candidate; and dissertations as work for the doctoral degree, such as the Doctor of Philosophy, Doctor of Education, and Doctor of Engineering. A separate listing is defined as being devoted exclusively to theses and/or dissertations, whether appearing once or serially; a work which carries a separate section or index of theses and dissertations; or a listing of theses and disserta-

tions carried in a bibliography section. Some items are also included which do not conform to these general limitations when the
number of theses and dissertations accounts for approximately half
of the work or, in a few instances, when the item is intrinsically
so valuable as to diminish the value of this bibliography by its
exclusion.

Since this bibliography is intended to be a working tool,
it does not include the general bibliographies of theses and dissertations of a single institution or a major general academic
unit of an institution, such as the Faculty of Philosophy of German universities, as these are considered to have limited value
for bibliographic verification and for subject access. On the
other hand, if a distinct instructional unit concerned with a particular subject or a group of related subjects, such as an Institute of Germanic Studies or a Faculty of Medicine, has produced
a separate listing this is included.

This bibliography does not include collections of the full
texts of theses and dissertations, manuscript or typescript
lists, or post-doctoral academic exercises, such as Habilitationsschriften.

Arrangement

The arrangement of this bibliography is primarily by subject,
patterned somewhat after Constance M. Winchell's Guide to Reference
Books. In establishing subject categories and in going from the
general to the specific within each category and sub-category, the
arrangement attempts to provide a mechanism for approximating relationships, for demonstrating the degree of comprehensiveness in
each category, and for extending the scope of the individual items
by making them complementary. Within the category, entries tend
to be subdivided into subject and institutional listings. The
subject portion is subdivided into general works representing a
broad coverage and then subdivisions for particular fields or
topics. The general subject listings are arranged by date of
publication and the institutional listings, representing the products of single institutions, are arranged alphabetically by
institution.

Entries

Entries for this work were drawn from a variety of sources,
many of which extend over a substantial period of time. As a
consequence, the form of main entry will sometimes vary from

current practice. The entry generally follows that used by the
Library of Congress at the time of initial cataloging. A further
caveat is in order in respect to transliteration. Because of the
technical limitations in producing this work it was necessary to
take considerable liberties in romanizing non-Roman languages,
especially Cyrillic. For Cyrillic the transliteration is based
upon the scheme developed by the U.S. Board of Geographic Names.

The bibliographic entry uniquely identifies each item. In
the event of a title change the latest title is used and the entry
carries a "Title varies" note. Frequency of the bibliography
always refers to the item itself and not to the larger or serial
work in which it appears. Whenever feasible that time when the
bibliography appears within the larger work is given. While an
attempt was made to verify and examine each item this was not
always possible. Accordingly, a single question mark (?) is used
to indicate those items for which the information is reliable but
incomplete and double question marks (??) are used for those items
which appeared in a secondary source but have not been validated.
Since many of the items are ephemeral in nature, all items which
appear in a numbered series carry the series note.

With few exceptions, the descriptive annotation is based
upon a personal examination of the item. The annotation is intended to suggest succinctly the range, character, coverage, and
noteworthy features of the work. It is not evaluative nor does
its length reflect the work's value. Many of the annotations are
in two parts. The initial portion is intended to expand and
clarify the bibliographic information in the entry and to relate
the entry to previous or similar efforts. The annotation itself
is intended to indicate the following elements: (1) the level of
work, theses or dissertations, and if completed or in progress;
(2) the number of items; (3) the years within which the studies
themselves were completed; (4) the institution, institutions, or
place in which the studies were undertaken; (5) the subject coverage of the bibliography, with representative topics, preferably
taken from headings in the bibliography itself; (6) the bibliographic arrangement, which in the case of a series or a work in
parts is based upon that followed in the latest piece of the work
(the term classified is used to indicate a hierarchical structure);
(7) the indexes. Additional information is provided in those
cases when the head of the candidate's committee is given, with
the note "Entry gives name of the adviser." The annotation also
notes if the bibliography indicates the items listed are published
in whole, in part, or as abstracts in some way other than within
the regular institutional requirement for publication. Unless
indicated all items give the level of degree, the date, and the
institution in which it was taken.

Indexes

Index of Institutions

If a bibliography contains works completed within a single institution or a distinctive unit within an institution, that institution or unit is listed in this index. If the listing contains studies from two or more different institutions the bibliography is considered as a general bibliography and entries for the separate institutions are not included in this index.

Index of Names and Titles

This index indicates the standard main entry for individuals and corporate bodies directly responsible for the compilation of the bibliography, as well as groups (not commercial publishers) associated with the work, individuals and groups involved in the preparation of items referred to in the annotation, and titles of journals. It does not list the titles of monographic works or the numbered series in which items in this bibliography appear.

Subject Index

This index includes and supplements those subject headings which appear in the body of the work. It is based in large part on the Sears List of Subject Headings. In order to complement the book's arrangement an attempt was made to group items under place and broad subject. Bibliographies of work produced in a particular area are included in the subject index under place with the notation (In) following the place. Since the subjects indicated in the annotations are representative of the content of the bibliography, rather than an exhaustive listing, no attempt is made to analyze each item for inclusion in this index. The table of contents should be used in conjunction with this subject index to ascertain the location of subjects and their relationship.

Editor's note: In establishing the limits of a bibliography and at
that juncture where a bibliography reaches a point when the time
expended in searching for additional items and the diminishing
success in obtaining materials make it impractical to continue, a
bibliographer should have a sense of disquietness which comes with
the decision to stop. Accordingly, this bibliographer welcomes comments on the scope of the work and any information concerning
other bibliographies of theses and/or dissertations, later information on the items listed, or information from persons familiar
with those items which are listed but are questionable. Details
should be forwarded to the editor c/o College of Library and
Information Services, University of Maryland, College Park, Maryland 20742. Hopefully, these as well as items published since
1973 will be published as a supplement to the main listing.

A. Universal

A1. BALDINGER, Ernst G. <u>Auszüge aus den neuesten Dissertationen</u>
<u>über die Naturlehre, Arzneiwissenschaft und alle Theile der-</u>
<u>selben</u> [1 (1769-1773)] Berlin and Stralsund: Gottlieb
Auguste Lange, 1769-1773.

Six numbers in vol. 1.

Abstracts of dissertations defended in Europe arranged by place. Entry gives praeses and respondent's name.

A2. LIDÉN, Johan H. <u>Catalogus disputationum in academiis et</u>
<u>gymnasiis Sveciae, atque etiam, a Svecis, extra patriam</u>
<u>habitarum.</u> Sectio 1-5. Uppsala: Typ. Edmannianis, 1778-
1780. 606, 221, 225, 54, 63 p.

Lists approximately 13,500 items, covering the period
to 1778. In five sections: (1) Disputationes Upsalienses; (2) Disputationes Lundenses; (3) Disputationes Aboënses; (4) Disputationes gymnasticas;
(5) Disputationes synodales. Each arranged alphabetically by praeses and then chronologically under
each, with the statement of the candidate. Index
of disputants in each section.

_____ _____ <u>Ad catalogum disputationum in academiis et</u>
<u>gymnasiis Sveciae Lidenianum supplementa.</u> Addidit. Gabriel
Marklin. Uppsala: Reg. Academiae Typ., 1820. 117 p.

Follows Lidén's arrangement. Index of disputants.

Continued by:

A3. MARKLIN, Gabriel. <u>Catalogus disputationum in academiis</u>

Scandinaviae et Finlandiae Lidenianus continuatus. Sectio 1-3. Upsaliae: Reg. Academiae Typ., 1820. 262, 179, 102 p.

Lists approximately 6,000 items for the period 1778-1819. Arranged in three parts: (1) Disputationes Upsalienses; (2) Disputationes Lundenses. Disputationes Christianienses; (3) Disputationes Aboënses.

Continued by:

A4.   Catalogus disputationum in academiis Sveciae et Fenniae habitarum, Lidenianus iterum continuatus. Sectio 1-3. Uppsala: Reg. Academiae Typ., 1856. 3 vols. in 1.

Also published in Stockholm in 1874.

Covers the period 1820-1855. In three parts: (1) Disputationes Upsalienses; (2) Disputationes Lundenses; (3) Disputationes Fennorum.

A5.   LECHNER, Johann J. Catalogus dissertationum cum veterum, tum recentiorum, varii argumenti, secundum literarum ordinem conscriptus. Norimbergae: 1826. 86 p.

Vol. 1, fasc. 1, A-Buder only.

A bookseller's catalog of approximately 5,000 dissertations, arranged alphabetically by praeses.

A6.   OXFORD. University. Bodleian Library. Catalogus dissertationum academicarum quibus nuper aucta est Bibliotheca Bodleiana MDCCCXXXII. Oxford: E. Typographeo Academico, 1834. 448, 63 p.

Lists the dissertations in the Library. Arranged alphabetically under the name of the praeses. Entry gives name of respondent. Index of respondents.

A7.   THEILE, Carl G. W. Thesaurus literaturae, theologicae academicae, sive Recensus dissertationum, programmatum aliarumque commentationum theologicarum philologicarum, philosophicarum, historicarum, paedagogicarum, quae ab antiquissimis usque ad recentissima tempora editae in collectione Weigeliana Lipsiensi sunt venales. Lipsiae: T. O. Weigel, 1841. 284 p.

A classified list, further arranged alphabetically.

A8.   CALVARY, S., & Co., Berlin. <u>Verzeichnis der im [Jahrg. 1</u> <u>(1863)-Jahrg. 6 (1868)] erschienen Universitäts- und Schul-</u> <u>Schriften als Habilitations-Schriften und Dissertationen des</u> <u>philosophischen Fakultäten.</u> Berlin: 1864-1869. Annual.

       German and Austrian dissertations.

A9.   PARIS. Bibliothèque nationale. <u>Catalogue d'une collection</u> <u>de thèses publiées dans les Pays-Bas donnée à la Bibliothèque</u> <u>nationale par le Service des échanges internationaux.</u> Paris: 1884. 2 vols. ?

       Vol. 1 consists of dissertations in law; vol. 2 other subjects.

A10.   PARIS. Bibliothèque nationale. Département des imprimés. <u>Catalogue des dissertations et écrits académiques provenant</u> <u>des échanges avec les universités étrangères et reçus par la</u> <u>Bibliothèque nationale</u> [1882-1924] Paris: Klincksieck, 1884-1925. 43 vols.

       Contains only theses and dissertations received from the end of 1882, as the exchange agreements between foreign universities and the French schools were concluded in the academic year 1881-1882.

       Primarily German universities represented in early volumes but includes a number of Swiss, English, Dutch, Swedish, Russian, and Belgian items. Arranged alphabetically by universities or academies. Publications of each institution are divided by date of printing and then by format. Publications of the same university in the same year and in the same format are arranged by faculty. One sentence description in French.

A11.   JOSEPHSON, Aksel G. S. <u>Avhandlingar ock program utgivna vid</u> <u>svenska ock finska akademier ock skolor under åren 1855-1890.</u> <u>Bibliografi.</u> Uppsala: Lundequistska Bokhandelen, 1891-1897. 2 vols.

       Includes dissertations. Arranged alphabetically by author. Entry occasionally gives the name of the praeses. Classified subject index.

A12. "TITLES of Theses Accepted for the Degree of Doctor [1925-
1928]" In Commonwealth Universities Yearbook 1927: 763-790;
1928: 763-798; 1929: 757-781.

> Represents studies, including the M.D., completed
> throughout the British Empire. Arranged by univer-
> sity. Entry gives publication information.

A13. DOCTORAL Dissertations Accepted by American Universities [no.
1 (1933/1934)-22 (1954/1955)] New York: H. W. Wilson, 1934-
1956. 22 nos. in 18 vols. Annual.

> Nos. 1 (1933/1934)-3 (1935/1936) compiled for the
> National Research Council and the American Council
> of Learned Societies by the Association of Research
> Libraries; nos. 4 (1936/1937)-22 (1954/1955) com-
> piled for the Association of Research Libraries.
>
> A classified listing of completed American and Can-
> adian published and unpublished dissertations sub-
> divided by university. Provides for each published
> dissertation bibliographic data as to publication
> as a separate or as part of a series or journal.
> "Publication and Presentation" section indicates
> institutional requirements for publication and depo-
> sition and for making dissertations available out-
> side the institution. Author index.
>
> Continued by:

A14. INDEX to American Doctoral Dissertations [1955/1956-1962/
1963] Ann Arbor, Mich.: University Microfilms, 1957-1964.
Annual. 8 vols.

> Compiled for the Association of Research Libraries.
>
> Issues for 1955/1956-1956/1957 combined with Disser-
> tation Abstracts (Item A17) index and appear as its
> vol. 16, no. 13 (1956) and vol. 17, no. 13 (1957)
> with references to Dissertation Abstracts for those
> studies listed therein; 1957/1958 issued as Disser-
> tation Abstracts 18, no. 7 (1957/1958); 1959/1960-
> 1962/1963 appear as no. 13 in Dissertation Abstracts
> 20 (1959/1960)-23 (1962/1963).
>
> Lists all dissertations completed in American and
> Canadian universities. Under such major headings
> as philosophy, religion, physical sciences, earth

sciences, humanities, the studies are arranged by
discipline and subdivided by institution. Table
provides information on publication, retention, and
availability. Author index.

Continued by:

A15. AMERICAN Doctoral Dissertations [1963/1964-   ] Ann Arbor,
Mich.: University Microfilms, 1965-   . Annual.

Classified listing of dissertations accepted by
American and Canadian universities. Under each subject, the studies are subdivided by university. A
table provides information on university practices
on the publication, retention, and lending of dissertations. Author index.

A16. MUNDT, Hermann. Bio-bibliographisches Verzeichnis von Uni-
versitäts- u. Hochschuldrucken (Dissertationen) vom Ausgang
des 16. bis Ende des 19. Jahrhunderts. Leipzig: Carlsohn,
1936-1942. 2 vols.

Incomplete: covers A-Ritter.

A dealer's catalog, representing Antiquariats Carlsohn, Leipzig. Attempts to include all German dissertations, but also includes items from Sweden,
Norway, and Holland. Entry includes biographical
information. Arranged by respondent or if more
than one respondent by praeses.

A17. DISSERTATION Abstracts; Abstracts of Dissertations and Monographs Available in Microfilm [1 (1938)-26 (June 1966)]
Ann Arbor, Mich.: University Microfilms, 1938-1966. Title
varies. Monthly.

Vols. 1 (1938)-11 (1951) published as Microfilm
Abstracts.

Abstracts of dissertations from those American and
Canadian universities associated with University
Microfilms and available for purchase in microfilm
or as xerographic reproductions. Arranged by subject categories, such as agriculture, economics,
education, language and literature, and subdivided
by university. Entry gives adviser. Vols. 12 (1952)
-15 (1955) contain author and subject indexes in

each issue, cumulating annually; listings in 16 (1956)-17 (1957) comprise part of entries in Item A14, which appeared as Dissertation Abstracts 16, no. 13 (1956) and 17, no. 13 (1957); 18, nos. 1-6 (1957/1958) and 19 (1958/1959) indexed in a separately published author index; 20 (1959/1960) and 21 (1960/1961) each have separate author index; subject indexing for vols. 16 (1956)-21 (1960/1961) through Index to American Doctoral Dissertations, 1955/1956-1960/1961; 22 (1961/1962)-25 (1964/1965) contain cumulated author and subject index as no. 12, pt. 2, in each volume.

Microfilm Abstracts Author Index, Covering Volumes 1-11, 1938-1951 of Microfilm Abstracts (Now Dissertation Abstracts). Compiled by the Georgia Chapter, Special Libraries Association. Atlanta: Georgia Chapter, Special Libraries Association, 1956. 27 p.

Continued in part by:

A18. DISSERTATION Abstracts. A: The Humanities and Social Sciences [27 (July 1966)-29 (June 1969)] Ann Arbor, Mich.: University Microfilms, 1966-1969. 3 vols. Monthly.

Lists those American and Canadian dissertations which are available from universities associated with University Microfilms for purchase in microfilm or as xerographic reproductions. Arranged under principal subject categories, such as accounting, economics, theater, and subdivided into fields. Entry gives adviser. Author and subject index in each issue. Cumulative keyword-in-title subject index and author index for each volume appear as no. 12, pt. 2.

Continued by:

A19. DISSERTATION Abstracts International. A: The Humanities and Social Sciences [30 (July 1969)-   ] Ann Arbor, Mich.: University Microfilms, 1969-   . Monthly.

Abstracts of those American, Canadian, and European dissertations from universities associated with University Microfilms which are available for purchase in microfilm or as xerographic reproductions. Arranged under principal subject category, such as economics, education, speech, and subdivided by

fields. Entry gives adviser. Keyword-in-title
and author index in each issue. Annual keyword-in-
title and author index.

A20. DISSERTATION Abstracts. B: The Sciences and Engineering
[27 (1966/1967)-29 (1968/1969)] Ann Arbor, Mich.: University Microfilms, 1966-1969. 3 vols. Monthly.

Continues in part Item A17.

Abstracts of those American and Canadian dissertations from universities associated with University
Microfilms which are available for purchase in microfilm or as xerographic reproductions. Arranged
under principal subject categories, such as agriculture, chemistry, health sciences, physics, and
subdivided into fields. Entry gives adviser.
Cumulative keyword-in-title subject index and author
index for each volume appear as no. 12, pt. 2.

Continued by:

A21. DISSERTATION Abstracts International. B: The Sciences and
Engineering [30 (July 1969)-   ] Ann Arbor, Mich.: University Microfilms, 1969-   . Monthly.

Abstracts of those American, Canadian, and European
dissertations from universities associated with
University Microfilms which are available for purchase in microfilm or as xerographic reproductions.
Arranged under principal subject category, such as
agriculture, engineering, health sciences, physics,
and subdivided by fields. Entry gives adviser.
Keyword-in-title and author index in each issue.
Annual keyword-in-title and author index.

A22. DISSERTATION Abstracts International. Retrospective Index,
Volumes 1-29. Ann Arbor, Mich.: Xerox University Microfilms, 1970. 9 vols. in 11.

Vol. 1: mathematics and physics; vol. 2: chemistry;
vol. 3: earth/life sciences; vol. 4: psychology/
sociology/political science; vol. 5: social sciences;
vol. 6: engineering; vol. 7: education; vol. 8: com-
munication/information/business/literature/fine
arts; vol. 9: author index.

An alphabetical permutated keyword-in-title index
(using the principal words) to Items A17, A18, A20.
Covers over 150,000 dissertations. Entry gives
institution and refers to original listing.

A23.   DISSERTATION Digest. B: A Guide to Doctoral Research in the
Physical Sciences and Engineering [1970-   ] Ann Arbor,
Mich.: University Microfilms, 1970-   . Monthly.

A classified list of dissertations which will be
abstracted in subsequent issues of Item A21. Arranged under such subjects as agriculture, engineering, psychology. Entry gives purchase information.

A24.   INDEX to Theses Accepted for Higher Degrees in the Universities of Great Britain and Ireland and by the Council for
National Academic Awards [1 (1950/1951)-   ] London: ASLIB,
1953-   . Title varies. Annual.

Vol. 1 (1950/1951) does not include theses accepted
at the University of London during Hilary and Trinity terms, 1951. With vol. 18 (1967/1968), includes
the Council for National Academic Awards.

A classified list of theses and dissertations subdivided alphabetically by institution. "Table of
Availability" provides information on availability
of theses at various institutions. Does not include
postgraduate diplomas of the University of London
or dissertations submitted for a higher degree in
conjunction with a written examination. Index to
subject headings and author index.

A25.   LIÈGE. Université. Bibliothèque. Répertoire des thèses de
doctorat européenes [1969/1970] Louvain: A. Dewallens, 1970.
1 vol. (unpaged)

Lists 10,663 dissertations received by the University of Liège Library on exchange from September 30,
1969, through September 30, 1970, though items may
have been written prior to 1969. Arranged under
the areas of philosophy and letters, law, medicine,
sciences, and applied sciences; subdivided in each
area by institution. Each area is separately indexed by a concordance of words in the title and is
arranged by language.

A26.   RÉPERTOIRE des thèses de doctorat soutenues devant les uni-
       versités de langue française [1969/1970-   ] Québec: Uni-
       versité Laval, Centre de documentation de la Bibliothèque,
       1970-   . Semiannual.

       Prepared for the Association des Universités entière-
       ment ou partiellement de langue française.

       Vol. 1, no. 1 also called 1. ed. 1970.

       Lists dissertations completed in French language
       institutions. In five parts: (1) a geographic
       index; (2) a subject index keyed to a classifica-
       tion of all subjects; (3) an index of advisers;
       (4) an author index; and (5) a listing by the num-
       ber assigned for each dissertation that gives bib-
       liographic information, the degree and date, and
       the name of the adviser.

A27.   MAKERERE UNIVERSITY. Library. Annotated List of Theses Sub-
       mitted to University of East Africa, and Held by Makerere
       University Library. Kampala: 1970. 52 p. (Its Publica-
       tions, no. 7)

       Lists 150 theses and dissertations accepted by the
       University of East Africa for June 1963-June 1970
       and by Makerere University College prior to June 29,
       1963, and held by the Makerere University Library.
       Arranged under broad subject. Author index.

A28.   JĀMI'AT al-Kuwayt. Qism al-Tawthīq. Dalīl al-risālāt al-
       'Arabīyah. Kuwait: 1972. 510 p.

       Lists 3,080 theses and dissertations completed in
       Arab universities in the period 1930-1970. Arranged
       by broad subjects. Author index.

B. National

Algeria

B1.   ALGIERS. Université. Bibliothèque. Liste des thèses.
Alger: 1950-1962. Annual.

      Arranged by faculty, i.e. law, medicine, pharmacy,
sciences, letters.

Australia

B2.   UNION List of Higher Degree Theses in Australian University
Libraries: Cumulative Edition to 1965. Edited by Enid
Wylie. Hobart: University of Tasmania Library, 1967.   568 p.

      First compiled in 1959 by Mary J. Marshall, with
supplements in 1961 and 1963.

      A classified listing of 6,500 theses and disserta-
tions submitted to ten Australian universities for
which a copy is held in the university library.
Does not include theses submitted for the bachelor's
degree with honours. A statement of loan conditions
for each contributing library is included. Author
index.

Austria

B3.   GESAMTVERZEICHNIS österreichischer Dissertationen [vol. 1
(1966)-   ] Wien: Verlag Notring der Wissenschaftlichen
Gesellschaften Österreichs, 1967-   . Annual.

      Lists all work completed at Austrian universities
for the doctorate. Arranged by institution and

alphabetically by author under the faculty within
which the work was done. Appendix in each volume
lists items not included in previous listings.
Author index and key word and person index.

B4. KURZAUSZÜGE österreichischer Dissertationen: Geistes- und
Sozialwissenschaften. Abstracts of Austrian Dissertations:
Humanities, Social Sciences [1967-   ] Wien: Verlag Notring der Wissenschaftlichen Gesellschaften Österreichs,
1970-   . Annual.

Complemented by:

B5. _____ Abstracts of Austrian Dissertations: Naturwissenschaf-
ten und Technik, Sciences, Technology [1967-   ] Wien:
Verlag Notring der Wissenschaftlichen Gesellschaften Österreichs, 1971-   . Annual.

Abstracts of dissertations completed in Austrian
institutions. Entry gives the adviser. The Gesamtverzeichnis österreichischer Dissertationen serves
to index the abstracts listed.

Belgium

B6. WALTHER, Christoph F. Catalogue méthodique des dissertations
ou thèses académiques imprimées par les Elzevir de 1616 à
1712, recueillies pour la première fois dans la Bibliothèque
impériale publique à Saint Petersbourg. Bruxelles: 1864.
107 p.

Appeared previously in Le Bibliophile belge (Bruxelles), ser. 2, vol. 8 (1862): 345-360; vol. 9 (1862):
3-25, 89-105, 217-228, 315-324, 409-415; vol. 10
(1863): 5-11, 149-154.

The 932 works listed follow the pattern of ownership
of the Elsevier firm. Under each imprint the items
are subdivided by broad categories, e.g. medicine,
theology, law.

_____ _____ "Supplément." Le Bibliophile belge, ser. 2,
vol. 10 (1863): 245-255.

Lists 147 items supplementing parts 1-3 of main work.

"Supplément." <u>Le Bibliophile belge</u>, ser. 3, vol. 2 (1867): 103-109.

Lists an additional 26 items not previously mentioned.

B7.   "THÈSES présentées pour l'obtention du grade de licencié ou de docteur dans les facultés de philosophie et lettres belges. Verhandlingen tot het bekomen van de graad van licenciaat of doctor voorgelegd in de Belgische faculteiten der letteren en wijsbegeerte [1923/1924-1966/1967]" <u>Revue belge de philologie et d'histoire</u> 3 (1924)-46 (1968). Annual.

Theses and dissertations listed separately under institution. Within each group, they are further subdivided into philosophy, history, classical philology, philology, and German philology.

B8.   BELGIUM. Ministère des affaires étrangères. <u>Répertoire des thèses de doctorat. Repertorium van doctorale proefschriften</u> [1971/1972-   ] Bruxelles: 1973-   . Annual.

An alphabetical author listing of dissertations completed in Belgian institutions. Subject index.

Bulgaria

B9.   <u>BĂLGARSKI knigopis</u> [60 (1956)-66 (1962)] Sofia: 1956-1966. Monthly.

Carries a separate listing of theses and dissertations.

<u>Prilozhenie</u> [67 (1963)-   ] Quarterly.

A subseries of <u>Bălgarski knigopis</u>.

Theses and dissertations are listed separately and arranged under broad area, such as philosophy, physics-mathematics, history, medical sciences.

B10.   STANISHEVA, Lazarina. <u>Bibliografija na disertacii zaštiteni v Bălgarija, 1929-1964</u>. Sofia: Univ. Bibl., 1969. 593 p.

A listing of 1,222 dissertations defended in Bulgaria between 1929 and 1964. In two parts: (1) candidate

and doctoral dissertations defended 1951-1964, and
(2) previous doctoral dissertations defended. Both
sections are classified and subdivided by institution, with the studies arranged chronologically
under institution. Contains a separate section of
summaries in English, German, and French. Author
and subject indexes.

Canada

B11. OTTAWA. National Library. Canadian Graduate Theses in the
Humanities and Social Sciences, 1921-1946. Ottawa: E. Cloutier, 1951. 194 p.

Compiled and published under the auspices of the
Humanities Research Council of Canada and the Canadian Social Science Research Council.

A listing, following Library of Congress classification, of 3,043 theses and dissertations. Arranged
under the two main headings of social sciences and
humanities and further subdivided into broad major
areas. For some entries provides the name of the
professor in charge and scope and content of the
study. Author index and English and French subject
indexes.

Continued by:

B12. OTTAWA. National Library. Canadian Theses; Thèses canadiennes, 1947-1960. Ottawa: 1973. 2 vols.

Captions in English and French.

Theses and dissertations accepted by Canadian universities between Spring 1947 and Spring 1960 inclusive. Arranged by subjects, such as agriculture,
economics, geography, linguistics, zoology; subdivided by institution. Author index.

Continued by:

B13. CANADIAN Theses. Thèses canadiennes [1960/1961-   ] Ottawa:
National Library of Canada, 1962-   . Annual.

Lists theses and dissertations accepted by Canadian

universities. Arranged by subject, based on the
Dewey decimal system, and subdivided by university.
Items not previously included in an academic year
are entered as information is supplied. Author
index.

B14. OTTAWA. National Library. Canadian Theses. A List of
Theses Accepted by Canadian Universities in 1952. Thèses
canadiennes. Une liste des thèses acceptées par les univer-
sités canadiennes en 1952. Ottawa: National Library of
Canada; Bibliothèque nationale du Canada, 1953. E. Cloutier
...Queen's Printer; Imprimeur de la Reine. 50 p.

Lists approximately 1,100 theses and dissertations
arranged under broad subjects. Under each subject
they are arranged alphabetically by institution.
Author index and an "Index of Persons as Subjects
of Theses."

B15. "CANADIAN Theses on Microfilm." Canadiana, pt. 3, July/Aug.
1967-   . Monthly.

First appeared in 1966 interfiled in pt. 1.

Pt. 3 is composed primarily of this series, which
represents theses and dissertations completed in
Canada or of Canadian interest available in the
Canadian National Library, Ottawa. Arranged by
Dewey decimal classification. Entry gives informa-
tion for the purchase of a microfilm copy.

Supplemented by:

B16. CANADIAN Theses on Microfilm; Catalogue, Price List. Thèses
canadiennes sur microfilm; Catalogue, prix. Ottawa: National
Library of Canada, 1969.

_____ Supplement [no. 1-   ] Ottawa: National Library of
Canada, 1969-   . Irregular.

A listing of theses and dissertations completed in
Canada or of Canadian interest available from the
National Library. Includes items dated prior to
1965, the first year of microfilming. Arranged by
accession (series) number.

Quebec

B17. QUÉBEC (City). Université Laval. Centre de documentation.
      Index des projets de recherche en cours dans les universités
      du Québec [1 (1967)-   ] Québec: 1967-   . Annual.

      Third edition 1969 (1970).

      In large part consists of theses and dissertations
      in progress. Entry includes degree sought. In
      five parts: (1) alphabetical author listing by
      institution and department, (2) key-word-in-title
      index, (3) subject index, (4) author index, (5)
      index of advisers.

Chile

B18. "TESIS doctorales...de Chile." Anuario español e hispano-
      americano del libro y de las artes gráficas con el Catálogo
      mundial del libro impreso en lengua española 10 (1956/1957):
      397-430, 443-448.

      Lists 763 items completed in Chilean universities
      in the period 1955-1958. (Coverage for each insti-
      tution varies.) Arranged by institution, subdivid-
      ed by school or department. Entry gives date of
      defense and publication date. Author index.

B19. CONSEJO DE RECTORES DE LAS UNIVERSIDADES CHILENAS. Centro
      Nacional de Información y Documentación. Tesis aprobadas
      en las universidades chilenas en 1962. Santiago de Chile:
      1965. 201 p. (Its Publicación técnica, no. 1)

      _____ _____ 1963. Santiago de Chile: 1967. 249 p. (Its
      Publicación técnica, no. 3)

      Listings of approved theses and dissertations.
      Arranged by institution, faculty, school, and depart-
      ment or concentration. Many items are abstracted.
      Author and subject indexes.

Costa Rica

B20. COSTA RICA. Universidad Nacional, San José. Biblioteca.

Lista de tesis de grado presentadas a la Universidad de
Costa Rica hasta 1957. San José: Ciudad Universitaria "Ro-
drigo Facio," 1961. 380 p. (Universidad de Costa Rica.
Serie bibliotecología. Publicaciones, no. 10)

Lists 2,649 theses completed between 1941 and 1957
arranged by faculty. Entry gives publication information. Author and subject indexes.

Lista de tesis de grado de la Universidad de Costa
Rica [1958-   ] San José: Ciudad Universitaria "Rodrigo
Facio," 1959-   . (Universidad de Costa Rica. Serie bib-
liotecología. Publicaciones, no. 11-   ) Annual.

Arranged by faculty. Entries include abstracts.

Czechoslovakia

B21. ČESKOSLOVENSKÉ disertace [1964-   ] Praha: Státní knihovna
CSSR, 1965-   . Annual.

Issued as a supplement to České knihy.

A classified listing of theses and dissertations
completed in Czech institutions. Under each subject, dissertations and theses are listed separately.
Author and subject index.

Denmark

B22. COPENHAGEN. Universitet. Bibliotek. Danish Theses for the
Doctorate, and Commemorative Publications of the University
of Copenhagen, 1836-1926; A Bio-Bibliography. Copenhagen:
Levin & Munksgaard, 1929. 395 p.

Preface signed Svend Dahl.

Pt. 1 is a systematic list, following Dewey's main
classes, of 937 theses and dissertations completed
at the University of Copenhagen and papers published
in the annual programmes and other commemorative
publications. Includes masters' licentiates as well
as doctors' degrees. Starting date of 1836 was
chosen because in that year the first theses were
written in Danish (all Latin before this). Since
1921 includes theses in any of the principal lan-

guages of Europe, if accompanied by a Danish summary. About half of the items are written by phy-
sicians. Pt. 2 is an alphabetical author listing
which includes biographical notes. Subject index.

B23. _____ Danish Theses for the Doctorate, 1927-1958; A Bibliography. Copenhagen: University Library, 1962. 249 p.
(Library Research Monographs, no. 6)

An alphabetical author listing of 1,389 dissertations completed at Danish universities. An English
translation of treatises with Danish titles is provided. Publication information and references to
summaries published in languages other than Danish
are provided. Subject index.

B24. COPENHAGEN. Universitet. Akademiske skrifter og dissertationer [1897-   ] København: 1897-   Annual.

Also issued in English as Theses Accepted for the
Doctorate and Other Publications Issued by the
University and in French as Liste de thèses et
d'écrits académiques.

Dissertations are listed separately and arranged
alphabetically by author. Entry gives discipline
in which work was done, publication information, and
indicates if a summary is included in a language
other than Danish.

Dominican Republic

B25. FLORÉN LOZANO, Luis. "Catálogo de las tesis presentadas en
las distintas facultades de la Universidad de Santo Domingo,
desde el año académico de 1938/39 a 1948/49." In Santo
Domingo. Universidad. Anales 21 (1956): 177-359.

A chronological listing of approximately 1,100 theses
and dissertations. Entry gives faculty. Chronological index by faculty, and an author index.

B26. "TESIS año academico [1945/1946-1950/1951]" In Anuario bibliográfico dominicano [1946-1951] Ciudad Trujillo: 1947-
1952. Annual.

None published for 1948.

Separate listings of theses and dissertations submitted to the University of Santo Domingo. Covers
all faculties, including medicine.

Finland

B27.   HJELT, Otto E. A. Det Finska universitets disputations-
och program-litteratur under åren 1828-1908 systemaliskt
ordnad. Dissertationes academicae et programmata Universitatis literarum Fennorum Helsingforsiae annis 1828-1908
edita. Helsingfors: Helsingfors Centraltryckeri, 1909.
162 p.

   Lists in a classified arrangement dissertations
   completed in Finnish universities. Author index.

B28.   KÄRMENIEMI, Kaija. Opinnäytteiden bibliografia; Luettelo
Helsingin yliopistossa, Turun yliopistossa ja Yhteiskunnall-
isessa Korkeakoulussa vuoteen 1956 mennessä humanististen
tietei den aloilta laadituista tutkielmista. Helsinki: Suo-
malaisen Kirjallisuuden Seura, 1959. 164 p. (Tietolipas,
no. 15)

   Alphabetical author listing of dissertations accepted
   in Finnish institutions of higher education from 1930
   through 1955. Entry gives date and institution.
   Subject index.

Formosa

B29.   CHUNG YANG T'U SHU KUAN, T'ai-pei. Chung-hua min kuo po
shih shuo shih lun wên mu lu. T'ai-pei: 1970. 272 p.
(Its Kuo li chung yang t'u shu kuan mu lu ts'ung k'an ti 3
chi)

   Lists 2,669 theses and dissertations completed between 1949 and 1968. In two major parts: (1) theses
   and dissertations completed in Formosa, which lists
   dissertations under law and literature, and theses
   under the topics humanities, sciences, public health,
   law, education, engineering, agriculture, and commerce; (2) theses and dissertations by military who
   have received degrees abroad. Author index.

France

B30. POUY, Louis E. F. <u>Iconographie des thèses; Notice sur les</u>
<u>thèses dites historiées soutenues ou gravées notamment par</u>
<u>des Picards</u>. Amiens: Caillaux, 1869. 44 p.

A bibliography of about 30 theses by Picards which
are significant because of the textual decoration,
the significance of the author, or the rarity of
the theses.

B31. FRANCE. Direction des bibliothèques de France. <u>Catalogue</u>
<u>des thèses de doctorat soutenues devant les universités</u>
<u>françaises</u> [fasc. 1 (1884/1885)-75 (1958)] Paris: 1885-1959.
75 pts. in 15 vols. Title varies. Annual.

The official listing of French dissertations. Fasc.
1 (1884/1885)-30 (1913) cover the academic year and
are arranged by university, subdivided by faculty.
Fasc. 31 (1914)-75 (1958) cover the calendar year
and are arranged by faculty, such as law, medicine,
letters, and subdivided by university. Five year
subject and author indexes through 1928. Fasc. 74
(1957)-75 (1958) have author indexes.

_____ _____ <u>Nouvelle série</u> [1959-   ] Paris: Cercle de
la librairie, 1960-   . Annual.

Arranged by faculty, subdivided by university and
type of doctorate. Author index.

B32. "THÈSES [1931-   ]" <u>Bibliographie de la France</u> 121 (1932)
. Paris: Cercle de la librairie, 1932-   . Annual,
appearing in fascicules.

Issued as 1. partie; Supplément D.

Lists dissertations received through legal deposit
in the Bibliothèque nationale. Arranged by broad
subjects, e.g. pharmacy, sciences, theology, subdivided by institution and type of doctorate received. Entry gives faculty in which work was done
and a series note if the study appears in a series.
Annual author and institutional indexes.

B33. "THÈSES de doctorat concernant les sciences philosophiques et théologiques soutenues en France pendant l'année [1951-1964]" <u>Revue des sciences philosophiques et théologiques</u> 36 (1952)-49 (1965). Title varies. Annual. Usually July issue.

A list classified by subject through 1961, including theses for doctorates in theology, canon law, philosophy, letters, law, and science from state and private Catholic universities in France. Citations give degree, institution, whether to be published. Vols. 46 (1962)-49 (1965) not arranged by subject.

B34. UNIVERSITÉ DE PARIS X: NANTERRE. <u>Répertoire raissoné des sujets en cours des doctorats d'État, lettres et sciences humaines inscripts en France 1965-juillet 1970</u>. Paris: Centre de documentation sciences humaines, C.N.R.S., n.d. 3 vols.

Lists approximately 6,000 dissertations in progress. Arranged by institution, subdivided by such subjects as history, ethnology, sociology, geography. Entry gives adviser. Author and subject indexes.

B35. <u>ANNUAIRE de docteurs (lettres) de l'Université de Paris et des autres universitaires françaises; Bibliographie analytique des thèses</u> [1 (1899/1965)-   ] Paris: n.d.-   .

Theses for the degree of Docteur de l'Université. Arranged by year, subdivided by institution. Author, proper name, subject, and place indexes.

Germany

B36. <u>JAHRESVERZEICHNIS der deutschen Hochschulschriften</u> [1885-   ] Bearb. von der Deutschen Bücherei. Leipzig: Verlag für Buch- und Bibliothekswesen, 1887-   . Title varies. Annual.

Vols. 1 (1885/1886)-51 (1936) published by the Königliche, later Staatsbibliothek Berlin; vols. 61 (1945)-64 (1948) published together in 1951.

Arranged by place and then by university; further subdivided by type of material, with the section for dissertations making up the substantial portion. From vol. 29 (1913) includes the dissertations of

technische Hochschulen; from 40 (1924) those of the
Hochschulen der Länder; vols. 55 (1939)-60 (1944)
include the territories in Austria, Czechoslovakia,
and Poland occupied by Germany. Entry gives publication information. Vols. 20 (1904)-37 (1921)
carry biographical information. Author and subject
indexes up to vol. 81 (1965); thereafter, author
indexes.

_____ _____ Sachregister zu I-V. 1891. 96 p.

Dissertations are listed alphabetically by author
under the institution.

B37. BIBLIOGRAPHISCHER Monatsbericht über neuerschienene Schul-
und Universitäts- und Hochschulschriften [1 (1889/1890)-54,
Hft. 2 (1943)] Leipzig: Gustav Fock, 1890-1943. 54 vols.
Title varies. Annual.

A dealer's catalog made up largely of dissertations
and Habilitationsschriften. Includes technological
institutions from vol. 20 (1908). Subject index
from vol. 4 (1892/1893). Author index.

B38. DEUTSCHE Nationalbibliographie [1931-   ] Leipzig: VEB
Verlag für Buch- und Bibliothekswesen, 1931-   .

None published during part of 1945-1946; since 1946
only the publications of the German Democratic Republic are included.

In Reihe B, "Neuerscheinungen Ausserhalb des Buchhandels" (1931-1967), dissertations make up a substantial portion. Entry gives publication information. Quarterly and annual author and subject
indexes.

_____ "Reihe C: Dissertationen und Habilitationsschrift
[1968-   ]" Monthly.

Supersedes Reihe B.

Consists primarily of dissertations. Arranged
under such topics as religion and theology; philosophy and psychology; belles lettres; medicine.
Entry gives publication information. Author and
subject indexes.

B39. NATIONALSOZIALISTISCHE DEUTSCHE ARBEITER-PARTEI. Partei-
Amtliche Prüfungskommission zum Schutze des NS. Schrifttums.
Hochschulschrifttum, Verzeichnis von Dissertationen und
Habilitationsschriften; Ausgewählt auf Grund des Erlasses
des Reichsministers für Wissenschaft, Erziehung und Volks-
bildung vom 20. 10. 1939 in der Zeit von 1939 bis 1941 über-
prüften Arbeiten. Berlin: F. Eher Nachf., 1942. 94 p.
(Nationalsozialistische Bibliographie, 4. Beiheft)

Abstracts of 337 studies classified under "The
People," social order, the Reich as political real-
ity and idea; politics; Germany in the world system.
Entry gives publication information. Author index.

B40. PROEHL, Friedrich-Karl. Verzeichnis ausgewahlter Hochschulschriften 1945 bis 1963. Hamburg: Stiftung Wissenschaft und
Presse, 1966. 47 p.

_____ _____ 1964 bis 1966. 11 p. at end.

A classified listing of selected German language
dissertations. Covers such areas as religion, journalism, law, economics, medicine, and sports.

B41. DEUTSCHE Bibliographie: Hochschulschriften-Verzeichnis
[1971-   ] Frankfurt am Main: Buchhändler-Vereinigung,
1972-   . Monthly.

Issued by Deutsche Bibliothek as Reihe H.

Lists dissertations and Habilitationsschriften completed in West German universities under such topics
as religion, theology, medicine, mathematics, natural sciences. Entry gives institution and faculty,
date, type of academic study, publication information, and information on exchange. Author, title,
and key word index in each issue. Annual author,
title, and key word index.

Ghana

B42. GHANA National Bibliography [1965-   ] Accra: Ghana Library Board, 1966-   . Annual.

"Theses" began to be listed separately in 1966.
This includes theses and dissertations, most of them

completed at Ghanaian institutions, but increasingly includes those by Ghanaians in other countries (principally the United States, Canada, and Great Britain). Items are listed alphabetically by author.

Guatemala

B43. GUATEMALA (City). Universidad de San Carlos. Escuela de Biblioteconomía. Tesario universitario, 1945-1960, vol. 1. Guatemala: 1961. 44 p. (Publicaciónes, no. 1)

Approximately 500 theses arranged alphabetically under faculty. Abstracts are given for some.

B44. BENDFELDT ROJAS, Lourdes. Tesario universitario; Facultad de Humanidadaes, 1945-65. Guatemala: Universidad de San Carlos, Departamento de Publicaciones, 1965. 91 p.

In three sections: (1) outlines of content of published and unpublished theses in alphabetical order by author; (2) alphabetical list of titles; and (3) list of theses arranged by department.

Hungary

B45. KANDIDÁTUSI es disszertációk katalógusa [1 (1952/1961)-] Budapest: 1962- . Semiannual.

No. 1 is a classified list covering the period 1952 to 1961.

Lists theses completed in Hungarian institutions of higher education. Author and opponents indexes.

India

B46. INTER-UNIVERSITY BOARD OF INDIA AND CEYLON. Bibliography of Doctorate Theses in Science and Arts Accepted by Indian Universities [1930/1934-1954/1958] N.p.: 1935-1961. 5 vols. Title varies. Irregular.

Volumes cover 1930/1934; 1943/1945; 1950/1952; 1952/1954; and 1954/1958.

Lists dissertations completed by institution, subdivided by field, such as philosophy, economics,
and history.

B47. INDIA (Republic). National Archives. <u>Bulletin of Research
Theses and Dissertations in the Union of India</u> [no. 1 (Jan.
1955)-4 (May 1966)] New Delhi: 1955-1968.

Nos. 1-3 include theses and dissertations; no. 4
carries dissertations only.

Theses and dissertations completed or in progress.
Arranged by institution, subdivided by work completed
or in progress. Subject index.

B48. JAIPUR, India (Rajasthan). University of Rajasthan. Library.
<u>Catalogue of Theses and Dissertations Available in the Rajas-
than University Library</u>. Jaipur: 1966. 316 p.

A catalog of 1,680 theses and dissertations. In
addition to representing the work done at the University of Rajasthan, includes many studies completed in other Indian institutions. Arranged by academic field and subdivided into dissertations and
theses. Author index and index of thesis supervisors.

B49. INTER-UNIVERSITY BOARD OF INDIA AND CEYLON. <u>Research in Progress; A Record of Subjects Taken Up for Research by Scholars
Registered for Doctoral Degrees with Indian Universities
during 1958-66</u>. New Delhi: 1968-1970. 4 vols.

Vol. 1: physical sciences; vol. 2: biological sciences; vol. 3: social sciences; vol. 4: humanities.

Classified arrangement of work for the doctorate
following Dewey decimal classification. For each,
entry gives title of thesis as registered with the
institution, institution and department, year research was begun and when it is likely to be completed, adviser, and a resume of the research topic.
Index of researchers in each volume.

B50. _____ <u>A Bibliography of Doctoral Dissertations Accepted by
Indian Universities, 1857-1970</u>. New Delhi: 1972- .

Separate volumes, each dealing with a distinct area.

Vol. 1 (1972), covering education, library science, journalism, lists 333 items; vol. 2 (1973), psychology, lists 211 items; vol. 3 (1973), political science, law, public administration, lists 609 items; vol. 4 (1973), sociology, lists 426 items.

The listings are classified. Titles in languages other than English are transliterated and the original language is indicated. Entry gives institution, date, and type of degree if other than Ph.D. Author index in each volume.

Uttar Pradesh

B51. "RESEARCH News from U.P. Universities." <u>Uttara Bharati</u> 1 (June 1954): 127-143; 2 (July 1955): 83-95.

First section lists doctoral work completed at Lucknow, Allahabad, and Agra Universities for 1949 through 1953. Arranged chronologically under school and faculty. Entry indicates the degree taken. Second section lists theses completed at Lucknow and Agra Universities from 1949 through 1954 in their Faculties of Medicine.

Israel

B52. <u>ISRAEL Science Bibliography: A Guide to Books, Dissertations and Periodicals Published in Israel</u> [no. 1 (Jan.-June 1954)- 2 (July-Dec. 1954)] Jerusalem: Israel Scientific Press, 1954. 2 vols.

In English, with titles in Hebrew.

Listed in broad subject classifications according to UDC in the natural sciences and humanities. Carries a separate section of dissertations in each classification. Entry indicates if parts are written in English. Some items carry abstracts.

Japan

B53. <u>NIHON hakushi roku</u> [1882-   ] Tokyo: Kyōiku Gyōsei Kenkyū-sho, 1956-   . Annual.

Supersedes <u>Dai Nihon hakushiroku</u>, 1921-1930.

Lists the dissertations conferred under the old system for awarding doctoral degrees. Vol. 1 lists approximately 40,000 dissertations completed from 1888 through 1955. Each volume covers a particular time period and is arranged by major areas, such as law, medicine, pharmacy, agriculture, etc. The dissertations are listed chronologically under the area. Author index.

B54. <u>NIHON hakushi roku</u> [1957-1965] Tokyo: Teikoku Chihō Gyōsei Kakkai, 1967. 4 vols.

Vol. 1 covers 1957-1961; vol. 2, 1962-1963; vol. 3, 1964; vol. 4, 1965.

Lists dissertations awarded under the new system (similar to the practice in the United States). Arranged by year, subdivided by institution and subject area. Index by type of degree and then alphabetically by author.

Mexico

B55. MEXICO. Biblioteca Nacional. <u>Boletín</u> [1904-1929, 1950-   ] Mexico, D.F.: 1904-   . Quarterly.

Special section dedicated to theses, organized by subject. Entry indicates university in which presented.

Netherlands

B56. "ACADEMISCHE proefschriften [1880-1892]" <u>Nieuwsblad voor den boekhandel</u>, jaarg. 1880-1892. Amsterdam: Vereeniging tot Bevorderingvande Belangen des Boekhandels, 1880-1892. Annual.

An alphabetical author listing of Dutch dissertations which appears as a subsection of the "Register" and gives their location in the <u>Nieuwsblad</u>.... In the work itself dissertations are listed under institution. (They were carried this way up to approximately 1907.)

B57. DÉE, M. A. <u>Academische proefschriften verdedigd te Leiden,</u> <u>Utrecht, Groningen en Amsterdam in de jaren 1877-1899</u>. Ley-den: D. Donner, 1900. 166 p. ?

B58. WIJNDELTS, J. W. <u>Catalogus van academische proefschriften,</u> <u>verdedigd aan de Nederlandsche universiteiten gedurende de</u> <u>jaren 1815-1900</u>. Groningen: G. A. Evers, 1901-1903. 2 vols.

> Supersedes Johannes J. Dodt, <u>Repertorium disserta-</u> <u>tionum belgicarum...1815 usque ad annum 1830...</u> (1830).

> Lists 1,076 dissertations from the Universities of Leyden, Utrecht, Groningen, and Amsterdam. Vol. 1 covers theology and vol. 2 covers literature. Ar-ranged chronologically by university. Author and subject indexes.

B59. UTRECHT. Rijksuniversiteit. Bibliotheek. <u>Catalogus van</u> <u>academische geschriften in Nederland verschenen</u> [jaarg. 1 (1924)-38 (1961)] Utrecht: 1925-1973. Title varies. Irregular.

> _____ _____ <u>Nieuwe reeks</u> [jaarg. 1. en 2. (1962/ 1963)-   ] Utrecht: 1966-   . Irregular.

> Jaarg. 1 (1924)-22 (1945) include the Dutch Indies; 1 (1924)-30 (1953) include other academic publica-tions, as well as dissertations. Jaarg. 18 (1941)-22 (1945) published together in 1949; 23 (1946)-26 (1949) published together in 1952. <u>Nieuwe reeks</u> covers two year period, arranged by year.

> Lists dissertations under institution, subdivided by faculty. Entry gives publication information. Author index.

> _____ _____ <u>Naam- en zaakregister</u> [1 (1924)-10 (1933)] 'sGravenhage: Nederl. Vereenig. van Bibliothecarissen, 1941. 122 p.

B60. "DOCTORAL Dissertations [1957-   ]" <u>Higher Education and</u> <u>Research in the Netherlands</u> 1 (1957)-   . Quarterly.

> Publication is the bulletin of the Stiching voor Internationale Sammenwerking der Universiteiten en Hogescholen.

Also issued in French, German, and Spanish editions.

Listings of dissertations completed in participating Dutch universities. Arranged by large subject such as theology, law, medicine, natural sciences, arts, economics, political and social sciences, technical sciences, agricultural sciences. Entry gives translation of title into English.

New Zealand

B61. JENKINS, D. L. <u>Union List of Theses of the University of New Zealand, 1910-1954</u>. Wellington: New Zealand Library Association, 1956. 1 vol. (unpaged)

Arranged under "Doctorate Theses," "Medical and Dental Theses," "Masterate Theses," then by subject. Includes "overseas theses of New Zealand interest and theses presented by New Zealanders while overseas." Location given when known. Author index.

Continued by:

B62. <u>UNION List of Theses of the Universities of New Zealand; Supplement 1955-1962; With Some Additions and Corrections to the 1910-1954 List.</u> Compiled by D. G. Jamieson. Wellington: New Zealand Library Association, 1963. 86 p.

Continued by:

B63. <u>UNION List of Higher Degree Theses of the Universities of New Zealand; Supplement 1963-1967.</u> Compiled by Catherine G. Swift. Wellington: New Zealand Library Association, 1969. 137 p.

Nigeria

B64. NATIONAL LIBRARY OF NIGERIA. <u>Theses and Dissertations Accepted for Higher Degrees in Nigerian Universities</u> [1966/1967-] Lagos: 1967- . Annual.

Entries arranged by subject. Includes an author index.

Panama

B65. PANAMA (City). Universidad. Biblioteca. Lista bibliográ-
fica de los trabajos de graduación y tesis presentados en la
Universidad, 1939-1960. Preparado por Carmen D. de Herrera.
Contribución al Tercer Seminario Bibliográfico de Centro
América y el Caribe. Panamá: 1960. 186 p.

> Supersedes its Lista de los trabajos de graduación
> correspondiente a los años 1957-1955 [sic] (1958).

> Lists approximately 1,400 theses by faculties, sub-
> divided by school. Entry gives date.

Philippines

B66. PHILIPPINES (Republic). National Science Development Board.
Compilation of Graduate Theses Prepared in the Philippines,
1913-1960. Compiled by Aurora R. Roxas. Manila: 1964.
437 p.

> Supersedes Science Review, suppl. 1 and 2, of the
> Philippines National Institute of Science and
> Technology.

> Lists 4,355 theses and dissertations from 69 schools,
> classified into 44 specialized subject fields. Of
> these, 1,728 are in education and 545 in law. In
> each field, entries are listed by type of degree.
> Entry gives institution and department and date.

B67. MANILA. National Library. Filipiniana Division. List of
Theses and Dissertations Available in the Filipiniana
Division. Manila: 1967. 54 p.

> Lists approximately 700 studies completed in Philip-
> pine institutions alphabetically by author. Entry
> gives degree, institution, and date.

B68. QUEZON, Philippines. University of the Philippines. Library. Readers Services Division. U.P. Theses and Dissertations, 1956-1968. Diliman, Rizal: University of the Philippines, Library, 1969.` 397 p. (University of the Philippines.
Library. Research Guides, no. 6)

An alphabetical author listing of 972 theses and
dissertations. Entry gives previous degrees and
the institutions where taken. Subject and chronological indexes and a roster of graduates by degree.

Poland

B69. KATALOG rozpraw doktorskich i habilitacyjnych [1959/1961-
        ] Warszawa: Państwowe Wydawn. Naukowe: 1962-   .
      Annual.

      A classified listing. Entry gives major adviser and
      carries an abstract. Author index.

B70. POLAND. Ministerstwo Oświaty i Szkolnictwa Wyższego. Kata-
      log rozpraw doktorskich i habilitacyjnych, 1965. Warszawa:
      Państwowe Wydawnictwo Naukowe, 1967. 827 p.

      Classified annotated bibliography of 2,328 studies.
      Entry indicates major adviser. Author index.

Romania

B71. RAUS, Lidia and Lucia Grigorcea. Teze de doctorat: 1948-
      1966; Repertoriu bibliografic. București: 1968. ??

Salvador

B72. SAN SALVADOR. Universidad Nacional. Biblioteca Central.
      Catálogo de tésis doctorales de las facultades de la Univer-
      sidad de El Salvador. Preparado por Raúl Humberto Flores.
      San Salvador: Editorial Universitaria, 1960. 582, 38 p.

      Dissertations presented to the University between
      1878 and 1960 and available at the University.
      Arranged by faculty; includes humanities, economics,
      jurisprudence and social sciences, chemistry and
      pharmacy, medicine, dentistry, engineering. Dis-
      sertations are arranged alphabetically by author
      under faculty. Entry gives publication information.

Singapore

B73. SINGAPORE (City). University. Library. <u>Academic Exercises,</u>
<u>Theses and Dissertations Submitted to the University of</u>
<u>Singapore and Deposited in the University of Singapore Lib-</u>
<u>rary, 1947-1969</u>. Singapore: University of Singapore, Libra-
ry, 1969. 59, 12, 16 p.

    Supersedes list published in 1962 and the 1964 sup-
    plement.

    Lists 1,029 studies arranged by department. Author
    and subject indexes.

South Africa

B74. ROBINSON, Anthony M. L. <u>Catalogue of Theses and Disserta-</u>
<u>tions Accepted for Degrees by the South African Universities;</u>
<u>Katalogus van proefskrifts en verhandelinge vir grade deur</u>
<u>die Suid-Afrikaanse universiteite goedgekeur, 1918-1941</u>.
Cape Town: 1943. 155 p.

    A classified bibliography of 1,757 completed theses
    and dissertations. Publication information provided.
    Indicates location. Note on the lending of theses
    by universities and other libraries. Subject and
    author indexes.

    Continued by:

B75. MALAN, Stephanus I. <u>Gesamentlike katalogus van proefskrifte</u>
<u>en verhandelinge van die Suid-Afrikaanse universiteite, 1942-</u>
<u>1958</u>. <u>Union Catalogue of Theses and Dissertations of the</u>
<u>South African Universities, 1942-1958</u>. Potchefstroom: Pot-
chefstroomse Universiteit vir Christelike Hoër Onderwys,
1959. 216 p.

    Arranged in nine broad subject areas and subdivided
    under each. Entries are arranged by university and
    then alphabetically by author. Some theses that are
    required for the bachelor's degree, as well as some
    in theology which have the same value as a master's
    degree, are included. Entry gives title in original
    language in which it was written, location of copies,
    and publishing information. Author index.

_____ _____ Aanvullung. Supplement [no. 1 (1959)-]
Potchefstroom: Universiteit vir Christelike Hoër Onderwys,
1959- . Annual.

Theses and dissertations classified under major
areas such as philosophy, pure sciences, biological
sciences; further subdivided by institution. Entry
indicates location of copies. Author index.

B76. SOUTH AFRICA. National Council for Social Research. Register van huidige navorsing in die humaniora aan die universi-
teite. Register of Current Research in the Humanities at
the Universities [1946-] Pretoria: 1946- . Annual.

In Afrikaans and English.

A listing of university and non-university research
in the humanities, social sciences, philology and
language, and theology. University research includes
many theses and dissertations in progress. Arranged
by institution and department. Entries include beginning and expected completion date and adviser.

South Korea

B77. HAN'GUK paksa mit sŏksa hagwi nonmun ch'ongmongnok [1 (1945/
1968)-] Seoul, Korea: 1969- . Irregular.

Vol. 1 (1945/1968) supersedes Han'guk Yŏn'gu
Tosŏgwan, Seoul, Korea. Han'guk sŏk, paksa hagwi
nonmun mongnok, 1945-1960 (1960).

Vol. 1 covers period 1945-1968; vol. 2 covers 1969-
1970 (1971).

Lists theses and dissertations completed in South
Korea. Each volume is in two parts, the social
sciences and humanities and the natural sciences.
These are further subdivided by fields, such as
economics, law, medicine, chemistry. Separate
indexes for authors of theses and for dissertations.

Spain

B78. MADRID. Universidad. Biblioteca. Catálogo de las publicaciones y tesis doctorales destinadas al cambio internacional de libros. Madrid: Gráfica universal, 1934. 65 p.

A subject listing representing dissertations from Spanish universities. Entry gives publication information.

B79. "RELACION de las tesis doctorales manuscritas existentes en la Biblioteca de la Universidad de Madrid." Anuario español e hispanoamericano del libro y de las artes gráficas con el Catálogo mundial del libro impreso en lengua española 5 (1949/1950): appendix, 213-246; 9 (1955/1956): 447-480.

Vol. 5 (1949/1950) list is a retrospective record of holdings of Spanish dissertations, largely from 1900 through 1949. Vol. 9 (1955/1956) list continues the coverage through 1955, with some 1956 items. Altogether approximately 3,000 dissertations are represented. Arranged under such fields as philosophy, law, sciences, medicine.

B80. MADRID. Universidad. Catálogo de las tesis doctorales manuscritas existentes en la Universidad de Madrid. Madrid: Gráficas González, 1952. 36 p.

Classified listing of manuscript dissertations. Largely represents work done at the University of Madrid, but also includes other Spanish universities.

Sweden

B81. WAHLBERG, Carl G. Förteckning öfver offentligen fösvarade akademiska afhandlingar vid Kongl. universiteten i Upsala och Lund (1852-77), Kongl. Carolinska medico-kirurgiska institutet i Stockholm (1842-77) och Kejserliga Alexanders-universitetet i Helsingfors (1853-77) jemte de under samma tid vid dessa högskolor utgifna program. Upsala: Esaias Edquist, 1877. 145 p.

Arranged by institutions and then by subjects. Author index.

B82. NELSON, Axel H. Akademiska afhandlingar vid Sveriges universitet och högskolor läsåren 1890/91-1909/10 jämte förteckning öfver svenskars akademiska afhandlingar vid utländska universitet under samma tid. Uppsala: Akademiska Bokhandeln, 1911-1912. 150 p.

Continues Item All.

Also appeared as Uppsala universitets årsskrift, 1911, bd. 2-1912.

Author and subject listings. Also includes Swedish dissertations submitted to institutions outside Sweden. Entry gives publication information.

Continued by:

B83. TUNELD, John. Akademiska avhandlingar vid Sveriges universitet och högskolor, läsåren 1910/11-1939/40; Bibliografi. Lund: Ohlsson, 1945. 336 p.

An alphabetical author listing of approximately 2,000 dissertations. Includes a separate list of work done at institutions outside Sweden. In two parts, an author list and a subject list with index. Entry gives brief biographical data and publication information. Classified index.

Switzerland

B84. JAHRESVERZEICHNIS der schweizerischen Hochschulschriften... Catalogue des écrits académiques suisses [1897/1898-   ] Basel: 1898-   . Title varies. Annual.

Vols. 1 (1897/1898)-27 (1923/1924) cover the school year; 28 (1925)-   cover the calendar year.

Primarily a listing of dissertations, arranged by institution. Pt. C, dissertations, is subdivided by faculty. Entry gives publication information. Early volumes give biographical information. From vol. 29 (1926) includes a catchword subject index. Title and subject and author indexes.

Verfasser-Registerzuden Jahrgängen 1897/1898-1922/ 1923. Basel: Universitätsbibliothek, 1927. 87 p.

B85. "VERÖFFENTLICHUNGEN ausserhalb des Buchhandels. Publications hors commerce." Schweizer Buch 44 (1943)-   . Bimonthly.

Issued as Series B.

In largest part consists of dissertations completed
in Swiss institutions of higher education. Arranged
under broad areas, such as history, folklore; philology, literary history; politics; economics, statistics; law, administration. Entry gives field and
publication information. Author and key word indexes.
Annual author and key word indexes. Indexed in
Schweizer Bucherverzeichnis.

U.S.S.R.

B86. EZHEGODNIK dissertatsiy [1936-1937] Moskva: Izdatel'stvo
Vsesoyuznaya knizhnoy palaty, 1938-1940. Annual.

Lists theses and dissertations completed in Russian
institutions. Arranged by fields, such as physics-
mathematics, medical sciences, geological-mineralogical sciences; subdivided under field into theses
and dissertations. Entry gives publication information. Author, subject, and institutional indexes.

B87. MOSCOW. Publichnaya biblioteka. Bibliografiya dissertatsiy:
doktorskie dissertatsiy [1941-1946] Moskva: 1946-1947.
2 vols.

Compiled by M. S. Vainov.

Vol. 1 covers the period 1941-1944; vol. 2 covers
1945.

Lists dissertations under broad subjects, such as
physics-mathematics, geography, philosophy, architecture. Entry gives the table of contents and
publication information. Author, subject, and
institutional indexes in each volume.

B88. "SPISOK tem dissertatsiy zashchishchennykh v [1952-1956] na
soiskanie uchenoy stepeni kandidata istoricheskikh nauk,
kandidata filosofskikh nauk i kandidata ekonomicheskikh
nauk." Vestnik vysshey shkoly, 1953, vyp. 8: 61-64; 1954,
vyp. 7: 57-63; 1955, vyp. 4: 59-62; 1957, vyp. 8: 94-96.

A listing of theses defended in the U.S.S.R. Each
year's work is arranged under such topics as the

history of the Communist Party, dialectic materialism, history of materialism, political economy.

B89. "SPISOK tem dissertatsiy zashchishchennykh vo vtorom polu-
godni [1953-1957] na soiskanie uchenoy stepeni kandidata
filosofskikh nauk." Vestnik vysshey shkoly, 1954, vyp. 1:
59-62; 1955, vyp. 2: 61-63, vyp. 3: 62-63; 1956, vyp. 4: 59-
62; 1957, vyp. 8: 94-96; 1958, vyp. 5: 95.

A listing of theses defended in the U.S.S.R. Each
year's work is under such topics as dialectic materialism, historical materialism, history of philosophy, logic.

B90. MOSCOW. Publichnaya biblioteka. Katalog kandidatskikh
dissertatsiy postupivshikh v Biblioteku [1955-1956] Moskva:
1956-1959. 4 vols.

Also lists pre-1955 items.

A classified listing of theses under such areas as
Marxism-Leninism, mathematics, mechanics and physics,
geology. Does not include medical sciences. Author
and institutional indexes.

B91. _____ Katalog doktorskikh dissertatsiy, postupivshikh v
biblioteku im V. I. Lenina v 1956 g. Sost. A. A. Kondrat'ev.
Moskva: 1957. 45 p.

A listing of 304 dissertations deposited in the
library in 1956. Arranged by fields, such as
mathematics-physics, chemistry, geology. Institutional and author indexes.

B92. _____ Katalog kandidatskikh i doktorskikh dissertatsiy,
postupivshikh v Biblioteku im V. I. Lenina i Gosudarstvennuyu
TSentral'nuyu nauchnuyu meditsinskuyu biblioteku [1957-   ]
Moskva: 1958-   . Semiannual.

Lists for 1957-1959 were issued quarterly.

A classified listing of U.S.S.R. theses and dissertations. Includes items completed prior to 1957.
Arranged under 29 fields such as Marxism-Leninism,
mathematics, chemistry, economic sciences. Titles
in non-Russian languages are transliterated. Author,

name, and institutional indexes.

B93. "AVTOREFERATY dissertatsiy [1954-1960]" Knizhnaya letopis',
1955-1960. Weekly.

A list of the published abstracts of Russian theses
and dissertations. (The full text is rarely published.) Classified into 31 fields, such as philosophical sciences, economic sciences, physics-math-
ematical sciences, architectural sciences. Dissertations and theses are listed separately under each
field. Indexed with other publications quarterly
and annually by author, subject, and geographic
area.

Continued by:

_____ Knizhnaya letopis'. Dopolnitel'nyi vypusk, 1961,
1964- . Monthly.

No lists included in 1962 and 1963 volumes. Quarterly author, subject, and geographical indexes.

Belorussia

B94. AKADEMIYA NAVUK BSSR, Minsk. Fundamental'naya bibliyatĕka.
Bibliografiya dissertatsiy, zashchishchennykh v Belorusskoĭ
SSR za 1945-1955 gody. Sost. L. A. Osipchik. Minsk: Izd-vo
Akademii nauk BSSR, 1958. 87 p.

Lists 704 theses and dissertations arranged under
such topics as philosophy, history, economics,
physics, and mathematics. Theses and dissertations
are listed separately under each topic.

Estonia

B95. TIIK, Leo. Tartu Riiklikus Ülikoolis 1946-1959 kaitstud
väiterkirjad; Bibliograafia. Tartu: 1961. 50 p.

A classified listing of six doctoral and 272 candidate studies. Entry gives publication information
and adviser.

Latvia

B96. YAKOBSON, M. and Peile, E. "Bibliografiya dissertatsiy zashchishchennykh v Latviyskoy SSR s 1945 po 1955 g. (1-e polugodie)." In Latvijas Padomju Socialistiskās Republikas Zinātnu Akadēmija. Vēstis, 1955, vyp. 9: 150-160.

A classified listing of approximately 300 theses and dissertations.

Lithuania

B97. PETRAUSKIENE, Z. and P. Valentelienė. Lietuvos TSR mokslininku disertacijos, 1945-1968; Bibliografiia. Vilnius: Lietuvos TSR Mokslų akademijos Centrinė biblioteka, 1971. 489 p.

Titles translated into Russian.

A classified listing of 2,692 theses and dissertations, listed separately. Author index.

Ukraine

B98. "AVTOREFERATI dissertatsiy." Litopys knyh 1 (1924)-Monthly.

A classified listing of theses and dissertations completed in the Ukrainian S.S.R., under such subjects as historical, geological-mineralogical, and economic sciences. Under each subject, theses and dissertations are listed separately.

Uzbekistan

B99. TASHKEND. Universitet. Fundamental'naya biblioteka. Ukazatel' doktorskikh i kandidatskikh dissertatsiy zashchishchennykh v 1936-1951 gg. Obshchestvennye nauki, Estestvennye nauki, mathematika. Red. D. F. Zheleznyakov i M. S. Viridarskii. Tashkent: SAGU, 1954. 174 p. (Sredneaziatskiy gosudarstvennyi universitet. Materialy k bibliografii, vyp. 4)

A classified list of theses and dissertations

defended in Uzbekistan in the social sciences,
natural sciences, and mathematics. Does not include
medical sciences. Arranged under social sciences;
natural sciences; geography, geomorphology, hydrology;
and biological sciences. Under each, dissertations
and theses are listed separately and chronologically.
Author index.

United States

B100. U.S. Library of Congress. Catalog Division. List of American Doctoral Dissertations Printed in 1912-1938. Washington: U.S. Government Printing Office, 1913-1940. 26 vols.
Annual. Title varies.

Includes only the printed dissertations received by
the Library of Congress. The original intention
was to acquire, classify, and catalog "every thesis
printed, whether separately or in another publication." Each volume contains (1) an alphabetical
author list of the dissertations for the year covered
and a supplementary list of dissertations received
by the Library of Congress which were printed prior
to the year covered; (2) a classified list according
to Library of Congress classification; (3) a subject
index; and (4) an alphabetical list arranged by the
institution. Entry, bibliographic and publication
information, and notes in the author listing follow
Library of Congress practice.

B101. WEST, Clarence J. and Callie Hull. "Doctorates Conferred in
the Arts and Sciences by American Universities, 1921-1922."
School and Society 17 (1923): 57-63, 106-109, 132-139.

Lists 297 dissertations in the arts and 442 in the
sciences for the academic year 1921/1922. Also
lists dissertations in the arts for the period
1916/1917-1920/1921. Arranged by subjects and then
institution.

B102. KANSAS. Fort Hays State College, Hays. Graduate Club. A
Partial List of Titles of Essays Written by Candidates for
the Master's Degree in Colleges and Universities in the
United States, 1929-30. Topeka: Kansas State Printing Plant,
1931. 60 p. (Its Current Problems in Research. Bulletin,
no. 1. Fort Hays Kansas State College Bulletin, vol. 33,

no. 3)

> Lists about 1,500 studies completed at 22 institutions between September 1929 and June 1930 under major subject disciplines.

B103. LESTER, Robert M. Doctoral Dissertations by...Recipients of Fellowship Grants from the Southern Fellowship Fund [1955/1958-   ] Chapel Hill, N.C.: 1958-   . (Southern Fellowship Fund. Report, no. 1-   ) Irregular.

> A series of reports, each providing an alphabetical listing of the recipients, their academic degrees, title of the dissertation, and latest reported position.

B104. MASTERS Abstracts; A Catalog of Selected Masters Theses on Microfilm [vol. 1-   ] Ann Arbor, Mich.: University Microfilms, 1962-   . Title varies. Quarterly.

> Vol. 1 (1962/1963) was semiannual; vols. 2 (1964)-quarterly.

> Subject list of brief abstracts from cooperating institutions in the United States. Inclusion limited to a selection of theses recommended for publication by the faculty of the awarding school

> Entry gives purchase information. Beginning with vol. 6 (1968) includes annual author index.

> _____ Cumulative Subject and Author Index [vol. 1 (1962)-5 (1967)] 1968. 51 p.

> _____ Cumulative Subject and Author Index [vol. 6 (1968)-10 (1972)] 1972. 145 p.

B105. COMPREHENSIVE Dissertation Index, 1861-1972. Ann Arbor, Mich.: Xerox University Microfilms, 1973. 37 vols.

> A classified index of dissertations accepted in the United States from 1861. In all, approximately 417,000 items are included. Listed under such subjects as chemistry, physics, agriculture, psychology. Within each subject items are listed by key word in title. Entry gives reference to location in Dissertation Abstracts. Vols. 33-37 comprise the author index.

Kentucky

B106. "BIBLIOGRAPHY of Graduate Theses Accepted by Kentucky Colleges and Universities through 1948." Compiled by Ellen Stutsman. Kentucky Historical Society Register 48 (1950): 128-172, 221-266, 331-357.

> Reprinted as Kentucky Library Association. College and Reference Section. Bibliography of Graduate Theses Accepted by Kentucky Colleges and Universities through 1948. Lexington: 1950.

> Lists 3,340 theses and dissertations. Arranged by subject, then by institution. Includes the Asbury Theological Seminary, Eastern Kentucky State, Kentucky, Louisville, Morehead State, Murray State at Morehead, Louisville Presbyterian Seminary, Transylvania, Women's Missionary Union Training School, and Western Kentucky State. Author index.

_____ "1949-1953." Compiled by Mildred A. Moore. Kentucky Historical Society Register 54 (1956): 153-184, 237-268, 373-388.

> Reprinted as Kentucky Library Association. College and Reference Section. Graduate Theses Accepted by Kentucky Colleges and Universities, 1949-1953. Lexington: 1956.

> Lists 1,518 theses and dissertations from institutions in previous list, adding the College of the Bible (Lexington) and excluding Murray State at Morehead and Transylvania. Arranged by subject and then by institution. Author index.

Montana

B107. HISTORICAL RECORDS SURVEY. Montana. Bibliography of Graduate Theses, University of Montana, Montana State University, Montana State College, Montana School of Mines. Prepared by Work Projects Administration, Service Division, The Inventory of Public Archives, Historical Records Survey Project. Bozeman, Mont.: The Inventory of Public Archives, Montana Historical Records Survey, 1942. 71 p.

> Approximately 470 theses and dissertations covering the period from 1902 arranged by broad subject classes.

Author index.

Oregon

B108. OREGON. State Board of Higher Education. <u>Graduate Theses:</u>
<u>University of Oregon, Oregon State College, University of</u>
<u>Oregon Medical School, 1932-1942</u>. Eugene: Oregon State
System of Higher Education, 1946. 198 p.

Supersedes its <u>Graduate Theses of the Oregon State</u>
<u>System of Higher Education</u> (1939). (<u>Its</u> Leaflet
Series, no. 2)

Contains (1) abstracts of all dissertations and
(2) lists of all graduate theses. Arranged by
school and department. Author index.

Yugoslavia

B109. BELGRAD. Univerzitet. Biblioteka. <u>Spisak prinova ruko-</u>
<u>pisnih doktorskih disertacija</u> [1963-   ] Beograd: 1964-
. Annual.

A record of accessions of Yugoslavian dissertations.
Arranged by fields, such as historical sciences,
mathematics, pharmacy, agriculture.

B110. <u>REFERATIVNI bilten doktorskih disertacija</u> [1-   ] Beograd:
Savezna Privredna Komora i Institut za Naucno-Tehničku Doku-
mentaciju i Informacije, 1968-   .

Issued in parts.

A classified listing of 2,534 Yugoslavian dissertations. Most items listed were completed in the
period 1945-1967. Entry carries an abstract.

_____ <u>Registar</u>. Beograd: n.d. 149 p. ?

Ljubljana

B111. KOKOLE, Jože. <u>Bibliografija doktorskih disertacij univerze</u>
<u>in drugih visokošolskih in znanstvenih ustanov v Ljubljani</u>

<u>1920-1968</u>. Ljubljana: Univerza, 1969. 232 p.

A classified listing of the 690 dissertations accepted for the doctorate at the University of Ljubljana and other institutions of higher education in Ljubljana. Entry gives publication information. Chronological index, index of dissertations by department, and author and adviser indexes.

C. Area Studies

General

C1. U.S. Department of State. Office of Intelligence Research and Analysis. <u>Abstracts of Completed Doctoral Dissertations for the Academic Year 1950/51</u>. Washington: 1952. 437 p. (<u>Its</u> Abstract Series, no. 1)

> Abstracts of 151 dissertations completed in American universities. Arranged under such areas as international organizations, American affairs, European affairs; subdivided by country and region. Institutional index.

C2. HORNA, Dagmar. <u>Current Research on Central and Eastern Europe</u>. New York: Mid-European Studies Center, Free Europe Committee, 1956. 251 p. (Mid-European Studies Center Publication, no. 28)

> Includes many dissertations from American and Canadian universities dealing with Albania, Austria, the Baltic States, Bulgaria, Czechoslovakia, Eastern Germany, Hungary, Poland, and Yugoslavia. Includes material on the Soviet Union only if one of the above countries is included as well. Arranged by country and covers the social sciences, geography, religion, language and linguistics, and law.

C3. "ORIENTALISTISCHE Dissertationen." <u>In</u> Deutsche Morgenländische Gesellschaft. <u>Zeitschrift</u> 105 (1955)-110 (1960). Annual.

> Lists dissertations which have been completed or are in progress in German universities. Arranged under field such as Egyptology; Islamic philology, literature, and cultural history; Japanology; and

Sinology. Entry gives status and adviser.

C4.   MOSER, Gerald M. <u>Brazilian and Portuguese Studies in Progress in the United States and Canada</u>. New York: New York
University, Brazilian Institute, 1962. 16 p.

   In part appears in his "Contemporary Portuguese
   Scholarship in North America." <u>Luso-Brazilian
   Review</u> 1 (1965): 19-59.

   Section B, "Ph.D. Dissertations and M.A. Theses in
   Progress or Completed in 1962" (p. 9-11, 13-14),
   lists 54 items. Entry indicates the country and
   subject covered.

   Continued by:

C5.   "BRAZILIAN and Portuguese Studies in Progress in the United
States and Canada [1962-1965/1966]" <u>Luso-Brazilian Review</u>
1 (1964)-3 (1966). Irregular.

   Contains separate sections of dissertations and
   theses completed and in progress. Entry gives
   adviser and date completed or expected to be completed.

C6.   CRUGER, Doris M. <u>A List of American Doctoral Dissertations
on Africa, covering 1961/62 through 1964/65; France, covering 1933/34 through 1964/65; Italy, covering 1933/34 through
1964/65</u>. Ann Arbor, Mich.: Xerox, University Microfilms
Library Services, 1967. 36 p.

   For Africa supersedes her <u>List of American Doctoral
   Dissertations on Africa</u> (1965) and <u>Supplement 1,
   1961/62 through 1963/64</u> (1965).

   Listing on Africa is intended to supplement Item
   C17, with an emphasis on items in the fields of the
   social sciences and humanities. The listing on
   France covers the modern period of French history
   from 1870 and the listing on Italy, the period from
   1861. The emphasis in these latter lists has been
   on the social sciences. Arranged chronologically
   under country.

C7.   _____   <u>A List of Doctoral Dissertations on Australia,</u>

covering <u>1933/34 through 1964/65; Canada, covering 1933/34</u>
<u>through 1964/65; New Zealand, covering 1933/34 through</u>
<u>1964/65</u>. Ann Arbor, Mich.: Xerox, 1967. 20 p.

Covers dissertations in economics, history, political
science, and sociology accepted by Canadian and American universities. There is a separate listing for
each country.

C8. PARIS. Université. Faculté de droit et des sciences économiques. Centre de documentation africaine. <u>Thèses et</u>
<u>mémoires relatif au tiers monde (moins l'Afrique) soutenues</u>
<u>et déposés, année 1967</u>. Paris: Département de droit et
économie des pays d'Afrique, 1968. 29 p.

In two parts: (1) separate listings of theses and
dissertations subdivided by field of the degree
(law, political science) and type of doctorate; and
(2) by subject.

C9. SCHERER, Anton. <u>Südosteuropa-Dissertationen, 1918-1960; Eine</u>
<u>Bibliographie deutscher, österreichischer und schweizerischer</u>
<u>Hochschulschriften</u>. Graz: Böhlau, 1968. 221 p.

Lists 2,234 dissertations dealing with the social,
cultural, and political history of Albania, Bulgaria,
Greece, Yugoslavia, Austro-Hungary, Romania, Slovakia,
Turkey, and Hungary. Each area is arranged by general topics. Some parenthetical notes. Author index.

C10. SCHWARZ, Klaus. <u>Verzeichnis deutschsprachiger Hochschul-</u>
<u>schriften zum islamischen Orient (1885-1970) Deutschland-</u>
<u>Österreich-Schweiz</u>. Freiburg im Breisgau: 1971. 280 p.
(Islamkundliche Materialien, Bd. 2)

Includes Petra Kappert and others, <u>Dissertationen</u>
<u>an deutschsprachigen Universitäten zur Geschichte</u>
<u>und Kultur des osmanischen Reiches</u> (1971).

Lists 2,394 dissertations. Arranged under such
fields as religion, law, medicine, history; subdivided by topic or place. Author and subject index.

C11. AKADEMIYA NAUK SSSR. Institut vostokovedeniya. <u>Doktorskie</u>
<u>i kandidatskie dissertatsiy zashchishchennye v Institute</u>
<u>vostokovedeniya Akademiya nauk SSSR s 1950-1970 gg.</u>;

Bibliograficheskiy ukazatel'. Sost. D. F. Brodskaya, 1972. 243 p.

> Lists theses and dissertations separately under department. Author and adviser indexes.

Africa

General

C12. WATTEL, Pierre. Bibliographie des mémoires de l'Institute des territoires d'outre-mer. Bruxelles: Commission belge de bibliographie, 1955. 95 p. (Bibliographia belgica, 11)

> A classified list of 903 theses in the colonial and administrative sciences, mainly dealing with the Belgian Congo and Ruanda-Urundi. Geographic index.

C13. COLEMAN, James S. "Research on Africa in European Centers." African Studies Bulletin 2, no. 3 (1959): 1-33.

> Appendix B: "Ph.D. Dissertations on African Subjects Completed at British Universities, 1950-1956" (p. 18-22); appendix E: "Doct. d'État Theses on African Subjects Completed at French Universities, 1951-1957" (p. 28-32). Each of these is arranged by general topic.

C14. HERRICK, Mary D. "Report on Africana in American Theological Collections." African Studies Bulletin 3 (May 1960): 5-12.

> "Unpublished Materials" (p. 9-11) is an alphabetical listing made up largely of theses.

C15. KÕHLER, Jochen. Deutsche Dissertationen über Afrika; Ein Verzeichnis für die Jahre 1918-1959. Hrsg. vom Wissenschaftlichen Ausschuss, Deutsche Afrika-Gesellschaft e. V. Bonn. Bonn: K. Schroeder, 1962. 1 vol. (unpaged)

> Lists 795 dissertations and Habilitationsschriften dealing with all aspects of Africa. Geographically subdivided. Entry indicates availability on exchange and publication information. Key word and author indexes.

C16. UNITED STATES and Canadian Publications on Africa [1960-   ]
Stanford, Calif.: Stanford University, Hoover Institution on
War, Revolution, and Peace, 1962-   . (Stanford University.
Hoover Institution on War, Revolution, and Peace Bibliogra-
phical Series) Annual.

The volume for 1960 was published by the Library of
Congress, African Section, and does not include theses
or dissertations.

Arranged by (1) works on Africa south of the Sahara,
in broad subjects, and (2) works dealing with specific
countries and regions. Each section is subdivided
by form of publication. Dissertations are included
with books and pamphlets. Author index.

C17. U.S. Library of Congress. African Section. A List of
American Doctoral Dissertations on Africa. Washington: U.S.
Government Printing Office, 1962. 62 p.

A revision and expansion of an earlier checklist
compiled jointly by Boston University's African
Studies Program and the Library of Congress African
Section, which appeared in African Studies Bulletin
4 (March 1961): 1-49.

An alphabetical author list of over 700 studies
accepted by United States and Canadian universities
from the late 19th century through the academic year
1960/1961. Entry gives publication information and
location of abstracts. Subject index.

Continued and supplemented by:

C18. DUIGNAN, Peter. United States and Canadian Doctoral Dissertations on Africa. Ann Arbor, Mich.: Xerox University
Microfilms, 1973. 33 p.

Lists over 1,000 dissertations related to sub-Saharan
Africa accepted in the United States from the nineteenth century through the academic year 1968/1969,
though most items listed were completed since 1961.
Arranged alphabetically by author. Entry gives
University Microfilms order number. Subject, geographical, and key-words-in-title index.

C19. "FOREIGN Area Fellowships." African Studies Bulletin 6 (May

1963): 24-27; 7 (May 1964): 20-23.

Lists doctoral candidates with work in progress on African topics and provides a brief description of their topics.

C20. INTERNATIONAL CENTRE FOR AFRICAN SOCIAL AND ECONOMIC DOCUMEN-
TATION. Bulletin of Information on Current Research on Human Sciences concerning Africa [no. 1 (1962/1963)-   ] Brussels: 1963-   . Title and frequency of publication vary.

In English and French.

A selective international listing of research in progress, a substantial portion of which consists of dissertations and some theses. Coverage takes in the range of the social sciences, as well as economics. Arranged alphabetically by researcher. Entry gives brief abstract in French (except for English language items), language in which the study will be written, the degree to be taken, depart-ment, and expected date of completion. Each number contains a section, "Following Up the Recensions Published in the Previous Bulletins," which indi-cates changes in the status of listings. Geographic and institutional indexes.

C21. "DOKTORSKIE i kandidatskie dissertatsiy, 1941-1961 gg." In Akademiya nauk SSSR. Institut Afriki. Bibliografiya Afriki, 1964, vyp. 1: 234-239.

Alphabetical author listing of 101 theses and dis-sertations completed in the U.S.S.R.

C22. STANDING CONFERENCE ON LIBRARY MATERIALS ON AFRICA. Theses on Africa Accepted by Universities in the United Kingdom and Ireland. Cambridge, England: W. Heffer & Sons, 1964. 74 p.

A listing of 1,142 theses and dissertations on Afri-can subjects prepared between 1920 and 1962 at 22 universities in the United Kingdom and Ireland. Arranged by region and country with each heading subdivided, when practical, into broad subject classes. Information on the availability of theses is given. Author index and index to tribes and peoples.

Continued by:

C23. UNITED KINGDOM Publications and Theses on Africa [1963-   ]
Cambridge, England: W. Heffer, 1966-   . Annual.

Prepared by the Standing Conference on Library
Materials on Africa.

Theses and dissertations, arranged geographically,
are listed in a separate section. Author index.

C24. DINSTEL, Marion. List of French Doctoral Dissertations on
Africa, 1884-1961. Boston: G. K. Hall, 1966. 336 p.

Lists 2,923 dissertations taken from the Catalogue
des thèses de doctorat soutenues devant les universités françaises and the French Doctoral Theses,
Sciences, 1951-53. Arranged by country and/or area
and alphabetically by author under each area. Entries give institution and type of degree and indicate from which of the above sources extracted.
Author, area, and subject indexes.

C25. "INVENTAIRE de thèses et mémoires africanistes de langue
française en cours [1969-   ]" In Centre d'analyse et de
recherche documentaire pour l'Afrique noire, Paris. Recherche, enseignement, documentation africanistes francophones 1 (1969)-   . Annual.

Lists theses and dissertations in progress in France
and in French language institutions outside France.
Arranged geographically, subdivided by such subjects
as archaeology and prehistory, art, economics, history, medicine and health. Entry gives adviser and
date when work began. Author, adviser, and subject
indexes.

C26. "INVENTAIRE de thèses et mémoires africanistes de langue
française, soutenues depuis [1966/1969-   ]" In Centre
d'analyse et de recherche documentaire pour l'Afrique noire,
Paris. Recherche, enseignement, documentation africanistes
francophones 1 (1969)-   . Annual.

Vol. 1 (1969) covers period 1966 to June 1969; vol.
2 (1970) covers period to 1970 and includes items
not listed in vol. 1.

Lists theses and dissertations completed in France
and in French language institutions outside France.
Arranged geographically, subdivided by such subjects
as archaeology and prehistory, art, economics, history,
medicine and health. Entry gives adviser. Author
and subject indexes.

C27. "DISSERTATIONS on Africa [1970/1971-   ]" African Studies
Newsletter 5 (1972)-   . Title varies. Irregular.

Vols. 1 (1968)-4 (1971) carry "Research in Progress,"
which also includes work for the degree.

American dissertations recently completed or in
progress arranged under broad subjects, e.g. art
history, economics, geography, history, music, literature, etc. Entry gives country or area of concern of the study.

C28. "MASTERS Theses on Africa [1972/1973-   ]" African Studies
Newsletter 6 (1973)-   . Annual.

An alphabetical author listing of American theses
in progress or recently completed.

C29. BRATTON, Michael and Anne Schneller. American Doctoral Dissertations on Africa, 1886-1972. Waltham, Mass.: American
Studies Association, 1973. 165 p.

Lists 2,540 dissertations completed between 1886
and 1972, arranged by geographical area and then by
subject. Subjects include the social sciences,
agriculture, natural sciences, health, religion,
language, linguistics, and fine arts. Author and
subject indexes.

Individual Institutions

C30. HOEHN, R. Philip and Jean Judson. "Theses on Sub-Saharan
Africa Accepted by the University of California at Berkeley."
African Studies Bulletin 12 (1969): 157-166.

Theses and dissertations cataloged by the University
Library through January 1969. Geographical arrangement.

C31. GARLICK, Peter C. "Theses on Africa Accepted by Howard University, Washington, D.C." African Studies Bulletin 11 (1968): 259-268.

> Covers theses and dissertations from 1936 through June 1968. Geographical arrangement.

C32. WISCONSIN. University. Library. Master's Theses on Africa Presented at the University of Wisconsin, 1914-1970; A List by Authors, with Indexes of Keywords from the Titles and of Academic Disciplines. By Michael J. Briggs and Georges D. Bokamba. Madison: 1970. 19 p.

> An alphabetical author list of 114 theses, the largest part of which are in history, political science, the social sciences, and journalism. Key word index.

East Africa

C33. ROGERS, M. H. "Theses on East African Topics; Completed and in Progress." In his Report of a Tour of East Africa, July-August, 1966, p. 55-62. Brighton: University of Sussex, Library, 1967.

> An alphabetical listing of approximately 100 references, mainly American with some from Germany and Great Britain. Indicates date of completion and provisional titles.

Ethiopia

C34. ADDIS ABABA. Haile Selassie I University. Institute of Ethiopian Studies. Register of Current Research on Ethiopia and the Horn of Africa [July 1963-   ] Addis Ababa: 1963-   . Annual.

> International in coverage with separate listings of dissertations and of theses in progress under each of the main subject areas. Entries give duration of the study and adviser.

C35. ADDIS ABABA. Haile Selassie I University. Reference Department. Theses on Ethiopia Produced in American Universities,

1920-1969. 1970. ??

Ghana

C36. GHANA. University. Balmi Library. Balmi Library Theses;
An Annotated List of Theses Accessioned. By J. K. T. Kafe.
Accra: 1969. 79, 5 p.

> Lists 202 theses and dissertations, a major portion
> of which deal with Ghana and/or the Gold Coast.
> These are arranged under broad subjects. The research
> represents work completed in large part outside of
> Ghana. The appendix, "Alphabetical List of Long
> Essays Submitted for the Associate Certificate and
> Post-Graduate Diploma in Education, University of
> Ghana" (p. 59-79), is an alphabetical author listing
> of 195 studies, which are not annotated. Author
> index.

C37. KAFE, Joseph K. Ghana: An Annotated Bibliography of Academic
Theses 1920-1970 in the Commonwealth, the Republic of Ireland
and the United States of America. Boston: Hall, 1973. 219 p.

> A classified bibliography of 522 theses and disser-
> tations in the main listing, covering all aspects
> of Ghana. An appendix carries an additional 118
> items, which may be relevant to Ghana. Entry
> frequently indicates location.

Nigeria

C38. AMOSU, Margaret. Nigerian Theses; A List of Theses on Nigerian Subjects and of Theses by Nigerians. Ibadan: Ibadan
University Press, 1965. 36 p.

> Subject listing of 489 theses and dissertations.
> Entry indicates whether a copy is held at the
> University of Ibadan Library. Author and subject
> indexes.

Anglo/American

General

C39. LEIPZIG. Universität. Verzeichnis der an der Universität Leipzig erschienenen Dissertationen und Fakultätsschriften auf englischem Gebiet. Leipzig: Verlag von dr. Seele & Co., 1900. 7 p.

A chronological listing by academic year of approximately 150 studies.

C40. KOPKA, Hans W. K. "Seit 1945 an Universitäten der DDR angenommene Dissertationen der Anglistik-Amerikanistik." Zeitschrift für Anglistik und Amerikanistik 1 (1953): 111.

An alphabetical author list covering the period to 1952. Entry gives adviser.

C41. "VERZEICHNIS der an philosophischen Fakultäten deutscher Universitäten von 1885[-1920] angenommenen anglistischen Dissertationen und Habilitationsschriften." Zeitschrift für Anglistik und Amerikanistik 2 (1954): 255-258, 365-370, 484-489; 3 (1955): 219-254, 383-384, 492-509; 4 (1956): 128-130, 257-260, 380-382.

Entries are numbered consecutively. Arranged alphabetically by author under academic year. Entry indicates if a dissertation or Habilitationsschrift.

Continued by:

C42. "AUS dem Jahresverzeichnis der deutschen Hochschulschriften [1921/1930-]" Zeitschrift für Anglistik und Amerikanistik 4 (1956)- . Irregular.

Arranged alphabetically by author under academic year. Later volumes cover shorter time spans. Items omitted from previous years are listed.

C43. LANGE, Hans. "Bibliographie in Arbeit befindliche Dissertationen." Zeitschrift für Anglistik und Amerikanistik 6 (1958)- . Irregular.

Title listing of dissertations in progress in German
and Austrian universities, arranged by country and
then by university. Entry gives adviser.

C44. ENGLISH and American Studies in German; Summaries of Theses
and Monographs [1968-   ] Tübingen: Max Niemeyer Verlag,
1969-   . Annual.

A supplement to Anglia.

English language summaries of dissertations and
Habilitationsschriften completed in German language
countries. Titles are also given in German. Entries
arranged under broad topics. Entry gives adviser
and publication information. Author, authors as
subjects, and subject indexes.

America

C45. THE UNITED STATES, 1865-1900; A Survey of Current Literature
with Abstracts of Unpublished Dissertations [Sept. 1941/Aug.
1942-Jan. 1/Dec. 31, 1944] Fremont, Ohio: Rutherford B.
Hayes-Lucy Webb Hayes Foundation, 1943-1945. 3 vols.

"Abstracts of Unpublished Dissertations Accepted in
1954..." in vol. 1 (p. 111-168). Index to the volume also includes dissertations completed in 1941
for which abstracts were published in the Hayes
Memorial Library, Fourth Annual Report. "Abstracts
of Unpublished Dissertations Accepted in 1943 [and
1944] Relating to American History from 1865 to 1900"
in vol. 2 (p. 259-287) and vol. 3 (p. 374-438).

Items are arranged under broad topic or by region
and state. Author indexes in each volume.

C46. "JAHRESBIBLIOGRAPHIE." In Deutsche Gesellschaft für Amerika-
studien. Mitteilungsblatt 1 (1954)-   . Annual.

Carries separate listing of dissertations and Habilitationen completed and in progress in German, Swiss,
and Austrian universities.

C47. KOPKA, Hans W. K. "Bibliographie an philosophischen Fakultäten deutscher Universitäten von 1885-1952 angenommene

amerikanistische Dissertationen." <u>Zeitschrift für Anglistik
und Amerikanistik</u> 2 (1954): 124-130.

> Dissertations on American topics grouped by time
> periods. Entry gives year of publication or com-
> pletion date.

C48. "DISSERTATIONS-in-Progress in American Studies." <u>American
Studies</u> 2, no. 2 (Nov. 1956): 5-7.

> An alphabetical author listing of approximately 120
> theses and dissertations in progress as of June
> 1956. Entry gives adviser.

> Continued by:

C49. "AMERICAN Studies Dissertations [1956-   ]" <u>American Quar-
terly</u> 9 (1957)-   . Title varies. Annual. Summer issue.

> An interdisciplinary bibliography of theses and
> dissertations in programs involving an American
> subject. Arranged under literature, regional
> studies, and history and biography. Each, in turn,
> is divided into new listings, completed, and with-
> drawn. Entry gives adviser.

C50. "THESES on American Topics in Progress and Completed at
British Universities." <u>Journal of American Studies</u> 4 (1970):
107-122; 6 (1972): 109-128.

> Compiled by the University of London Institute of
> United States Studies.

> A listing under broad subjects of theses and disser-
> tations covering the period 1966-1967. Covers
> economics, economic history, education, history,
> international relations, literature, philosophy,
> politics and government, religion and theology, and
> sociology. Entry gives adviser and indicates if
> completed.

Arizona

C51. HINTON, Harwood P. "Arizona Theses and Dissertations: A
Preliminary Checklist." <u>Arizona and the West</u> 7 (1965):

239-264.

Lists 275 theses and 46 dissertations completed in
American universities from 1902 on all aspects of
Arizona, including agriculture, art, anthropology,
sociology, speech. Listed under the temporal subdivisions Spanish, Mexican, territorial, since
statehood.

Louisiana

C52. "THESES on Louisiana." In Louisiana Library Association.
Bulletin 1, no. 3 (Dec. 1932): 3-14.

A listing of approximately 100 theses on Louisiana
arranged under subject. Represents theses completed
at Tulane University and Louisiana State University
only.

C53. WYLIE, Margery B. Bibliography of Tulane University Theses
Relating to Louisiana, 1893-1963. New Orleans, La.: Tulane
University, Howard-Tilton Memorial Library, 1965. 52 p.

An alphabetical author listing of 560 theses and
dissertations (some theses for the bachelor's degree
are also included). Subject index.

_____ _____ First Supplement, 1964-1968. New Orleans, La.:
Howard Tilton Memorial Library, 1970. 6 p.

An alphabetical author listing of 44 theses and
dissertations through 1968. Subject index.

New Jersey

C54. DORRIS, Charles and Julia Sabine. "Theses and Dissertations
on Subjects Relating to New Jersey." In New Jersey Historical Society. Proceedings 60 (1942): 153-171.

Alphabetical author listing covering the period 1912
to 1941. Indicates if available in the Newark Public
Library. Subject index.

New York State and New York City

C55. BELTH, Pauline. "Selected New York City and New York State
      Dissertations and Theses." Municipal Reference Library
      Notes 35 (1961): 133-142.

      Classified listing of research done at American
      institutions on New York City and New York State.

Oklahoma

C56. MORRIS, Mary E. Bibliography of Theses on Oklahoma in the
      University of Oklahoma Library. Norman, Okla.: University
      of Oklahoma, Institute of Community Development, 1956.
      104 p.

      A listing by department of bachelors' and masters'
      theses and dissertations completed at the University
      which are concerned with Oklahoma, her people, history,
      and resources. Entry gives adviser.

Pacific Northwest

C57. APPLETON, John B. The Pacific Northwest; A Select Biblio-
      graphy Covering Completed Research in the Natural Resource
      and Socio-Economic Fields...1930-39. Portland, Or.: North-
      west Regional Council, 1939. 454 p.

      Subject matter includes "natural resources and the
      various interrelated economic, social, and political
      factors which have a bearing on the human occupance
      of the region." The area covered includes Oregon,
      Washington, British Columbia, Alaska, Idaho, and
      Montana. Many theses and dissertations included in
      "Part I: Completed Research--Published and Unpub-
      lished." Arrangement is by subject, then alphabe-
      tically by author.

C58. TODD, Ronald. "Theses Related to the Pacific Northwest:
      University of Washington Checklist." Pacific Northwest Quar-
      terly 35 (1944): 55-64.

      Lists all theses and dissertations from beginning
      of the graduate school. Arranged alphabetically.

Entry indicates subject.

Continued by:

_____ _____ *Pacific Northwest Quarterly* 40 (1949): 65-69.

Covers the years 1943-1947.

C59. BROMBERG, Erik. "Bibliography of Theses and Dissertations Concerning the Pacific Northwest and Alaska." *Pacific Northwest Quarterly* 40 (1949): 203-252.

"...an effort to bring together all the M.A. and Ph.D. theses written in the Pacific Northwest in the field of social sciences which pertain to Alaska or to the Northwest or any part thereof."--Introd. "Social sciences" is interpreted broadly to include such subjects as English, drama, forestry, and agriculture. Listed under broad subject headings. Subject index.

_____ "A Further Bibliography of Theses Concerning the Pacific Northwest and Alaska." *Pacific Northwest Quarterly* 42 (1951): 147-166.

Has same subject matter and arrangement as main listing but lists work completed at institutions outside the Pacific Northwest.

_____ _____ "Supplement, 1949-1957." *Oregon Historical Quarterly* 59 (March 1958): 27-84.

South Carolina

C60. ENGLISH, Elisabeth D. "Author List of Caroliniana in the University of South Carolina Library." *University of South Carolina Bulletin*, no. 134 (1923): 302-316.

Appendix B, "University of South Carolina M.A. Theses," lists theses and dissertations completed at the University of South Carolina in the period from 1909 to 1923. The majority of the items deal with South Carolina topics.

The West

C61. "A LIST of Dissertations [1968/1969-   ]" <u>Western Histori-</u>
<u>cal Quarterly</u> 1 (1970)-   . Annual.

    Appears as a separate section in "Sources and Lit-
erature for Western American History."

    Dissertations completed in American institutions,
which are concerned with the history of the American
West in its broadest sense. Arranged under such
topics as language and literature, theatre, speech,
economics, Indians, anthropology, government and
politics.

Wisconsin

C62. RUKA, Mary L. <u>Wisconsin Region: A Bibliography of Theses in</u>
<u>the Social Sciences and Humanities</u>. Madison, Wis.: Univer-
sity of Wisconsin Centennial Committee, 1949. 1 vol. (various pagings)

    Also includes work done at out-of-state institutions,
published and unpublished. Includes "all theses,
within the geographical limits, having a social and
cultural value, regardless of the fields in which
they were prepared." Contains a separate list of
bachelors' theses.

C63. WYMAN, Roger E. <u>A Guide to Theses on Wisconsin Subjects</u>.
Madison, Wis.: State Historical Society of Wisconsin and
University of Wisconsin Extension Division, 1964. 88 p.

    Supersedes the Committee on the Study of American
Civilization, <u>The Wisconsin Region: A Bibliography</u>
<u>of Theses in the Social Sciences and Humanities</u>
(1949). Some items in this earlier listing were
eliminated as being too technical or too limited to
be of value.

    A classified listing of "all Doctor's, Masters, and
Bachelors Theses having a broad social or cultural
value to the area of Wisconsin studies." Includes
items prepared at institutions other than the University of Wisconsin. Author index.

Continued by:

C64. CHISWICK, Jeanne H. A Guide to Theses on Wisconsin Subjects,
Supplement [no. 1-] Madison: State Historical Society
of Wisconsin, 1966- . Irregular.

Includes theses and dissertations completed at the
University of Wisconsin on Wisconsin subjects since
September 1964, as well as those completed at various
times in other institutions. All items are located
at the University of Wisconsin or the Wisconsin
Historical Society. Arranged under broad subjects,
such as agriculture, arts, biography, government,
Indians, social history, politics, religion.

Canada - Western Canada

C65. KOESTER, Charles B. A Bibliography of Selected Theses on
[i.e. in] the Library of the University of Alberta (Edmonton)
Relating to Western Canada, 1915-1965. Edmonton: 1965.
21 p.

Compiled for the Western Canada Research Project.

Represents theses and dissertations completed in the
University of Alberta, Edmonton. Does not include
technical, agricultural, or educational studies
unless they are confined to the immediate region.
Arranged by such subjects as agriculture, history,
biology, economics, literature.

Great Britain

C66. BELL, Peter. Social Reform and Social Structure in Victorian
England; A Handlist of University Theses. Leicester: Univer-
sity of Leicester, Victorian Studies Centre, 1972. 16 p.
(Victorian Studies Handlist, 5)

Lists approximately 150 British theses and dissertations and American dissertations completed through
1971 (some 1972). In two sections: (1) social reform and (2) social structure. These are subdivided
to include such topics as poverty, the poor, public
health, urban and working conditions, family, migration, social class. Entry gives publication information.

Wales

C67. DAVIES, Alun E. <u>Traethodau Ymchwil Cymraeg a Chymreig a</u> <u>dderbyniwyd gan brifysgolion Prydeinig, Americanaidd ac</u> <u>Almaenaidd, 1887-1971</u>. <u>Welsh Language and Welsh Disserta-</u> <u>tions Accepted by British, American and German Universities,</u> <u>1887-1971</u>. Caerdydd (Cardiff): Gwasg Prifysgol Cymru ar ran y Bwrdd Gwybodau Celtaidd, 1973. 205 p.

> Lists 1,636 theses and dissertations. Does not include works which deal with Wales and Great Britain as a single unit. Arranged by classes, following the Library of Congress classification. Author and subject indexes.

Yorkshire and Derbyshire

C68. HALL, John and R. Wells. <u>Sheffield University Theses Relat-</u> <u>ing to Yorkshire and Derbyshire, 1920-1970</u>. Sheffield, England: Sheffield University Library, 1971. 11 p. (University of Sheffield. Library. Information Service Guides, 5/71)

> A listing of approximately 80 theses and dissertations. Includes items deposited in the University Library and in the Departments of Economic History and Town and Regional Planning. Arranged, generally, by the departments in which they were done. If relevance is not clear from the title, the locality is given.

Asia

General

C69. MULLER, Frederik, & Co., Amsterdam. <u>Catalogus dissertation-</u> <u>um et orationum orientem et litteras orientales spectantium.</u> <u>Defensarum et habitarum ab a. 1650 usque ad 1851 in academiis</u> <u>Germaniae, etc. praesertim Neerlandiae. Quae venales pros-</u> <u>tant apud Fredericum Muller...</u> Amstelodami: 1851. 6, 1 p.

> A dealer's catalog listing 130 items. In two parts, (1) quarto and (2) octavo.

C70. <u>BULLETIN of Oriental Studies; An Annual Record of Work in</u>

Progress in Britain [1951-1961] Cambridge, England: Association of British Orientalists, 1951-1961. Title varies.
Annual.

Not issued 1952, 1953, 1958.

Included in part one is a substantial number of
theses and dissertations completed or in progress.
Items are listed only once unless titles are changed.
Arranged by region and period, i.e. ancient East,
Near East in post-Christian period, Middle East,
Southeast Asia, India, Pakistan, and Ceylon.

C71. COLUMBIA UNIVERSITY. Libraries. East Asiatic Library.
Columbia University Masters' Essays and Doctoral Dissertations on Asia, 1875-1956. New York: 1957. 96 p.

Includes all titles of graduate work on the East,
Far East, Central, Southeast, and South Asia completed at Columbia University, regardless of faculty. Arranged by area and by subject within area.
Analytical index to authors, subjects, biographies,
some proper and place names. Updated record of
essays and dissertations is maintained at the East
Asiatic Library.

C72. SCHMIDT, Earl R. A Bibliography of Ph.D. Theses on Asia,
1940-1960. Philadelphia: 1960. 29 p.

Covers only Southwest Asia and includes some pre-
1940 items.

Lists 580 completed American dissertations arranged
alphabetically by author under the following headings: B.C. period; Islamic studies (language, history,
and literature); general; Israel; Egypt; Jordan,
Syria, Lebanon, Iraq, and Arabia; Central Asia (Iran
and Afghanistan); and Turkey.

C73. CHICAGO. University. Far Eastern Library. The University
of Chicago Doctoral Dissertations and Masters' Theses on
Asia, 1894-1962. Chicago: 1962. 52 p.

A geographically arranged listing of 630 items completed at the University of Chicago on East, Southeast, and South Asia. Most items deal with the pre-
1949 period. Two hundred seventy four are on China,

145 on India and Pakistan, and 90 on Japan.

C74. VOCHELE, Jaroslav. "Survey of Graduation Theses in the Field of Far Eastern Studies Presented by Students of the Department of Asian and African Studies of the Faculty of Philosophy, Caroline University Prague." Orientalia Pragensia 2 (1962): 81-86.

A subseries of the Prague. Universita Karlova. Acta Universitatis Carolinae Philologica.

Separate chronological listings of 35 theses in Sinology, 12 in Korean language and literature, and 11 in Japanology. Covers the period 1951-1961. Some studies are abstracted.

C75. "LIST of Doctoral Dissertations, 1961/1962." In Association for Asian Studies. Newsletter 9 (Dec. 1963): 48-59.

A listing of items found in Dissertation Abstracts, excluding items on the physical, earth, and biological sciences. Arranged by geographical areas and subdivided by subject.

C76. SYRACUSE UNIVERSITY. An Annotated Bibliography of Theses and Dissertations on Asia Accepted at Syracuse University, 1907-1963. Compiled under the direction of Donn V. Hart. Syracuse, N.Y.: Syracuse University Library, 1964. 46 p.

Lists 161 theses and dissertations accepted as of late 1963 at Syracuse University (including those accepted at the New York State College of Forestry). Arranged alphabetically by author with annotations. Subject and author index.

C77. BLOOMFIELD, Barry C. Theses on Asia Accepted by Universities in the United Kingdom and Ireland 1877-1964. London: Frank Cass & Co., 1967. 126 p.

Lists 2,571 theses and dissertations which in some way deal with Asian and Oriental studies. Covers the whole continent of Asia and its islands together with Oceania. Excludes Georgia and North Africa. Arranged by region, then country and then subject. Contains a section indicating the availability of material. Author index.

Continued by:

C78. _____ "Theses on Asia: 1964-65." In Association of British Orientalists. Bulletin, new ser. 4 (1968): 56-65.

Lists approximately 150 theses and dissertations on Asian subjects accepted by British universities during the 1964/65 session. Extracted from ASLIB, Index to Theses Accepted for Higher Degrees..., vol. 15 (1967). Arranged by major geographic region and then by area, country, or large topic. Includes material for law, religion, Jews, social sciences, agriculture, history, geography, languages, and linguistics.

C79. STUCKI, Curtis W. American Doctoral Dissertations on Asia, 1933-June 1966, including Appendix of Masters' Theses at Cornell University 1933-June 1966. 3d ed. Ithaca, N.Y.: Cornell University, 1968. 304 p. (Cornell University. Dept. of Asian Studies. Southeast Asia Program. Data Paper, no. 71)

First edition 1959; second edition 1963.

Attempts to cover the whole range of doctoral studies, published and unpublished, on Asia in the fields of social sciences and humanities. Items are listed in chronological order under each country and subject. Author index.

C80. SHULMAN, Frank J. "Doctoral Dissertations." In Association for Asian Studies. Newsletter 14 (May 1969)-16 (1971).

An international listing of dissertations completed or in progress. Listings gradually expanded to include items for an increasingly larger number of Asian countries. Arranged by region and subdivided chronologically and by subject.

Continued by:

C81. "DOCTORAL Dissertations [1971-   ]" Asian Studies Professional Review, no. 1 (Fall 1971)-   . Semiannual.

An international listing of dissertations completed or in progress. Arranged by subject or historical

period under region or country. For non-English
language items the title is translated into English.
Entry gives University Microfilms number. Some
items carry short descriptive note and indicate the
department in which work was done.

C82. BIBLIOGRAPHY of Asian Studies [1970-   ] Ann Arbor, Mich.:
Association for Asian Studies, 1972-   . Annual.

Arranged by place and subdivided by topic. A separate listing for theses and dissertations is provided under each topic. The coverage is international.

C83. BISHOP, Enid. Australian Theses on Asia; A Union List of
Higher Degree Theses Accepted by Australian Universities to
31 December 1970. Canberra: Australian National University,
Faculty of Asian Studies, 1972. 35 p. (Australian National
University, Canberra. Faculty of Asian Studies. Occasional
Paper, 12)

Lists 306 theses and dissertations which deal with
some aspect of Asian studies, including science and
technology. Arranged by region, by country, and
then by broad subject headings. Author index.

Southeast Asia

General

C84. DEMIÉVILLE, Paul. "Organization of East Asian Studies in
France." Journal of Asian Studies 18 (1958): 163-181.

Section entitled "List of Theses Concerning East
Asia Completed in France 1946-1958" (p. 177-181) is
a chronological listing covering literature, history,
political science, sociology, religion, and linguistics.

C85. "HARVARD Ph.D. Theses on East Asian Subjects since 1930."
In Harvard University. East Asian Studies at Harvard
University, p. 50-57. Cambridge, Mass.: 1964.

Appendix B lists dissertations for the period 1931-
1964, inclusive, chronologically.

C86. PENNINGTON, Juliana and Paul Marsh. The University of Southern California Doctoral Dissertations and Master's Theses on
East and Southeast Asia, 1911-1964. Los Angeles: University
of Southern California, 1965. 54 p.

> A preliminary checklist of some 350 theses and dis-
> sertations on the Far East and Southeast Asia ac-
> cepted at the University of Southern California.
> Deals primarily with the pre-1949 period. Arrange-
> ment by country and by subject under country.
> Author index.

C87. JACKSON, James C. Recent Higher Degree Theses on Social,
Political and Economic Aspects of Southeast Asia, Presented
in the Universities of the United Kingdom and in the Univer-
sities of Malaya and Singapore. Hull: University of Hull,
Dept. of Geography, 1966. 1 vol. (unpaged) (University of
Hull, Dept. of Geography. Miscellaneous Series, no. 6)

> Contains 143 theses and dissertations arranged
> under individual countries. Based upon Index to
> Theses Accepted for Higher Degrees in the Univer-
> sities of Great Britain and Ireland, 1950/51-1963/64.

C88. LIAN The and Paul W. van der Veur. Treasures and Trivia;
Doctoral Dissertations on Southeast Asia Accepted by Univer-
sities in the United States. Athens, Ohio: Ohio University,
Center for International Studies, 1968. 141 p. (Papers in
International Studies. Southeast Asia Series, no. 1)

> Approximately 900 dissertations arranged by country
> and then by broad subject. Includes 79 items com-
> pleted prior to 1941. Contains material in the
> biological sciences, as well as history, philosophy,
> religion, language and literature, education, and
> the social sciences. Author index.

C89. KOZICKI, Richard J. and Peter Ananda. South and Southeast
Asia: Doctoral Dissertations and Masters' Theses Completed
at the University of California at Berkeley 1906-1968.
Berkeley: University of California, Center for South and
Southeast Asia Studies, 1969. 49 p. (Occasional Paper,
no. 1)

> Lists 287 theses and dissertations completed in
> the period from 1913 through 1968, arranged by
> country within the region and alphabetically by

author within discipline. The emphasis is on the
social sciences and humanities, but material in
agriculture and agricultural economics is also
included. Entry indicates department in which work
was done. Author and subject index.

C90. SarDESAI, D. R. and Bhanu D. SarDesai. Theses and Dissertations on Southeast Asia; An International Bibliography in
Social Sciences, Education and Fine Arts. Zug, Switzerland:
Inter Documentation, 1970. 176 p. (Bibliotheca asiatica,
no. 6)

A list of 2,814 items representing work done in the
United States, Canada, Eastern and Western Europe,
and Asia. Arranged by broad subjects, then by
country. Non-Roman language entries are Romanized
and an English translation is provided. Author
index.

C91. SHULMAN, Frank J. Japan and Korea: An Annotated Bibliography of Doctoral Dissertations in Western Languages, 1877-
1969. Chicago: American Library Association for the Center
of Japanese Studies, University of Michigan, 1970. 360 p.

This is an enlarged edition of and supersedes Peter
G. Cornwall, "Unpublished Doctoral Dissertations
Relating to Japan, Accepted in the Universities of
Australia, Canada, Great Britain and the United
States, 1946-1963." In Association for Asian Stu-
dies. Newsletter 10 (1964): 53-88. Cornwall list
was also issued as a separate by the University of
Michigan Center for Japanese Studies (1965).

An interdisciplinary bibliography of approximately
2,600 items from 26 countries in 14 languages, which
is intended to cover every Western language dissertation throughout the world. It is arranged with
sections for Japan and Korea and within the section
by subject, such as anthropology and sociology/com-
munity studies. The entry includes identification
numbers of Dissertation Abstracts and University
Microfilms. An annotation or listing of the table
of contents and related publications by the author
are also included. Indexed by author, by degree
granting institution, and by personal name, if
dissertation is primarily biographical.

C92. _____ Doctoral Dissertations on South Asia, 1966-1970; An Annotated Bibliography Covering North America, Europe, and Australia. Ann Arbor, Mich.: University of Michigan, Center for South and Southeast Asian Studies, 1971. 228 p. (Michigan Papers on South and Southeast Asia, no. 4)

   Lists 1,362 dissertations, of which 1,254 cover 1966-1970 and 108 works completed in 1971, which deal wholly or in part with the former civilization and the contemporary affairs of Ceylon, India, Nepal, and Pakistan. Includes material in the natural sciences, as well as the human and the social sciences. Covers the United States and Canada through 1970 and Great Britain through 1969. It is not comprehensive for dissertations completed in Western Europe, includes Australian dissertations from the Australian National University, and excludes those from South Asia and the Soviet Union. Arranged on the basis of country and then by specific subject or time period. Entry provides reference to Dissertation Abstracts International. Author, institutional, and subject indexes.

China

C93. "THESES on Social and Educational Conditions in China." Education for Victory 1 (April 15, 1943): 16.

   Eight theses, with abstracts, on file and available in the U.S. Office of Education Library.

C94. BERTON, Peter and Eugene Wu. Contemporary China; A Research Guide. Edited by Howard Koch, Jr. Stanford, Calif.: Stanford University, The Hoover Institution on War, Revolution, and Peace, 1967. 695 p. (Hoover Institution Bibliographic Series, no. 31)

   Prepared for the Joint Committee on Contemporary China of the American Council of Learned Societies and the Social Science Research Council.

   Limited almost exclusively to post-1949 Mainland China and post-1945 Taiwan.

   Appendix B, "Dissertations and Theses" (p. 556-584), is a listing of roughly 340 theses and dissertations accepted by American universities. It is arranged into four categories: (1) the People's Republic of

China, (2) the Republic of China, (3) the overseas
Chinese, (4) China policy. Subject index and
author-title index.

C95. MODERN China Studies; International Bulletin [no. 1 (1970)-
      ] Semiannual.

      Published by the China Quarterly.

      Consists largely of dissertations in progress.
      International in coverage. Arranged by subject or
      place, such as anthropology and sociology, arts,
      biography, Hong Kong. Entry gives department, ex-
      pected date of completion, and an abstract. Author
      index.

C96. GORDON, Leonard H. D. and Frank J. Shulman. Doctoral Disser-
      tations on China; A Bibliography of Studies in Western Lan-
      guages, 1945-1970. Seattle: Published for the Association
      of Asian Studies by the University of Washington Press, 1972.
      317 p. (Association for Asian Studies, Reference Series,
      no. 1)

      A classified bibliography of 2,217 dissertations on
      China, Mongolia, Tibet, and the overseas Chinese
      communities, covering history, law, education, the
      social sciences, humanities, and the natural sciences.
      Also includes dissertations which partially deal with
      the area of China. Though representing work completed
      principally in the United States, France, Germany,
      Great Britain, and the U.S.S.R., it includes many
      studies completed in other countries as well. Dis-
      sertations in the social sciences are arranged by
      historical period and a topical arrangement is used
      for the humanities and natural sciences. Entry
      includes English translation of title when necessary.
      Brief annotations are provided if the title does not
      indicate the work's contents. Author, institutional,
      and subject indexes.

India

C97. JANERT, Klaus L. Verzeichnis indienkundlichen Hochschul-
      schriften: Deutschland, Österreich, Schweiz. Wiesbaden:
      Harrassowitz, 1961. 80 p.

A classified bibliography of 933 dissertations
covering the period 1884 through 1959, dealing with
all aspects of India. Entry gives information on
publication. Author and subject indexes.

C98. IYER, K. P. "Ph.D. Theses on India Accepted by Universities
in the United Kingdom and Ireland, 1877-1964." In Sinha,
Mansas R. A Bunch of Current Indian Studies, p. 103-126.
Bombay: Asian Studies Press, 1969.

An alphabetical author listing of 1,063 theses and
dissertations, including law and medicine.

Japan

C99. JAPAN INSTITUTE, INC., New York. Doctoral Dissertations on
Japan Accepted by American Universities, 1912-1939. New
York: 1940. 17 p.

A classified listing of 89 published and unpublished
dissertations concerning Japan or Japanese affairs,
national, international or colonial, or which, inci-
dent to their main subject, discuss such affairs at
some length.

Pakistan

C100. EBERHARD, Wolfram. Studies on Pakistan's Social and Economic
Conditions; A Bibliographical Note. Berkeley: University of
California Institute of International Studies, Center for
South Asia Studies, 1958. 47 p.

"A working bibliography prepared for the South Asia
Colloquium, May, 1958...Most of these studies are
theses and dissertations which are unpublished but
available in the libraries of the different departments of the University of Punjab and the Library
of the Agricultural College in Lyallpur." Some
printed and foreign studies, and some titles dealing
with East Punjab (India) have been included. A
brief descriptive note is often included, as well as
location.

Europe

East Europe and the U.S.S.R.

General

C101. MATL, Joseph and Anton Scherer. "Wiener (bzw. Grazer) Dissertationen über den Südosten (1918-1948)." Osteuropa 7 (1951): 149-151.

Dissertations primarily from the various faculties of the University of Vienna. Arranged by area and by country.

C102. HANUSCH, Gerhard. "Osteuropa-Dissertationen [1945/50-1958/60]" Jahrbücher für Geschichte Osteuropas, neue Folge, vol. 1, no. 4, suppl. (1953); vol. 2, no. 2, suppl. (1954); vol. 3, no. 1, suppl. (1955); vol. 4, no. 3, suppl. (1956); vol. 6, no. 4, suppl. (1958); vol. 8, no. 2, suppl. (1960).

In all 239 pages numbered consecutively.

Lists 2,546 dissertations on Eastern Europe accepted by American and West European universities from 1945 to 1960. Covers social sciences, humanities, literature, theology, philosophy, medicine, psychology, and education. Arranged alphabetically under broad subject.

C103. DISSERTATIONEN zur Problematik des böhmisch-mährischen Raumes. München: Sekretariat des Sudetendeutschen Archivs, 1955-1956. 2 vols. (Schriftenreihe des Sudetendeutschen Archivs, Heft 1-2)

Two separate classified listings, totaling 443 dissertations, covering such areas as history, economics, law, sociology, agriculture, and politics. Represents work done in western Europe and the U.S. for the period 1940-1955. Each piece contains separate subject and author indexes.

C104. PESCHL, Otto. "Wiener slavistische Dissertationen aus den Jahren 1882-1962 in der Universitätsbibliothek Wien." Wiener slavistisches Jahrbuch 10 (1963): 195-205.

A chronological listing of the 167 dissertations
completed at the University of Vienna and still
available in the University Library.

_____ "Supplement, 1963." Wiener slavistisches
Jahrbuch 11 (1964): 216-218.

Lists dissertations submitted to the University of
Vienna only.

C105. DOSSICK, Jesse J. "Doctoral Dissertations on Russia, the
Soviet Union and Eastern Europe Accepted by American, Cana-
dian and British Universities [1964/1965-   ]" Slavic
Review 24 (1965)-   . Annual. Dec. issue.

Continues Item C113.

Completed dissertations dealing directly with Russia,
the Soviet Union, and Eastern Europe, or auxiliary
dissertations which, while not primarily on those
countries, contain sufficient material of interest
or value to warrant inclusion. In two parts: (1)
American and Canadian dissertations on Russia and
the Soviet Union and Eastern Europe, subdivided by
subject; (2) British dissertations. Under each subject, auxiliary dissertations are listed separately.

C106. ASSOCIATION OF RESEARCH LIBRARIES. Slavic Bibliographic and
Documentation Center. Dissertations-in-Progress in Slavic
and East European Studies [1970-   ] Washington: 1971-   .
Annual.

An international listing of dissertations and Habilitationsschriften. Arranged by broad subject in two
parts: U.S. and Canadian dissertations and German
dissertations. Entry indicates expected date of completion and adviser.

C107. SEYDOUX, Marianne and Mieczysław Biesiekierski. Répertoire
des thèses concernant les études slaves, l'U.R.S.S. et les
pays de l'Est européen, et soutenues en France de 1824 à
1969. Paris: Institut d'Études slaves, 30)

Supersedes Marianne Seydoux, "Thèses concernant la
Russie et l'U.R.S.S. soutenues en France de 1888 à
1964." Cahiers du monde russe et soviétique 6
(1965): 437-466, and its annual supplements for

1965 to 1967 in the Cahiers du monde russe et soviétique 7 (1966)-9 (1968); 12 (1971).

Classified listing of 1,357 dissertations. Following
a general section, the studies are arranged by country,
e.g. U.S.S.R., Czechoslovakia, Poland, Yugoslavia,
Bulgaria, Romania, Hungary, and Albania. Includes
economics and sociology; law and institutions; history
and politics; linguistics and philology; religion,
ideas, and literature; education; art and music;
science and medicine; nationalities and minorities;
and emigration. Author index.

Hungary

C108. "DISSERTATIONS." Hungarian Studies Newsletter, no. 1 (1973)-
. Three times per year.

Abstracts of dissertations completed in American
universities.

Poland

C109. "POLISH Problems in Doctoral Dissertations (Partial List)."
Polish Review 1 (Spring 1956): 151-154.

A chronological listing covering the period 1948-
1955, representing the work done at European and
American universities.

The U.S.S.R.

C110. FOCK, Gustav, firm, booksellers, Leipzig. Doktorarbeiten
über Russland...[1895-1933] Leipzig: 1934. 11 p.

A price list of 319 dissertations.

C111. COLUMBIA UNIVERSITY. Russian Institute. Report on Research
and Publication [Sept. 1946/Aug. 1948-   ] Irregular.

Carries separate listings of dissertations completed
within the Institute and of research in progress,
which consists largely of dissertations. Both list-

ings are arranged by such subjects as economics, education, government and law, history, international relations, and literature.

C112. DOSSICK, Jesse J. <u>Doctoral Research on Russia and the Soviet Union</u>. New York: New York University Press, 1960. 248 p.

A list of 960 doctoral dissertations completed in American, British, and Canadian universities in the period 1900 to 1959, classified under 23 subjects. Pt. 2: "American and Canadian Dissertations..."; pt. 3: "British Dissertations." Each part also lists "auxiliary theses, in all 325, which, while not primarily on Russia or the Soviet Union, contain material contributing to a larger frame of reference."

Continued by:

C113. _____ · "Doctoral Dissertations on Russia and the Soviet Union Accepted by American, British, and Canadian Universities, 1960-1964." <u>Slavic Review</u> 23 (1964): 797-812.

Continued by Item C105.

Approximately 400 titles, a large portion of which are in the social sciences, language, and literature. However, dissertations in education, geography, agriculture, religion, and philosophy are also represented. Also includes auxiliary dissertations which, while not directly on Russia or the Soviet Union, contribute to the frame of reference. In two parts: (1) American and Canadian dissertations, 1960-1964; (2) British dissertations, 1960-1963, each subdivided by subject.

Moscow

C114. "DISSERTATSIY po voprosam izucheniya Moskvy i Moskovskoy oblasti, zashchishchennye v 1944-1959 gg." <u>Voprosy geografii</u>, sbornik 51 (1961): 187-188.

An alphabetical author listing of 29 theses and dissertations completed between 1944 and 1959, covering such subjects as geography, history, economics, architecture.

Tadzhikistan

C115. SHEVCHENKO, Zinaida M. <u>Katalog kandidatskikh i doktorskikh</u>
<u>dissertatsiy, zashchishchennykh na materialakh Tadzikskoy</u>
<u>SSR 1960-1965 gg</u>. Dushanbe: "Donish," 1970. 133 p.

A listing of 655 theses and dissertations arranged
under such fields as medicine, philosophy, geography,
chemistry. Author index.

Ukraine

C116. HORBACH, Olexa. "Ukraïnistichni pratsi po universitetakh
zakhidnoï Nimechchini ta Avstriï v 1945-1957 rr."
<u>Ukrains'kyie samostiienyk</u> 11 (1960), ch. 11: 20-25, ch. 12:
17-20.

A listing of dissertations on Ukrainian subjects
completed in West German and Austrian institutions
in 1945-1957. Some descriptive notes are provided.

C117. DANKO, Joseph W. "European and American Doctoral Dissertations on the Ukraine, 1945-1960." <u>In</u> Ukrainian Academy of
Arts and Sciences in the United States. <u>Annals</u> 9, nos. 1
and 2 (1961): 313-333.

A classified listing of 215 dissertations and Habili-
tatsschrifte dealing with the Ukraine in whole or in
part. Of these 55 are from various German universities; 53 from the Ukrainian Free University, Munich.
Covers the fields of history, church history, language, and literature.

France

C118. UTRECHT. Rijksuniversiteit. Bibliotheek. <u>Lijst van proef-</u>
<u>schriften over Fransche taal- en letterkunde</u>. Utrecht:
1928-1939. 4 vols.

Vols. 1-3 edited by M. A. Rombach; vol. 4 by E. J.
Gras, I. J. Hogewind, and D. Ruys.

An alphabetical international listing of theses and
dissertations in the Library. Vol. 4 includes items

collected to 1935. Entry gives title in original
language and publication information. Separate
subject indexes in vols. 3 and 4.

C119. GREEN, Frederick L. "Thèses inédites de littérature, histoire, philosophie et art français soutenues devant les universités de Grande Bretagne de 1939 à 1949." In Association
internationale des études françaises. Cahiers 2 (1952):
112-121.

A subject list of approximately 170 dissertations,
arranged by periods and centuries.

C120. TAYLOR, Alan C. Bibliography of Unpublished Theses on French
Subjects Deposited in University Libraries of the United
Kingdom, 1905-1950. Oxford: Published for the Society for
French Studies by B. Blackwell, 1964. 45 p. (French Studies.
Supplementary Publication, no. 2)

A classified listing of all unpublished theses on
French subjects for the M.A., B.Litt., M.Litt.,
D.Phil., Ph.D., and D.Litt. deposited in the libraries of the universities and university colleges
of Great Britain and Northern Ireland up to and
including 1949/1950. Includes material on linguistics and stylistics; literature; and studies of
writers, anonymous works, and historical persons or
fictitious characters (French or foreign). Entries
carry notes on the availability of theses. Includes
a few titles which appeared after 1950 which do not
appear in the Index to Theses Accepted for Higher
Degrees in the Universities of Great Britain and
Ireland.

Continued by:

C121. _____ Current Research in French Studies at Universities
and University Colleges in the United Kingdom [1960/1961-
] Compiled for the Association of University Professors of French and the Society for French Studies in association with the Modern Humanities Research Association.
London: Association of University Professors of French,
1961- . Title varies. Annual.

Approximately half the items listed are theses and
dissertations completed and in progress. Covers
linguistics and stylistics; genres; literature

movements and tendencies; literature by periods;
and writers, characters, and anonymous works. Entry
gives degree sought and status of the work.

Southern France

C122. "THÈSES de doctorat: Faculté de droit." Revue d l'économie
méridionale 6 (1958): 333.

Dissertations on the region, completed between 1933
and 1958 at the University of Montpellier. Covers
law, economics, history, political science.

Germanic

General

C123. LONDON. University. Institute of Germanic Studies. Theses
in Germanic Studies; A Catalogue of Theses and Dissertations
in the Field of Germanic Studies, excluding English, Approved
for Higher Degrees in the Universities of Great Britain and
Ireland between 1903 and 1961. Edited by Frederick Norman.
London: 1962. 46 p. (Its Publication, 4)

An alphabetical listing of 455 items covering Germanic work in Gothic, German, Dutch, Old Norse, and
the modern Scandinavian languages. Excludes Old
English. Subject index.

Continued by:

C124. _____ Theses in Germanic Studies, 1962-67: A Catalogue of
Theses and Dissertations in the Field of Germanic Studies
(excluding English) Approved for Higher Degrees in the Universities of Great Britain and Ireland between 1962 and 1967.
London: 1968. 5, 18 p. (Its Publications, 10)

Contains 156 items, submitted for the Ph.D. and
D.Phil., arranged alphabetically. Copies located
at the Institute are marked. Subject index.

Continued by:

C125. <u>THESES in Progress at British Universities and Work Due to be Published</u> [1967-   ] London: University of London, Institute of Germanic Studies, 1968-   . Title varies. Annual.

    Lists theses and dissertations in progress. Arranged by (1) general reference works, editions, and translations; (2) Germanic language; (3) general works on German literature; (4) Germanic literature by periods and individuals; (5) history, society, institutions. Each number includes a section of works due to be published.

Austria

C126. HASSINGER, Hugo and Herbert Hassinger. <u>Wegweiser für Landes- und Volksforschung in Österreich; Abgeschlossen am 1. Juli 1950</u>. Horn, N.-Ö.: In Kommission bei F. Berger, 1951. 181 p.

    Arranged by region, indicating the research facilities. Under the universities, relevant dissertations and Habilitationsschriften are listed separately under the various institutes and faculties. Author and subject indexes.

C127. BEHOFSITS, Stefan. "Dissertationen über das Burgenländ." <u>Burgenländische Heimblätter</u>, neue Folge, 2 (1965): 96; 4 (1967): 185-186.

    Abstracts of eight Austrian dissertations.

Krems an der Donau

C128. KÜHNEL, Harry. "Dissertationen über Kremser Themen." <u>In</u> Krems an der Donau, Austria (City). Stadtarchiv. <u>Mitteilungen</u> 7 (1967): 179-182.

    Abstracts of dissertations completed at the University of Vienna between 1962 and 1967.

Germany

C129. SNELL, John L. "Dissertationen zur deutschen Zeitgeschichte

an amerikanischen Universitäten, 1933-1953." <u>Vierteljahrs-</u>
<u>hefte für Zeitgeschichte</u> 1 (1953): 289-296.

A classified listing of approximately 200 American
dissertations completed or in progress on contemporary Germany. Includes such areas as history,
economics, sociology, political science, and international relations. In two parts, dissertations
completed to 1952 and dissertations in progress
1952-1953.

Saar

C130. CARTELLIERI, Walther. <u>Verzeichnis der Saardissertationen.</u>
Berlin: Geschäftsstelle "Saar-Verein," 1933. 23 p.

Classified listing of 126 dissertations from German
universities on the Saar region.

Westphalia

C131. SCHÖLLER, Peter. "Ungedruckte Dissertationen über Westfalen
aus den Jahren 1942 bis 1947; Verzeichnis mit Kurzreferaten."
<u>Westfälische Forschungen</u> 9 (1956): 199-208.

Approximately 70 German dissertations arranged under
history, geography, and economics; folklore and
literature; art; medicine; and law. Entry gives
faculty and indicates if available in the University
of Münster Library.

Supplemented and continued by:

C132. DETERMANN, Magdalene. "Ungedruckte Dissertationen über
Westfalen aus den Jahren 1942 bis 1947; Verzeichnis mit
Kurzreferaten. Zusätze, Berichigungen und Nachträge."
<u>Westfälische Forschungen</u> 10 (1957): 190-192.

Includes a list of published dissertations.

Supplemented and continued by:

C133. _____ "Ungedruckte Dissertationen über Westfalen aus den
Jahren 1948-1953." <u>Westfälische Forschungen</u> 10 (1957):

192-199; 11 (1958): 152-169.

Lists dissertations completed in German institutions.
Arranged under history; geology, geography, and
economics; folklore, language, and literature; art;
medicine. Entry gives adviser. Many entries carry
abstracts.

Northern Europe

General

C134. MEYEN, Fritz. The North European Nations as Presented in
German University Publications, 1885-1957. Bonn: H. Bouvier;
Charlottesville, Va.: Bibliographical Society of the University of Virginia, 1959. 124 p. (Bonner Beiträge zur Bib-
liotheks- und Bücherkunde, 4)

Topically arranged listing of 1,099 dissertations
and Habilitationsschriften accepted within the
German Empire (Strasbourg included to 1918 and 1940-
1945, and Austria from 1938 to 1945) that "exclusively or predominantly treat a theme relative to
Denmark, Sweden, Norway, Iceland or Finland." Emphasis is on linguistics, literature, history, and
the social sciences. Entry gives publication information. Author and subject indexes in German.

Continued by:

C135. _____ "Die nordeuropäischen Länder im Spiegel der deutschen
Universitätsschriften [1958-1963/1964]" Nordisk Tidskrift
for Bok- och Biblioteksvasen 48 (1961): 130-132; 50 (1963):
104-108; 51 (1964): 146-148; 53 (1966): 80-83.

Includes items omitted from main work. Arranged by
broad subjects. Entry gives faculty in which the
degree was taken and indicates if a Habilitationsschrift.

Iceland

C136. BENEDIKZ, Benedikt S. and Ólafur F. Hjartur. "Skrá um dok-
torsritgerthar og oprentathar, 1666-1963." In Reykjavík.

Landsbókas-afnith. <u>Ärbók</u>, 1962-1963 (Är. 19-20): 171-197.
Reykjavík: 1964.

A chronological international listing of 150 studies.
Entry gives publication information. Some have contents notes. Subject, author, and institutional
indexes.

Sweden

C137. CEDERHAMN, Per. <u>Catalogus dissertationum, quae ad illustran-
das res Svecicas faciunt, praesertim in argumentis historicis,
ecclesiasticis, juridicis, literariis, oeconomicis, physicis,
& historia naturali</u>. Holmiae: Literis & Impensis Direct.
Laur. Salvii, 1765. 214, 48 p.

A title listing. Entry gives praeses and respondent.
Index of respondents and an index of praeses.

Ireland

C138. BELFAST. Queen's University. Institute of Irish Studies.
<u>Theses on Subjects Relating to Ireland Presented for Higher
Degrees 1950-1967</u>. Belfast: Queen's University of Belfast,
1968. 28 p.

Theses and dissertations listed chronologically
under the department or faculty in which the degree
was taken.

Italy

C139. "DIPLÔMES d'études supérieures." <u>Revue des études italiennes</u>,
n.s. 2 (1955): 111-117.

Theses completed in French institutions. Arranged
chronologically under institution. Entry gives
adviser.

C140. MARRARO, Howard R. "Tesi Ph.D. sull' Italia (1950-1960)."
<u>Quadrivio</u> 5 (1962): 51-84.

Italian studies completed in American institutions.

Arranged by institution, subdivided by discipline.

Latin America

General

C141. KANTOR, Harry. <u>A Bibliography of Unpublished Doctoral Dis-
sertations and Masters Theses Dealing with the Governments,
Politics, and International Relations of Latin America</u>.
Prepared for the Committee on Latin American Affairs of the
American Political Science Association. Gainesville, Fla.:
1953. 85 p. (Inter-American Bibliographical and Library
Association. Publications, ser. 1, vol. 13)

A preliminary edition was published by the University of Florida, 1953.

Arranged in broad classifications, then by country
or subject subdivisions.

C142. <u>SURVEY of Investigations in Progress in the Field of Latin
American Studies</u> [no. 1 (1953)-   ] Washington: Pan American Union, 1953-   . Title varies. Irregular.

A joint publication of the Pan American Union Department of Cultural Affairs and the University of
Florida School of Inter-American Studies. No. 1
edited by Edward Marasciulo (1953); no. 2 by Frederick E. Kidder (1956); no. 3 by Basil C. Hedrick
(1959); no. 4 by Philip F. Flemion and Murdo J.
MacLeod (1962); no. 5 by Selma F. Rubin (1965).

Classified listings of theses and dissertations in
progress at American and Canadian universities.
Entry gives institution or address of researcher,
expected date of completion, and the time spent on
research. Country and author indexes.

C143. PAN AMERICAN UNION. Columbus Memorial Library. <u>Theses on
Pan American Topics, Prepared by Candidates for Degrees in
Colleges and Universities in the United States</u>. Washington:
1962. 124 p. (<u>Its</u> Bibliographic Series, no. 5, 4th ed.)

Earlier editions appeared in 1931, 1933, and 1941,
and contained theses as well as dissertations. This

edition compiled by Frederick E. Kidder and Allen D. Bushong.

An alphabetical author listing of 2,253 completed dissertations from American and Canadian institutions covering the period 1869 to 1960. Includes dissertations for doctoral degrees other than the Ph.D., such as law, theology, education, and the sciences. If published, the published title is given and the nature and date of publication are indicated. Institutional and subject indexes.

Continued by:

C144. KIDDER, Frederick E. "Doctoral Dissertations in Latin American Area Studies [1959/1960-1962/1963]" _Americas_ 18 (Jan. 1962): 304-310; 19 (1962)-21 (1964). Oct. issue.

Lists completed American and Canadian dissertations. Arranged alphabetically by author. Entry gives publication information.

Continued and supplemented by:

C145. BUSHONG, Allen D. "Doctoral Dissertations on Pan American Topics Accepted by United States and Canadian Colleges and Universities, 1961-1965, Bibliography and Analysis." _Latin American Research Review_ 2, no. 2 (1967): suppl. 57 p.

An author listing of 950 dissertations covering all disciplines and geographic areas, including non-Hispanic areas in Latin America. Also includes regions in the United States if the study involves the time when it was part of the Spanish empire in America. Institutional, geographical, and biographical indexes.

C146. LONDON. University. Institute of Latin American Studies. _Theses in Latin American Studies at British Universities in Progress and Completed_ [no. 1 (1966/1967-   ] London: 1967-   . Annual.

Arranged by university. Entry gives adviser and expected date of completion.

C147. BLOOMFIELD, Valerie. West Indian and Latin American Theses at U.K. Universities. London: University of London, Institute of Commonwealth Studies, 1969. 22 p. ?

C148. TEXAS. University. Institute of Latin American Studies. Latin American Research and Publications at the University of Texas at Austin, 1893-1969. Austin: 1971. 187 p. (Guides and Bibliographies Series, no. 3)

    A revision of its Seventy-Five Years of Latin American Research at the University of Texas (1959), of which an earlier edition appeared in 1952.

    The second section contains "Doctoral Dissertations of Latin American Interest, 1893-1969" (p. 21-93) and "Masters Theses of Latin American Interest, 1893-1969" (p. 94-146). Both listings are arranged chronologically and indicate the department in which the work was taken. For the dissertations an abstract is included. Combined author and subject indexes.

C149. ZUBATSKY, David S. Doctoral Dissertations in History and the Social Sciences on Latin America and the Caribbean Accepted by Universities in the United Kingdom, 1920-1972. London: University of London, Institute of Latin American Studies, 1973. 16 p.

    Lists approximately 250 items. Does not include languages and literature. Arranged by country or geographical region.

Caribbean

General

C150. DOSSICK, Jesse J. "Current Dissertations on the Caribbean; Doctoral Research on the Caribbean and Circum-Caribbean Accepted by American, British and Canadian Universities, 1966-1967." Caribbean Studies 8 (July 1968): 89-96.

    Lists 134 dissertations arranged under region or country. Heavy representation of American dissertations in the social studies. Also material in language, linguistics, and education. No Canadian dissertations listed.

C151. BAA, Enid M. Theses on Caribbean Topics, 1778-1968. San Juan, Puerto Rico: University of Puerto Rico, Institute of Caribbean Studies and University of Puerto Rico Press, 1970. 146 p. (University of Puerto Rico. Institute of Caribbean Studies. Caribbean Bibliographic Series, no. 1)

Another edition was previously published as Doctoral Dissertations and Selected Theses on Caribbean Topics Accepted by Universities of Canada, United States and Europe from 1778 to 1968 (1969) by the Virgin Islands Bureau of Public Libraries and Museums.

Two separate author listings of 1,005 dissertations and 236 theses. International in coverage but primarily represents work done in the United States, Canada, Great Britain, and France. University, geographical subject, and chronological indexes.

C152. HILLS, Theo L. Caribbean Topics: Theses in Canadian University Libraries. 3d ed. Montreal: McGill University, Centre for Developing Area Studies, 1971. 21 p.

First edition 1967.

Canadian theses and dissertations covering the period 1927-1970, arranged by institution and subdivided by subject area, such as history, geography, sociology, economics.

Cuba

C153. MEDEROS, Amelia. "A Contribution to a Bibliography of Published and Unpublished Theses Written by Cubans or on Cuba, Located at Harvard University Library: Appended is a List of Theses Submitted at the University of Miami; Working Paper No. 11." In Seminar on the Acquisition of Latin American Library Materials. Final Report and Working Papers, 15th Toronto, 1970, vol. 2: 177-189. Washington: Organization of American States, 1971. (Pan American Union. Columbus Memorial Library. Reuniones bibliotecologicas, no. 20-21)

Rosa Abella compiled the University of Miami list.

The Harvard listing contains approximately 60 theses and dissertations, covering the period 1897-1968. The University of Miami listing contains 30 theses and dissertations completed between 1955 and 1969.

Jamaica

C154. KULHAWIK, Leonard R. "Jamaica: A Bibliography of Doctoral Dissertations Relating to Jamaica Accepted by United States Colleges and Universities to 1959." Southeastern Latin Americanist 4 (June 1960): 2-3.

An alphabetical author list covering the period from 1928.

Puerto Rico

C155. KIDDER, Frederick E. and Allen D. Bushong. "Bibliography of Doctoral Dissertations Relating to Puerto Rico Accepted by United States Colleges and Universities through 1955-56." Southeastern Latin Americanist 2 (Sept. 1958): 5-12.

An alphabetical author listing of 127 studies dealing with some aspect of Puerto Rico, covering the period 1917-1956. The bulk of the items are in the social sciences, including geography; 25 are in the natural sciences.

_____ _____ "Supplement, 1956-57." Southeastern Latin Americanist 2 (Dec. 1958): 4-5.

Lists 21 dissertations.

C156. DOSSICK, Jesse J. Doctoral Research on Puerto Rico and Puerto Ricans. New York: New York University Press, 1967. 34 p.

A classified list of more than 300 dissertations accepted in American universities, a large portion of which are by Puerto Ricans. Author index.

Colombia

C157. BUSHONG, Allen D. "Doctoral Dissertations on Colombia Accepted by United States Universities through the 1958/59 Academic Year." <u>Southeastern Latin Americanist</u> 4 (March 1961): 5-7.

> An alphabetical author listing covering materials completed from 1926. Subjects included represent history, education, and the social sciences.

Mexico

C158. DOSSICK, Jesse J. "Doctoral Dissertations on Mexican Topics Accepted by Universities in the United States of America." <u>Mexicana Review</u> 2 (Spring 1942): 3-17.

> A classified list of 220 titles.

Middle East

General

C159. SELIM, George D. <u>American Doctoral Dissertations on the Arab World, 1883-1968</u>. Washington: U.S. Government Printing Office, 1970. 103 p.

> Prepared in the Near East Section of the Library of Congress Orientalia Division.

> An author listing of 1,032 dissertations from United States and selected Canadian universities. Included is material on all Arabic-speaking countries of the Near East and North Africa and all other communities where Arabic is spoken. Also titles related to Islam as a religion are included. There is an appendix of dissertations on the Middle and Near East. Index of subjects and key words in title.

Israel and Palestine

C160. SHULMAN, Frank J. <u>American and British Doctoral Disserta-</u>

tions on Israel and Palestine in Modern Times. Ann Arbor,
Mich.: Xerox University Microfilms, 1973. 25 p.

A classified listing of 530 American and British
dissertations completed since 1945 and dealing in
whole or in part with the land of Israel since the
early 1800's. Covers such subjects as Palestine
under the British mandate, Zionism in Europe and
the United States, kibbutzim, Palestine Arab language
and culture. Entry gives purchase information.

Turkey

C161. SUZUKI, Peter T. French, German, and Swiss University Dissertations on Twentieth Century Turkey: A Bibliography of
593 Titles, with English Translations. Wiesbaden: Germant,
wds-Schnelldruck, 1970. 138 p.

An alphabetical author listing. Includes 169 French
dissertations from 1900 to 1967; 312 German dissertations from 1900 to 1965; 88 Swiss dissertations
from 1900 to 1968; 23 Austrian dissertations; and
one Dutch dissertation. There is a separate listing
of ten dissertations in progress (p. 135). Subject
index.

Pacific Islands

General

C162. DICKSON, Diane and Carol Dosser. World Catalogue of Theses
on the Pacific Islands. Honolulu: University of Hawaii
Press, 1970. 123 p.

Supersedes South Pacific Commission, Index of Social
Science Theses on the South Pacific (1957).

A geographical listing based on the microfilm Library
of Theses on the Pacific Islands of the Australian
National University Department of Pacific History,
the University of Hawaii Library, the Berlin Museum
für Völkerkunde, examinations of thesis catalogs,
and solicitations to universities known to be inter-
ested in post-doctoral Pacific studies. Lists all
dissertations, master of arts theses or their equiva-

lent, a few university prize essays, and B.A. (Honors) and Dip.Ed. theses considered to be a significant contribution to the region. In the case of Hawaii, all listings below the doctorate were selective and those whose themes were not concerned with the Pacific Islands or were purely of local interest were excluded. Includes items through June 1968. Entry gives publication information and occasionally a note. Author index.

Philippines

C163. KIM, Yung-Min and Filomenia C. Mercado. "Doctoral Dissertations on the Philippines in American Universities, 1923-1962." Philippine Journal of Public Administration 7 (1963): 230-237.

An alphabetical author listing covering the period 1916 through 1962.

C164. ONORATO, Michael P. The Philippines; A List of Doctoral Dissertations in American Universities in the Fields of Economics, History, Political Science, and Sociology (1916-1964). Rev. ed. New York: New York State University, Foreign Area Materials Center, 1964. 4 p.

An alphabetical author listing covering the period 1916 through 1962.

C165. MANILA. National Library. Filipiniana Division. The National Library; Guide to Doctoral Dissertations on Microfilm (1937-1968) in the Filipiniana Division. Prepared by Concepcion S. Baylen. Manila: 1971. 92 p. (Its TNL Research Guide Series, no. 3)

An alphabetical author listing of 218 dissertations dealing with the Philippines. In large part represents work done in American universities. Index.

D. Special/Racial Groups

As Subjects

American Indians

D1.   JOBLIN, Elgie E. M. <u>The North American Indians</u>. Toronto:
University of Toronto, Ontario College of Education, Dept.
of Educational Research, 1947. 29 p. (Toronto. University.
Ontario College of Education. Bibliography Series, no. 15)

> Pt. A, Section III, "Indian Education in Canada and
> the United States: Research Studies in Indian Edu-
> cation" (p. 4-10), lists theses and dissertations
> completed since 1930, nearly all done in the United
> States.

D2.   JONES, John A. <u>List of Unpublished Doctoral Dissertations
and Masters Theses in the Field of Anthropology Bearing on
North American Indians North of Mexico</u>. Washington: U.S.
Dept. of Justice, 1953. 19 p.

> Classified listing covering the period 1904 to 1952.

D3.   DOCKSTADER, Frederick J. <u>The American Indian in Graduate
Studies; A Bibliography of Theses and Dissertations</u>. New
York: Museum of the American Indian, Heye Foundation, 1957.
399 p. (Museum of the American Indian, Heye Foundation
Contribution, no. 15)

> An alphabetical author listing of 3,684 theses and
> dissertations which deal in any way with the Indians
> of North, Central, and South America and with the
> Eskimos, completed in the United States, Canada,
> and Mexico from 1890 to 1955. Entry gives publica-
> tion information. Occasional notes and comments are
> included for ambiguous titles and in cases where

items include significant material. Subject index.

Asians in America

D4.   LUM, William W. <u>Asians in America: A Bibliography of Theses</u>
<u>and Doctoral Dissertations</u>. Davis, Calif.: University of
California, Davis, Asian American Studies Division, 1970.
78 p. (Asian American Research Project, Working Bibliography, no. 2)

> A classified bibliography of 750 theses and disser-
> tations on subjects relevant to understanding the
> Asian experience in America. Studies represent only
> work done at American institutions. Includes mater-
> ial dealing with emigration and immigration, social
> organization, identity, discrimination, overseas
> Asians, and contributions. Author index.

Blacks

D5.   KNOX, Ellis O. "The Negro as a Subject of University Research in [1932-1951]" <u>Journal of Negro Education</u> 2 (1933)-
21 (1952). Annual. Fall or Spring issue.

> Analysis and evaluations of theses and dissertations
> completed in American institutions. Contents vary:
> vols. 2 (1933)-5 (1936) list both theses and disser-
> tations; vols. 7 (1938)-21 (1952) list dissertations
> only; vols. 9 (1940)-14 (1945) contain abstracts of
> selected dissertations.

D6.   REID, Ira De A. <u>Negro Youth: Their Social and Economic Back-</u>
<u>grounds: A Selected Bibliography of Unpublished Studies,</u>
<u>1900-1938</u>. Washington: American Council on Education, Amer-
ican Youth Commission, 1939. 71 p.

> A subject listing, primarily of theses with some
> dissertations and bachelors' papers, from a selec-
> ted group of institutions in the United States.

D7.   WEST, Earle H. "Summaries of Doctoral Research...Related to
the Negro and Negro Education [1963-1965]" <u>Journal of Negro</u>
<u>Education</u> 34 (1965)-36 (1967). Annual. Winter issue.

Following an analysis of the studies under such
topics as educational administration, elementary and
secondary education, higher education, history and
politics, literature, psychology, and sociological
studies, the dissertations are listed by Dissertation Abstracts number.

D8. SPANGLER, Earl. Bibliography of Negro History: Selected and
Annotated Entries, General and Minnesota. Minneapolis: Ross
and Haines, Inc., 1963. 101 p.

Section 6, "Unpublished Materials" (p. 79-86),
includes theses pertaining to the Negro in
Minnesota.

D9. SINCLAIR, Donald A. The Negro and New Jersey: Checklist of
Books, Pamphlets, Official Publications, Broadsides, and
Dissertations, 1754-1964, in the Rutgers University Library.
New Brunswick: Rutgers University Library, 1965. 56 p.

Pt. 3, "Broadsides, and Dissertations, 1754-1964"
(p. 50-56), is primarily an alphabetical listing of
undergraduate papers, theses, and dissertations.
Includes items from institutions other than Rutgers
University.

D10. WEST, Earle H. A Bibliography of Doctoral Research on the
Negro, 1933-1966. Washington: Xerox, 1969. 134 p.

A classified bibliography of 1,452 dissertations
completed in the United States available from
University Microfilms. Author index indicates cost
of full or microfilm texts.

Chinese in Canada

D11. CON, Ronald J. "University Research on Chinese-Canadians."
Canadian Ethnic Studies (Calgary. University. Research
Centre for Canadian Ethnic Studies) 1, no. 1 (1969): 1-2.

Lists nine Canadian and American theses and dissertations.

Dutch in Canada

D12. BREUGELMANS, René. "University Research on Netherlandic-
Canadians; A Preliminary Checklist of Dissertations and
Theses." Canadian Ethnic Studies (Calgary. University.
Research Centre for Canadian Ethnic Studies) 1, no. 1 (1969):
54-55.

   Lists eight Canadian and American studies.

Germans in Canada

D13. CARDINAL, Clive H. and Alexander Malycky. "University Research on German-Canadians; A Preliminary Check List of Dissertations and Theses." Canadian Ethnic Studies (Calgary.
University. Research Centre for Canadian Ethnic Studies)
1, no. 1 (1969): 7-12.

   An alphabetical author listing of 49 Canadian and
   American studies.

Japanese in America

D14. CALIFORNIA. University. University at Los Angeles. Japanese American Research Project. Dissertations and Theses on
Japanese Americans. Los Angeles: University of California
at Los Angeles Library, 1969. ??

Jews

D15. PATAI, Raphael. Current Jewish Social Research. New York:
Theodor Herzl Foundation, 1958. 102 p.

   A classified bibliography covering Jewish studies
   undertaken in the United States. Lists 1,128 items,
   including a substantial number of dissertations,
   rabbinical theses, and works in progress.

D16. KIRSCH, Guido and Kurt Roepke. Schriften zur Geschichte der
Juden; Eine Bibliographie der in Deutschland und der Schweiz,
1922-1955, erschienenen Dissertationen. Tübingen: Mohr,
1959. 49 p. (Leo Baeck Institute of Jews from Germany,

Schriftenreihe Wissenschaftlicher Abhandlungen, Bd. 4)

An expansion of the bibliography covering the period 1922-1928 which appeared in the Zeitschrift für die Geschichte der Juden in Deutschland 3 (1931): 117-123.

A classified list of 381 dissertations.

Continued by:

D17.   KIRSCH, Guido. Judaistische Bibliographie. Ein Verzeichnis der in Deutschland und der Schweiz von 1956 bis 1970 erschienenen Dissertationen und Habilitationsschriften. Basel: Helbing & Lichtenhahn, 1972. 104 p.

A classified listing of 508 dissertations. Entry gives institution and faculty and publication information. Subject and author indexes.

D18.   BIHL, Wolfdieter. Bibliographie der Dissertationen über Judentum und jüdische Persönlichkeiten, die 1872-1962 an österreichischen Hochschulen (Wien, Graz, Innsbruck) approbiert wurden. Wien: Notring der Wissenschaftlichen Verbände Österreichs, 1965. 51 p.

Lists 448 dissertations representing all faculties, including theology, arranged by broad subjects. An appendix contains a listing of relevant titles from Franz Kroller's Dissertationen-Verzeichnis der Universität Graz, 1872-1963 (Graz, 1964), p. 48-51. Index to biographical dissertations and an author index.

D19.   GRAEBER, Isacque. "Jewish Themes in American Doctoral Dissertations, 1933-1962." YIVO Annual of Jewish Social Science 13 (1965): 279-304.

Lists 452 dissertations completed at 52 universities and seminaries. Arranged chronologically under religion and philosophy; sociology, psychology, anthropology, and economics; literature and languages; history; and education. Education covers the period 1953-1962 and continues the author's "Research in Jewish Education" (Item G189).

D20.   DOCTORAL Dissertations and Master's Theses Accepted by Amer-

ican Institutions of Higher Learning [1963/1964-   ] New
York: YIVO Institute for Jewish Research, 1966-   . Annual.
(Guides to Jewish Subjects in Social and Humanistic Research,
1-   )

Lists American theses, dissertations, and works in
progress of Jewish interest, arranged by broad subject, such as anthropology and archaeology, art,
Bible, education, sociology, speech, and theater.
Author index.

D21.   MALYCKY, Alexander. "University Research on Jewish-Cana-
dians; A Preliminary Check List of Dissertations and Theses."
Canadian Ethnic Studies (Calgary. University. Research
Centre for Canadian Ethnic Studies) 1, no. 1 (1969): 40-43.

Lists 26 Canadian and American studies.

Pennsylvania Dutch

D22.   YODER, Don. "Lutheran Theses." Pennsylvania Dutchman 2
(Aug. 1950): 6.

A list of 24 B.D. and S.T.M. theses prepared by
students between 1926 and 1940 at the Philadelphia
Lutheran Seminary, Mt. Airy, dealing with Pennsylvania Dutch religious history.

D23.   SHOEMAKER, Alfred L. "Ohio State Theses." Pennsylvania
Dutchman 4 (Oct. 1952): 3.

A list of 17 theses and dissertations completed at
Ohio State University which deal with the folk
culture of the Pennsylvania Dutch country. Some
items are annotated.

D24.   SHOEMAKER, Alfred L. "Pittsburgh Theses." Pennsylvania
Dutchman 4 (Nov. 1952): 14.

Fifteen theses and dissertations on the folk culture
of the Pennsylvania Dutch completed at the University of Pittsburgh.

D25.   SHOEMAKER, Alfred L. "Gettysburg Theses." Pennsylvania

Dutchman 4 (Jan. 15, 1953): 3-4.

> A listing of bachelors' and masters' theses complet-
> ed at the Lutheran Theological Seminary at Gettys-
> burg that deal with the cultural history of the
> Pennsylvania Dutch area.

D26.   SHOEMAKER, Alfred L.   "Theses [Franklin and Marshall Col-
lege]"   Pennsylvania Dutchman 4 (Aug. 1953): 3.

> Bachelors' and masters' theses on the Pennsylvania
> Dutch completed at Franklin and Marshall College.

Russians in Canada

D27.   ROSVAL, Sergei J.   "University Research on Russian-Canadians;
A Preliminary Check List of Dissertations and Theses."
Canadian Ethnic Studies (Calgary. University. Research
Centre for Canadian Ethnic Studies) 1, no. 1 (1969): 59-60.

> Lists 12 Canadian and American studies.

Spanish Speaking in the United States

D28.   U.S.   Cabinet Committee on Opportunity for the Spanish Speaking.   The Spanish Speaking in the United States: A Guide to
Materials.   Washington: 1971.   175 p.

> "Dissertations and Other Published Materials" (p. 83-
> 103) consists largely of American theses and disser-
> tations.   Arranged alphabetically by author.

Ukrainians in Canada

D29.   MALYCKY, Alexander.   "University Research on Ukrainian-
Canadians."   Canadian Ethnic Studies (Calgary. University.
Research Centre for Canadian Ethnic Studies) 1, no. 1 (1969):
72-76.

> Lists 28 Canadian and American studies.

As Authors

Arabs

D30. "ABSTRACTS of a Selection of Doctoral Dissertations Written by Arab Students on Subjects Relating to the Arab World." Arab Journal 1 (1964): 4-48.

Covers the period 1961-1964. In addition to items for which abstracts are provided, there is a list of titles of other dissertations by Arab students on scientific and technical subjects.

Bas-Alpins

D31. LIEUTAUD, Victor. Une Pléiade nouvelle du ciel bas-alpin. Digne: Chaspoul, 1908. 12 p.

Doctoral dissertations by natives of the Department of the Basses-Alpes.

Blacks

D32. "BIBLIOGRAPHY [of Dissertations by Negroes]: Doctors' Dissertations, Masters' Theses [1935-1959]" The Journal of Negro Education 2 (1933)-28 (1959). One to two issues per year.

None in vols. 23 (1954), 26 (1957), 27 (1958). The list in vol. 28 (Fall 1959) is a short section of unpublished masters' theses from Florida A. and M. University.

Dissertations and theses in separate lists, then arranged by subject area (art, economics, education, history, etc.)

D33. GREENE, Harry W. Holders of Doctorates among American Negroes; An Educational and Social Study of Negroes Who Have Earned Doctoral Degrees in Course, 1876-1943. Boston: Meador Publishing Co., 1946. 275 p.

An analysis of 368 dissertations. Each chapter is

devoted to a broad subject and includes an alphabetical directory of recipients. Information on each
individual includes current position, other degrees
held and where awarded, major field, and title of
dissertation. Appendix A, "List of Names of Holders
of Doctorates, 1876-1943" (p. 255-266), is an alphabetical listing indicating field of work.

D34. WALKER, Geogre H., Jr. "Master's Theses under Way in Negro
Colleges and Universities [1950/1951-1960/1961]" Negro
Education Review 2 (1951)-13 (1962). Annual.

Represents work in all fields. Arranged alphabetically under topics.

D35. _____ "Masters Theses under Way in Selected Colleges and
Universities, 1972-1973." Negro Education Review 24 (1973):
144-156.

A classified listing of approximately 130 studies,
arranged under such topics as Afro-American studies
and Black studies, secondary education, guidance,
earth science, urban studies.

Chinese

D36. "THESES and Dissertations by Chinese Students in America."
In China Institute in America. Bulletin, no. 4 (1927):
1-42; no. 7 (1928): 1-12; Jan. 1934: 1-31; Oct. 1936: 1-31;
vol. 3 (March 1939): 164-176.

Classified lists of masters' and doctors' theses,
totaling 2,110 items, covering the period 1902-1938.

D37. YÜAN, T'ung-Li. A Guide to Doctoral Dissertations by Chinese
Students in America, 1905-1960. Washington: Sino-American
Cultural Society, 1961. 248 p.

An alphabetical author arrangement (Chinese names
are given) of 2,789 dissertations within three
parts: pt. 1: humanities, social and behavioral
sciences; pt. 2: physical, biological, and engineering sciences; pt. 3: Canadian dissertations,
1926-1960. Entry gives publication information.
Index by field of study.

Continued by:

D38. LI, Tze-Chung. <u>A List of Doctoral Dissertations by Chinese Students in the United States, 1961-1964</u>. Chicago: Chinese American Educational Foundation, 1967. 84 p.

Contains 843 dissertations arranged by subject. Includes some items completed prior to 1961 and not included in Yüan. Author index.

D39. YÜAN, T'ung-Li. "Doctoral Dissertations by Chinese Students in Great Britain and Northern Ireland, 1916-1961." <u>Chinese Culture</u> 4 (March 1963): 107-137.

A special supplement to <u>Chinese Culture</u> 4, no. 4, issued as a separate (1963).

Lists 344 dissertations accepted by British universities, arranged alphabetically by author in two sections: (1) the humanities and social sciences; and (2) the biological, physical, and engineering sciences.

D40. _____ <u>A Guide to Doctoral Dissertations by Chinese Students in Continental Europe, 1907-1962</u>. Washington: 1964. 154 p.

Reprinted from <u>Chinese Culture Quarterly</u> 5 (March 1964): 98-156; 5 (June 1964): 81-149; 6 (Oct. 1964): 79-98, as a special supplement.

An arrangement of 1,574 dissertations by country and by faculty. Entry provides name in Chinese.

Discalced Carmelites

D41. LOUVAIN. Convent of Discalced Carmelites. [Dissertationes quas defendent] Lovanii [Bruxelles, etc.]: 1726-1766. 2 vols.

Includes 24 Thomastic dissertations by Discalced Carmelites of Louvain, Brussels, Antwerp, and Ghent.

Felician Sisters

D42. HILBURGER, Mary C., Sister. <u>Writings of the Felician Sisters in the United States</u>. Chicago: Felician Sisters, 1955. 63 p.

Theses and dissertations completed by members of the Felician Sisters for the period 1924-1946 are listed on p. 18-29. Theses and dissertations for the period 1946-1954 are listed on p. 44-56. (The 1924-1946 listing is a revision of her article in <u>Polish American Studies</u> 3 (1946): 75-84; the 1946-1954 list also appeared in <u>Polish American Studies</u> 11 (1954): 78-97. Some items are annotated.

Finns

D43. LEINBERG, Karl G. "Dissertationes academicae Fennorum extra patriam. Ett bidrag till Finlands kulturhistoria." <u>In</u> Finska vetenskapssocieteten, Helsingfors. <u>Bidrag till Kännedom af Finlands natur och folk</u> 58 (1900): 347-523.

Also appeared as a separate.

Lists dissertations by Finns at universities outside of Finland. Arranged by institution and covers the Universities of Uppsala, Lund, Dorpat, Pernau, and Griefswald. Author index.

Iraqis

D44. BAGDAD. Jami 'at Baghdad. al-Maktabah al-Markazīyah. <u>A List of Theses and Dissertations of Iraqis Kept in the Central Library of Bagdad, Arranged in Shelf List Order</u>. Compiled by Nazar M. Qassim. Bagdad: 1967. 163 p.

Lists more than 550 theses and dissertations in English, French, and German. Most represent work done outside of Iraq. Entry gives institution, date, and degree. Author and subject indexes.

————— —————— <u>Supplement I</u>. Bagdad: 1969. 86 p.

Approximately 280 additional items received.

Koreans

D45. KUKHOE TOSŎGWAN, Seoul, Korea. Ippŏp Chosaguk. <u>Han'gugin</u>
<u>paksarok</u>. Seoul: Min'guk Kukhoe Tosŏgwan, 1967. 122 p.

A translation of Ki P. Yang, <u>Guide to Doctoral Dis-</u>
<u>sertations Written by Korean Students in the United</u>
<u>States, 1910-1965, and Those Written by Americans</u>
<u>on Korean Affairs</u> (1965). Unpublished.

A listing of 620 dissertations completed by Korean
students in the United States in the period 1910
through 1965. Arranged by such areas as humanities,
social sciences, and engineering. Entry gives a
Korean translation of English titles. Author index.

Romanians

D46. BENGESCU, George. <u>Bibliographie franco-roumaine du XIX</u>e
<u>siècle</u>. Tome premier. Bruxelles: P. Lacomblez, 1895.
218 p.

No more published.

French works published in France dealing in whole
or in part with Romania, or by Romanians. Contains
a separate list of theses by Romanians at French
universities (p. 175-216).

Women

D47. BOEDEKER, Elisabeth. <u>25 Jahre Frauenstudium in Deutschland;</u>
<u>Verzeichnis der Doktorarbeiten von Frauen, 1908-1933</u>. Han-
nover: Trute, 1935-1939. 4 vols.

Lists approximately 10,000 dissertations. Vol. 1:
general and humanities; vol. 2: philology and literature; vol. 3: social sciences; vol. 4: applied
and pure sciences. In each volume the dissertations are arranged chronologically under areas, e.g.
philosophy, mathematics, orientalia. Author index
in each volume.

D48. EELLS, Walter C. "Earned Doctorates for Women in the Nine-

teenth Century." In American Association of University
Professors. Bulletin 42 (1956): 644-651.

Lists the names and fields of study of the 229
women awarded doctorates. Arranged by date under
institution.

D49. PANAMA (City). Universidad. Biblioteca. Bibliografía de
las tesis de mujeres universitarias presentadas en la Universidad de 1940-1965. Panama: 1965. 145 p.

Approximately 1,400 theses, arranged by faculty
and by school.

E. Applied Sciences

Agriculture

General

E1. GERMANY. Reichsforschungsstelle Landwirtschaftliches Market-
     wesen. <u>Verzeichnis der Dissertationen aus dem Gebiet des</u>
     <u>Obst- , Gemuse- und Gartenbaues sowie Weinbaues.</u> Berlin:
     1933. 22 p.

>   A chronological listing of 263 dissertations com-
>   pleted in German universities from 1903 to 1933.

E2. "NEUE Dissertationen: Schweizerische Dissertationen [1945/
     1947-1957/1959]" <u>Das Schrifttum der Bodenkultur</u> 1, no. 4
     (1948/1949)-12 (1960). Irregular.

>   Arranged under subject, such as agriculture and
>   forestry. Entry gives publication information.
>   Does not include the Hochschule für Bodenkultur
>   (Wien) and dissertations in veterinary medicine
>   for the period 1945-1955.

E3. "HOCHSCHULNACHRICHTEN." <u>Der Diplomlandwirt</u> 1 (Dec. 1951)-?.
     Monthly.

>   Carries lists of dissertations completed in German
>   institutions on agricultural subjects arranged by
>   institution.

E4. "AUSZÜGE aus Dissertationen und Forschungsaufträgen."
     <u>Forschung und Beratung</u> 1 (1952)-   . Annual.

>   Appears in Reihe A.

Abstracts of dissertations completed in North Rhine-
Westphalian scientific institutions and the Bonn
University Landwirtschaftlichen Fakultät on nutrition,
forestry, and agriculture.

E5.   DUX, Werner and Curt Fleischhack. Bibliographie der landwirtschaftlichen Hochschulschriften; Ein systematiches Verzeichnis der Titel aller in deutscher Sprache in den Jahren
1945-1952 an deutschen, schweizerischen und österreichischen
Universitäten und Hochschulen veröffentlichten Dissertation-
en und Habilitationsschriften aus dem Gebiet der Land- und
Forstwirtschaftswissenschaften. Leipzig: Verlag für Buch-
und Bibliothekswesen, 1954. 172 p. (Sonderbibliographien
der deutschen Bücherei, 1)

A classified bibliography of 1,992 references, including non-European German language items, dealing
with all aspects of agriculture, broadly defined,
and includes historical, sociological, legal studies,
etc. Citations indicate faculty within which the
work was completed. Author index and index to geographical topics.

_____ _____ ...1953-1956... Leipzig: Verlag für Buch- und
Bibliothekswesen, 1958. 339 p. (Sonderbibliographie der
deutschen Bücherei, 14)

Lists 3,452 additional dissertations, following
same arrangement as earlier work. Author and geographic indexes.

E6.   FORSCHUNGSGESELLSCHAFT FÜR AGRARPOLITIK UND AGRARSOZIOLOGIE.
Verzeichnis von Dissertationen aus Agrarökonomik und Agrar-
sociologie, 1945-1955; Übersicht über abgeschlossene und
laufende Untersuchungen. Bonn: 1955. 117 p.

Lists German language dissertations. In two parts:
(1) list of 725 completed dissertations, and (2)
list of 307 dissertations in progress. Each part
is arranged by institution. Subject index.

E7.   _____ Dissertationen aus Agrarökonomik und Agrarsoziologie;
Kurzauszüge [1 (1945/1955-   ] Bonn: 1956-   . Irregular.

Vols. 1-4 cover 1945-1955; vols. 5-6 cover 1945-
1957; vol. 7 covers 1957-1964.

Abstracts of dissertations completed in German
universities dealing with the social science aspects
of agriculture, including economics, sociology,
cooperation. Indexed in Item E6. Each volume
carries a separate subject index.

E8.   "DISSERTATSIY raboty po sel'skomu khozyaystvu." Vestnik
       sel'skokhozyaystvennoi nauki 1956, no. 2: 140-142; 1957,
       no. 1: 156-160, no. 2: 155-157, no. 3: 159-160, no. 4: 154-
       156, no. 6: 157-158, no. 7: 156-158, no. 8: 157-159, no. 9:
       158-159, no. 10: 158-159; 1960, no. 1: 156-158, no. 2: 156-
       158, no. 3: 157-158, no. 4: 156-158, no. 5: 157-158, no. 6:
       155-158, no. 7: 156-158, no. 9: 157-158; 1961, no. 1: 156-
       157, no. 2: 157-158, no. 5: 158.

       A classified listing of theses and dissertations
       defended in the U.S.S.R. between 1939 and 1955,
       deposited in the Lenin State Library (Moscow).

E9.   "SPISOK tem dissertatsiy zashchishchennykh na soiskanne
       uchenoy stepeni kandidata istoricheskikh nauk." Vestnik
       sel'skokhozyaystvennoi nauki, 1956-1961. Monthly. Irregular.

       A classified listing of theses and dissertations
       in the Lenin State Library (Moscow) defended in the
       period 1939-1961.

E10.   FORSCHUNGSGESELLSCHAFT FÜR AGRARPOLITIK UND AGRARSOZIOLOGIE.
       Forschungsarbeiten aus Agrökonomik und ländlicher Soziologie
       [Folge 1 (1945/1957)-   ] Bonn: 1957-   . Title varies.
       Irregular.

       Folge 1 edited by Theodore Dams; Folge 2 (1962),
       covering 1957-1960, edited by Joachim Lunze.

       Lists dissertations completed and in progress in
       German institutions. Arranged by institution and
       subdivided into works completed and works in progress.
       Items keyed to Item E7. Each volume has keyword index.

E11.   SOUTH AFRICA. Department of Agricultural Technical Services.
       Agricultural Research [1961-   ] Pretoria: 1961-   .
       Annual.

       Pt. 2, "Theses on Agricultural Research," is a
       classified listing of abstracts of theses and dis-

sertations completed in the Union of South Africa.
Entry gives adviser.

E12. BOLETÍN bibliográfico agricola (Turrialba, Costa Rica) 1
(1964)- . Quarterly.

In its "Nuevas publicaciones," carries a separate
listing of theses and dissertations acquired by the
Inter-American Institute of Agricultural Sciences
Library. International in coverage, but the majority
of items are from Latin American universities.

E13. GAURI, K. B. Dissertations in Agricultural and Animal Sciences, 1948-1965; With Keyword Index. Ludhiana: Punjab
Agricultural University Library, 1966. 88 p.

A classified bibliography of 585 theses and dissertations from all campuses of Punjab University, as
well as Chandigarh. Author index.

E14. INDIAN COUNCIL OF AGRICULTURAL RESEARCH. Library. Classified List of Theses Available in I.C.A.R. Library. New
Delhi: 1967. 64, iv, vii, 7 p.

Covers theses and dissertations received by the
Library from 1954 to 1966. Author and subject indexes
and an index of degrees.

E15. SANDOVAL GUERRERO, Margarita. Lista de tesis presentadas
en las escuelas de agricultura, ganaderia y medicina veterinaria de la Republica Mexicana, 1856-1967. Chapingo: Escuela Nacional de Agricultura, Biblioteca Central, 1970.
1 vol. (various pagings)

An alphabetical author listing of 5,450 studies.
Subject index and an index to those geographic
locations specially treated in the studies.

E16. INTER-AMERICAN INSTITUTE OF AGRICULTURAL SCIENCES. Centro
Interamericano de Documentación e Información Agrícola.
Indice latinoamericano de tesis agrícolas. Turrialba,
Costa Rica: 1972. 778 p. (Bibliotecología y documentación,
no. 20)

Lists 7,242 theses presented at 78 institutions

during the period 1957-1967. KWIC subject index
and author index.

Individual Institutions

E17. CHAPINGO, Mexico. Escuela Nacional de Agricultura. Biblioteca Central. Relación de tesis existentes en la Biblioteca de la Escuela Nacional de Agricultura y del Colegio de
Post-Graduados. Mexico, D.F.: 1965. 86 p.

Subject listing of theses submitted at the Escuela
Nacional de Agricultura. Also includes some theses
and dissertations from other Mexican universities,
as well as from universities outside Mexico.

E18. _____ Tesis sobre agricultura méxicana durante los años
1957-1967. Chapingo: 1968. 135 p. ?

E19. HERNÁNDEZ DE CALDAS, Angela and Lucía Valencia M. Tesis de
grado presentadas a la Facultad Nacional de Agronomía de
Medellín. Medellín, Colombia: Facultad Nacional de Agronomía,
1954. 27 p.

First edition published in 1953.

An author listing of 246 theses completed from 1932
to 1952. Entry gives publication information.
Subject index.

E20. RODRIQUÍZ, Amelia. Tesis de grado presentadas a la Facultad
Nacional de Agronomía de Medellín. Medellín, Colombia: 1963.
10 p.

An alphabetical author listing of 72 theses covering
the period 1954-1961. Subject index.

E21. COLOMBIA. Universidad, Bogotá. Facultad de Agronomía del
Valle, Palmira. Resúmenes de tesis de los graduados,
promoción 1963. 1 vol. (unpaged)

Abstracts of 20 theses.

E22. COSTA RICA. Universidad Nacional, San José. Departamento de Publicaciones. Bibliografía de tesis de grado, Facultad de Agronomía, 1931-1954. San José: 1955. 20 p. (Departamento de Publicaciones, Publ. no. 428)

Supersedes 1953 edition.

An alphabetical author listing of approximately 225 theses. Some of those listed are not available.

E23. GIESSEN. Universität. Institut für landwirtschaftliche Betriebslehre. Abteilung für Wirtschaftsberatung. Ergebnisse landwirtschaftlicher Forschung an der Justus Liebig-Universität. Auszüge aus den Dissertationen der Landwirtschaftlichen Fakultät [2 (1955/1957)-   ] Giessen: 1959-   . Annual.

Abstracts of dissertations, arranged by institute.

E24. CHAPMAN, T. and E. Herrera. "List of Completed Research Work Carried Out in the Imperial College of Tropical Agriculture on Crop Husbandry." Journal of the Agricultural Society of Trinidad and Tobago 61 (1961): 489-503; 62 (1962): 72-91.

Arranged by crop. Each section is divided into published work and the unpublished theses and reports presented for the associateship and the diploma from the mid-1920's. Entry indicates adviser.

E25. INTER-AMERICAN INSTITUTE OF AGRICULTURAL SCIENCES. Resúmenes analíticos de tesis de grado en el Programa de Extensión Agrícola: De 55 estudiantes que han recebido su título de Magister Scientiae en este Programa desde su iniciación en 1956 hasta el 31 de marzo de 1968. Compiled by D. G. Peña C. Turrialba, Costa Rica: 1968. 23 p. ?

E26. MALUGANI, María D. and Alfredo Alvear. Tesis de la Escuela para Graduados, 1948-1968; Resúmenes. 2. ed. rev. y ampl. Turrialba, Costa Rica: Instituto Interamericano de Ciencias Agrícolas, Biblioteca y Servicio de Documentación, 1969. 234 p. (Inter-American Institute of Agricultural Sciences. Bibliotecología y documentación, no. 3)

Supersedes Inter-American Institute of Agricultural Sciences. Graduate School. Tesis de magister agriculturae de la Escuela para Graduados, 1947-1963

(1964), the 1963 edition, and the supplement, "Tesis de Magister Agriculturae de la Escuela para Graduados, 1964-1965." Boletin bibliográfica agricola (Costa Rica) 3 (1966):137-154.

Abstracts of 314 theses submitted at the Institute, classified under the disciplines taught. Entry gives publication information. Author and subject indexes.

E27.   INTER-AMERICAN INSTITUTE OF AGRICULTURAL SCIENCES. Southern Zone.   Teses brasileiras em ciencias agrícolas e afins, 1957-1967. Rio de Janeiro: 1968.   38 p.   ??

E28.   JERUSALEM.   Hebrew University.   Faculty of Agriculture. Abstracts of M.Sc. Agr. Theses [no. 1-   ] Rehovoth: 1960-   .

In Hebrew with English language abstracts.

Arranged by department.

E29.   LA MOLINA, Peru.   Universidad Agraria.   Biblioteca.   Relación de la existencia de tesis a diciembre de 1953.   La Molina, Lima: 1953.   47 p.

An alphabetical author listing of approximately 450 theses covering the period up to 1953.   Includes some items from institutions other than the Escuela Nacional de Agricultura of Peru.

E30.   LANDBOUWHOGESCHOOL, Wageningen.   Dissertation Abstracts of the Agricultural University of Wageningen, the Netherlands, 1918-1968.   Wageningen: H. Veenam, 1968.   349 p.   (Its Miscellaneous Papers, no. 1)

Supersedes its Lijst van dissertaties van de Landbouwhoogeschool to Wageningen (1956).

Abstracts of 423 dissertations, representing those taken at Wageningen, arranged chronologically, and 73 prepared at Wageningen but defended at other universities, arranged by institution.   Entry gives publication information.   Author, subject, and major adviser indexes.

E31. MANIZALES, Colombia. Universidad de Caldas. Biblioteca
Central. Lista de tesis de agronomía que se encuentran en
la Biblioteca. Manizales: 1965. 8 p. ?

_____ _____ II. Boletin informativo 4, no. 11 (1963): 1-
2, 4-9. ??

Includes agronomy and veterinary medicine.

E32. BARREIRO, Adolfo. Reseña historica de la enseñanza agrícola
y veterinario en México. Mexico: Tipografía El Libro de
Commercio, 1906. 105 p.

"Tesis originales (existentes) en el archivo de la
Secretaría de la Escuela" (p. 94-105) lists chronologically the theses submitted to the Escuela Nacional
de Agricultura y Veterinaria for the degrees of
Ingeniero Agrónimo, Perita Agrícola and Médico Veterinario.

E33. MOSCOW. Moskovskaya sel'skokhozyaystvennaya akademiya imeni
Timiryazeva. TSentral'naya nauchnaya biblioteka. Bibliografiya dissertatsiy zashchishchennykh v Akademii v 1936-
1952 gg. Sost. L. IA. Shraiber and E. P. Ostrovskaya. Moscow: 1953. 117 p.

Lists 71 dissertations and 730 theses completed at
the Academy. Arranged under economics, geology,
chemistry, biology, and technology. Under each subject theses and dissertations are separate and are
listed chronologically. Author, subject, and geographical indexes.

E34. RANCHI AGRICULTURAL COLLEGE. Abstract of Theses Submitted
in Partial Fulfillment of the Requirements for the Degree
of Master of Science in Agriculture. Ranchi. Annual.

Vol. 4 (1967).

Arranged under agronomy, agricultural botany, land
development, agricultural economics.

E35. SÃO PAULO, Brazil (City). Universidade. Escola Superior de
Agricultura "Luiz Quieroz," Piracicaba. Resumos de tesis
(dissertation abstracts) [1967-   ] Piracicaba: 1968-   .
Annual.

Abstracts of theses and dissertations. Author index.

E36. "RELACIÓN de tesis de la Facultad de Agronomía: Tesis sobre horticultura, tesis sobre fito-mejoramiénto." Agronomía (Peru) 29 (1962): 214-222.

List of theses approved by the Faculty of Agronomía of the Universidad Agraria, La Molina, from about 1935.

E37. "RELACIÓN de tesis sobre algodón, arroz, maíz, trigo, etc." Agronomía (Peru) 30 (1963): 48-62.

An alphabetical author listing of studies completed between 1916 and 1961 at the Universidad Agraria, La Molina, arranged under cotton, rice, maize, wheat, and other field crops.

E38. "DAS DOKTORAT der Bodenkultur [1906/1907-1971/1972]" In Vienna. Hochschule für Bodenkultur in Wien. 100 [Hundert] Jahre Hochschule für Bodenkultur in Wien, 1872-1972, vol. 1: 361-408. Wien: 1972-1973.

Supersedes listings in Das Schrifttum für Bodenkultur 1 (1948)-12 (1960).

A chronological listing of approximately 1,000 dissertations completed at the Hochschule.

E39. "NEUE Dissertationen; New Doctoral Dissertations; Nouvelles thèses de doctorat (Hochschule für Welthandel Wien)." Das Schrifttum für Bodenkultur 1, no. 3 (1960): 23-25.

Lists only those dissertations which are on agricultural topics or are in related fields. Covers 1945-1947.

E40. WARSAW. Szkola Główna Gospodarstwa Wiejskiego. Bibliografia prac magisterskich, kandydackich, doktorskich i habilitacyjnych, przyjętych w Szkole Głównej Gospodarstwa Wiejskiego w Warszawie w latach 1918-1963. Wyd. 2, uzup. i popr. Warszawa: Dział Wydawn. SGGW, 1966. 2 vols. (Its Prace Biblioteki Głównej, nr. 3)

First edition: Bibliografia prac dyplomowych, kandy-

dackich, doktorskich i habilitacyjnych, złozonych w
Szkole Głównej Gospodarstwa Wiejskiego do roku 1958
(1959-1960).

Lists 5,815 studies by subjects, subdivided by type
of degree. Author and promoter's index and subject
index.

Special Subjects

Agricultural Economics

E41. "DOCTORAL Degrees Conferred in Agricultural Economics [1951-
]" American Journal of Agricultural Economics 34 (1952)-
. Title varies. Annual. May issue.

Vols. 34 (1952)-39 (1957) include dissertations in
progress and a separate listing of theses completed
and in progress.

Alphabetical author listing arranged by university.
Entry indicates previous degrees (institution and
date).

E42. HUTCHISON, John E. Agricultural Economics Dissertations,
1924-1962, Department of Agricultural Economics, University
of Maryland. College Park, Md.: 1962. 38 p.

A chronological listing, with brief abstracts, of
theses and dissertations submitted by students of
the Agricultural Economics Department of the University of Maryland. Entries are keyed to categories
of topics and also provide the name of adviser.
Subject index.

E43. HLADKÁ, L. Bibliografický súpis záverečných zpráy, dizertačných a habilitačných prác v Ústrednej pŏsohospodárskej
knižnici. Nitra: 1966. 109 p.

Abstracts of dissertations arranged by type of
degree. Author and subject indexes.

E44. TEXAS A. & M. UNIVERSITY, College Station. Department of
Agricultural Economics and Sociology. A List of Research

Publications, Technical Papers, Theses and Dissertations, Information Reports in the Dept. of Agricultural Economics and Rural Sociology [1970-   ] College Station: 1970-   .
Annual.

> Theses and dissertations are listed separately.
> Entry gives adviser.

Agricultural Engineering

E45.   ACTA agronómica 1 (1950)-   . Palmira, Colombia: Universidad Nacional de Colombia, Facultad de Agronomia, 1951-   .
Quarterly.

> Summaries of theses presented for the Ingenieros Agrónomos. Summaries are in Spanish and English. Annual author and subject index.

E46.   "GRADUATE Theses in Agricultural Engineering." Agricultural Engineering 36 (1955): 339-340.

> Theses dated from September 1935. Arranged by institution. Indicates place where available for reference use.

E47.   CONCEPCIÓN, Chile. Universidad. Escuela de Agronomía. Extracto de tesis presentadas a la Facultad de Agronomía [1960-   ] Chillan: 1961-   . (Extracto de tesis no. 1-) Title varies. Irregular.

> Abstracts of theses in agricultural engineering. Entry gives adviser.

E48.   AMERICAN SOCIETY OF AGRICULTURAL ENGINEERS. Committee on Runoff. Bibliography of Theses Concerning Runoff Prepared by Graduate Students at Various Universities and Colleges. N.p.: 1961. 68 p. (Its Contribution no. 1)

> Theses and dissertations arranged by schools in alphabetical order and chronologically under schools. Entry gives publication information.

E49.   GUAYASAMÍN DE LÓPEZ, Zoila. Tesis de grado de ingenieros agrónomos colombianos, 1917-1968. Pasto, Colombia:

Universidad de Nariño, Instituto Tecnológico Agrícola,
Biblioteca y Hemeroteca Agrícolas, 1968. 205 p. (Serie
bibliográfica, no. 7; Universidad de Nariño. Instituto
Tecnológico Agrícola. Publicación 8)

    An alphabetical author listing of 1,052 theses com-
pleted in Colombian institutions. (A few dissertations by Colombians submitted to institutions outside Colombia are also listed.) Subject index. Index
by faculty.

E50. YASEMTSIK, F. C. <u>Dissertatsionnye raboty po problemam remota</u>
<u>i ekspluatatsii mashinnotraktornogo parka; Bibliogr. ukazatel'</u>
<u>za 1940-1968 gg</u>. Moskva: 1970. 107 p.

    A classified listing of 835 theses and dissertations
defended in the U.S.S.R. Under subject the studies
are arranged chronologically.

Agricultural History

E51. NORDIN, Dennis S. "Graduate Studies in American Agricultural
History." <u>Agricultural History</u> 41 (1967): 275-305.

    A classified bibliography of approximately 1,000
theses and dissertations completed in the history
departments of American universities. Author index.

Animal Husbandry

E52. PAYNE, Loyal F., W. J. Mellen, and J. H. Bruckner. <u>Poultry</u>
<u>Theses, Presented for Advanced Degrees at Land Grant Colleges</u>
<u>in the United States of America, 1896-1950</u>. Ithaca, N.Y.:
Cornell University, James E. Rice Memorial Poultry Library,
1952. 106 p. (James E. Rice Memorial Poultry Library Publication, no. 1)

    An earlier edition was published by the Kansas State
University Department of Poultry Husbandry in 1944.

    Lists 1,140 dissertations and theses of which three
quarters are theses in poultry or in allied fields
and which contain results of value to persons inter-
ested in poultry science and husbandry. Pt. 1 is
an alphabetical author listing and pt. 2 is a subject

listing.

E53.   WOOL BUREAU, INC., New York. <u>Theses and Dissertations on</u>
<u>Wool Fiber Grading, Preparation and Utilization and the</u>
<u>Economics of Wool Production and Marketing, Accepted by Amer-</u>
<u>ican Universities.</u> New York: 1954. 23 p.

Arranged by institution.

E54.   WILSON, P. N. and E. Herrera. "List of Completed Research
Work Carried Out at the Imperial College of Tropical Agriculture on Animal Husbandry and Grassland Husbandry." <u>Journal</u>
<u>of the Agricultural Society of Trinidad and Tobago</u> 61 (1961):
63-86.

Covers the period from 1933. Arranged by broad
topic. Under each topic unpublished theses and
reports for the associateship and the diploma are
listed separately. Entry gives adviser.

E55.   LA MOLINA, Peru. Universidad Agraria. Facultad de Zootec-
nia. <u>Catálogo de tesis, 1907-1966.</u> La Molina, Peru: 1966.
49 p.   ??

Cereals

E56.   BERLIN. Versuchsanstalt für Getreideverwertung. <u>Das</u>
<u>Getreide und seine Verarbeitung. Universitätsschriften aus</u>
<u>den Jahren 1900-1950.</u> Berlin: 1950-1954. 5 pts. in 1 vol.

A classified bibliography of dissertations issued
in five separate pamphlets: "Anbau und Ernte,"
"Untersuchung und Berwertung," "Verarbeitung," "Er-
nährungsphysiologie," "Wirtschaft und Organization."
Entries are listed chronologically under each heading. Each part carries a separate author index.

_____ <u>Nachtragsband; Universitätsschriften der Jahre</u>
<u>1951-1955.</u> Berlin: 1958. 31 p.

Includes items omitted from main work. Author index.

_____ <u>Nachtrag 2; Universitätsschriften der Jahre</u>
<u>1956-1960.</u> Berlin: 1963. 48 p.

E57. "DISSERTATSIY po kul'tura risa." In Krasnodar. Kubanskiya risovanaya opytnaya stantsiya. Kratkie itogi nauchno-issledovatel'skoy raboty za 1959-1960 gg., p. 203-206. Krasnodar: 1962.

A classified listing of 45 theses and dissertations completed in the U.S.S.R. between 1936 and 1960.

E58. SCHNEIDER, Jakob. Deutschsprachige Dissertationen über das Bier und verwandte Gebiete: Eine Bibliographie Titelerfassung deutscher und ausländischer Hochschulschriften. N.p.: Gesellschaft für die Geschichte und Bibliographie des Brauwesens, 1965. 91 p. ?

Tobacco

E59. POHL, Emma W. Theses on the Subject of Tobacco Written at North Carolina State University at Raleigh. Raleigh: North Carolina State University, D. H. Hill Library, 1970. 17 p.

A listing of approximately 150 theses and dissertations on the growing, marketing, and economics of tobacco, arranged by broad topic. Represents work completed in the various departments of North Carolina State University. Author index.

E60. CHEEK, Emory. List of Theses and Dissertations on Tobacco and Tobacco Related Research. Athens, Ga.: University of Georgia, College of Agriculture Experiment Stations, 1973. 88 p. (Georgia. Agricultural Experiment Stations. Research Report 158)

An alphabetical author listing of 602 American theses and dissertations. Subject index.

Engineering

General

E61. WALTHER, Karl. Bibliographie der an den deutschen technischen Hochschulen erschienenen Doktor-Ingenieur-Dissertationen, 1900-1910. Berlin: J. Springer, 1913. 131 p.

Classified listing of 1,274 dissertations. Entry
gives publication information. Author index.

E62. TROMMSDORFF, Paul. Verzeichnis der bis Ende 1912 an den
technischen Hochschulen des deutschen Reiches erschienenen
Schriften. Berlin: Springer, 1914. 183 p.

Contains separate listings of dissertations for the
doctorate in engineering. Arranged by institution,
subdivided by department. Entry gives publication
information.

Continued by:

E63. "VERZEICHNIS von Doktor-Ingenieur-Dissertationen der deutschen
technischen Hochschulen aus dem Gebiete des Bauingenieurwesens
und seiner Grenzgebiete [1918-1930] in sachlicher Anordnung."
In Deutsche Gesellschaft für Bauingenieurwesen, Berlin.
Jahrbuch 2 (1926): 184-213; 4 (1929): 170-181; 6 (1931): 116-
129.

Vol. 2 (1926) covers 1918-1926; 4 (1929) covers 1926-
1928; 6 (1931) covers 1928-1930.

Altogether approximately 700 dissertations are
listed. In each list the dissertations are listed
under such subjects as mathematics-surveying, bridge
building, sanitary engineering, steel construction.
Author index in each volume.

E64. NIEMANN, Willy B. and M. W. Neufeld. Verzeichnis der Dr.-
Ing.-Dissertationen der deutschen technischen Hochschulen
und Bergakademien des Deutschen Reiches [1913-1927] Charlot-
tenburg: 1924-1931. 2 vols.

Vol. 1, edited by Willy B. Niemann, includes technological institutions only for the period 1913-1922;
vol. 2 also covers schools of mining and covers the
period 1923-1927 only.

A classified listing. Author and key word subject
indexes.

E65. "LISTE der Doktordissertationen des Verbandes der Laboratoriums-Vorstände an deutschen Hochschulen für d. J. 1921
auf 1922-1926/27." In Verband der Laboratoriums-Vorstände

an Deutschen Hochschulen. Berichte 24 (1928): 1-289. ?

E66. "TITLES of Graduate Engineering Theses Submitted in American Schools in 1939." Engineering Education 31 (1941): 508-531, 586-610.

Lists 1,141 theses and dissertations under such subjects as chemical engineering, civil engineering, electrical engineering, mechanical engineering, mineral industries. Under subject the studies are subdivided by institution.

E67. MASTER'S Theses Accepted by U.S. Colleges and Universities in the Fields of Chemical Engineering, Metallurgical Engineering and Physics [1955/1956-   ] Lafayette, Ind.: Purdue University, School of Mechanical Engineering, 1957-   . Title varies. Annual.

Vol. 3, pt. 2 (1959) includes 2,846 dissertations for the 1956/1957 school year.

Arranged by disciplines and subdivided alphabetically by university under each discipline. Excludes mathematical and life sciences. Date is given if different than year covered by volume.

E68. BUDAPEST. Müszaki Egyetem. Központi Könyvtär. A magyar Müszaki Egyetemeken elfogadott doktari dissertáciök jegyzéke [1958/1963-   ] Budapest: 1964-   . Biennial.

First number covers period 1958-1965.

Abstracts of dissertations accepted by Hungarian technical universities. Arranged by institution. Entry gives adviser. Author and subject indexes.

Individual Institutions

E69. AACHEN. Technische Hochschule. Die Technische Hochschule zu Aachen 1870-1920, eine Gedenkschrift. Aachen: 1920. 486 p.

"Dissertationen" (p. 468-473) lists approximately 140 dissertations chronologically under architecture and metallurgy.

E70. CALIFORNIA. University. College of Engineering. <u>Forefront</u>
[1947/1948-   ] Berkeley: 1948-   . Title varies. Annual.
1968/1970 (1970): double issue.

> Abstracts of dissertations completed at the College.
> Arranged under faculty, such as engineering, civil
> engineering, nuclear engineering. Entry gives
> adviser.

E71. CALIFORNIA. University. University at Los Angeles. School
of Engineering and Applied Science. <u>Research Development
and Public Service</u> [July 1950-   ] Los Angeles: 1951-   .
Annual.

> Pt. 3 carries separate lists of theses and of dis-
> sertations completed at the School.

E72. COLORADO. State University, Fort Collins. Department of
Civil Engineering. <u>Research Reports, Papers, Bulletins, and
Theses, 1948 through 1963</u>. Fort Collins: 1963. 1 vol.
(various pagings)

> Section F (p. F1-F9): "Theses, Dissertations and
> Master's Reports," listed in chronological order.
> Author index.

E73. DELFT. Technische Hoogeschool. <u>Bibliografie van de dissertaties ter verkrijging van de titel van doctor in de technische wetenschappen en lijst van de promoties honoris causa
1905-1966</u>. Uitg. ter gelegenheid van het 25. lustrum van de
Technische Hogeschool. [Bibliography of Doctoral Dissertations and List of Doctores Honoris Causa 1905-1966. Published on the occasion of the 125th anniversary of the
University] 's-Gravenhage: Staatsdrukkerij- en Uitgeverij-
bedrif, 1967. 245 p.

> Supersedes first edition (1955) and supplement
> (1966).

> A chronological listing of 733 dissertations.
> Entry gives adviser. Subject and geographic indexes.

E74. HAIFA. Technion, Israel Institute of Technology. Graduate
School. <u>Taktsire hibure ha-mehkar</u> [1960/1961-   ] Annual.

> In Hebrew and English.

Abstracts of theses and dissertations are listed
separately. Entry gives adviser. Author index.

E75. HANOVER. Technische Universität. <u>Dissertationen der Technischen Universität Hannover Studienjahre</u> [1954/1955-   ]
Hanover: 1956-   . Title varies. Annual.

Abstracts of dissertations completed in the University, arranged by faculty, subdivided by departments.
Entry gives brief biographical information. Author
index.

E76. ILLINOIS. University. College of Engineering. <u>Engineering
Departmental Reports and Theses; Abstracts of Engineering
Departmental Reports and Titles of Theses</u> [1958/1959-?]
Urbana: 1959-? Annual.

Separate lists of dissertations and theses at the
end of each record of departmental research. Author
and subject indexes.

E77. INDIAN INSTITUTE OF TECHNOLOGY, Madras. <u>Ph.D. Dissertation
Abstracts, 1965-1968</u>. Madras: 1969. 49 p.

Abstracts of dissertations, arranged by department
and year.

E78. BOLTON, John H. <u>Theses, College of Engineering, Iowa State
University, 1940-1962</u>. Ames, Iowa: 1963. 56 p. (Iowa
State University of Science and Technology. Engineering
Experiment Station. Engineering Report no. 41)

Supersedes Iowa State University of Science and
Technology Engineering Experiment Station, <u>List of
Research Reports: Master and Doctoral Theses</u> (1959).

A chronological listing of theses and dissertations
submitted for advanced degrees at the College of
Engineering. Within each year the entries are arranged by department. Author index.

E79. "THESES and Reports." <u>In</u> Kansas. State University of Agriculture and Applied Science. Engineering Experiment Station.
<u>Research Activities, 1960</u>, p. 40-43. Manhattan, Kans.: 1960.
(<u>Its</u> Bulletin, no. 91)

Lists by department unpublished studies completed
in 1960 in association with the Engineering Experiment Station.

_____ In Kansas. State University of Agriculture and Ap-
plied Science. Engineering Experiment Station. Research
Activities, 1961, p. 49-52. Manhattan, Kans.: 1961. (Its
Bulletin, no. 92)

Lists by department unpublished studies completed
in 1961 in association with the Engineering Experiment Station.

E80. POPOVA, L. M. and E. E. Motornaya. Dissertatsiy, zashchishchennye vo L'vovskom politekhnicheskom institute v 1946-1960
gg.; Bibliogr. ukazatel'. L'vov: 1961. 93 p.

Lists 198 dissertations defended at the Institute,
with a supplement of 73 items defended by the staff
of the Institute.

E81. MASSACHUSETTS INSTITUTE OF TECHNOLOGY. Library. Subject
List of Theses in Civil and Sanitary Engineering in the
Library: A Twenty-Five Year Record, 1913-1938. Compiled by
Ralph R. McNay. Cambridge, Mass.: 1939. 68 p.

Lists approximately 1,650 bachelors' and masters'
theses completed at the Massachusetts Institute of
Technology.

E82. NEWARK, N.J. College of Engineering. Catalog of Dissertations and Theses, 1949-1972. Newark: 1972. 85 p.

Supersedes its Master of Science Theses, 1950/1964
(1964?).

A listing by department of approximately 1,050
theses and dissertations. Under department theses
and dissertations are listed separately. Title
and author indexes.

E83. NORTHWESTERN UNIVERSITY, Evanston, Ill. Technological Institute. Faculty Publications, 1958-1959. Evanston: 1959.
28 p.

Contains separate lists of dissertations and theses

arranged by department (p. 21-28). Entry gives
major adviser.

E84. OKLAHOMA. State University of Agriculture and Applied
Science, Stillwater. College of Engineering. Abstracts of
Theses Directed by Members of the Staff of the College of
Engineering, Oklahoma State University. Stillwater: 1965.
1 vol. (unpaged)

Abstracts of theses and dissertations completed in
1965, arranged by school and by the faculty member
who directed the study. Each entry indicates the
scope and method of the study and the findings and
conclusions.

E85. PENNSYLVANIA. State University. College of Engineering.
Theses Abstracts [1968/1969-   ] University Park: 1969-
. Irregular.

Abstracts of theses and dissertations submitted to
the College. Arranged by department, i.e. aerospace,
architectural, civil, electrical. Entry gives adviser. Title and author indexes.

E86. PURDUE UNIVERSITY, Lafayette, Ind. Engineering Experiment
Station. Abstracts of Engineering Staff Publications and
Theses [1955/1956-   ] Lafayette: 1957-   . Annual.

Abstracts of theses and dissertations are listed
separately by department.

E87. BROLISH, A. A. Dissertatsiy, zashchishchennye v Rizhskom
politekhnicheskom institute 1958-1966. Bibliogr. ukazatel'.
Riga: 1968. 38 p.

In Latvian and Russian.

Classified listing of 146 dissertations defended
at the Institute. Author index.

E88. ODQVIST, Dagmar. Förteckning över Kungl. tekniska högskolans
doktorsavhandlingar 1928-1963: List of Royal Institute of
Technology Doctoral Dissertations 1928-1963. Stockholm:
Kungl. Tekniska högskolans Bibliotek, 1964. 28 p. (Kungl.
Tekniska hogskolans. Bibliotek. Publikation, no. 4)

Supersedes 1962 edition, edited by C. Ringius.

Lists the doctoral dissertations completed at the Royal Institute of Technology (Stockholm) from 1928 to 1963 arranged under physics, mechanical engineering, aeronautics and shipbuilding, electrical engineering, civil engineering, chemical engineering, mining and metallurgy, architecture and surveying. Entry gives publication information. Author index.

Continued by:

_____ _____ 1964-1970. Editor: John Linders. Stockholm: 1972. 27 p. (Kungl. Tekniska högskolans bibliotek. Publikation 14)

Title and description are in English. Author index.

E89. STUTTGART. Technische Hochschule. Stuttgarter Dissertationen, 1953-1955. In Auszügen. Stuttgart: 1957. 384 p.

Abstracts of 200 dissertations, arranged by faculty.

E90. VAINIO, Virpi and Elin Törnudd. Väitöskirjat, 1911-1968. Doktorsavhandlingar. Theses. Otaniemi: Teknillinen Korkeakoulu, Tekniska högskolan, Finland's Institute of Technology, 1969. 24 p. (Teknillinen Korkeakoulu. Tieteellisiä tutkimuksia, no. 29)

Supersedes Teknillinen Korkeakoulu, Helsingfors. List of Dissertations for the Degree of Technology, 1911-1953 (1953).

Alphabetical author listing of 167 dissertations. Entry gives publication information. Subject index.

E91. VIENNA. Dokumentationszentrum für Technik und Wirtschaft. Die Dissertationen der Technischen Hochschule Wien aus den Jahren 1901-1953. Hrsg. vom Österr. Dokumentationszentrum für Technik und Wirtschaft mit Unterstützung des Notringes der Wissenschaftlichen Verbände Österreichs. Bonn: 1955. 202 p. (Its Abhandlungen, Heft 26)

A classified list of 1,824 dissertations covering civil engineering, architecture, chemistry, engineering, mathematics, physics, and surveying. Subject and author indexes.

Continued by:

E92.   VIENNA. Technische Hochschule. Bibliothek. <u>Die Disserta-</u>
<u>tionen der Technischen Hochschule Wien aus den Jahren 1953-</u>
<u>1965</u>. Wien: Verlag Notring, 1967. 55 p.

A classified bibliography of 523 dissertations in
engineering, surveying, architecture, chemistry,
mathematics, and physics. Subject and author
indexes.

E93.   "PUBLICATIONS and Graduate Theses, College of Engineering
[1953-   ]" <u>Trends in Engineering at the University of</u>
<u>Washington</u> 5 (1953)-   . Annual. Vols. 5-11, Oct. issue;
vols. 12-   Jan. issue.

Lists completed theses and dissertations. Vol. 5
(1953) lists are retrospective to cover period from
1940.

E94.   ZURICH. Eidgenössische Technische Hochschule. Bibliothek.
<u>Dissertationenverzeichnis, 1909-1971; Répertoire des thèses,</u>
<u>1909-1971</u>. Zürich: 1972. 480 p. (<u>Its</u> Schriftenreihe,
Nr. 15)

Supersedes Schriftenreihe Nr. 1 and Nr. 3.

A classified listing of the 5,013 dissertations
accepted by the Swiss Federal Institute of Technology
since the introduction of the doctorate. Author
index.

Special Subjects

Architecture

E95.   "COMPLETE List of Masters' Theses Written at Oberlin College
under the Guidance of Clarence Ward." <u>In</u> Society of Architectural Historians. <u>Journal</u> 7 (July-Dec. 1948): 21-22.

A chronological listing of 41 theses written between
1928 and 1947.

E96.   "SUMMARIES of Masters' Theses on Topics from the History of

Architecture, Written at Oberlin College under the Guidance of Clarence Ward." In Society of Architectural Historians. Journal 7 (July-Dec. 1948): 22-32.

E97. GERO, John S. Post-Graduate Research Theses in the Dept. of Architectural Science. Sydney, Australia: University of Sydney, Dept. of Architectural Science, 1971. 60 p. (Sydney. University. Dept. of Architectural Science. Education Report, ER3) ?

Chemical Engineering

E98. MASSACHUSETTS INSTITUTE OF TECHNOLOGY. Libraries. M.I.T. Chemical Engineering Department Theses in the Institute Library, 1921-1947, Inclusive. Cambridge: Massachusetts Institute of Technology, 1948. 581 p. (Its Technical Reference List, no. 3)

M.S. theses and Sc.D. dissertations arranged by year and subdivided within each year into those courses concerned with chemical engineering and with chemical engineering practice. Author index.

E99. "RESEARCH Roundup [1951-   ]" Chemical Engineering Progress 48 (1952)-   . Title varies. Annual. Jan. issue.

Lists dissertations completed in American universities. Arranged under such topics as adsorption, bioengineering, chemical reactors, fluid dynamics, metallurgy. Entry gives adviser and indicates if work is being continued.

E100. "DISSERTATIONEN auf dem Gebiet der chemischen Technik und ihrer Grundlagen sowie auf angrenzenden Fachgebieten [1953-1958]" Chemie-Ingenieur-Technik 25 (1953)-32 (1960). Annual.

Dissertations completed in German institutions. Arranged under such areas as heat, chemical methods, materials, and construction. Entry gives adviser and publication information.

E101. "DISSERTATSIY po neftepromyslovomu delu, zashchishchennye v Institute nefti Akad. nauk SSSR 1951-1958 gg." In Akademiya nauk SSSR. Institut geologii i razrabotki goriuchikh iskopaemyk. Trudy 2 (1960): 200-201.

Lists three dissertations and 20 theses completed at the Institute between 1951 and 1958.

Electrical Engineering

E102. MAYNARD, Katherine and Murray F. Gardner. A Classified List of Theses in Electrical Engineering Presented at Massachusetts Institute of Technology, 1902-1929, including also Recent Research Reports. Cambridge, Mass.: Technology Press, 1929. 108 p. (Massachusetts Institute of Technology. Dept. of Electrical Engineering. Contribution, serial no. 65)

Bachelors' and masters' theses and dissertations listed chronologically under subject.

E103. "DISSERTATSIY." Elektrichestvo, 1946, no. 7: 84-90, no. 10: 79-80; 1947, no. 2: 89-92, no. 3: 89-91, no. 4: 88-94, no. 5: 90-93, no. 6: 88-90, no. 10: 91-92.

An annotated listing of approximately 250 theses and dissertations completed in the period 1939-1947. Arranged by institution.

E104. "DISSERTATSIY zashchishchennye v Moskovskom elektrotekhnicheskom institute svyazi v 1953-1954 uchebnom gody." Vestnikh svyazi, 1955, no. 1: 32-33, no. 2: 32-33.

Annotated listing of 42 studies arranged under departments.

E105. ILMENAU (City). Technische Hochschule. Bibliothek. Bibliographie deutschesprachiger Hochschulschriften der Electrotechnik und ihrer Grundlagenwissenschaften. Ilmenau: n.d. Semiannual.

Edited by Karl H. Körtner.

Folge 3: 2. Halbjahr 1963.

A classified listing of German and German language Swiss dissertations and Habilitationen.

Applied Sciences

E106. RAFAJ, Emil. <u>Bibliografia dizertačných a diplomových prác obhájených na Vysokej škole dopravnej</u>. Martin: Matica Slovenská, 196?

> Vol. 2, "Fakulta Strojnícka a Elektrotechnícká, 1957-1965," lists 1,019 abstracts chronologically under type of degree. Author and subject indexes.

Electronic Data Processing

E107. GOLDBERG, Albert J. "Dissertations [1959/1964-1970]" <u>Journal of Educational Data Processing</u> 3 (1966): 83-87; 4 (1967): 106-110; 5 (1968): 92-95; 6 (1969): 124-127; 7 (1970): 255-258.

> Alphabetical author listings of dissertations, with some theses. The numbering of items is consecutive.

Gearing

E108. SEHERR-THOSS, Hans C. and Stefan Fronius. "Die deutsch-sprachigen Dissertationen zur Zahnrad-Wissenschaft." <u>In their Die Entwicklung der Zahnrad-Technik; Zahnformen und Tragfähigkeitsberechung</u>, p. 510-519. Berlin: Springer Verlag, 1965.

> A chronological listing of approximately 130 dissertations and Habilitationsschriften covering the period 1901 through 1963. Entry gives publication information.

Hydraulics

E109. MAVIS, Frederic T. <u>Two Decades of Hydraulics at the University of Iowa: Abstracts of Theses, Publications, and Research Reports, 1919-1938</u>. Iowa City, Iowa: 1939. 80 p. (University of Iowa Studies in Engineering. Bulletin, no. 19)

> Consists in large part of work submitted to the Department of Mechanics and Hydraulics for the master and doctorate degrees.

Industrial Engineering

E110. COLUMBIA UNIVERSITY. Department of Industrial Engineering and Management Education. <u>Reports in Industrial Engineering; A Cumulative Bibliography of Ph.D. Dissertations, Master's Reports and Selected Course Papers</u>. New York: 1949. 61 p.

Lists approximately 325 studies under subject.

_____ _____ <u>Supplement</u> [1950/1951-1957/1958] New York: 1951-1958. Annual.

Follows same plan as main work with (1) studies listed under subject and (2) an author list.

Mechanical Engineering

E111. CALIFORNIA. University. College of Engineering. Division of Mechanical Engineering. <u>Theses and Reports on Fluid Mechanics and Related Fields (1900-1945) and Publications of Fluid Mechanics Laboratory (1926-1945)</u>. Compiled by J. W. Johnson. Berkeley, Calif.: 1945. 35 p.

Pt. 1 (p. 1-26) is a classified bibliography of 263 bachelors' and masters' theses and dissertations.

Mechanics

E112. LOZINSKAYA, L. A. and L. A. Tarasova. <u>Dissertacii po mehanike zaščiščenyje sotrudnikami institutov an USRS v 1968</u>. Kiev: 1968. ?

Metallurgy

E113. "DISSERTATSIY na soiskanie uchenykh stepeney." <u>Metallovedenie i termicheskaya obrabotka metallov</u>, 1955-1961. Irregular.

Separate lists of theses and dissertations defended in the U.S.S.R. Arranged under physics-mathematics, chemical sciences, and technological sciences.

E114. GENTZSCH, Gerhard. <u>Umformtechnik; Dissertationsreferate</u>,

<u>1945-1967</u>. Düsseldorf: VDI-Verlag, 1968. 160 p.

A classified annotated bibliography of 311 German
language dissertations. Author, institutional,
date of completion, and subject indexes.

Mining

E115. "ISTORIYA gornogo dela i metallurgii." <u>In</u> Akademiya nauk
SSSR. Institut istorii estestvoznaniya i tekhniki. <u>Trudy</u>
3 (1955): 236-237.

Lists two dissertations and 13 theses.

E116. HARTMAN, Howard L. "Bibliography of Theses on Mining in U.S.
Institutions." <u>Colorado School of Mines Quarterly</u> 51 (April
1956): 1-70.

Also issued separately.

Attempts to list all theses in mining engineering
to date of publication. Contains items from 23
participating schools. Arranged by subject with
short annotation when available. "List...by School
of Origin" arranged by date, giving key number or
thesis number and publishing information if known.
"List of Theses by Author" gives no reference to
location in main list.

E117. BRADY, Alice J. <u>Theses of the College of Mines, University
of Idaho, 1911-1957</u>. Moscow, Idaho: 1957. 26 p. (Idaho.
Bureau of Mines and Geology. Information Circular, no. 2)

Divided into geology, metallurgy, and mining. Also
includes dissertations and bachelors' theses. Author
index.

E118. MICHIGAN. College of Mining and Technology, Houghton.
Library. <u>Graduate Theses, 1928-1957, Available in the College Library</u>. Houghton: 1958. 14 p.

Masters' degrees, arranged by title.

E119. STANFORD UNIVERSITY. School of Mineral Sciences. <u>Theses</u>

and Publications of the School of Mineral Sciences 1951 to
1961, Inclusive. Stanford, Calif.: 1961. 11 p.

In two major parts: alphabetically by author and
under general subject.

Refrigeration

E120. PRILUTSKIY, David N. Bibliograficheskiy spravochnik doktorskikh i kandidatskikh dissertatsiy. Dissertatsiy po kholodil'noy tekhnike, 1936-1962 gg. Moskva: Gostorgizdat Izd.
Torgovoy Literaturya, 1963. 148 p.

A classified listing of 572 theses and 100 dissertations on refrigeration completed in the U.S.S.R.
Author and institutional indexes.

Continued by:

E121. _____ "Dissertatsiy v oblasti kholodil'noy tekhniki i tekh-
nologii za 1963-1965 gg." Kholodil'naya tekhnika i tekh-
nologiya, 1966, no. 3: 50-52.

Lists 46 theses and dissertations.

Supplemented and continued by:

E122. _____ _____ "1964-1966 gg." Kholodil'naya tekhnika, 1968,
no. 1: 42-43.

Lists 33 theses and dissertations completed in the
U.S.S.R.

Continued by:

_____ _____ "1966-1968 gg." Kholodil'naya tekhnika, 1969,
no. 4: 50-52.

Lists 37 theses and dissertations.

Continued and supplemented by:

_____ _____ "1966-1969 gg." Kholodil'naya tekhnika, 1970,
no. 2: 56-58.

Lists 53 theses and dissertations.

Surveying

E123. SANDER, Willy and Franz Manek. <u>Deutschsprachige Disserta-</u>
<u>tionen und Habilitationen über Bildmessung</u>. Dresden: Gesell-
schaft für Photogrammetrie in d. DDR, 1963. 345 p. ?

Forestry

General

E124. OSBORNE, Katherine H. <u>Forestry Theses Accepted by Colleges</u>
<u>and Universities in the United States, 1900-1952</u>. Subject
index by Ray A. Yoder and William I. West. Corvallis, Ore.:
Oregon State College, 1953. 140 p. (Oregon State College,
Corvallis. Library. Bibliographic Series, no. 3)

> Earlier listings were compiled by Oregon State Uni-
> versity Library as <u>Theses Submitted for Advanced</u>
> <u>Degrees in the Subject Field of Forestry...</u> in 1935,
> 1938, and 1942.

> Theses and dissertations arranged by institution
> and chronologically under each. Author and subject
> indexes.

> _____ _____ <u>Supplement, 1953-1955, Including Additions for</u>
> <u>1904-1952</u>. Subject index by Louis H. Powell and William I.
> West. Corvallis, Ore.: Oregon State College, 1957. 44 p.
> (Oregon State College, Corvallis. Library. Bibliographic
> Series, no. 5)

> Continued by:

E125. _____ _____ "Supplement [Jan. 1956/June 1958-July 1968/
June 1969]" <u>Forest Science</u> 5 (1959)-16 (1970). Sept. issue
except vols. 11 (1965)-14 (1968) in June issue.

> Subject indexes prepared by Ray A. Yoder, William
> I. West, and Martha H. Brookes.

> Theses and dissertations are arranged alphabetically
> by author under institution. Author and subject
> indexes with each list.

E126. "FORSTWIRTSCHAFTLICHE Dissertationen." Forstarchiv 25 (1954): 60-63, 186-188.

> A classified listing of dissertations completed in forestry faculties, covering the period from 1945. In two parts: pt. 1 lists 93 dissertations from Freiburg, Hamburg, Munich, and Hannover Münden; pt. 2, 54 dissertations from Elberswalde, Vienna, and Zurich.

E127. SMITH, Anne Marie, Robert W. Wellwood, and Leonid Valg. "Canadian Theses in Forestry and Related Subject Fields, 1913-1962." Forestry Chronicle 38 (1962): 375-400.

> Contains 388 theses and dissertations, arranged chronologically by institution. Author and subject indexes.

E128. POLSKIE TOWARZYSTWO LEŚNE. Wykaz stopni i tytułów naukowych nadanych w dziedzinie leśnictwa i drzewnictwa polskiego w latach 1918-1964. Warszawa: Państwowe Wydawnictwo Rolnicze i Leśne, 1966. 86 p.

> In two major parts, covering the periods 1918-1939 and 1945-1964. Under each, arranged chronologically by institution. Entry gives publication information.

Individual Institutions

E129. WALTERS, John. An Annotated Bibliography of Reports, Theses, and Publications Pertaining to the Campus and Research Forests of the University of British Columbia. Vancouver, B.C.: University of British Columbia, Faculty of Forestry, 1968. 71 p.

> An alphabetical author listing of studies completed between 1935 and 1967. Theses and dissertations are listed separately in the index. Subject index.

E130. CHILE. Universidad, Santiago. Escuela de Ingeniéria Forestal. Reseña de tesis, 1954-1964. Santiago: 1965. 22 p. (Its Boletin Técnico, no. 10)

> Abstracts of 35 theses completed at the School for the degree of Ingeniero Forestal. Author index.

E131. FLORIDA. University, Gainesville. School of Forestry. Theses in Forestry and Related Subjects Accepted at the University of Florida through June, 1966. Gainesville: 1967. 194 p.

Classified bibliography with abstracts of more than 315 theses and dissertations. Covers such areas as products, technology, wildlife, economics, recreation, and education. Index to genera and species. Author and subject index.

E132. LENINGRAD. Lesotekhnicheskaya akademiya. Ukazatel' dissertatsiy, zashchishchennykh v Leningradskoy lesotekhnicheskoy akademii (1934-1961). Leningrad: 1962. 90 p.

Lists dissertations defended at the Academy.

E133. CROW, Alonza B. Master's Theses in Forestry, Game Management, and Related Subjects at Louisiana State University, 1926 to 1958. Baton Rouge, La.: 1958. 6 p. (LSU Forestry Notes, no. 22)

Continued by:

_____ Theses and Dissertations in Forestry, Game Management, and Related Subjects at Louisiana State University, A Supplement, August 1958 to August 1961. Baton Rouge, La.: 1961. 4 p. (LSU Forestry Notes, no. 45)

Continued by:

_____ _____ Supplement, January 1962 to August 1963, Including Additions for 1961. Baton Rouge, La.: 1963. 3 p. (LSU Forestry Notes, no. 54)

Continued by:

_____ _____ Supplement, January 1964 to August 1965. Baton Rouge, La.: 1965. 3 p. (LSU Forestry Notes, no. 64)

Continued by:

_____ _____ Supplement, January 1965 to August 1967. Baton Rouge, La.: 1967. 4 p. (LSU Forestry Notes, no. 73)

Subdivided into (1) dissertations and (2) theses, then into forestry, game management, and fisheries. Each of the parts is arranged chronologically.

E134. MÉRIDA, Venezuela (City). Universidad de los Andes. Facultad de Ciencias Forestales. Tesis de grado y trabajos de ascenso presentadas...1957-1967. Mérida: 1968. 25 p. ?

E135. CASTAÑOS M., León Jorge. "Tesis profesionales de especialistas en bosques egresados de la Escuela Nacional de Agricultura." Mexico y sus bosques 2, no. 8 (1964): 18-25.

A chronological listing of 185 theses covering the period 1936-1963. Author and subject indexes.

_____ _____ "1964." Mexico y sus bosques 2, no. 11 (1964): 12.

_____ _____ "1965-1966." Mexico y sus bosques 3, no. 13/14 (1967): 13-14.

_____ _____ "1967-1972." Mexico y sus bosques 11, no. 4 (1972): 29-32.

The supplements continue numbering of main listing. Each has author and subject indexes.

E136. MOSCOW. Lesotekhnicheskiy institut. Doktorskie i kandidatskie dissertatsiy, zashchishchennye v Moskovskom Lesotekhnicheskom institute s 1948 po 1956 gg. Moskva: 1957. 24 p.

Theses and dissertations defended at the Institute.

E137. NEW YORK STATE COLLEGE OF FORESTRY, Syracuse University. Graduate Theses, 1944-1954. Compiled by Genevieve L. Reidy. Syracuse, N.Y.: State University of New York, College of Forestry, 1955. 116 p.

Classified list of 150 theses and dissertations completed at Syracuse University, with abstracts. Represents a variety of studies in fields relating to forestry, forest utilization, and forest products. Appendix contains a listing in chronological order of work accepted from 1914 to 1943. Subject index.

Continued by:

E138. _____ _____ 1955-1960. Compiled by J. Vincent Thirgood. Syracuse, N.Y.: State University of New York, College of Forestry, 1961. 111 p.

A listing of abstracts of 228 theses and dissertations completed at Syracuse University, arranged under broad subjects. Author and subject indexes.

E139. SMITH, Bernice F. <u>Theses in Forestry</u>. Seattle: University of Washington, Institute of Forest Products, 1967. 36 p. (Washington (State). University. Institute of Forest Products. Library Series. Contribution no. 3)

A chronological listing of theses and dissertations submitted to the University of Washington Graduate School from 1904 through 1966 in the forest sciences. Entry indicates if taken in a department other than the College of Forest Resources. Author and subject indexes.

<u>Theses in Forestry, 1967-1969</u>. 7 p. (Washington (State). University. Institute of Forest Products. Library Series. Contribution no. 3, suppl. 1970)

E140. YALE UNIVERSITY. School of Forestry. <u>Theses Accepted for ...Degrees</u> [June 1949-   ] New Haven, Conn.: 1949-   . Annual.

Theses and dissertations completed in the School.

Transportation

E141. RUSSIA. Ministerstvo putey soobshcheniya. TSentral'naya nauchno-tekhnicheskaya biblioteka. <u>Dissertatsiy po zhelez-nodorozhnoy tematike, zashchishchennye s 1934-1955 gg</u>. Moskva: Gos. Transp. zhel. dor izd.-no, 1957. 155 p.

A listing under subjects of 137 dissertations and 1,805 theses dealing with railroads, completed in Russian institutions. Author and institutional indexes.

E142. REHBEIN, Gerhard. <u>Dissertations- und Habilitationsschriften auf dem Gebiet des Verkehrs, Transport- und Nachrichten-wesens seit 1945</u>. Hamburg: Auto und Erdöl Presse-Verlag, 1962. 141 p.

A classified bibliography of German, Austrian, and Swiss German language studies.

E143. NORTHWESTERN UNIVERSITY, Evanston, Ill.   Transportation
Center Library. Doctoral Dissertations on Transportation,
1961-1967, and Addendum December 1967-July 1968: A Bibliography. Evanston: Northwestern University Transportation
Center, 1968. 45 p.

> Supersedes its Ph.D. Dissertations in Intercity and
> Local Transportation, 1961-1966 (1967), expanded to
> include urban transportation and traffic from 1961
> to 1967.

> Lists 420 items completed in American institutions
> in the main work and 61 in the addendum. Arranged
> by subject. Entry indicates if available in the
> Transportation Center Library. Geographic and sub-
> ject indexes.

_____ _____ [1969-   ] Evanston: Northwestern University
Transportation Center, 1970-   . Irregular.

> Continues numbering of main work.

E144. SOKOLL, Alfred H.   Hochschulschriften zur Aero- und Astro-
nautik; Deutschsprachige Bibliographie 1910-1965. München:
Alkos Verlag, 1968. 134 p. (Bibliothek der Aero- und
Astronautik, Bd. 6)

> A chronological listing of dissertations and
> Habilitationsschriften, including items from Austrian
> and Swiss universities. Author and subject indexes.

E145. WHEELER, James. Research on the Journey to Work. Monticello,
Ill.: 1969. 21 p. (Council of Planning Librarians. Exchange Bibliography, no. 65)

> On p. 20-21, theses and dissertations are listed
> alphabetically by author, covering the period
> 1950-1967.

F. Communication and Mass Media

Communication

F1.   STUDIES in Public Communication [no. 1 (Summer 1957)-]
      Chicago: University of Chicago, 1957-   . Irregular.

> Originally published by the University of Chicago
> Committee on Communication and continued by an
> editorial board of the University of Chicago.
>
> Contains abstracts of students' papers. No. 1 con-
> tains a listing of masters' theses in communication,
> 1954-1957, completed within the University of
> Chicago (p. 49).

F2.   CHICAGO. University. Committee on Communication. Masters'
      Theses in Communication, 1954 to 1959. Chicago: 1959. 77 p.
      (Its Studies in Public Communication, no. 2)

> Twenty-two theses completed at the University of
> Chicago.

F3.   KNOWER, Franklin H. Bibliography of Communications Disser-
      tations in American Schools of Theology. N.p.: 1961. 45 p.

> Reprinted in Speech Monographs 30 (1963): 105-133.
>
> The listing was prepared by circularizing the 124
> member schools of the American Association of
> Theological Schools at the request of the Religious
> Interest Group of the Speech Association of America.
> Contains 453 baccalaureate theses, 256 masters'
> theses, and 154 dissertations completed through
> 1960, selected on the basis of some relevance to
> communication activities. Arranged chronologically
> by schools.

Film

F4.   THIEL, Reinhold E. "Filmdissertationen an deutschen Hoch-
      schulen, 1907-1954." Publizistik 1 (1956): 310-315, 372-
      378.

      A classified listing of approximately 200 disserta-
      tions covering aesthetics, history, censorship, law,
      economics, instructional aspects, psychology and
      medicine, and sociology. Entry gives publication
      information.

F5.   FIELDING, Raymond. "Theses and Dissertations on the Subject
      of Film at U.S. Universities, 1916-1967; A Bibliography."
      Journal of the University Film Association 20 (1968): 46-53.

      A listing of 386 theses and dissertations dealing
      with the motion picture completed at Iowa, Boston,
      Michigan, Southern California, California at Los
      Angeles, Northwestern, Stanford, and Ohio State
      Universities. Arranged alphabetically by author
      under institution.

      Continued by:

F6.   _____ "Second Bibliographic Survey of Theses and Disserta-
      tions on the Subject of Film in U.S. Universities, 1916-
      1969." Journal of the University Film Association 21 (1969):
      111-113.

      Lists an additional 107 studies, most completed in
      1968 and 1969, but some from as early as 1925. Ar-
      ranged by institution.

F7.   MANCHEL, Frank. Film Study; A Resource Guide. Rutherford,
      N.J.: Fairleigh Dickinson University Press, 1973.

      Appendix 6, "A Selective List of Dissertations on
      Films" (p. 356-362), lists approximately 50 items
      completed at American universities between 1955 and
      1971.

Journalism

F8.   REDFORD, Edward H. "Survey of College and University Theses

Which Discuss High School Journalism and Publications."
Education 57 (1936): 239-243.

Lists 54 theses completed in the period 1933-1934.

F9.   MOTT, Frank L. "A List of Unpublished Theses in the Field
      of Journalism on File in the Libraries of American Universi-
      ties." Journalism Quarterly 13 (1936): 329-355.

      A subject list of theses (apparently including some
      dissertations though most are theses) completed
      from 1902 through 1935.

      Continued by:

F10. SWINDLER, William F. "Graduate Theses in the Field of Jour-
      nalism: 1936-1945." Journalism Quarterly 22 (1945): 231-254.

      Theses and dissertations arranged by subject.

      Continued in part by:

F11. PRICE, Warren C. "Doctoral Dissertations in the Field of
      Journalism, 1946-1949." Journalism Quarterly 27 (1950):
      164-167.

      Includes items from departments and schools other
      than journalism. Arranged by subject.

      Continued by:

F12. "REPORT on Graduate Research in Journalism and Communication
      [1949/50-1969]" Journalism Quarterly 27 (1950)-46 (1969).
      Title varies. Annual. Winter issue, 1954-1959; Summer
      issue, 1960-1969.

         In two parts: pt. 1 contains two sections, (a) an
         annotated list of Ph.D.'s accepted and (b) Ph.D.
         titles approved; pt. 2: "Masters Theses Completed
         in Journalism." In vols. 31 (1953)-38 (1961), pt.
         1 carries staff as well as doctoral research. Both
         parts are classified. Entry indicates the institu-
         tion.

         Continued by:

F13. "PH.D. Dissertations Completed [1969/1970-1970/1971]" Journalism Quarterly 47 (1970): 625-629; 48 (1971): 768-774.

An alphabetical author listing compiled primarily from Journalism Abstracts (Item F25). Entry gives adviser.

F14. FRANZMEYER, Fritz. Press-Dissertationen an deutschen Hochschulen, 1885-1938; Auf Grund der Jahresverzeichnisse der deutschen Hochschulschriften und der Verzeichnisse für die Ostmark und das Protektorat Böhmen. Leipzig: Börsenverein der Deutschen Buchhändler, 1940. 167 p.

Supersedes Karl Bömer, Bibliographisches Handbuch der Zeitungswissenschaft (1929), which had, in turn, incorporated the material appearing in Karl Jaeger, Von der Zeitungskunde zur publizistischen Wissenschaft (1926).

A chronological listing of 1,353 dissertations. Author and subject index.

Continued by:

F15. _____ Press-Dissertationen an deutschen Hochschulen. Nachtrag 1. 1939. Berlin: Walther Heide, 1941. 15 p.

Lists 74 additional dissertations.

_____ "Presse-Dissertationen an deutschen und schweizerischen Hochschulen. Nachtrag 1940." Zeitungswissenschaft 17 (1942): 148-155.

In two parts: (1) a list of 88 dissertations completed in German universities in 1940 and earlier, and (2) a list of ten Swiss dissertations completed in 1940 or earlier. Entry gives publication information. Some carry descriptive note.

_____ _____ "Nachtrag 1941." Zeitungswissenschaft 18 (1943): 13-20.

In two parts: (1) a list of 91 dissertations completed in German universities in 1941 or earlier, and (2) three Swiss dissertations completed in 1941. Some carry descriptive note.

_____ _____ "Nachtrag 1942." Zeitungswissenschaft 19

(1944): 127-130.

> Lists 58 dissertations completed in Germany or in countries occupied by Germany. Some carry descriptive notes.

————— —————— "1943." _Zeitungswissenschaft_ 19 (1944): 258-262.

> Lists 48 dissertations completed in Germany or in countries occupied by Germany. Some carry descriptive notes.

F16.　————— "Schweizerische Press-Dissertationen." _Zeitungswissenschaft_ 16 (1941): 68-73.

> Continued by Item F15.

> Lists 88 dissertations completed in Swiss universities between 1897 and 1938. Arranged by institution. Author index.

F17.　————— "Französiche Presse-Dissertationen 1885-1937." _Zeitungswissenschaft_ 18 (1943): 390-408.

> Alphabetical author listing of 219 dissertations. Some entries carry notes.

F18.　————— "Presse-Dissertationen an amerikanischen Universitäten." _Zeitungswissenschaft_ 19 (1944): 162-168.

> An alphabetical author listing of 119 dissertations completed in the period 1933-1941.

F19.　NEBRASKA. University. School of Journalism. _Graduate Theses in Journalism, 1945-1947_. Lincoln: 1948. 16 p. (Contributions to Bibliography in Journalism, no. 1)

> A subject listing of approximately 150 American theses and dissertations completed in the period 1945-1947, inclusive.

F20.　BIGMAN, Stanley K. "Unpublished Theses on Journalism at Columbia University." _Journalism Quarterly_ 27 (1950): 28-45.

Masters' theses written in departments other than
journalism but pertaining to the subject, dating
from 1900. A classified list.

F21. WEIGLE, Clifford F. "Master's Dissertations in the Field of
Journalism, 1946-49." Journalism Quarterly 27 (1950): 168-
185.

Continues Item F9 and Item F10, giving the same
information, but including only masters' theses.

Lists theses in schools and departments of journalism under subject. Includes some items from other
disciplines.

Continued by:

F22. SWANSON, Charles E. "Masters' Theses in the Field of Journalism [1949-1952]" Journalism Quarterly 28 (1951): 100-
107; 29 (1952): 78-84; 30 (1953): 115-117, 391.

Completed theses, arranged under subject.

F23. _____ "Report on Journalism Research in Progress [1950-
1953]" Journalism Quarterly 28 (1951): 93-99; 29 (1952):
74-78; 30 (1953): 112-114.

Lists works "by staff members and doctoral candidates in American schools and departments of journalism." Arranged by subject, giving status of
investigator and whether in progress or completed.

F24. KIESLICH, Günter. "Fachliche Dissertationen an deutschen
und deutschsprachigen Universitäten und Hochschulen seit
1945." Publizistik 1 (1956): 113-118, 182-186, 249-253;
2 (1957): 51-56.

Dissertations completed in German and Austrian universities to 1955. Arranged chronologically under
institution. Coverage for each varies: Freie Universität (Berlin), 1951-1955; Westfälische Wilhelms-
Universität (Münster), 1947-1955; Ludwig-Maximilians-
Universität (München), 1946-1951; Hochschule für
Wirtschafts- und Sozialwissenschaften (Nürnberg),
1948-1956; Universität Wien, 1945-1949. Entry gives
faculty in which work was done and publication

information.

F25. JOURNALISM Abstracts [1 (1963)-   ] Minneapolis [etc.]:
Association for Education in Journalism, 1963-   . Annual.

Lists theses and dissertations in journalism and
mass communication completed in schools and departments of journalism and communication in the United
States. In two parts, (1) dissertations and (2)
theses. Entry gives adviser. Author index.

F26. SPIESS, Volker. Verzeichnis deutschsprachiger Hochschulschriften zur Publizistik, 1885-1967. Berlin: Verlag Dokumentation, 1969. 231 p.

Alphabetical author listing of 4,766 dissertations
and Habilitationsschriften representing work done
in Austria, Switzerland, and East and West Germany.
Covers (1) media as sources of research, (2) research
methodologies from other disciplines which have
relevance to mass communication, (3) individuals
identified with mass communication, (4) technique
and political journalism. Entry indicates faculty
in which work was taken and publication information. Classified index and geographical subject
index.

Radio and Television

F27. CHEYDLEUR, Raymond D. A Compilation of Radio Theses in
American Colleges and Universities, 1918-1950. Huntington,
W. Va.: Marshall College, 1950. 73 p.

A listing of theses and dissertations. In addition
to the obvious subjects, such as speech, education,
and journalism, items are also included in such areas
as civil and electrical engineering and physics,
when radio is the major topic.

F28. INDIANA. University. Department of Radio and Television.
A List of Masters' Theses and Doctoral Dissertations Written
at Indiana University since 1920 on the Subject of Broadcasting. Bloomington: 1957. 2, 3 p.

Includes work done in all departments of the univer-

sity. Dissertations and theses are listed separately.
Entry gives the department in which the work was done.

F29. "DOCTORAL Dissertations in Radio and Television." Journal
of Broadcasting 1 (1957): 377-383.

An alphabetical list taken from lists compiled by
Cheydleur (Item F27) and Golter (Item G224).

Lists 202 items dating from 1920 to 1957 and dealing with the program, business, or educational aspects of radio and television. Entry gives publication information.

F30. LERG, Winifred B. "Rundfunkdissertationen an deutschen Hochschulen, 1920-1953 [1957]" Publizistik 2 (1957): 185-188,
249-252, 310-315.

A classified listing of 216 dissertations and Habilitationsschriften. Covers sociology, law, history,
economics, administration, and technology. Entry
gives publication information.

Translated in part in:

F31. LEE, E. Franck. "Doctoral Dissertations in Radio and Television at German Universities, 1920-1957." Journal of
Broadcasting 2 (1958): 369-375.

Lists 121 non-technical and engineering dissertations selected from Item F30. Arranged by subject
under radio and television.

F32. SUMMERS, Robert E. "Graduate Theses in Broadcasting: A
Topical Index, 1920-1956." Journal of Broadcasting 2 (Winter 1957/1958): 55-90.

Based on Item F27 and Item F29.

A classified list of 1,275 non-technical theses and
dissertations dealing specifically with radio and
television broadcasting, covering such topics as
acting, announcing, and advertising.

Continued by:

F33. KNOWER, Franklin H. "Graduate Theses and Dissertations on Broadcasting [1956/1958-]" _Journal of Broadcasting_ 4 (Winter 1959/1960)- . Irregular.

Arranged alphabetically by author under subject.

F34. BARCUS, Frances E. "A Bibliography of Studies of Radio and Television Program Content, 1928-1958." _Journal of Broadcasting_ 4 (1960): 355-369.

Many dissertations are included in pt. 2, "Bibliography" (p. 358-365). Pt. 3, "Masters' Theses" (p. 365-369), is a classified list.

F35. SPARKS, Kenneth R. _A Bibliography of Doctoral Dissertations in Television and Radio._ Syracuse, N.Y.: Syracuse University, School of Journalism, 1962. 32 p.

Author listing of 352 dissertations completed at American universities through 1961, covering every phase of broadcasting except engineering.

F36. "THESES and Dissertations." _In_ Television Information Office. Library. _Television in Government and Politics; A Bibliography_, p. 51-54. New York: 1964.

An annotated list of 26 theses and dissertations.

F37. PRAGUE. Ústřední tělovýchovná knihovna. _Diplomové práce FTVS-UK a závěrečné práce Trenérské školy při FTVS, obhájené v roce 1965_. Prague: 1966. 18 p. ?

Edited by Miloslavia Waitová.

G. Education

General

G1. ILLINOIS. University. Bureau of Educational Research.
     <u>Titles of Masters' and Doctors' Theses in Education Accepted</u>
     <u>by Colleges and Universities in the United States</u> [1 (1917/
     1919)-6 (1925/1927)] Urbana: 1920-1928. 6 vols. Title
     varies. Irregular.

     Compiled by Walter S. Monroe.

     A classified listing, covering such areas as educa-
     tional history, biography, higher education, religious
     education, exceptional children. Within each subject
     further subdivided into dissertations and theses.
     Altogether 1,038 dissertations and 5,785 theses are
     listed. Entry gives publication information.

     In part cumulated in:

G2. MONROE, Walter S. <u>Ten Years of Educational Research, 1918-</u>
     <u>27</u>. Urbana, Ill.: University of Illinois, 1928. 367 p.
     (Illinois. University. College of Education. Bureau of
     Educational Research. Bulletin no. 42)

     Pt. 2 contains a separate "List of Doctors of Phil-
     osophy of Education by Institution, 1918-1927."
     Entry gives publication information. Topical index.

G3. "THESES Written in California Universities in Candidacy for
     Graduate Degrees in Education during the Academic Year
     [1928/1929-1933/1934]" <u>Journal of Secondary Education</u> 5
     (1929)-10 (1934). Title varies. Annual. Oct. issue.

     Arranged by institution and subdivided by level of
     degree.

G4.   U.S. Office of Education. Library. Bibliography of Re-
      search Studies in Education [1926/1927-1939/1940] Washing-
      ton: U.S. Government Printing Office, 1929-1942. Annual.

      Classified listing of published and unpublished
      studies, a substantial number of which are theses
      and dissertations, reported to the Office of Educa-
      tion covering all aspects of education and all
      levels of instruction. Entry gives publication
      information. Many entries are annotated. Subject,
      institutional, and author indexes.

      Supplemented by:

G5.   "SELECTED Theses on Education." School Life 18, no. 5 (Jan.
      1933)-36, no. 1 (Oct. 1953). Title varies.

      Originally called "Recent Theses in Education,"
      these short lists appeared monthly in almost every
      number of School Life. They included selected
      dissertations and outstanding theses, usually com-
      pleted in the year immediately preceding listing,
      received by the U.S. Office of Education and on
      file in the Federal Security Agency Library (later
      the Health, Education, and Welfare Department
      Library). Entries are listed alphabetically by
      title and give publication information. Vols. 29
      (1946/1947)-33, no. 8 (May 1951) carry annotations.

      Supplemented by:

G6.   "RECENT Theses." Education for Victory 1 (1942)-3 (1945).

      Lists recent theses and dissertations which could
      be borrowed from the U.S. Office of Education
      Library. The lists appear in almost every issue,
      in the section "Educators' Bulletin Board." Begin-
      ning with vol. 2 (1943) short annotations are
      included.

      Supplemented by:

G7.   U.S. Office of Education. Recent Theses in Education: An
      Annotated List of 242 Theses Deposited with the Office of
      Education and Available for Loan. Washington: U.S. Govern-
      ment Printing Office, 1932. 41 p. (Its Pamphlet, 1931, no.
      26)

Lists 132 dissertations and 110 theses, most completed during 1930-1931, arranged alphabetically under subject. Annotated.

In part superseded by:

G8. GRAY, Ruth A. Doctor's Theses in Education; A List of 797 Theses Deposited with the Office of Education and Available for Loan. Washington: U.S. Government Printing Office, 1935. 69 p. (U.S. Office of Education. Pamphlet, 1935, no. 60)

Lists all dissertations deposited prior to September 15, 1934, arranged alphabetically by author, subject, and institution. Entry gives publication information.

G9. GOOD, Carter V. "Doctors' Dissertations under Way in Education [1930/1931-1945/1946]" Journal of Educational Research 23 (1931)-39 (1945/1946). Title varies. To 1944 in Jan. issue; Feb. 1945; Feb., March 1946.

Entries obtained from lists sent in by American universities. Alphabetical author list of Ph.D. and Ed.D. dissertations. Entry gives adviser. Except for vols. 28-30 and 39, topical index included in each list.

Continued by:

G10. "DOCTORS' Dissertations under Way in Education." Phi Delta Kappan 28 (1947)-33 (1952). Annual.

With vol. 32 (1951) a subject classification was introduced, which was later continued in Research Studies in Education (Item G30). Entry gives adviser.

G11. NEW YORK (State). University. Committee on Cooperation in Educational Research. Needed Educational Research in New York State and Research Studies in Progress, 1931-1932. Albany: University of the State of New York Press, 1932. 24 p.

Pt. 2, "Research Studies in Progress, 1931-1932," is a classified listing of theses, dissertations, and other work in progress. Entry indicates probable date of completion.

G12. EBY, Frederick and S. E. Frost, Jr. <u>Graduate Theses and
      Dissertations Written in the Field of Education at Baylor
      University</u>, Southern Methodist University, Texas Christian
      University, Texas Technological College, the University of
      Texas and West Texas State Teachers College... Austin, Tex.:
      University of Texas, 1934. 77 p.

> Arranged by the different schools. Author index.

G13. GEORGE PEABODY COLLEGE FOR TEACHERS, Nashville, Tenn. <u>Bib-
      liography of Master's Theses Produced in the United States</u>.
      Nashville, Tenn.: 1934. 64 p,

> Covers studies produced in 11 teachers' colleges
> through 1933. Arranged by institution.

G14. "RESEARCH Studies in Kansas; Brief Abstracts of Theses Devel-
      oped at the Graduate Schools of the State." <u>Kansas Teacher</u>
      42, no. 4 (Feb. 1936): 24-25; 42, no. 5 (March 1936): 24;
      43, no. 1 (April 1936): 15; 43, no. 2 (May 1936): 32; 43, no.
      3 (June 1936): 27; 43, no. 4 (Sept. 1936): 13.

> Some theses included are on subjects other than ed-
> ucation. Entry gives adviser.

G15. SMITH, Albert H. and others. <u>A Bibliography of Canadian
      Education</u>. Toronto: University of Toronto, Dept. of Educa-
      tional Research, 1938. 302 p. (Toronto. University. Dept.
      of Educational Research. Bulletin, no. 10)

> A fairly complete list of Canadian theses and dis-
> sertations in education arranged by province. En-
> try gives publication information. Author and sub-
> ject indexes.

G16. KOENINGER, Rupert C. <u>Follow-up Studies: A Comprehensive
      Bibliography</u>. Lansing, Mich.: Michigan State Board of Edu-
      cation, Michigan Study of the Secondary School Curriculum,
      1942. 50 p.

> "Theses--Masters and Doctors" (p. 30-38) is an
> annotated author list of 67 items, primarily repre-
> senting research completed in Michigan institutions.

G17. "ABSTRACTS of Masters Theses." <u>Utah Educational Research</u>

Bulletin 1, no. 3 (1946): 6-36.

Represents work accepted at Brigham Young University, the University of Utah, and Utah State University from September 1946 to September 1947. Arranged by institution. Author index.

G18.   "THESES Accepted for Master's Degrees in Utah [1946]" Utah Educational Research Bulletin 1, no. 1 (1946): 3; no. 2: 41-43.

Arranged by institution.

G19.   "BIBLIOGRAPHY of Studies on File at Utah Colleges and Universities." Utah Educational Research Bulletin 1, no. 1 (1946): 3-27.

A listing of 412 theses and some dissertations, nearly all completed in Utah. Arranged under such subjects as child study, tests and testing, curriculum studies, secondary education, higher education. Author and institutional indexes.

Continued by:

G20.   "BIBLIOGRAPHY of Studies Completed at Utah Colleges and Universities since 1946." Utah Educational Research Bulletin 3, no. 3 (1952): 1-29.

Lists theses completed between September 1946 and October 1951 and the 21 dissertations completed at the University of Utah to October 1951. Lists dissertations alphabetically by author and theses under such subjects as adult education, educational philosophy, theory, principles, health, physical education, recreation. Author and institutional indexes.

Continued by:

G21.   "BIBLIOGRAPHY of Studies Completed at Utah Colleges and Universities [1952-1956]" Utah Educational Research Bulletin 4 (1953)-7 (1957). Annual, in issue no. 1.

Whole issues.

Lists for 1954 and 1955 in vol. 6 (1956).

Lists theses and dissertations. Author and institutional indexes.

Continued by:

G22.   "ANNOTATED Bibliography of Studies in Education Completed at Utah Graduate Schools [1957-   ]" Utah Educational Research Bulletin 8 (1958)-   . Annual.

Published by the Utah Educational Research Council.

In two parts: (1) an alphabetical author listing of dissertations, and (2) a classified listing of theses. Author indexes.

G23.   "DOCTORAL Dissertations in Education Accepted by California Institutions [1949-   ]" California Journal of Educational Research 1 (1949)-   . Title varies. Annual. Usually Nov. issue.

Vols. 1 (1950)-5 (1953) include separate listings of theses accepted by California institutions.

A classified listing under such areas as administration of schools, teaching profession, curriculum development, education discussed by levels and kinds.

G24.   BLACKWELL, Annie M. A List of Researches in Education and Educational Psychology Presented for Higher Degrees in the Universities of the United Kingdom, Northern Ireland, and the Irish Republic, from 1918 to 1948. London: Newnes Educational Publishing Co., for National Foundation for Educational Research, 1950. 173 p. (National Foundation for Educational Research in England and Wales. Publication, no. 1)

_____ _____ A Second List...[for] the Years 1949, 1950, and 1951. London: 1952. 127 p. (National Foundation for Educational Research in England and Wales. Publication, no. 5)

_____ _____ Supplement I, for the Years 1952 and 1953. London: 1954. 57 p. (National Foundation for Educational Research in England and Wales. Publication, no. 7)

_____ _____ Supplement II for the Years 1954 and 1955. London: 1956. 62 p. (National Foundation for Educational Research in England and Wales. Publication, no. 9)

_____ _____ Supplement III for the Years 1956 and 1957.
London: 1958. 64 p. (National Foundation for Educational
Research in England and Wales. Publication no. 11)

> Includes theses and dissertations for the B.Litt.,
> Ed.B., M.A., M.S., M.Ed., M.Litt., and Ph.D. degrees.
> Entries are arranged in a modified Dewey decimal
> system and chronologically within subdivisions.
> The main work is divided into (1) educational psy-
> chology and (2) education. Entry gives publication
> information. Subject and author indexes in each
> volume, except for the author index of vol. 1, which
> is combined in vol. 2.
>
> Continued by:

G25. NATIONAL FEDERATION FOR EDUCATIONAL RESEARCH IN ENGLAND AND
WALES. Current Researches in Education and Educational
Psychology [1959/1960-1961/1963] Slough, Bucks: 1961-1963.
Biennial. ?

> A topical listing of research in progress in Great
> Britain. Entry gives note on the study, adviser,
> and estimated duration.

G26. "UNIVERSITAIRE proefschriften en verhandelingen. Thèses et
mémoires universitaires [1 (1950)-   ]" Paedagogica
belgica academica. Anvers: "De Sikkels," 1951-   .
Title varies. Annual.

> Issued as Part A of Paedagogica belgica from vol.
> 3 (1952).
>
> Titles in French, Dutch, and English.
>
> Lists abstracts of theses and dissertations submitted
> to Belgian institutions in psychology and educational
> psychology. Abstracts are in French or Dutch. Ar-
> ranged under institution. Entry gives adviser.
> Author and subject indexes.

G27. CANADIAN EDUCATION ASSOCIATION. Graduate Theses in Education, 1913-1952; A Partial List. Toronto: 1952. 33 p.

> An alphabetical author listing of over 500 theses
> and dissertations completed in Canadian institutions
> as well as those on Canadian education completed in

American institutions.

_____ _____ Supplement A. Toronto: 1954. 10 p.

Adds items not included in main listing.

G28. "DOCTORAL Studies Completed in Education, 1949-1950." Phi Delta Kappan 33 (1952): 355-372.

The first subject compilation of completed dissertations and reports for the Ph.D. in Ed. and Ed.D.
since the U.S. Office of Education discontinued
its annual listing (Item G4).

Continued by:

G29. LYDA, Mary L. and Stanley B. Brown. Research Studies in
Education; A Subject Index of Doctoral Dissertations, Reports,
and Field Studies, 1941-1951. Boulder, Colo.: 1953. 121 p.

_____ _____ Supplement, 1952. Boulder, Colo.: 1954. 63 p.

A classified bibliography of dissertations, theses,
reports, and field studies accepted for the Ph.D.
and Ed.D. degrees. Items are arranged under 30 topics,
which cover administration, education of particular
types, learning, and teaching.

Continued by:

G30. RESEARCH Studies in Education; A Subject Index of Doctoral
Dissertations, Reports and Field Studies; And a Research
Methods Bibliography [1953-   ] Bloomington, Ind.: Phi
Delta Kappa, 1955-   . Annual.

Continues Item G10.

In four parts: (1) a classified listing of American
and Canadian dissertations completed, (2) author
index, (3) research methods bibliography, and (4)
ERIC Documents Index related to research methods

G31. PLANCKE, R. L. Paedagogica belgica. Bibliographie et aperçu
périodiques des études pédagogiques belges. II (1951).
Ghent: Ghent université, Institut supérior de sciences pédagogiques, 1952. 158 p.

In French and Flemish.

Contains a complete list of doctoral theses and
mémoires in education from 1925 to 1951, and tables
of contents of the University theses and mémoires
for 1951. Subject index and a list of names.

G32. "SUMMARIES of Graduate Theses in Education [1950-1959]"
Canadian Education 8 (1953)-15 (1960). Annual. June issue.

Vol. 8 (1953) covers 1950-1952; none published for
1953.

Abstracts of theses and dissertations completed in
Canadian institutions, arranged by institution.

Continued by:

G33. "SUMMARIES of Graduate Theses in Education [1960-1965]"
Canadian Education and Research Digest 1 (1961)-6 (1966).
Annual. June issue.

Abstracts of theses and dissertations completed in
Canadian universities. Arranged by university.

Continued by:

G34. CANADIAN EDUCATION ASSOCIATION. Information Division.
Education Studies Completed in Canadian Universities [1966/
1967-1967/1968] Toronto: 1967-1968. Annual.

An alphabetical author listing of abstracts of
theses and dissertations. Entry gives publication
information. Subject index.

Continued by:

G35. DIRECTORY of Education Studies in Canada. Annuaire d'études
en éducation au Canada [1968/1969-   ] Toronto: Canadian
Education Association, 1969-   . Annual.

English and French.

A classified listing of theses and dissertations,
as well as studies by the staff of teaching institutions and educational agencies. Arranged under

such topics as reading, arts, counselors and counseling, school buildings. Entry carries an abstract. Author index.

G36. AUSTRALIAN COUNCIL FOR EDUCATIONAL RESEARCH. Library. <u>Theses in Education and Educational Psychology Accepted for Degrees at Australian Universities, 1919 to 1950</u>. Melbourne: 1953. 36 p.

A classified bibliography of 294 items, mostly bachelors' and masters' theses, with a few dissertations. Includes theses accepted at Sydney University only for 1951 and 1952 and in the Australian Council for Educational Research Library, and those at the University of Queensland only for 1951. Several theses by Australian students at overseas universities are included. Some entries contain a brief note. Author and subject indexes.

_____ <u>Theses in Education and Educational Psychology Accepted for Degrees at Australian Universities; Supplement 1951 to 1953</u>. Melbourne: 1955. 34 p.

A classified bibliography of about 210 bachelors' and masters' theses. Includes theses accepted at Melbourne University in 1954, as well as studies not included in main work. Some entries annotated. Author and subject indexes.

G37. <u>MASTER'S Theses in Education</u> [1951/1952-   ] Cedar Falls, Iowa: Research Publications, 1953-   . Annual.

Attempts to include all theses accepted at American and Canadian institutions. Over time the number of contributing institutions has increased. Classified topical arrangement, then alphabetically by author. Institutional and subject indexes. Beginning with vol. 5 (1955/1956) includes an author index.

G38. "DISSERTATIONES doctorales." <u>Scientia Paedagogica</u> 1 (1955)-   . Title varies. Annual.

In French and English.

An international listing of theses and dissertations in education. Lists only those American works about which additional information was received above that which appears in Research Studies in Education (Item G30). Classified arrangement under such subjects as geography of education, history of education, biography of educationists, special didactics. Entry gives adviser. Many are abstracted.

G39. VIRGINIA. Department of Education. The Cooperative Program in Educational Research. Sponsored by the Education Departments of the College of William and Mary, the University of Virginia, Virginia Polytechnic Institute, Virginia State College, and the Research Service of the State Department of Education. Richmond: 1955. 225 p. (Virginia. State Board of Education. Bulletin, vol. 38, no. 2)

First edition published as Virginia State Board of Education Bulletin, vol. 35, no. 10 (1953).

Contains "A List of Authors and Titles of Selected Theses Which Are in the Files of the Cooperating Institutions" (p. 27-32), which lists 97 items; "Classified Abstracts of Theses and Dissertations Which Are Regarded as Being Generally Useful and Applicable in Virginia" (p. 33-219), representing 136 studies completed during the 1940's and 1950's at the cooperating institutions and including statements on purpose, method employed, findings, and interpretation; and "A List of Authors and Titles Only of Problems under Study at Present in the Cooperating Institutions" (p. 221-223), containing 66 studies in progress. Classified index of studies.

G40. "BIBLIOGRAPHIE der deutschen Hochschulschriften im Bereiche der Pädagogik und Psychologie [1950-1956]" Pädagogik 11 (1956)-13 (1958). Irregular.

Lists educational and education-related studies completed in German universities. Entry carries a descriptive note.

G41. U.S. Office of Education. The Core Program: Abstracts of Unpublished Research, 1946-1955. Prepared by Grace S. Wright. Washington: U.S. Government Printing Office, 1956. 70 p. (Circular, no. 485)

An alphabetical author listing of 54 dissertations and 20 theses. Entry gives adviser. Abstracts provide problem statement, procedure, and major findings and conclusions. Subject index.

G42. BREHAUT, Willard. Quarter Century of Educational Research in Canada: An Analysis of Dissertations (English) in Education Accepted by Canadian Universities, 1930-1955. Toronto: Toronto University, Ontario College of Education, 1958. 283 p. (University of Toronto. Ontario College of Education. Dept. of Educational Research. Information Series, no. 10)

Also appeared in Ontario Journal of Educational Research 2 (1960): 186-222.

Appendix A, "Theses (English) in Education by Canadian Universities, 1930-1955" (p. 120-165), lists 574 theses and dissertations alphabetically by author.

G43. "SURVEY of Educational Research in Canada, 1953 to 1955-56." Ontario Journal of Educational Research 1, no. 1 (Oct. 1958). 141 p.

Includes separate sections of theses and disserta- tions in "Completed Studies" and "Current and Planned Research." Arranged by province, then school and department.

G44. CANADIAN EDUCATION ASSOCIATION. Research and Information Division. Registry of Canadian Theses in Education, Series 1 to 1955 [nos. 1/59-4/61] Toronto: 1959-1961. 13 nos.

Appeared as inserts in the CEA News Letter from November 1959 to April 1960.

A retrospective listing of theses and dissertations completed in Canadian universities or on Canadian education in American universities. Arranged under such subjects as administration, church and educa- tion, English language, geometry. Entry carries a descriptive note.

G45. EELLS, Walter C. American Dissertations on Foreign Educa- tion; Doctor's Dissertations and Master's Theses Written at American Universities and Colleges Concerning Education or Educators in Foreign Countries and Education of Groups of Foreign Birth or Ancestry in the United States, 1884-1958. Washington: National Education Association, Committee on

International Relations, 1959. 300 p.

A bibliography of 5,716 items concerned with education and educators in foreign countries, comparative
education, and the education of foreign born or
those of foreign ancestry in the United States.
Many of the items deal with higher education. Arranged by continent and then by country. Full bibliographical information, including the author's
birth and death dates when available, clarifying
notes in some cases, and the item's availability on
microfilm. Subject and author indexes.

G46. "DISSERTATIONEN und Habilitationen in Pädagogik [1951/1958-
]" Zeitschrift für Pädagogik (Berlin) 5 (1959)-   .
Annual.

Vols. 5 (1959)-11 (1965) list only items completed
in West Germany.

Lists of German language educational studies in
Germany, Austria, and Switzerland. Arranged by
country, subdivided by institution. Entry gives
adviser.

G47. CANADIAN EDUCATION ASSOCIATION. Research and Information
Division. Education Studies in Progress in Canadian Univer-
sities [1959-1966] Toronto: 1960-1967. Title varies.
Annual.

Listing for 1959 issued as the Research and Information Division Report 12 (1959/1960); from 1960,
listings are issued as Research and Information
Division Bulletins.

Carries a separate listing of theses and dissertations in progress. Arranged by subject. Institutional index with graduate studies listed separately
under each institution.

G48. "[FIRST-FOURTH] Survey of Educational Research Completed or
in Progress in Ontario [July 1, 1959/June 30, 1960-July 1,
1963/June 30, 1965]" Ontario Journal of Educational Research
3 (Oct. 1960): 39-83; 4 (Autumn 1961): 1-30; 7 (Autumn 1964):
61-98; 8 (Spring 1966): 287-323.

Editor varies.

Includes separate listings of theses in progress
and completed in education and related fields in
Ontario teachers colleges and university departments
of education. The first survey lists about 30 theses
and dissertations from the University of Ottawa
School of Psychology and Education (p. 69-71) and
about 40 theses and dissertations from the Ontario
College of Education of the University of Toronto
(p. 75-77).

G49. "LIST of Researches in Education and Educational Psychology
Presented for Degrees in Scottish Universities [1958/1961-
]" In Scottish Council for Research in Education.
Annual Report [1961/1962-   ] Edinburgh: 1962-   . Annual.

First list is retrospective to 1958. Succeeding
lists cover only works completed in previous year.

Classified listing of theses and dissertations.

G50. "RESEARCH in Education at Certain Connecticut Colleges and
at the University of Connecticut." Teacher Education
Quarterly 19 (1961)-23 (1965). Annual. Usually in no. 1.

Vol. 19 (1961) covers Central Connecticut State
College for 1957-1961, Danbury for 1957-1961, Southern Connecticut for 1955-1961, University of Connecticut for 1950-1961, Trinity for 1953-1960, Willi-
mantic State College for 1959-1961. Vol. 20 (1962)
covers 1961/1962; vol. 23 (1965) covers 1964/1965.

Lists theses and dissertations by institution.

G51. VISHNYAKOV, I. M. and I. V. Lepilin. Doktorskie dissertatsiy
po pedagogicheskim naukam; Bibliograficheskiy ukazatel'.
Moskva: 1961. 178 p.

Abstracts of approximately 100 dissertations completed in U.S.S.R. institutions between 1937 and
1959. Arranged under broad topics.

G52. BULGAKOV, B. Dissertatsiy zashchishchennye v institutakh
Akademii pedagogicheskikh nauk RSFSR za 1944-1961 gg.
Moskva: 1962. 164 p.

Lists approximately 1,220 theses and dissertations

in the Russian Socialist Federated Soviet Republic.

G53. "DISSERTATIONS." Studies in Philosophy and Education 3
(1963)-   . Irregular.

Alphabetical author listing of dissertations recently completed in American universities from 1958.

G54. COLORADO. Department of Education. Division of Research
and Statistics. Colorado Graduate Research Studies in Education [1957 and 1958-1961 and 1962] Prepared in cooperation with the Colorado Council on Educational Research.
Denver: n.d.-1964. 3 vols.

Compiled by Lee Ann Heckman.

Lists 1,085 theses and dissertations on education
completed in Colorado institutions. Arranged by
subject, then alphabetically by author. Author
indexes.

G55. "DISSERTATIONES." Paedagogica Historica 4 (1964)-   .
Title varies. Annual.

A classified international listing of dissertations.
Covers all aspects of education in its historical
development, such as educators; comparative, national,
and local history; teacher training. Entry gives
publication information. With vol. 8 (1968) also
includes a list of dissertations and theses in
progress arranged by country and university.

G56. "CHRONICA." Scientia paedagogica experimentalis 1 (1964)-
. Semiannual.

Under country, theses and dissertations, completed
or in progress, which are brought to the attention
of the editorial staff are listed by institution.

G57. CORDASCO, Francesco and Leonard Covello. Educational Sociology: A Subject Index of Doctoral Dissertations Completed at
American Universities, 1941-1963. New York: Scarecrow Press,
1965. 226 p.

A classified listing by broad subject of 2,146 titles.

Author index.

G58. WIKSTROM, Thomas N. West Virginia Graduate Research Studies
      in Education, 1894-1965; A Bibliographical Listing. Charles-
      ton, W. Va.: West Virginia Dept. of Education, 1965. 150 p.

      Supersedes West Virginia University, Graduate Re-
      search in Education, West Virginia University,
      1898-1959 (1959).

      Lists 1,667 theses and problems and 13 dissertations
      completed at West Virginia University and Marshall
      University. Entries are arranged alphabetically
      under 31 broad categories. Author index.

G59. LUFER, Margarete. Bibliographie der pädagogischen Disser-
      tationen und Habilitationsschriften der Deutschen Demokra-
      tischen Republik, der Deutschen Bundesrepublik und West-
      berlins, 1945 bis 1965. Zusammengestellt und bearb. in der
      Abteilung Dokumentation und Information des Deutschen
      Pädagogischen Zentralinstituts. Berlin: Volk und Wissen,
      1966. 248 p.

      In three parts: (1) the German Democratic Republic;
      (2) the German Federal Republic; (3) West Berlin.
      Each part is classified and the entries are arranged
      chronologically under each topic. Altogether 1,263
      items are represented. Author and institutional
      indexes.

G60. NATIONAL COUNCIL OF EDUCATIONAL RESEARCH AND TRAINING.
      Educational Investigations in Indian Universities, 1939-
      1961; A List of Theses and Dissertations Approved for Doc-
      torate and Master's Degrees in Education. New Delhi: 1966.
      276 p.

      First published in 1963 in mimeographed form.

      Lists 85 dissertations and 2,856 M.Ed. theses com-
      pleted up to December 31, 1961. Pt. 1: doctoral
      theses; pt. 2: theses in full satisfaction of the
      M.Ed. degree; pt. 3: theses in partial fulfillment
      of the M.Ed. degree (inclusive of M.A. in Educa-
      tion in Calcutta University). Arranged by univer-
      sity and chronologically. If written in regional
      language, the title is translated into English and
      the original language is indicated. Author and

subject indexes.

Continued by:

G61. NATIONAL COUNCIL OF EDUCATIONAL RESEARCH AND TRAINING.
Educational Investigations in Indian Universities, 1962-1966;
A List of Theses and Dissertations for Doctorate and Master's
Degrees in Education. Compiled by Satnam Singh. New Delhi:
1968. 304 p.

> Lists 2,224 studies. In three parts: (1) disserta-
> tions, (2) theses in fulfillment of the requirement
> for the M.Ed. degree, and (3) theses in partial ful-
> fillment of the requirement for the M.Ed. degree.
> Under each, the studies are listed by institution
> and subdivided chronologically. Studies in regional
> languages are translated into English and the
> original language is indicated. Author and subject
> indexes.

G62. "DOCTORAL Dissertations in Progress and Completed." Comparative Education Review 11 (1967)-   . Irregular.

> Separate listings of primarily American disserta-
> tions completed (from 1965) and in progress.

G63. "THESES Abstracts." Leyte-Samar Studies 1 (1967)-   .
Tacloban City, Philippines: Divine World University, Graduate School, 1967-   .

> Abstracts of theses completed at St. Paul College
> and at Divine World University. Retrospective in
> coverage. Abstract indicates problem, methodology,
> and summary. Entry gives adviser and purchase
> information.

G64. DAVISON, Hugh M. Doctoral Theses in Education; Selected
Material from Abstracts of Theses. N.p.: the author, 1968.
54 p. ??

G65. ROHLOFF, Hans-Joachim. Erziehungswissenschaftliche Hochschulschriften; Bibliographie der Dissertationen und
Habilitationsschriften in Deutschland (BRD und DDR) 1945
bis 1967. Bearb. von Lydia Franke. Weinheim: J. Beltz,
1968. 564 p. (Pädagogisches Zentrum. Veröffentlichungen.

Reihe A: Dokumentation, Bd. 7)

An alphabetical author list of 2,319 items. Pt. A:
German Democratic Republic; pt. B: German Federal
Republic. Includes relevant work in psychology,
sociology, medicine, law, etc. Subject index.

G66. NAUËKAÏTIS, P. "Dissertatsii--Nauch. Trudy Byssh Ucheb.
zavedeniy Lit SSR." Pedagogika i psichologija, 1969, no.
10: 139-143. ?

Lists 79 dissertations in education and related
areas completed in Lithuania in 1968.

G67. KNIEFEL, David and Tanya S. Kniefel. Annotated Bibliography
and Descriptive Summary of Dissertations and Theses on Rural-
ity and Small Schools. University Park, N.M.: New Mexico
State University, ERIC Clearinghouse on Rural Education and
Small Schools, 1970. 51 p.

ED 039 962.

Abstracts of 76 American dissertations completed
between 1963 and 1968. Arranged alphabetically by
author. Subject index.

G68. JOOS, Elisabeth. Bibliographie der schweizerischen paedago-
gischen Dissertationen. Bibliographie des thèses pédagogiques suisses, 1896-1969. Bern: Schweizerische Landsbib-
liothek, Bibliographische Aufkunfsstelle, 1971. 116 p.

A classified list of 644 dissertations. Entry gives
publication information. Geographic and author
indexes.

G69. PARKER, Franklin. American Dissertations on Foreign Education; A Bibliography with Abstracts. Troy, N.Y.: Whitston
Publishing Co., 1971- .

Vol. 1 (1971) covers Canada with 171 items; vol. 2
(1972) India: 191 items; vol. 3 (1972) Japan: 57
items; vol. 4 (1973) Africa: 291 items.

Each volume is arranged alphabetically by author.
Some Canadian dissertations are included. Entries
include abstracts if available (usually when

abstract is in <u>Dissertation Abstracts</u>). Subject
index in each volume.

Individual Institutions

G70. KNILL, William D. <u>A Classification of Theses in Education</u>
<u>Completed at the University of Alberta, 1929-1966</u>. 3d rev-
ised ed. Edmonton: University of Alberta, 1967. 67 p.

>   First edition 1949.

>   Lists 580 theses and dissertations completed at the
>   University of Alberta under curriculum; special
>   areas (e.g. library, guidance, health services);
>   personnel; facilities; organization, administration,
>   and finance; higher education.

G71. BANARAS HINDU UNIVERSITY. <u>Abstracts of the Theses Accepted</u>
<u>for the Ph.D. and M.Ed. Degrees of Banaras Hindu University</u>
<u>in Education and Allied Subjects</u>. Banaras: ?

>   Vol. 3 published in 1964.

G72. CAIRO. Jāmi'at 'Ayn Shams. Kullīyat al-Tarbiyah. <u>al-Kitāb</u>
<u>al-sanawī il-mulakhkhas al-buhūth al-'ilmīyah</u> [1959-   ]
Cairo: 1959-   . Irregular.

>   Abstracts of theses and dissertations in the College
>   of Education.

G73. EDWARDS, Elva D. "Digest of Theses Accepted in Partial Fulfillment of Requirements for Higher Degrees in Education at
the University of California [May 1930-March 1933]" <u>Univer-</u>
<u>sity High School Journal</u> 10 (1930): 251-265; 11 (1931): 14-
19, 294-300; 12 (1932/1933): 46-50, 221-226; 13 (1933): 23-
25.

>   Lists theses and dissertations. Abstracts give scope
>   of study and findings.

>   In part superseded by:

G74. CALIFORNIA. University. <u>Abstracts of Doctors' Theses in</u>
<u>Education at the University of California, 1898 to March</u>

1933. Compiled by Arnold E. Joyal. Los Angeles: Printed by Frank Wiggins Trade School, 1933. 104 p.

An alphabetical author listing of abstracts of 90 dissertations. Entry gives publication information. Subject index.

Continued by:

G75. _____ School of Education. Abstracts of Doctors' Theses in Education at the University of California, March 1933 to March 1946. Compiled by Fletcher H. Swift. Los Angeles: 1949. 80 p.

An alphabetical author listing of 92 dissertations. Entry gives adviser. Index of advisers.

G76. "ANNOTATED Bibliography of Doctoral Dissertations at the University of California, 1954-1958." Scientia Paedagogica 7 (1961): 92-125.

An alphabetical author listing. Entry gives adviser.

G77. CALIFORNIA. University. University at Los Angeles. School of Education. A Subject Index of Theses and Dissertations in Education for 1934-1962. Los Angeles: 1963. 124 p.

Alphabetical subject list. Author index.

G78. "THE CATHOLIC University Research Abstracts." Catholic Educational Review 45 (1947)-67, no. 2 (Nov. 1969).

Abstracts of theses and dissertations (not necessarily both in each issue) in education. Entry gives degree and abstract. Publication information is provided for dissertations. With vol. 55 (1957) abstracts appear in the periodical's yearly index in varying ways. In vols. 55 (1957)-60 (1962) they are grouped under "Research Abstracts"; from vol. 61 (1963) included in general index.

G79. "THE CATHOLIC University Research Studies." Catholic Educational Review 47 (1949): 263-266.

A partial list of dissertations written under the

direction of the Department of Education of the
Catholic University of America and published by
the Catholic University Press during the years
1932-1944.

G80. CENTRAL INSTITUTE OF EDUCATION, Delhi. A Decade in Retro-
spect, 1947-1958. Delhi: 1958. 16 p.

Research studies completed by candidates for the
Master of Education.

G81. CHICAGO. University. Department of Education. Annotated
List of Graduate Theses and Dissertations: The Department of
Education, the University of Chicago, 1900-1931. Chicago:
University of Chicago, 1932. 119 p.

An alphabetical list of 1,116 theses and 119 dissertations, giving a short descriptive note. Topical index.

Continued in part by:

G82. _____ Annotated List of Ph.D. Dissertations, the Department
of Education [1932/1935-1936/June 1951] Chicago: 1936-1951.
2 vols. Title varies.

Vol. 1 (1932/1935) includes theses and dissertations;
vol. 2 (1936-June 1951) includes dissertations only.

Alphabetical author listings. Each volume has a
subject index.

G83. CINCINNATI. University. Teachers College. Abstracts:
Graduate Theses in Education [1927-1954] Cincinnati: 1931-
1955. 5 vols.

Vol. 1 contains abstracts for 1927-1931; vol. 2 for
1931-1936; vol. 3 for 1937-1939; vol. 4 for 1940-1943;
vol. 5 for 1944-1954. Vol. 1 lists all theses for
1924-1931, but abstracts theses only for 1927-1930
and dissertations only for 1927-1931; all other
volumes contain only lists of theses but have lengthy
abstracts of all dissertations, including selected
bibliographies.

G84. "DISSERTATION Research Capsules [1961/1962-   ]" Colorado

Journal of Educational Research 1 (1962/1963)-   . Irregular.

> Abstracts of dissertations in education completed
> at the University of Northern Colorado. Classified
> arrangement under such subjects as industrial arts,
> science, special education, psychology, and guidance.

G85.   "NEW Studies in Education." Teachers College Record 25, no.
       2 (1924)-43, no. 8 (1942). Irregular.

> Primarily contains abstracts of Columbia University
> Teachers College doctoral dissertations.

G86.   COLUMBIA UNIVERSITY. Teachers College. Register of Doctor
       of Education Reports [1 (1935/1945)-   ] New York: Teachers
       College, Bureau of Publications, 1935-   . Irregular.

> Vol. 1: January 1935-March 1945; vol. 2: March
> 1945-December 1951; vol. 3: January 1952-June 1957;
> vol. 4: July 1957-June 1963.

> Cumulated volumes supersede annual supplements which
> appear in Teachers College Record.

> Lists those reports which are a requirement for the
> Ed.D. degree (first conferred in 1935). Entry indi-
> cates if microfilm copies are available. Subject
> and author indexes.

G87.   _____ Register of Doctoral Dissertations Accepted in Partial
       Fulfillment of the Requirements for the Degree of Doctor of
       Philosophy [1899/1936-   ] New York: Columbia University,
       Teachers College, 1937-   . Irregular.

> Vol. 1: 1899-1936; vol. 2: 1937-1941; vol. 3: 1942-
> 1946; vol. 4: 1947-1953; vol. 5: 1954-1959; vol. 6:
> 1959-1963.

> Vol. 1 supersedes its Register of Teachers College
> Doctors of Philosophy, 1899-1928.

> Cumulated volumes supersede annual supplements in
> the Teachers College Record to 1959. From 1960
> supplements are issued separately.

> A chronological listing. Entry indicates if

microfilm copies are available. Subject and author
indexes.

G88. "RECENT Ph.D. Studies." Teachers College Record 44 (1942)-
49 (1948); 51 (1950). Title varies. Irregular.

Abstracts of Columbia University Teachers College
dissertations, many of which were published in full
in the Columbia University Teachers College "Contributions to Education" series.

G89. "DOCTOR of Education Project Reports." Teachers College
Record 50, no. 2 (1948)-53, no. 8 (1952).

Abstracts of selected reports completed at Columbia
University Teachers College.

G90. DAYTON, Ohio. University. School of Education. Abstracts
of Research Projects Submitted to the Graduate Committee...
in Partial Fulfillment of the Requirements for the Degree
of Master of Science in Education [vol. 1-   ] Dayton:
1968-   . Annual.

The 1968 volume contains the abstracts of 104
research projects completed for the Master of
Science in Education degree during the period 1963
through 1967, arranged by author. Beginning with
vol. 2 (1969) the coverage is for the preceding
calendar year.

G91. PHI DELTA KAPPA. Alpha Sigma Chapter, University of Denver.
Abstracts of Theses in Education, University of Denver,
July 1, 1930 to June 30, 1938; With Supplemental List Prior
to July 1, 1930. Denver, Colo.: 1939. 62 p. (Its Educational Research Bulletin, no. 1)

Alphabetically by subject. Author index.

G92. DUBLIN. University College. Library. List of Research
Work in Education and Educational Psychology Presented at
University College Dublin, 1912-1968: A Provisional List.
Dublin: 1969. 20 p.

Theses and dissertations arranged by the Dewey
decimal system. Subject index and index of

authors and persons who were subjects of research.

G93. GEORGE PEABODY COLLEGE FOR TEACHERS, Nashville, Tenn. Chronological Check List of Contributions to Education 1920-1933; A Chronological List of Doctoral Dissertations Accepted by the George Peabody College for Teachers. Nashville: 1935. ?

Supersedes its "Contributions to Education." Peabody Reflector and Alumni News 5 (1932): 303-305.

G94. _____ Abstracts of Dissertations [1942-1962] Nashville: 1942-1962. Annual.

Dissertations completed at the College. All deal with some aspects of education. Arranged alphabetically by author.

G95. PHI DELTA KAPPA. Gamma Theta Chapter, Florida State University, Tallahassee. Abstracts of Dissertations in Education Accepted by Florida State University, 1952-1962. Tallahassee: Florida State University, School of Education, 1964. 61 p.

A chronological listing of 135 dissertations in the School of Education and the School of Music. Table of contents provides arrangement by broad subject. Entry gives adviser. Subject and author indexes.

G96. FLORIDA. University, Gainesville. College of Education. Abstracts of Doctoral Studies in Education [1952-1962] Gainesville: 1953-1962. Annual. 11 vols.

Volume for 1952 contains a listing of recipients for the period 1948-1951 with titles of their dissertations (p. 37-38).

Abstracts of dissertations completed in the College of Education. Abstract indicates problem, procedure, findings, and conclusions. Entry gives biographical sketch.

G97. COX, John M. and Ely R. Day. Advanced Studies in Education; Theses and Dissertations Accepted in Partial Fulfillment of the Requirements for Graduate Degrees, 1940-1959. Houston, Tex.: University of Houston, 1960. 50 p. (University of

Houston. Bureau of Education Research and Services, Publication no. 1)

Supersedes James T. Griffis, Annotated Bibliography of Graduate Research Studies; Complete Listing of Masters' Theses and Doctors' Dissertations Accepted by College of Education, the University of Houston, 1940 to 1953 (1953).

A classified annotated listing of theses and dissertations in education completed at the University of Houston. Theses and dissertations from the Department of Psychology which present research applicable to public schools are also included (p. 35-48). Author index.

G98. ILLINOIS. Northern Illinois University, De Kalb. Graduate School. Abstracts of Selected Qualifying Papers: College of Education [1963-   ] De Kalb: 1963-   . (Illinois. Northern Illinois University. Bureau of University Research. Research Bulletins, no. 12-   ) Annual.

Covers the period from 1963. Abstracts are arranged alphabetically by author under broad topic.

G99. GREGG, Russell T. and Thomas T. Hamilton, Jr. Annotated Bibliography of Graduate Theses in Education at the University of Illinois. Urbana: University of Illinois, 1931. 80 p. (University of Illinois. College of Education. Bureau of Educational Research. Bulletin no. 55)

Alphabetical author listing of 228 theses and 25 dissertations completed in the College of Education from 1910 to February 1931. Entry includes a brief annotation. Topical index.

G100. INDIANA. University. School of Education. Phi Delta Kappa. Alpha Chapter. Abstracts of Theses and Dissertations Presented in Education at Indiana University [June 1924-1933] Bloomington: 1927-1934. (Its Bulletin, no. 1-7) Title varies. Annual.

No. 7 (1934) contains a chronological listing covering the period 1910-1933, which supersedes its List of Theses Submitted to Date, October 19, 1929 (1930).

Alphabetical author lists. Entry gives previous
degrees and where taken. Abstract indicates problem, procedure, and findings.

G101. _____ Theses Presented to the School of Education, Indiana
University. Bloomington: 1931. 56 p.

Summary of theses and dissertations in education
presented in June and October 1930.

G102. INDIANA. University. School of Education. Studies in Education [nos. 1 (1945/1949)-20 (1968)] Bloomington: 1960-
1968. Annual.

No. 1 published as Indiana University Bulletin of
the School of Education, vol. 26, no. 4, with title
"Studies in Education: Abstracts of Theses."

Abstracts of all Indiana University dissertations
for the Ed.D., as well as some Ph.D. dissertations
with a major in education. Abstracts indicate
problem, sources of data, procedure, conclusions,
and recommendations.

G103. IOWA. University. Abstracts of Studies in Education. Compiled by Epsilon Chapter of Phi Delta Kappa. Iowa City:
1920. 19 p. (University of Iowa Studies. Aims and Progress
of Research, vol. 1, no. 9, New Series no. 31, May 1920)

In three sections: "Current Studies" contains abstracts of seven dissertations completed in the
College of Education during 1919-1920; "Sentence
Summaries of Studies" is an annotated listing of
theses completed in 1919; "Bibliography of Studies,
1900 to 1919," by Frank D. Mesner, lists dissertations and theses chronologically in separate listings
(p. 12-17).

G104. PHI DELTA KAPPA. Alpha Delta Chapter, Kansas State Univer-
sity of Agriculture and Applied Science, Manhattan.
Abstracts of Masters' Theses in Education Approved by Kansas
State College, 1915-1940. Manhattan, Kans.: 1941. 130 p.
(Its Bulletin, no. 1)

Arranged alphabetically by author. At end: "Theses
in Home Economics Education, Kansas State College,"

for 1927-1941, arranged by date.

G105. KANSAS. University. Bureau of School Service and Research. "Titles and Authors of Theses Written for Graduate Degrees in Education, 1922-30." In Kansas. University. Bulletin of Education 2, no. 2 (Dec. 1928): 24-30; 3, no. 2 (Dec. 1930): 27-30.

Vol. 2 covers theses completed from 1922 through 1928 and vol. 3, the years 1929 and 1930.

G106. KANSAS. University. School of Education. Graduate Research in Education and Abstracts of Doctoral Dissertations in Education, 1940 to 1943. Lawrence: 1944. 31 p. (Kansas University Studies in Education, vol. 3, no. 10)

Supersedes Abstracts of Doctoral Studies in Education Completed in 1940 (1941) (Kansas University. Kansas Studies in Education, vol. 2, no. 6)

Lists all theses and dissertations from January 1940 to January 1, 1944, completed in the School of Education.

G107. KENTUCKY. University. College of Education. Theses in Education [1912/1932-1937/1943] Lexington: 1933-1943. 3 vols. (Its Bureau of School Service Bulletin 5, no. 4 (1933); 10, no. 1 (1937); 15, no. 3 (1943))

An alphabetical author listing of theses and dissertations completed at the College of Education. Separate subject and author indexes in each volume.

G108. _____ Doctoral Theses in Education [1966-   ] Lexington: 1967-   . Annual. (Its Bureau of School Service Bulletin 39, no. 4 (1967)-   )

An alphabetical author listing of abstracts of dissertations completed at the College of Education. A brief biographical sketch is provided.

G109. ABSTRACTS of M.Ed. Dissertations [1963/1964-   ] Kurukshetra: Kurukshetra University, Dept. of Education, 1966-   . Annual.

Abstracts of theses accepted by the Department of
Education. Abstract indicates problem, objectives,
procedure, and findings. Each volume also carries
a listing of Ph.D. and M.Ed. work in progress.

G110. WEERSING, Frederick J. Annotated Index of Theses and Dissertations in Education. Los Angeles: Alpha Epsilon Chapter of
Phi Delta Kappa, University of Southern California, School
of Education, 1936. 133 p.

This third edition combines and adds to material in
the previous edition published in 1931 and the 1932
supplement.

Research completed at the University of Southern
California in the period 1911-1935. Arranged by
author. Subject index.

G111. LOUISIANA. State University and Agricultural and Mechanical
College. Bureau of Educational Materials and Research.
Theses and Dissertations: Department of Education, Louisiana
State University, 1917-1960. Baton Rouge: 1961. 44 p.

Arranged in two sections: pt. 1: masters' theses,
1917-1960; pt. 2: dissertations completed, 1936-
1960. Chronologically arranged.

G112. MAHARAJA SAYAJIRAO UNIVERSITY OF BARODA. Faculty of Education and Psychology. Research Abstracts [no. 1 (1962/1963)-
] Baroda: 1963-   . Annual.

Abstracts of theses and dissertations completed in
the University in the fields of education and
psychology. In two parts: M.Ed. and M.A. (Psychology).
The abstract indicates problem, objectives, procedure,
and findings. Entry gives adviser.

G113. MARYLAND. University. College of Education. Dissertation
Abstracts, 1969. College Park: Maryland University, College
of Education, Bureau of Field Services, 1969. 155 p.

Abstracts of theses and dissertations completed in
the College of Education.

G114. MELBOURNE. University. Educational Studies and Investigations; Summaries of Investigations Submitted in 1936-1939 by Students in the Second Year of the Course for the Bachelor of Education Degree at the University of Melbourne. Melbourne: Melbourne University Press, 1940. 240 p.

Abstracts of studies for advanced degrees. Arranged alphabetically by author under year. Abstract gives problem statement, method, and conclusions. Subject index.

G115. MICHIGAN. University. Bureau of Educational Reference and Research. Abstracts of Dissertations and Theses in Education at the University of Michigan [1917/1931-1931/1932] Ann Arbor, Mich.: 1932-1933. (Its Monograph, nos. 1 and 2)

Contains "digests of all dissertations and theses accepted in connection with advanced degrees up to January 1933." No. 1 lists 34 doctoral dissertations and 29 masters' theses. No. 2 has four dissertations and 105 theses. Arranged according to degree, then in alphabetical order for each year. Author index.

Continued by:

G116. "DISSERTATIONS, Research Reports, and Theses in Education, 1932-1962." In Michigan. University. School of Education. Bulletin 4 (1932)-35 (1964). Title varies. Annual. Jan. issue from vol. 12 (1943).

Vols. 4 (1932)-14 (1943) list only theses; specialists' degrees appear in vols. 34 (1963)-35 (1964).

Alphabetical listing of research accepted in the College of Education in connection with graduate degrees, arranged under type of degree. Entry gives adviser.

G117. ENGLEHARDT, Fred and Henry J. Otto. Master's and Doctor's Theses in Education, University of Minnesota, 1912-1928. Minneapolis: The University of Minnesota Press, 1929. 32, vi p.

Chronological annotated listings of the 178 theses and the 30 dissertations completed in the College of Education. Author index.

Continued by:

G118. GRINNELL, J. E. and James G. Umstattd. Abstracts of Master's and Doctor's Theses in Education, July 1, 1928-July 1, 1929. Minneapolis: University of Minnesota, College of Education, 1931. 26 p. (Phi Delta Kappa, Eta Chapter. Educational Research Bulletin, no. 1)

Summarizes 29 studies.

Continued by:

G119. _____ Abstracts of Master's and Doctor's Theses in Education, July 1, 1929-July 1, 1930. Minneapolis: University of Minnesota, College of Education, 1932. 35 p. (Phi Delta Kappa, Eta Chapter. Educational Research Bulletin, no. 2)

Summarizes the problems, procedures, and findings in 37 studies.

Continued by:

G120. MINNESOTA. University. College of Education. Abstracts of Master's and Doctor's Theses in Education...July 1, 1930-July 1, 1931. Prepared by Stuart D. Fink and James G. Umstattd. Minneapolis: 1932. 72 p. (Its Educational Research Bulletin, no. 4)

Includes all theses and dissertations submitted to the graduate faculties between July 1, 1930, and July 1, 1931, and some earlier ones not previously abstracted. Arranged by broad subject. For each item there is a statement of the problem, procedure, and results. Author index.

G121. MISSOURI. University. College of Education. Abstracts of Dissertations in Education Accepted by the College of Education, the University of Missouri--Columbia [1916/1938-   ] Columbia: 1938-   . Title varies. Irregular.

Vol. 1 (1916-1938) edited by A. G. Capps and H. M. Clements; vol. 2: 1937-1946; vol. 3: 1946-1950; vol. 4: 1951-1953.

Alphabetical author listing of abstracts of dissertations completed in the College of Education.

G122. "SPIS prac doktorskich, 1953-1963." <u>Kwartalnik Pedagogizny</u> (Warsaw) 9 (1964): 203-208.

> Lists the dissertations completed in the University of Moscow Department of Education.

G123. NEBRASKA. University. Teachers College. <u>Summaries of Doctoral Dissertations and Masters' Theses Accepted during 1936</u>. Lincoln: University of Nebraska, Extension Division, 1937. 40 p. (Educational Monographs, no. 10. Nebraska. University. Extension Division. University of Nebraska Publication, no. 121)

> Short summaries of two dissertations and 40 theses.

G124. NEW YORK. City College. School of Education. <u>Abstracts of Theses for the Degree of Master of Science in Education, 1923-1939</u>. New York: 1939. 118 p.

> Supersedes its <u>Annotated Bibliography and Topical Index of Master of Science in Education Theses, 1923-1931</u> (1931) and supplements.

> Contains 381 theses listed alphabetically by author under year. Topical and author indexes.

G125. NEW YORK UNIVERSITY. School of Education. <u>Abstracts of Theses Submitted in Partial Fulfillment of the Requirements for the Degrees of Doctor of Philosophy and Doctor of Education</u> [1930-1949/1950] New York: New York University, 1930-1951. Annual.

> Abstracts of dissertations completed in the College of Education. Coverage from 1942 does not include items published on microfilm.

G126. DOSSICK, Jesse J. <u>Doctoral Research at the School of Education, New York University, 1890-1970; A Classified List of 4,336 Dissertations with Some Critical and Statistical Analysis</u>. New York: New York University Press, 1972. 236 p.

> Supersedes Herbert A. Tonne, <u>Index of Dissertations of the School of Education</u> (1930 and 1932); and Nouvart Tashjian, <u>List of Doctor's and Master's Theses in Education, New York University, 1890-June 1936</u> (1937) and <u>Supplement, Oct. 1936-June 1940</u>

(1941).

Includes an author index.

G127. NORTHWESTERN UNIVERSITY, Evanston, Ill. <u>Abstracts of Master's Theses in Education by Forty-Five Graduate Students Who Received Master's Degrees at Northwestern University in 1931 and 1932</u>. Evanston, Ill.: School of Education, 1933. 129 p. (Northwestern University Contributions to Education. School of Education Series, no. 10)

Selected from those theses completed in 1931 and 1932 in the School of Education.

G128. DWYER, Justin, Brother. <u>A Summary of Master's Degrees in Education Done at the University of Notre Dame from 1918-1935</u>. South Bend, Ind.: University of Notre Dame, 1936. 250 p. (M.A. Thesis, Notre Dame, 1936)

A classified listing of abstracts of the 144 theses submitted to the Department of Education from 1921 to 1935. The abstract gives the problem, method, and findings. Of the theses, 85 were written by nuns; 33 deal with the history of education. A majority of the theses deal with the histories of religious orders and communities. Author and topical indexes.

G129. "GRADUATE Degrees and Dissertations in Education." <u>Educational Research Bulletin</u> (Ohio State University. Bureau of Educational Research) 3 (1924)-4 (1925), 6 (1927)-8 (1929). Title varies. Feb. issue.

Theses and dissertations presented for degrees at Ohio State University, Columbus, during the year preceding each listing. First two lists include only those degrees granted in school administration.

G130. PLUNKETT, Josephine. <u>A Survey of Masters' Theses in Educational Research at Oklahoma Agricultural and Mechanical College</u>. 134 p. (M.S., Oklahoma Agricultural and Mechanical University, 1938)

A classified annotated listing of 342 theses and reports in the departments of Education and allied fields on educational problems. Covers the period 1917-1937. Author, adviser, and institutional and

subject indexes.

G131. SMITH, Leonard G. and Franklin Parker. History of Education, Philosophy of Education, and Comparative Education; An Annotated Bibliography of Doctoral Dissertations Accepted at the University of Oklahoma, 1932-1964. Norman: University of Oklahoma, College of Education, 1964. 41 p.

An alphabetical author listing. The annotation consists of the dissertation's table of contents and gives purpose of the research. Entry gives adviser. Author and subject index.

G132. PARKER, Franklin. "History of Education Dissertations Accepted at the University of Oklahoma; Briefly Annotated Bibliography." Paedagogica Historica 7 (1967): 562-567.

An alphabetical author listing of 32 dissertations completed between 1936 and 1963. Entry indicates the purpose of the research.

G133. PENNSYLVANIA. State University. School of Education. Abstracts of Studies in Education at Pennsylvania State College. State College: 1931-1951. 11 vols. (Its Studies in Education, nos. 2, 4, 8, 9, 12, 14, 19, 21, 22, 24; Studies in Education and Psychology, no. 26)

The eleven pieces are numbered consecutively.

No. 1 (1931) carries brief abstracts of approximately half of the theses and dissertations submitted up to 1931, which were of sufficient interest for publication. No. 11 (1951) covers the period 1942-1950. No. 11 (1951) also contains separate chronological lists of theses in psychology and education, 1928-1939; early theses in the Department of Education, 1917-1927; School of Physical Education theses, 1933-1939; and Department of Agricultural Education theses 1933-1939. These lists indicate if an item has been published in the series.

Abstracts of selected theses and dissertations completed at the School of Education. Abstracts generally state the problem and give the findings and the conclusion.

G134. PENNSYLVANIA. University. Directory of Those Granted the
Degree of Doctor of Philosophy in Education by the University
of Pennsylvania. Philadelphia: University of Pennsylvania,
School of Education, Educational Service Bureau, 1942. 21 p.
(Pennsylvania University. School of Education. Educational
Service Bureau. Publication, no. 2)

> Alphabetical listing of 140 dissertations completed
> from 1896 to June 1941.

G135. _____ Studies in Education: Abstracts of Studies for the
Degree of Doctor of Philosophy and the Degree of Doctor of
Education [1944/1948-1965/1966] Philadelphia: n.d.-1967.
8 vols. Irregular.

> Abstracts of all dissertations in education submitted
> to the University. These include the 57 Ph.D.'s under
> the jurisdiction of the Graduate School of Arts and
> Sciences and the 182 Ed.D.'s under the jurisdiction of
> the School of Education. Entry gives previous degrees.

G136. PHILADELPHIA. Temple University. Teachers College. Teachers College, Studies in Education and Psychology (Abstracts).
Edited by Dean George E. Walk and others. Philadelphia:
Published by the Graduate Division of Teachers College in
cooperation with Alpha Eta Chapter of Phi Delta Kappa, 1934.
64 p. (Temple University. Bulletin, vol. 1, June 1934)

> Limited to 31 theses and dissertations presented
> during the university year 1932/1933. Contains a
> list of dissertations (covering 1927-1933) and theses
> (covering 1922-1933) that have been accepted by
> Teachers College.

G137. _____ Abstracts of Dissertations and Titles of Theses Accepted in Partial Satisfaction of the Requirements for
Graduate Degrees, 1940-1949. Philadelphia: 1951. 293 p.

> Most of the dissertations have been published in
> whole or in part.

G138. PITTSBURGH. University. School of Education. Directory of
Holders of Graduate Degrees in Education with Titles of
Theses and Dissertations. 3d ed. Compiled by John A. Nietz.
Pittsburgh: Xi Chapter of Phi Delta Kappa, 1945. 90 p.

First edition entitled <u>Annotations of Theses and Dissertations in Education</u> (1934).

Lists 1,065 theses and dissertations completed in the University of Pittsburgh College of Education.

G139. PUNJAB, Pakistan (Province). University, Lahore. Institute of Education and Research. <u>Bibliography of Master's Projects in the Field of Education Completed by M.A. Education and M.Ed. Students, 1964-1965</u>. Lahore: n.d. 24 p.

A classified listing of 152 theses.

G140. RHODE ISLAND COLLEGE, Providence. <u>Master of Education Theses</u> [1924/1943-1956/1960] Providence: 1943-1960. 3 vols. Title varies.

Vol. 1 covers 1924-1943; vol. 2 covers 1948-1955; vol. 3 covers 1956-1960.

Theses completed at the College arranged under such fields as secondary school administration, geography, music, English. Each volume carries a chronological index.

G141. _____ <u>Abstracts of Masters Theses in Education, 1943/1947</u>. Providence: 1947. 58 p.

Abstracts are listed under such fields as art, English language, mathematics. Carries a separate section of biographical sketches.

G142. ST. JOHN COLLEGE, Cleveland, Ohio. <u>Abstracts of Theses for the Master of Arts in Education Submitted to the Committee on Graduate Studies of Saint John College...1943-1949</u>. Cleveland: St. John College, Committee on Graduate Studies, 1949. 63 p.

Approximately 55 studies arranged under the subjects education, English, social science, and sociology. Entry gives the religious order of the candidate.

G143. SOUTH DAKOTA. University. College of Education. <u>Theses, Research Studies and Dissertations in Education</u>. Vermillion: 1967. 26 p.

First edition 1934.

Lists approximately 600 studies covering the period
1917 to July 1967. Theses and research reports are
listed under such subjects as curriculum, audio-
visual education, measurements, transportation.
Dissertations are listed separately, alphabetically
by author.

G144. SHUNK, William R. and Franklin Parker. History of Education,
Philosophy of Education, and Comparative Education: Annotated
Bibliography of Doctoral Dissertations at the University of
Texas, 1923-1958. Austin: University of Texas, Dept. of
History and Philosophy of Education, 1959. 64 p.

Also appeared in Scientia Paedagogica 6 (1960): 79-
103; 7 (1961): 19-38.

An alphabetical author listing of 81 selected dissertations completed in the various departments of
the University of Texas. Lists chapters, purpose,
sources, and findings. Author and subject index.

G145. PITTENGER, Benjamin F. The Pittenger Report; Doctorates in
Education, the University of Texas at Austin, May, 1923-
January, 1970. Austin, Tex.: University of Texas, 1971?
1 vol. (various pagings)

Supersedes Texas. University. College of Education. Abstracts of Masters' and Doctors' Theses in
Education, the University of Texas (1941).

Dissertations listed chronologically under such
categories as curriculum and instruction, educational psychology, educational administration,
physical and health education.

G146. TORONTO. University. Ontario College of Education. Department of Educational Research. Theses in Education, since
1898 (Including Theses in Pedagogy from Queen's University,
1911-1925). Toronto: 1949-1952. 32 p. (Its Educational
Research Series, no. 20)

Includes theses and dissertations. From Queen's
University only dissertations are included. Pt. 1,
arranged by author, includes brief annotations for
items in the 1919-1949 period; pt. 2 is a chronolo-

gical list of those completed since 1898 and is updated to include those up to 1952.

G147. "CONDENSATION of Masters' Theses in Education." In Washington (State). State University, Pullman. Dept. of Education.
Research Studies 9 (1941): 261-348.

Whole number.

Abstracts of 14 theses completed in the Department.
Abstract gives the problem, procedure, findings and
interpretation, and significance of the study.

Places

Africa

General

G148. PARKER, Franklin. "U.S.A. Doctoral Dissertations Pertaining
to the History of African Education." Paedagogica Historica
4 (1964): 232-233.

An alphabetical author listing of 24 dissertations
completed to 1959.

G149. _____ African Education; A Bibliography of 121 U.S.A. Doctoral Dissertations. Washington: World Confederation of
Organizations of the Teaching Profession, 1965. 48 p.

Previously published in part as American Doctoral
Dissertations on African Education (1963), which in
turn was reissued with the title African Education:
A Partial Bibliography of U.S.A. Doctoral Dissertations (1964).

Author listing. Includes abstracts, if these are
available. Subject index.

South Africa

G150. EELLS, Walter C. "American Doctoral Dissertations on Education in South Africa." <u>Tydskrif vir Maatskaplike Navorsing</u> (Journal for Social Research) 6 (1955): 43-44.

An alphabetical author listing of 17 dissertations dealing in whole or in part with education in South Africa. Covers the period 1910 through 1953. Some items have brief note.

Australia

G151. EELLS, Walter C. "American Doctoral Dissertations in Education in Australia." <u>In</u> Australia. Commonwealth Office of Education. <u>Educational Research Being Undertaken in Australia, 1955,</u> appendix, p. 55-56. Sydney: 1956.

Lists 13 dissertations completed between 1933 and 1944 by institution.

G152. PARKER, Franklin. "Australian Education; A Bibliography of American Doctoral Dissertations and Master's Theses." <u>In</u> Australian Council for Education Research. <u>Library Bulletin,</u> no. 71, suppl. (Nov. 1963): 1-3.

Lists 29 dissertations and 19 theses separately.

Canada

G153. EELLS, Walter C. "American Doctoral Dissertations on Education in Canada." <u>University of Toronto Quarterly</u> 25 (1956): 249-258.

A listing of 111 dissertations completed between 1908 and 1954, arranged by province.

G154. PARKER, Franklin. "Canadian Education: A Bibliography of Doctoral Dissertations." <u>Education Office Gazette</u> (Halifax, Nova Scotia) 11, no. 3 (1962): 23-29.

An alphabetical author listing of 132 items completed between 1907 and 1959 in American universities.

G155. _____ "Canadian Education; A Bibliography of Doctoral Dissertations." <u>McGill Journal of Education</u> 2 (1967): 175-182;

3 (1968): 63-70.

> Supersedes his <u>Canadian Education; A Bibliography of 131 Doctoral Dissertations</u> (1959) and his <u>Doctoral Dissertations Pertaining to the History of Canadian Education</u> (1959).

> An alphabetical author listing of 171 American and Canadian dissertations completed between 1913 and 1965.

Alberta

G156. EELLS, Walter C. "U.S. Dissertations on Education in Alberta." <u>A.T.A.</u> [Alberta Teachers Alliance] <u>Magazine</u> 38 (April 1958): 43-45.

> Lists 26 dissertations and 15 theses dealing wholly or in part with education in Alberta. Covers the period 1934-1956.

British Columbia

G157. EELLS, Walter C. "U.S. Dissertations on Education in British Columbia." <u>The B.C. Teacher</u> 38 (1959): 202-205.

> Separate lists of 16 dissertations and 27 theses. A few of the items are annotated.

Manitoba

G158. EELLS, Walter C. "United States Dissertations on Education in Manitoba." <u>The Manitoba Teacher</u> 36 (Jan./Feb. 1958): 32-34.

> Abstracts of 11 dissertations and a listing of eight theses completed in the period 1913-1956.

New Brunswick

G159. EELLS, Walter C. "United States Dissertations on Education in New Brunswick." <u>Educational Review</u> 72 (Jan./Feb. 1958):

40-42.

> Lists 13 dissertations and three theses. Entry
> gives publication information. Some items include
> abstracts.

Newfoundland

G160. EELLS, Walter C. "U.S. Dissertations on Education in Newfoundland." N.T.A. (Newfoundland Teachers Association)
Journal 39 (Nov. 1957): 34-35.

> Lists six dissertations and three theses.

Nova Scotia

G161. EELLS, Walter C. "Dissertations on Education in Nova Scotia."
Nova Scotia Teacher's Bulletin 34 (Feb. 1958): 38-39.

> An alphabetical author listing of nine dissertations
> and six theses completed at American institutions.
> The earliest is dated 1923. Entry gives publication
> information.

Saskatchewan

G162. EELLS, Walter C. "United States Dissertations on Education
in Saskatchewan." Saskatchewan Bulletin 33 (Oct. 1957):
29-30.

> An alphabetical author listing of 16 dissertations
> and five theses. The earliest item is dated 1923.
> Entry gives publication information. Some entries
> are annotated.

Germany

G163. EELLS, Walter C. "Amerikanische Doktor-Dissertationen über
Erziehung in Deutschland." Bildung und Erziehung 9 (1955):
425-434.

> An alphabetical author listing of 87 dissertations,

covering the period to 1954. Entry is in English,
with German translation of the title.

India

G164. NARANG, H. L. "North American Doctoral Dissertations on
Indian Education: A Bibliography." Education Libraries
Bulletin (London. University. Institute of Education), no.
43 (Spring 1972): 31-49.

An author listing of approximately 250 studies,
many by Indians, completed at American institutions
through 1969.

Italy

G165. EELLS, Walter C. "Tesi dottorali negli Stati Uniti sulla
pedagogia Italiana." Scuola e citta (Florence) 7 (1956):
149-151.

Lists 41 American dissertations completed from 1894
to 1954. Entry gives explanatory note.

Japan

G166. EELLS, Walter C. The Literature of Japanese Education, 1945-
1954. Hamden, Conn.: Shoe String Press, 1955. 210 p.

Items listed also appear in his "American Essays
on Japan Increasing." Nippon Times (Tokyo), June
22, 1955, p. 4, and in his "Dissertations on Japanese Education." Phi Delta Kappan 36 (1955): 367-
368.

An alphabetical listing by author or title. Thirty-
three entries are for dissertations and 19 are for
theses, which are listed separately in the index.
Entry gives publishing information and a brief annotation. Index of authors, titles, and subjects.

G167. PASSIN, Herbert. Japanese Education: A Bibliography of
Materials in the English Language. New York: Columbia University, Teachers College Press, 1970. 135 p.

Arranged by major topics, e.g. students, teachers, women. Dissertations are listed separately under topic. The dissertations listed were completed in American institutions in the period 1940-1970.

Latin America

General

G168. PARKER, Franklin. Latin American Education Research; An Annotated Bibliography of 269 United States Doctoral Dissertations. Austin, Tex.: University of Texas, Institute of Latin American Studies, 1963. 63 p.

Dr. George I. Sanchez of the University of Texas utilized annotations from some Spanish works for this bibliography.

An alphabetical author listing. Subject and institution indexes.

G169. _____ "History of Latin American Education; Annotated Bibliography of 108 United States Doctoral Dissertations." Paedagogica Historica 4 (1964): 503-523.

Also published as a separate in 1964.

An alphabetical author listing covering the period to 1962. Entry gives publication information.

G170. _____ "U.S. Doctoral Dissertations Dealing with Latin American Education." Phi Delta Kappan 45 (1964): 227-229.

An annotated list of 28 dissertations.

Mexico

G171. PARKER, Franklin. Mexican Education Research; Annotated Bibliography of 67 United States Doctoral Dissertations. Austin, Tex.: 1964. 15 p.

Taken from Item G168.

Puerto Rico

G172. PARKER, Franklin. Puerto Rican Education Research; Annotated Bibliography of 66 United States Doctoral Dissertations. Norman, Okla.: University of Oklahoma, 1964. 15 p.

> Taken from Item G168.

> An alphabetical author list.

Middle East

G173. EELLS, Walter C. American Doctoral Dissertations on Education in Countries of the Middle East: Afghanistan, Ceylon, Cyprus, Egypt, Eritrea, Ethiopia, India, Iran, Iraq, Israel, Lebanon, Libya, Pakistan, Somaliland, Syria, Turkey. Washington: The Middle East Institute, 1955. 28 p.

> Lists 184 dissertations arranged by country. More than half are on India. Covers the period 1899-1954. Entry gives publication information. An appendix lists seven dissertations submitted between 1940 and 1950 to foreign institutions.

Philippines

G174. EELLS, Walter C. "American Doctoral Dissertations on Education in the Philippines." The Philippine Educator 10 (Nov. 1955): 51-54.

> A list of 45 dissertations completed between 1909 and 1954, arranged alphabetically by author.

Special and Racial Groups

Blacks

G175. WILKERSON, Doxey A. "University Research in the Field of Vocational Education and Guidance for Negroes." Journal of Negro Education 9 (Jan. 1940): 126-130; 9 (April 1940): 264-266.

Lists 130 theses and dissertations covering the period 1921-1938, arranged alphabetically under topic. April 1940 list is a supplement to the main list.

G176. CARNEY, Mabel. "Doctoral Dissertations and Projects Relating to the Education of Negroes." Advanced School Digest 7 (Feb. 1942): 41-44.

Contains a chronological list of work completed at Columbia University Teachers College under the separate headings of dissertations and projects, as well as a list of Black candidates who matriculated for the Ph.D. and Ed.D. Entry gives publication information.

G177. "SELECTED 1944[-1947] References on Rural Life and Education." Journal of Negro Education 14 (1945)-16 (1948). Annual. Spring issue.

An author list of dissertations and theses primarily from American Negro universities, on Negro rural life and education.

G178. WASHINGTON, Alethea and Irene E. Dunlap. "Selected 1947 References on Rural Life and Education." Journal of Negro Education 17 (1948): 215-230.

Under "Doctor's Dissertations" lists five items, and under "Master's Theses" 44 references are cited.

G179. PARKER, Franklin. "Negro Education in the U.S.A.; A Bibliography of Doctoral Dissertations." Negro History Bulletin 24 (1961): 190-192.

Also appeared as a separate in 1960.

Lists 113 dissertations.

G180. _____ "American Doctoral Dissertations Pertaining to the History of Negro Education." Paedagogica Historica 1 (1961): 393-394.

Alphabetical author listing of 18 dissertations completed in American institutions to 1956 dealing with Negro education in the United States.

G181. _____ "Fisk University (Nashville, Tennessee) Master's Theses Concerning the History of Education, Mainly of the Negro in the South." Paedagogica Historica 3 (1963): 480-481.

An alphabetical author listing of 33 theses completed to 1958.

Catholics

G182. PARKER, Franklin. Catholic Education: A Partial List of 189 [i.e. 185] American Doctoral Dissertations. Austin, Tex.: 1961. 12 p.

An alphabetical author listing.

G183. _____ "Dissertations on Catholic Education." Catholic School Journal 62 (1962): 29-32.

An alphabetical author listing of approximately 175 American dissertations completed from 1904 through 1958 on Catholic education on all school levels and covering the United States and elsewhere.

Continued by:

G184. KINCHELOE, H. Karen and Franklin Parker. "Additional Dissertations on Catholic Education." Catholic School Journal 64 (March 1964): 112, 130, 138, 146.

Also issued as a separate in 1962.

An alphabetical author listing of approximately 80 dissertations completed to 1961, and including earlier studies not listed previously.

G185. PARKER, Franklin. "American Doctoral Dissertations Pertaining to the History of Catholic Education." Paedagogica Historica 2 (1962): 168-171.

An alphabetical listing of 61 dissertations completed to 1958 dealing with Catholic education. Not limited solely to the United States.

G186. "RECENT Doctoral Dissertations on Catholic Education." In
National Catholic Education Association. Bulletin 60, no.
4 (May 1964): 20-43; 61, no. 4 (May 1965): 9-22; 63, no. 4
(May 1967): 33-51; 65, no. 2 (Nov. 1968): 58-67.

Includes dissertations completed since 1958 or under
way in Catholic and non-Catholic institutions in the
United States. Listing is alphabetical by author
under broad subject headings. These headings are
consistent in all articles and consecutive numbering
in each subject carries through all articles. Entries
are cross-referenced and there are indexes to precise
subjects.

Jews

G187. SOLTES, Mordecai. "Doctoral Dissertations and Master's
Theses on Jewish Education and Kindred Themes." Jewish
Education 11 (1940): 189-195.

Supersedes listing in Jewish Education 7 (1935):
112-113.

A classified list of American theses and dissertations covering the period 1900 through 1939 on Jewish topics. This includes education, religion and
customs, Palestine, Hebrew language, Biblical and
Talmudic literature, history, biography, and sociology. Dissertations and theses are presented in
separate listings under each topic.

Continued and supplemented by:

G188. EELLS, Walter C. "American Graduate Dissertations on Jewish
Education outside the U.S.A." Jewish Education 28 (Winter
1957/1958): 61-63.

Theses and dissertations dealing with Jewish education and educators both inside and outside the
United States, covering the period 1909-1956. Includes works which do not appear in Item G187.
Dissertations and theses are arranged in separate
lists. Entry gives publication information.

G189. GRAEBER, Isacque A. "Research in American Jewish Education."
Jewish Education 24 (1954): 49-55, 57.

Lists 67 American theses and dissertations on the education of Jews in America, the history of Jewish education, American Jewish education, and Jewish education in Palestine. Covers the period 1890-1953.

G190. PARKER, Franklin. "Jewish Education: A Partial List of American Doctoral Dissertations." Jewish Journal of Sociology 3 (1961): 192-194.

Appeared previously in part in Franklin Parker and Judah Pilch, "Doctoral Dissertations in Jewish Education and Related Areas." Jewish Education 31 (Spring 1961): 60-62.

Includes dissertations completed from 1916 to 1958 dealing with all phases of Jewish education.

G191. PARKER, Franklin. "American Doctoral Dissertations Pertaining to the History of Jewish Education." Paedagogica Historica 2 (1962): 171-172.

An alphabetical listing of 22 dissertations completed to 1957. Not limited to the United States.

Women

G192. EELLS, Walter C. "American Doctoral Dissertations on Education Written by Women in the Nineteenth Century." Educational Horizons 35 (Winter 1956): 53-56.

An alphabetical list of 26 items. Entry includes year of bachelor's degree and institution where completed, and date of birth.

G193. _____ "American Doctoral Dissertations on the Education of Women in Foreign Countries." In National Association of Deans of Women. Journal 19 (1956): 79-81.

Thirty-one dissertations completed between 1916 and 1954. Arranged by continent and then country.

Special Subjects

Administration

G194. MORRIS, Lyle, Everett B. Sackett, and Whit Brogan. "An Annotated Bibliography of Researches in Educational Publicity to June 1927." Teachers College Record 30 (1928): 40-45.

> The same items contained in Carter Alexander, "Research in Educational Policy." Teachers College Record 29 (1928): 479-487.

> Twenty-eight studies in this field (all that could be found from the beginning), including 11 theses and dissertations.

G195. NATIONAL ASSOCIATION OF SECONDARY SCHOOL PRINCIPALS. Abstracts of Unpublished Masters' Theses in the Field of Secondary School Administration, 1929-1934. Berwyn, Ill.: 1929-1934. 6 vols. (Its Bulletin, no. 24 (1929), 34 (1930), 36 (1931), 39 (1932), 43 (1933), 47 (1934))

> Each Bulletin is devoted to a different institution and has a different editor. Bulletin no. 24: the University of Chicago, 1927-1928; nos. 34 and 36: the University of Southern California, 1925-1930; no. 39: Ohio State University, 1925-1931; no. 43: George Peabody College for Teachers, 1921-1932; no. 47: the University of Minnesota, 1927-1932.

G196. ALEXANDER, Carter. Educational Finance Studies; Summaries and Evaluations for School Administrators of Recent Educational Finance Dissertations at Teachers College, Columbia University. New York: Columbia University, Teachers College, 1931. 92 p.

> Summarizes and evaluates 19 works, primarily theses and dissertations, written about 1924-1929 on public school finance. Arranged by subject.

G197. "ABSTRACTS of Doctors' Theses." In National Association of Secondary School Principals. Bulletin 20 (May 1936): 5-28.

> Long abstracts of 14 dissertations.

G198. GOOD, Carter V. "Recent Graduate Theses in School Law."
Yearbook of School Law 5 (1937): 138-144; 6 (1938): 133-147;
7 (1939): 166-196; 8 (1940): 157-182; 9 (1941): 180-197; 10
(1942): 183-197. Title varies.

> Theses and dissertations completed in American univer-
> sities. The first number, "Doctoral Dissertations in
> the Field of Educational Law, 1918-1935," is an alpha-
> betical author list obtained primarily from Item G2
> and Item G4. All succeeding numbers include "I. Re-
> cent Doctoral Dissertations," each accompanied by a
> short abstract, and "II. Recent Masters' Theses."
> Entry gives publication information.

G199. NEBRASKA. University. Teachers College. Summaries of
Masters' Theses in School Administration, Teachers College,
University of Nebraska, 1925-1940. Lincoln: University of
Nebraska, Extension Division, 1940. 94 p. (Nebraska.
University. Extension Division. University of Nebraska
Publication, no. 136)

> Short descriptive abstracts giving scope of the
> study and the findings.

G200. NEW ENGLAND SCHOOL DEVELOPMENT COUNCIL. Thesis Abstracts:
Digests of Recently Completed Research in New England on
Problems Confronting Public Schools. Cambridge, Mass.: 1956.
52 p.

> Abstracts of 12 selected theses.

G201. CARPENTER, William W. and Arlie G. Capps. Areas of Educational Administration Considered in Doctoral Dissertations,
University of Missouri. Columbia, Mo.: College of Education,
1957. 51 p. (The University of Missouri Bulletin, vol. 58,
no. 27. Education Series, no. 67)

> A subject bibliography of the 360 dissertations in
> education accepted by the University of Missouri
> from 1916 through 1956. Author index.

G202. EELLS, Walter C. and Ernest V. Hollis. Administration of
Higher Education; An Annotated Bibliography. Washington:
U.S. Office of Education, 1960. 410 p. (U.S. Office of
Education. Bulletin, 1960, no. 7)

A subject arrangement of 2,708 items, 475 of which
are Ph.D.'s or Ed.D.'s. Includes only dissertations
which are published independently or abstracts of
which have been printed. Reference to source of
dissertations cited. Index of individuals, institutions, organizations, and principal topics.

G203. _____ The College Presidency, 1900-60; An Annotated Bibliography. Washington: U.S. Government Printing Office, 1961.
143 p.

A bibliography on the college president and his re-
sponsibilities. The subject index entry for doctoral
dissertations provides a separate listing for 36
studies.

G204. UNIVERSITY MICROFILMS, Ann Arbor, Mich. Doctoral Dissertations: School Administration, 1964. Ann Arbor: 1965. 13 p.

A subject bibliography of dissertations published
by University Microfilms in school administration
and related fields during 1964. Purchasing information provided.

G205. NOLTE, Mervin C. Bibliography of School Law Dissertations,
1952-1968. Eugene, Ore.: Oregon University, 1969. 43 p.
(ERIC Clearinghouse on Educational Administration. Bibliography Series, no. 13)

Lists 503 dissertations on school law completed in
American universities arranged under 25 major subject
categories.

Adult Education

G206. "RESEARCH and Investigations in Adult Education." Adult
Education 5 (1955)-17 (1967). Annual. Usually Summer issue.

A classified review of current research in adult
education complete or in progress in the U.S. since
the beginning of 1954. Most studies listed are
theses and dissertations. For each study there is
a summary of the purpose of the research, major
findings and where it is available.

G207. EELLS, Walter C. "American Doctoral Dissertations on Adult Education in Foreign Countries." Adult Education 6 (Winter 1956): 117-119.

>A classified list of 62 dissertations beginning in 1916.

G208. PARKER, Franklin. "Doctoral Dissertations Pertaining to the History of Adult Education." Paedagogica Historica 2 (1962): 393-394.

>An alphabetical author listing of 18 dissertations completed in American institutions up to 1958. Coverage not limited to the United States.

G209. LITTLE, Lawrence C. A Bibliography of Doctoral Dissertations on Adults and Adult Education. Revised ed. Pittsburgh: University of Pittsburgh Press, 1963. 163 p.

>A preliminary edition was published in 1962 for use in a research seminar.

>An alphabetical author listing of over 2,500 dissertations dealing with the experiences and needs of adults and with the many patterns of adult education. Refers to abstracts appearing in Microfilm Abstracts and Religious Education.

G210. PARKER, Franklin. Adult Education; A Partial Bibliography of 358 American Doctoral Dissertations. Austin, Tex.: University of Texas, 1964. 35 p.

>Supersedes his 1961 and 1963 listings.

>Alphabetical author listing covering the period to 1961.

G211. DE CROW, Roger and Nehume Loague. Adult Education Dissertation Abstracts: 1963-1967. Syracuse, N.Y.: ERIC Clearinghouse on Adult Education, 1971. 309 p. (Ed 044 537)

>A classified bibliography of 505 dissertations relative to the education or training of adults. Entry gives publication information. Author, institution, and methodological indexes.

Continued by:

G212. GRABOWSKI, Stanley M. and Nehume Loague. Adult Education
Dissertations: 1968-1969. Washington: Adult Education
Association of the U.S.A., 1971. 227 p.

ED 052 450

A classified listing of 303 abstracts of dissertations relevant to the education or the training of
adults. The abstracts are arranged under such areas
as adult education as a profession and field of
study, instruction methods, instructional devices,
occupational training. Author, institutional, and
methodological indexes.

Agricultural Education

G213. AMERICAN VOCATIONAL ASSOCIATION. Agricultural Education
Section. Summaries of Studies in Agricultural Education; An
Annotated Bibliography of 373 Studies in Agricultural Educa-
tion with a Classified Subject Index... Washington: U.S.
Government Printing Office, 1935. 196 p. (U.S. Office of
Education. Vocational Division. Vocational Education
Bulletin, no. 180. Agriculture Series, no. 18 [i.e. 17])

_____ _____ Supplement [no. 1-16] Washington: U.S. Government Printing Office, 1943-1965. Irregular.

No. 1 published by Danville, Ill.: Interstate Printers and Publishers; nos. 2-   issued as U.S. Office
of Education Bulletin and as its Agricultural Series.

Each is a separate alphabetical author listing, consisting primarily of theses or problem studies and
dissertations. The numbering, however, is consecutive and, in all, 3,399 items are represented,
covering the period 1917-1963. The abstracts indicate purpose, method, findings, and interpretation.
Each piece has a subject index.

_____ Summaries of Studies in Agricultural Education, Bibliography [1963/1965-   ] Danville, Ill.: American Association of Teacher Educators, 1968-   . Biennial.

An alphabetical author listing of theses, dissertations, and some staff research, arranged by academic

year. Summary indicates the purpose, method, and findings of the research. Classified subject index.

G214. AMERICAN VOCATIONAL ASSOCIATION. Committee on Research in the Education of Farm Veterans. Education of Veterans in Farming. Washington: 1952. (AVA Research Bulletin, no. 5)

Contains an alphabetical author listing of approximately 70 studies, primarily theses, completed in the United States in the period 1947-1952 (p. 91-94).

G215. QUEZON, Philippines. University of the Philippines. College of Agriculture. Summaries of Studies in Agricultural Education in the Philippines; An Annotated Bibliography of Studies. Laguna: 1959. 60 p.

Abstracts of 54 bachelors' and masters' theses completed in the public institutions of the Philippines, concerned with training teachers of agriculture on the secondary school level. Also included are some American dissertations. Most of the studies were completed between 1950 and 1959. Entry gives location of copies. The abstract includes purpose, method and findings, and interpretation.

G216. "RESEARCH in Agricultural Education: Studies Completed in [1961/1962-   ]" Agricultural Education 37 (1964)-   . Annual.

Vol. 37 (1964) covers the work completed in 1961/1962 and in 1962/1963 in two separate listings.

Primarily completed theses and dissertations arranged under such topics as curriculum development, cooperative extension education, agricultural education in other countries, evaluation, learning processes, and teaching methods.

Art Education

G217. NATIONAL ART EDUCATION ASSOCIATION. Information Studies Committee. "Survey of Research." Art Education 14 (Dec. 1961): 10-15.

Lists over 100 research studies and creative projects
underway or completed during the 1959/1960 academic
year. Includes historical, descriptive, and action
research and creative projects in visual and written
expression. More than half are in fulfillment of an
advanced degree.

G218. LANIER, Vincent. Doctoral Research in Art Education; Completed in Universities in the United States and Canada. Los
Angeles: 1962. 52, 20 p.

An alphabetical author listing of 498 items coded
to indicate subject category.

_____ _____ Supplement...1963. 13 p.

Continued and supplemented by:

G219. _____ Doctoral Research in Art Education. Eugene, Ore.:
1968. 101 p.

Sponsored by the United States Office of Education
and the University of Oregon.

An alphabetical author listing of dissertations
completed in American universities through 1968.
Approximately half of the items listed are for pre-
1962 items which were not listed in 1962 list.
Entry gives subject category and information on
the availability of an abstract.

Audio-Visual Education

G220. GOODMAN, David. "Experimental Research in Audio-Visual
Education." Educational Screen and Audio-Visual Guide 20,
no. 6 (June 1941)-25, no. 1 (Jan. 1946).

A feature appearing in nearly all issues during
this period, consisting of an abstract of a study
in the field, nearly always a doctor's or master's
thesis.

G221. LARSON, Lawrence C., Charity E. Runden, and others. Bibliography of Research in Audio-Visual Education and Mass Media,
1930-1950. Bloomington, Ind.: Indiana University, Audio-

Visual Center, 1950. 86 p.

_____ _____ Supplement 1, August 1, 1950. Bloomington,
Ind.: Indiana University, Audio-Visual Center, 1950. 81 p.

_____ _____ Supplement 2. Bloomington, Ind.: Indiana
University, Audio-Visual Center, 1952. 49 p.

> In largest part consists of theses and dissertations,
> arranged alphabetically. The supplements include
> materials not previously listed.

G222. McCLUSKY, Frederick D. The A-V Bibliography. Revised ed.
Dubuque, Iowa: W. C. Brown Co., 1955. 218 p.

> Pt. 7 (p. 190-198) contains a chronological listing
> of dissertations in the audio-visual field completed
> in United States universities from 1921 to 1954.
> Not a complete list, but comprehensive. Entry gives
> publication information.

G223. MOLSTAD, John. "Doctoral Dissertations in Audio-Visual Education." Audio-Visual Communication Review 4 (Fall 1956):
291-333.

> Lists 459 titles from 59 colleges and universities
> in the United States, representing all those found
> in the field to March 1956. Alphabetical arrange-
> ment with number reference to a subject classifica-
> tion table.

_____ _____ "Supplement I." Audio-Visual Communication
Review 6 (1958): 33-48.

> Lists 118 dissertations representing work completed
> March 1956-September 1957.

_____ _____ "Supplement II." Audio-Visual Communication
Review 7 (1959): 142-153.

> Lists 52 items completed September 1957-September
> 1958 and 31 additions to the previous lists in a
> separate alphabetical arrangement.

_____ _____ "Supplement III." Audio-Visual Communication
Review 9 (1961): 220-229.

> Lists 102 studies.

G224. GOLTER, Bob J. Bibliography of Theses and Dissertations Relating to Audio-Visuals and Broadcasting. Prepared by Bob J. Golter, through the research facilities of the Dept. of Church School Curriculum, the Methodist Publishing House. Nashville, Tenn.: 1958. 185 p.

      _____ _____ Addenda. 9 p.

> Arranged alphabetically by name of college or university and then by author. Based on earlier listings and a questionnaire sent to American institutions offering graduate degrees.

G225. PARKER, Franklin. Audio-Visual Education; A Bibliography of Doctoral Dissertations. Austin, Tex.: 1959. 17 p.

> An alphabetical author list of 209 American dissertations.

G226. _____ "Dissertation Subjects Reveal Variety of Audio-Visual Methods Researched: A Bibliography of 209 Doctoral Dissertations on Audio-Visual Education." Film World and A-V News 19 (1963): 114, 157-158, 199.

> An alphabetical author listing of American dissertations on audio-visual techniques in education completed in the period 1941-1959.

G227. PARKER, Franklin and Herman L. Totten. "Audio Visual Education Research: A Bibliography of 356 Doctoral Dissertations." Audio Visual Coordinators of Oklahoma 18 (April 1966): 5. ?

> Also appeared as a separate.

Business Education

G228. "NEW YORK UNIVERSITY Graduate Theses in Business Administration, 1925-1930." In New York University. Department of Business Education. Research Bulletin in Commercial Education 2 (Dec. 1930): 17-20.

> A chronological list. Within each academic year dissertations and theses are listed separately.

G229. "GRADUATE Theses at N.Y.U." Journal of Business Education 6 (Sept. 1931): 14, 22.

> Eleven theses completed at the School of Education, 1930-1931.

G230. TONNE, Herbert A. "Theses in Business Education." Journal of Business Education 6 (Oct. 1931): 25-26; 6 (Nov. 1931): 25-26.

> Alphabetical listing of 181 theses and dissertations completed or in progress from 1910 in typing, office practice, business English, penmanship, etc. Does not include N.Y.U. theses for 1930-1931.

> Supplemented by:

G231. _____ "Theses in Business Education." Journal of Business Education 7 (Feb. 1932): 23-24; 7 (March 1932): 25-27.

> Subject listing of works in Item G230. Some additions are made to previous list.

G232. HAYNES, Benjamin R. and Jessie Graham. Research in Business Education. Los Angeles: C. C. Crawford, 1932. 232 p.

> "Abstracts of Theses in Business Education," p. 136-213. Masters' degrees, nearly all of which are from the University of Southern California, with some from Stanford and the University of California.

G233. "RESEARCH Studies Completed and in Progress." In National Association for Business Teacher Training Education. Bulletin, nos. 3, 5, 9, 11, 15, 17, 20, 24, 27, 33, 36 (1933-1945). Title varies.

> Classified listings of theses and dissertations underway or completed in the field. Includes also work done at non-member institutions.

> Continued by:

G234. "RESEARCH in Business Education Completed or Under Way [1951/1952-1969]" National Business Education Quarterly 20 (1952)-38 (1970). Annual. Spring (March) issue.

A classified list of theses and dissertations divided according to "Studies Completed" and "Studies Under Way."

Continued by:

G235. "RESEARCH Studies in Business Education Completed or Under Way [1970-   ]" Business Education Forum 25 (1971)-   . Annual. March issue.

A classified bibliography of theses and dissertations. Under each topic items are subdivided into studies completed and studies under way.

G236. REED, La Vor, Harold Kirby, and Dale Jordan. "A Bibliography Related to the Teaching of Bookkeeping." National Business Education Quarterly 9 (Dec. 1940): 42-63.

Pt. 1, "Graduate Theses" (p. 42-44, 46-47), lists theses and some dissertations completed or in progress from about 1924. Entry gives publication information.

G237. FREEMAN, Max H. Bibliography of Research Studies in Business Education, 1920-1940; A Cumulative Author, Institutional, and Subject Index of Research Studies in Business Education Listed in the United States Office of Education Bibliography of Research Studies in Education, Bulletins, 1926-1941. Sponsored by Delta Pi Epsilon Fraternity. New York: Business Education World, 1943. 55 p.

An alphabetical listing of 1,148 theses and dissertations registered with the Office of Education from 1920 through 1940 and appearing in Item G4. Subject and institutional indexes.

Continued by:

G238. INDIANA. University. Department of Business Education. Bibliography of Research Studies in Business Education, 1941-1948. Prepared by the Dept. of Business Education of Indiana University in cooperation with Delta Pi Epsilon. Compiled and classified by Gertrude M. Dubats, C. Howard Lunquest, and Ralph W. Wilson. Bloomington: Indiana University, School of Business, Bureau of Business Research, 1949. 78 p. (Indiana Business Studies, Study no. 32)

An alphabetical author list of 1,272 theses and
dissertations in business education and related
fields completed from 1941 to 1948, inclusive.
Some pre-1940 items not included in Item G237 are
also listed. Subject index.

G239. "REVIEW of Research." Review of Business Education, 1943
ser., nos. 1/2: 40-43. (Oklahoma State University. Bulletin,
vol. 40, no. 4)

Abstracts of seven theses in business education
completed at Oklahoma State University during the
Spring and Summer of 1942.

G240. PI OMEGA PI. Alpha Tau Chapter, University of Southern
California. Selected Research Studies in Business Education,
University of Southern California...1943, Supplemented 1944.
Los Angeles: 1945. 70 p.

An alphabetical listing of abstracts of significant
theses and dissertations completed from 1939 to
1942/1943 at the University of Southern California.
Author and subject indexes.

G241. BROWNFIELD, Lelah. "Research Studies Completed and in Process." In National Association for Business Teacher Training Education. Bulletin 45 (June 1948): 40-52.

A listing of approximately 200 theses and dissertations completed or in progress for the period 1940
through 1947. Arranged under broad topics. Topics
include business and economic surveys, business education surveys, curriculum, evaluation of courses,
teaching methods, tests and research techniques, and
history and theory of business education.

G242. VEON, Dorothy H. Theses Completed at the George Washington
University of Interest to Business Educators. Washington:
1948. 76 p.

A classified list of theses and dissertation abstracts.

G243. DELTA PI EPSILON. 100 Summaries of Studies and Research in
Business Education, 1952. Columbus, Ohio: 1954. 101 p.

An alphabetical author list of abstracts of theses
and dissertations from American universities. Subject index.

Continued by:

G244. "SUMMARIES of Studies and Research in Business Education
[1953-1968]" National Business Education Quarterly 23
(1954)-38 (1969). Annual. Whole Fall (Oct.) issue.

Compiled by Delta Pi Epsilon.

Alphabetical author list of abstracts of completed
theses and dissertations. Entry includes subject,
purpose, method and sources, and summary of findings.
Subject index.

Secretarial Education

G245. VIETTI, Edward. "A Selected Bibliography Regarding the
Teaching of Typewriting: Graduate Theses." National Business
Education Quarterly 8 (March 1940): 61-62; 8 (May 1940): 61-
66.

A classified listing. Section 10, "Graduate Theses"
(p. 63-66), contains 118 items, primarily theses,
covering the period from 1916.

G246. RAHE, Harves. "A Review of Research in Typewriting Progno-
sis." National Business Education Quarterly 20 (1952): 44-
53.

Lists 71 items, mostly theses, covering the period
from 1917.

G247. _____ Typewriting Research Index; A Complete List of Re-
search Studies in Typewriting from 1904 to March 1963,
Classified by Author, Subject, University, and Date. New
York: Gregg Division, McGraw-Hill Book Co., 1963. 57 p.

First published in 1952 and revised in 1954.

Limited to those research reports which include some
form of the word type or typewriter in their titles.
Consists in large part of theses. Pt. 3, "College

and University Index," is an index by institution
of each thesis or report completed in partial fulfillment of a degree requirement.

G248. _____ Shorthand-Secretarial Research Index; A Complete List
of Research Studies in the Work and Training of Stenographers
and Secretaries, from 1891 to 1965, Classified by Author,
Subject, University, and Date. New York: Gregg Division,
McGraw-Hill, 1965. 68 p.

First edition published at Southern Illinois University as Bibliography of Research Studies in Steno-
graphic-Secretarial Training and Work Prior to 1959
(1959).

Of the 964 items indexed, theses and dissertations
make up the major portion. In five parts: (1) alphabetical author listing, (2) classified subject
index, (3) index of colleges and universities, (4)
chronological index, (5) summary analysis.

Counseling and Student Personnel

G249. NATIONAL REHABILITATION ASSOCIATION. Theses and Dissertations Related to Rehabilitation Counselor Education. By
James H. Hall and Jacob O. Bach. Washington: National Rehabilitation Association, Rehabilitation Counselor Education
Research, 1958. 2 vols. (Its Provisional Reports on Rehabilitation Literature, nos. 1-2)

Vol. 1 lists 1,077 American theses and dissertations.
Coverage for the theses is 1947-1956; for dissertations 1947-1955. Arranged by institution and subdivided into theses and dissertations. Broad coverage
to include work done in such areas as sociology,
political science, psychology, management, religious
education. Vol. 1 contains an author index. Vol. 2,
"Indexed Topical Analysis of Titles of Theses and
Dissertations Related to Rehabilitation Counselor
Education," provides an intensive subject index.

G250. U.S. Office of Education. Research in School and College
Personnel Services; Summaries of Unpublished Studies, Sep-
tember 1956-September 1958. Washington: 1960. 136 p. (Its
Bulletin, 1960, no. 10)

The greatest number of the studies summarized are
theses and dissertations. Subject arrangement.
For each study gives the director, problem statement,
research procedures, and major findings.

G251. PARKER, Franklin. "Mental Health and Education: A Bibliography of 177 Doctoral Dissertations and 11 Master's Theses."
Journal of Human Relations 14 (1966): 306-322.

An alphabetical author listing. In two parts: (1)
doctoral dissertations, and (2) Master of Arts or
Master of Education theses.

G252. ALSTON, Jerry G., Arthur L. Casebeer, and Thomas A. Leemon.
A Bibliography of Doctoral Dissertations Completed 1965-69
and Doctoral Dissertations in Progress 1969-70 by Persons
Enrolled in College Student Personnel Graduate Programs.
Carbondale, Ill.: Southern Illinois University, 1970. 43 p.

Approximately 400 studies, arranged under such topics
as achievement, admissions, attitudes and values,
housing, religion, student personnel services, student rights and government, and vocational development. Entry gives adviser.

Continued by:

G253. LEEMON, Thomas A. A Bibliography of Doctoral Dissertations
in the Field of College Student Personnel Work Containing
Those Dissertations Completed between January 1, 1970 and
December 31, 1970. Washington: American College Personnel
Association, 1970. 57 p.

Edited for Commission XII: The Professional Education
of Student Personnel Workers in Higher Education of
the American College Personnel Association.

Lists 160 studies representing work completed in
American institutions with graduate programs in college level student personnel work. Arranged in two
parts: alphabetically by author, and by topics, such
as student rights and government; admissions, achievement and attrition; student characteristics, attitudes
and values and behavior. Entry gives adviser.

G254. "DISSERTATIONS [1970-   ]" Journal of College Student

Personnel 12 (1971)-   . Annual.

Lists dissertations completed in American universities under such topics as student characteristics, attitudes and values, behavior and behavior modification, student culture and college environment, student rights and college government.

Desegregation

G255. PARKER, Franklin. "Public School Desegregation; A Partial Bibliography of 113 Doctoral Dissertations." Negro History Bulletin 26 (1963): 225-228.

A less complete listing appeared earlier in the Journal of Human Relations 10 (1961).

An alphabetical author listing.

Elementary Education

G256. "BIBLIOGRAPHY of Studies in Elementary Education, 1924-1929." In Pittsburgh. University. School of Education. Journal 4 (March-April 1929): 93, 104.

Lists 31 theses and dissertations completed at the University of Pittsburgh. Annotated.

G257. "RECENT Research Studies in Elementary Education Completed at Utah Colleges and Universities." Utah Educational Research Bulletin 4, no. 2 (1953): 1-33.

Whole number.

A bibliographic essay, presenting abstracts of theses and dissertations. The bibliography of studies cited is arranged by institution.

Exceptional Children

G258. GAFFNEY, Theresa W. and others. Abstracts of Theses on the Gifted Child Done between 1923 and 1957 at Boston University and Columbia University. Boston: Boston University, 1958.

67 p. (M.A. Thesis, Boston University)

Contains 20 theses and dissertations.

Supplemented by:

G259. DACEY, Elizabeth F. and others. <u>Abstracts of Unpublished</u>
<u>Theses on the Gifted Child Found in the School of Education</u>
<u>Library Which Were Not Included in the Gaffney Theses of</u>
<u>1958</u>. Boston: 1960. 121 p. (Ed.M. Thesis, Boston Univer-
sity)

> Thirty-one theses, dissertations, and service papers
> done at the Boston University Graduate School of
> Education, 1927-1959. Contains studies done in 1958
> and 1959, as well as those done since 1927 not in-
> cluded in the Gaffney list.

G260. GOWAN, John C. <u>An Annotated Bibliography on the Academically</u>
<u>Talented</u>. Washington: National Education Association Project
on the Academically Talented Student, 1961. 156 p.

> Research done since 1950, including, within the
> alphabetical listing, dissertations. Emphasis is
> on research, theory, bibliographies, and heuristic
> materials. Entry gives publication information.

G261. _____ "Annotation of Recent Dissertations of Creativity in
Teaching." <u>Gifted Child Quarterly</u> 12 (Autumn/Winter 1968):
186-187, 247-250.

> An annotated author listing of dissertations from
> American institutions covering the period 1963-1967.

G262. "BIBLIOGRAPHY of Recent Theses on Creativity and Problem
Solving." <u>Journal of Creative Behavior</u> 6 (1972)-   .
Irregular.

> Alphabetical author listings of dissertations as
> reported in <u>Dissertation Abstracts</u>. Entry gives
> primary interest area.

Health, Physical Education, and Recreation

G263. BROWNE, A. D. "A Classification of Completed Theses and

Selected Subjects Written by Students of Physical Education in Various Colleges and Universities for the Degree of
Master of Arts or Master of Science." Research Quarterly
2 (Oct. 1931): 119-151.

A listing of over 600 American theses completed or
in progress, arranged under topic.

G264. AFFLECK, George B. "Selected Bibliography of Graduate
Theses, Springfield College, 1929-1934." Research Quarterly
6, no. 2 (May 1935): suppl. p. 126-128.

A chronological listing of theses.

_____ "Master's Theses, Springfield College, Division of
Health and Physical Education." Research Quarterly 12, no.
2 (May 1941): suppl. p. 490-513.

Covers the period 1935-1940. Arranged chronologically.

G265. NEATE, Erminie A. Methods of Locating Theses and Dissertations in the Field of Health, Physical Education, and Recreation, with a Classified List of All Theses and Dissertations Written since 1929. Baton Rouge, La.: 1940. 176 p.
(M.S. Thesis, Louisiana State University, 1940)

Pt. 2 is a classified listing of "all" theses and
dissertations written in these fields. Under each
heading theses and dissertations are listed separately.

G266. BASS, Ruth. "Studies for the Years 1937-1939 Listed in the
Files of the Committee for Research of the National Associa-
tion of Directors of Physical Education for College Women."
Research Quarterly 11 (May 1940): 150-168.

Lists studies completed or "well under way." Includes
all types of research but about half are theses or
dissertations. Classified by subject. Entry gives
publication information.

_____ "Additions to the Files of the Committee for Research
of the National Association of Directors of Physical Education for College Women, 1939-1941." Research Quarterly 13
(Oct. 1942): 388-396.

Continued by:

G267. HODGSON, Pauline. "Studies Completed by Members of the National Association of Physical Education for College Women [1941/1943-1943/1945]" Research Quarterly 15 (Oct. 1944): 225-231; 16 (Dec. 1945): 293-301.

> First list arranged by subject, second list alphabetically by author. Entry gives publication information. Second list has "Subject Matter Index" at end. In both lists about half are theses or dissertations.

G268. CURETON, Thomas K. "Doctorate Theses Reported by Graduate Departments of Health, Physical Education and Recreation, 1930-1946, Inclusively." Research Quarterly 20 (March 1949): 21-59.

> Also appeared as a separate.

> An analysis and listing of 420 dissertations, arranged alphabetically. For each the topic emphasis and research method are indicated.

G269. _____ Masters Theses in Health, Physical Education, and Recreation. Washington: American Association for Health, Physical Education, and Recreation, 1952. 292 p.

> Lists 3,878 titles from 108 institutions. Contains considerable introductory analytical material, graphs of distribution, etc. Entry gives topical emphasis and research method. Subject index.

G270. _____ University of Illinois Thesis Abstracts in Physical Education, 1924-1953. Urbana, Ill.: 1953. 1 vol. (unpaged)

> Theses and dissertations completed at the University of Illinois.

G271. ILLINOIS. University. College of Physical Education. University of Illinois Abstracts of Graduate Theses in Physical Education, Recreation and Health Education [1924/1953-1963] Urbana: 1954-1964. Annual. Title varies.

> Theses and dissertations arranged under the headings physical education, recreation, and health education. Each volume contains a commentary, with the abstracts listed separately. Entry gives

purpose, methodology, and conclusions.

G272. CURETON, Thomas K. Effects of Physical Education and Athletics Upon College Men. Urbana, Ill.: 1955. 70 p.

A classified bibliography of 237 unpublished theses and dissertations.

G273. AMERICAN ASSOCIATION FOR HEALTH, PHYSICAL EDUCATION, AND RECREATION. Research Council. Thesis Abstracts in Health, Physical Education and Recreation [1954/1955-1956/1957] Compiled by Alfred W. Hubbard. Urbana: University of Illinois, 1956-1958. 2 vols.

A compilation of dissertations completed at selected American universities; also some lists from individual institutions. Arranged by institution. Entry gives adviser. Abstract gives purpose, method, and conclusions. Vol. 2 contains an author and subject index.

Continued by:

G274. _____ Completed Research in Health, Physical Education, Recreation Including International Sources [1958-   ] Washington: 1959-   . Title varies. Annual.

Pt. 3, "Theses Abstracts," contains theses and dissertations from American and Canadian institutions with graduate programs in health, physical education, recreation, and allied areas. Arranged by institution. Entry gives adviser and sometimes area of concentration. Pt. 1 is a subject index.

G275. CURETON, Thomas K., Carolyn W. Bookwalter, and Raymond A. Weiss. Graduate Thesis Abstracts, 1938-1953, from New York and Indiana Universities. Urbana, Ill.: 1956. 1 vol. (various pagings)

Abstracts of 37 Ed.D. and Ph.D. dissertations from New York University and 51 dissertations from Indiana University.

G276. CURETON, Thomas K. Graduate Thesis Abstracts, 1937-1954; From University of Oregon, University of Southern California, Springfield College, University of Utah. Urbana, Ill.: 1956.

1 vol. (various pagings)

Graduate theses and dissertations in health, physical education, and recreation. Arranged by institution and represents 48 abstracts from the University of Oregon for 1944-1954; 61 abstracts from the University of Southern California for 1940-1951; 57 abstracts from Springfield College for 1937-1954; and 31 abstracts from the University of Utah for 1947-1951. Abstracts indicate purpose, method, and conclusion.

G277. EELLS, Walter C. "American Doctoral Dissertations on Health, Physical Education, and Recreation in Foreign Countries." Research Quarterly 27 (March 1956): 119-121.

Lists 30 dissertations covering the period from 1909, arranged by country under continent.

G278. VAN VLIET, Maurice L. "Graduate Theses and Projects by Canadians." In his Physical Education in Canada, p. 306-315. Scarborough, Ont.: Prentice-Hall of Canada, 1965.

An alphabetical listing of 171 theses and dissertations completed in Canadian and American institutions.

G279. PRAGUE. Universita Karlova. Fakulta tělesné výchovy a sportu. Seznam diplomových prací [1966/1967-   ] Annual.

Compiled by Miloslava Waitová.

A classified listing of theses completed in the Faculty. Entry gives adviser.

G280. SOLLEDER, Marian K. "Theses, Dissertations, and Periodical References." In her Evaluation Instruments in Health Education. An Annotated Bibliography, p. 9-23. Washington: American Association for Health, Physical Education, and Recreation, 1969.

Lists studies completed in American institutions. Arranged under (1) elementary school, (2) junior high school, (3) senior high school.

G281. ABERNATHY, Thomas D. An Analysis of Master's and Doctoral

Studies Related to the History of Physical Education, Completed in the United States between 1930 and 1967. Urbana, Ill.: 1970. 109 p. (M.S. Thesis, University of Illinois)

Contains references to 203 theses and dissertations under such subjects as colleges and universities, physical education, biographies, physical education in foreign countries. Theses are listed under each topic and dissertations are abstracted.

G282. BEYRER, Mary K. Topical List of Theses and Dissertations in Health Education. Washington: American Association for Health, Physical Education, and Recreation, 1970. 42 p.

Compiled from Item G274; Research Quarterly, March 1958-May 1969; Health, Physical Education and Microcard Bulletin, 1949-1969; and Dissertation Abstracts 20 (1960)-29 (Feb. 1969).

A classified listing, covering such areas as community and public health, professional preparation, school health services, research. Entry gives adviser and reference to source where found.

G283. REED, James L. A Compendium of Selected Theses on Intramural Programs. Urbana, Ill.: 1971. 176 p. (M.S. Thesis, University of Illinois)

Lists abstracts of 55 theses under such topics as facilities and equipment, philosophy and history of intramurals, program evaluation, extramurals. Covers the period 1932-1965. Author index.

Recreation and Sports

G284. GLOSS, G. M. "Bibliography of Master's Theses and Doctoral Studies in the Field of Recreation (to December, 1939)." Research Quarterly 11 (March 1940): 150-163.

Lists approximately 400 items completed in American institutions, listed alphabetically by author.

G285. NAUCHNYE osnovy fizicheskogo vospitaniya i sport; Referativnyy sbornik dissertatsiy [1 (1958)-] Moskva: 1958- .

Abstracts of theses and dissertations defended in
the U.S.S.R. Arranged under such subjects as anatomy,
physiology, hygiene, physical culture, history, theory,
methods, gymnastics.

G286. "DISSERTATIONS: Their Authors and Titles." Parks and Recreation 42 (1959): 228-229.

Theses and dissertations of "contemporary" research
interest completed in American and Canadian universities related to parks and recreation. Arranged
by institution and type of degree.

G287. WEIDIG, Ursula. Bibliographie der Dissertationen aus Körperkultur, Körpererziehung, Sport und verwandten Gebieten; In-
und ausländische Dissertationen in deutscher Sprache sowie
an deutschen Universitäten verteidigte fremdsprachige Dissertationen von 1648 bis 1959. Mit einem Anhang: Habilitationsschriften. Hrsg. von der Bibliothek der Deutschen Hochschule
für Körperkultur. Leipzig: 1960. 128 p. (Veröffentlichung-
en der Bibliothek der Deutschen Hochschule für Körperkultur.
Sportbibliographien, 6)

_____ _____ Nachtrag [1-] Leipzig: 1962- . (Veröffentlichungen der Bibliothek der Deutschen Hochschule für
Körperkultur, 7-) Irregular.

With supplement 4 (1970) coverage is for German language dissertations only.

Arranged by broad subject groupings, i.e., philosophy, education; natural science; legal, governmental,
economic; medical and veterinary; and subdivided by
year. Supplements contain items omitted from earlier
numbers. Cumulative author and subject indexes.

G288. MESSINA, Vincent J. "Swimming--Theses and Dissertations."
Bulletin of Bibliography and Magazine Notes 24 (Jan.-April
1964): 62-68.

Also published as Bibliography of Swimming Theses
and Dissertations (1962).

Lists 280 items covering the period prior to June
1962, solicited from 436 colleges in the United
States. Includes some bachelor theses. Arranged
by state and institution within the state.

G289. PARKER, Franklin. "History of Sports and Physical Education; A Partial Bibliography of U.S.A. Doctoral Dissertations and Master's Theses." Paedagogica Historica 5 (1965): 503-510.

    In two parts: a listing of 49 Ph.D. and Ed.D. dissertations and a listing of 55 M.A. or M.Ed. theses. Covers the period to 1960. Entry gives reference to an abstract.

G290. ADELMAN, Melvin L. An Assessment of Sports History Theses in the United States, 1931-1967. Urbana, Ill.: 1970. 230 p. (M.S. Thesis, University of Illinois)

    The appendix contains (1) a classified list of 325 theses and dissertations under such subjects as the administration of intercollegiate athletics, biographical history, foreign culture, sports; and (2) an alphabetical author listing of abstracts of dissertations.

G291. VAN DER SMISSEN, Margaret E. and Donald V. Joyce. Bibliography of Theses and Dissertations in Recreation, Parks, Camping and Outdoor Education, 1970. Washington: National Recreation and Park Association, 1970. 555 p.

    Supersedes and integrates Margaret E. Van der Smissen, Bibliography of Research Related to Recreation (1962; first edition 1955, revised 1958) and its supplement by the National Recreation and Park Association, Research in Recreation, Part I (1965) and the thesis and dissertation section of the American Camping Association, Bibliography Related to Camping and Outdoor Recreation (1962) and Supplement (1966).

    An alphabetical author listing of nearly 4,000 theses and dissertations, many of which are described. Institution index and topical index for (1) camping and outdoor recreation and (2) recreation and parks.

G292. TRAVIS, Richard W. The Spatial Organization of Recreation: A Bibliography of Theses and Dissertations on the Geography of Recreation. Monticello, Ill.: 1972. 18 p. (Council of Planning Librarians Exchange Bibliography, no. 350)

    A listing of 195 theses and dissertations completed in American and Canadian geography departments during the period 1950-1971, arranged under broad

topics. Topics include impact of recreation on the
environment, economic impact of tourism and recreation, recreation resource legislation, perception of
recreation resources and recreational behavior,
demand, and planning. Activities and location indexes.

Higher Education

G293. EELLS, Walter C. Bibliography on Junior Colleges. Washington: U.S. Government Printing Office, 1930. 167 p. (U.S.
Office of Education. Bulletin, 1930, no. 2)

An alphabetical annotated bibliography. Twelve
dissertations and 61 theses are listed separately
in the index.

G294. MINNESOTA. University. College of Education. Committee on
Educational Research. Collegiate Educational Research,
University of Minnesota; The Report of the Committee on Edu-
cational Research for the Biennium [1928/1930-1930/1932]
Minneapolis: 1931-1933. 2 vols. (University of Minnesota
Bulletin, vol. 34, no. 7 (Feb. 1931); vol. 36, no. 1 (Jan.
1933))

On p. 128-148 of 1928/1930 volume is a list of
approximately 70 theses and dissertations completed
at the University of Minnesota in higher education.
Entry indicates contents. The volume for 1930/1932
(p. 30-31) provides a supplementary annotated listing of four dissertations and 25 theses.

G295. EELLS, Walter C. "Dissertations in the Junior College Field."
Community and Junior College Journal 2 (1932): 275-282.

Lists 117 theses and 20 dissertations written in
American institutions from 1916 to 1931. Author-
title list, arranged by institution, with reference
to its appearance in the author's Bibliography on
Junior Colleges (1930) (Item G293) or the "Bibliography on Junior Colleges," in Community and Junior
College Journal, where annotation may be found.

G296. ENGLEMAN, Lois E. and Walter C. Eells. The Literature of
Junior College Terminal Education. Prepared for the Commission on Junior Terminal Education. Washington: American

Association of Junior Colleges, 1941. 322 p. (Terminal Education Monograph, no. 1)

> An extensively annotated bibliography of all significant materials on the problems of terminal education at the junior college level published up to 1941. There are separate listings under theses and dissertations in the index.

G297. "HIGHER Education Theses." <u>American Education</u> 1, no. 1 (Jan. 1, 1945): 12; 1, no. 3 (Feb. 1, 1945): 12; 1, no. 4 (Feb. 15, 1945): 12; 7, no. 4 (Oct. 15, 1950): 45-46. Title varies.

> Annotated lists of dissertations and some theses on file in the U.S. Office of Education Library.

G298. HACKETT, Roger C. "Educational Research in Progress." <u>Community and Junior College Journal</u> 22 (1951): 219-223.

> A listing of 43 dissertations concerned with the junior college.

G299. EELLS, Walter C. <u>College Teachers and College Teaching; An Annotated Bibliography on College and University Faculty Members and Instructional Methods</u>. Atlanta: Southern Regional Education Board, 1957. 282 p.

> _____ _____ Supplement 1. Atlanta: Southern Regional Education Board, 1959. 134 p.

> _____ _____ Supplement 2. Atlanta: Southern Regional Education Board, 1962. 192 p.

> _____ _____ Supplement 3. Compiled by Maurice L. Litton and W. Hugh Stickler. Atlanta: Southern Regional Education Board, 1967. 124 p.

> A classified bibliography in which doctoral dissertations (and masters' theses in Supplements 1 and 2) are included. These are listed separately in the index of each volume.

G300. PARKER, Franklin. "American Doctoral Dissertations Pertaining to the History of the Community Junior College." <u>Paedagogica Historica</u> 1 (1961): 393.

An alphabetical author listing of 15 dissertations
completed in American institutions to 1958.

G301. EELLS, Walter C. "Dissertations on Improvement of College
Teaching--1960." Improving College and University Teaching
11 (1963): 51-54.

An alphabetical author listing of 121 dissertations
completed in the academic year 1960/1961. Entry
gives publication information.

G302. PARKER, Franklin and Anne Bailey. The Junior and Community
College: A Bibliography of Doctoral Dissertations, 1918-1963.
Washington: American Association of Junior Colleges, 1965.
47 p.

Supersedes Stanley Hergenroeder, Bibliography of
Doctoral Dissertations Accepted for Degrees in
Junior and Community College Education, 1934-1962
(1962); Franklin Parker, "American Doctoral Dissertations Pertaining to the History of the Community
Junior College." Paedagogica Historica 2 (1961):
393; Franklin Parker, "Community Junior College,
l'Enfant Terrible of American Higher Education: A
Bibliography of 225 Doctoral Dissertations." Community and Junior College Journal 32 (1961): 193-
204; and Walter C. Eells, "Junior College Doctoral
Dissertations--Supplementary List." Community and
Junior College Journal 33 (1962): 16-19.

Lists approximately 600 dissertations completed in
American institutions alphabetically by author
within 14 subject headings. Entry gives institution
and date. Author index.

G303. OGILVIE, William K. Abstracts of Graduate Studies in the
Community (Junior) College, 1961-1966. DeKalb, Ill.: Northern Illinois University, Community College Service Center,
1966. 79 p.

ED 013 607

Abstracts of 21 theses completed at Northern Illinois
University (DeKalb). Includes work done in departments other than education. Entry gives adviser.

G304. ROUECHE, John E. The Junior and Community College: A Bibliography of Doctoral Dissertations, 1964-1966. Los Angeles: University of California, ERIC Clearinghouse for Junior College Information, 1967. 16 p.

>ED 013 656.

>Published by the American Association of Junior Colleges.

>An alphabetical author listing of 214 dissertations completed in American institutions. Entry gives major subjects covered. Subject and institution index.

G305. "DISSERTATIONS Completed: Dissertations in Progress." Community and Junior College Journal 39 (1968/1969)-42 (1971/1972). Annual.

>In two parts, dissertations completed and dissertations in progress. Dissertations completed cover those completed from 1967 or not included in Item G304. Dissertations in progress section gives title and institution.

History of Education

G306. PARKER, Franklin. "Biographies of Educators; A Partial Bibliography of 153 Doctoral Dissertations." Peabody Journal of Education 40 (1962): 142-149.

>Supersedes his Biographies of Educators; A Partial Bibliography of 120 Doctoral Dissertations (1959). Also appeared in Paedagogica Historica 2 (1962): 389-393.

>Covers the period 1924-1962.

G307. AHLUWALIA, Sudarshan P. "Investigations in the History of Education (Conducted and Completed by Candidates Who Were Awarded Doctoral Degrees in Education--D.Litt./Ph.D./D.Phil. --by the Indian Universities during the Period 1939-1961)." Paedagogica Historica 5 (1965): 198-200.

>Lists 25 dissertations.

_____ _____ "1962-1966." <u>Paedagogica Historica</u> 10 (1970): 621-622.

Lists 13 dissertations.

G308. PARK, Joe. <u>The Rise of American Education; An Annotated Bibliography</u>. Evanston, Ill.: Northwestern University, 1965. 216 p.

Section 10, "Doctoral Dissertations Available on Microfilm" (p. 183-188), is an alphabetical listing of approximately 70 items located in <u>Dissertation Abstracts</u>.

G309. PARKER, Franklin. "History of Educational Foundations; Partially Annotated Bibliography of 36 Doctoral Dissertations." <u>Paedagogica Historica</u> 6 (1966): 241-244.

Lists dissertations completed in the United States up to 1963 alphabetically by author.

G310. HISTORY OF EDUCATION SOCIETY. <u>A List of Theses for Higher Degrees in British Universities Completed in</u> [1968-   ] Cambridge, Eng.: Cambridge University, Institute of Education [1969-   ] Title varies. Annual. ?

Compiled by T. G. Cook.

Home Economics Education

G311. WELCH, Lila M. and Mary R. Lingenfelter. <u>Studies of the Home-Economics Curriculum: An Annotated Bibliography</u>. Columbus, Ohio: Bureau of Educational Research, 1930. 46 p. (Ohio State University. Bureau of Educational Research. Bibliographies in Education, no. 1, June 1930)

Compiled for the American Vocational Association. Research Committee. Home Economics Subcommittee.

Contains a separate retrospective listing of 65 theses accepted by departments of home economics during the period 1914-1929 (p. 37-42). Arranged by institution. Subject index.

G312. "ABSTRACTS of Theses in Home Economics Education Completed during the Year 1930-31." In U.S. Federal Board for Vocational Education. Suggestions for Studies and Research in Home Economics Education, p. 57-74. Washington: 1932. 77 p. (Its Bulletin, no. 166; Home Economics Series, no. 15)

> A classified listing of theses and dissertations covering curriculum, methods of instruction, administration, and education. Entry gives scope and method of study, and outstanding findings and conclusions. Index.

G313. U.S. Office of Education. Bibliography of Studies of the Home Economics Curriculum, 1926-1934. Prepared by a Committee of the Home Economics Section of the Association of Land-Grant Colleges and Universities. Washington: 1934. 70 p. (Its Vocational Education Bulletin, no. 179; Home Economics Series, no. 17)

> The majority of the studies listed are theses and dissertations. Arranged under the headings adult education, college, elementary school, secondary school, and miscellany. Author and subject indexes.

G314. U.S. Office of Education. Vocational Division. Studies and Research in Home Economics Education Reported by Colleges and Universities. Washington: 1937. 98 p. (Its Miscellany 1163 rev.)

> First edition published in 1932 as its Miscellany 1163 and subsequently revised in 1934 and 1936.
>
> Lists theses completed in the period 1905-1935. Arranged by state, subdivided by institution.

_____ Subject Index of the Theses Studies in Home Economics Education. Washington: 1937. 32 p. (Its Miscellany 1173 rev.)

> First edition published as its Miscellany 1173 (1936).

G315. U.S. Office of Education. Abstracts of Studies in Home Economics Education, 1934-1938. Home Economics Education. September 1938. Washington: 1938. 43 p. (U.S. Office of Education. Vocational Division. Miscellany 2114)

> Abstracts of theses and graduate studies completed

in American universities. Arranged by academic
year, subdivided into administration, curriculum,
measurement, and methods of instruction.

G316. MATHER, Marguerite. Studies in Home Economics Education,
1918-1940, Reported in Published Form, Home Economics
Education, May 1940. Washington: U.S. Office of Education,
Vocational Division, 1940. 20 p. (U.S. Office of Education.
Vocational Division. Miscellany 2381)

"Colleges and Universities" (p. 1-8) lists approximately 50 theses and dissertations completed in
American universities by institution. Subject index.

G317. U.S. Office of Education. Vocational Education Division.
Studies on the Teaching of Home Economics in Colleges and
Universities, 1955-1956. Compiled by Ivol Spafford in coop-
eration with Edna P. Amidon. Washington: 1959. 144 p.
(Its Bulletin, no. 276; Home Economics Series, no. 31)

An analysis of theses and dissertations which includes
work done in years other than indicated in title.
Citations for theses and dissertations appear as
footnotes in the text. Index.

Language Teaching

G318. FOSTER, Richard A. and Margaret Hampel. "Unpublished Studies
in Elementary School English." Elementary English 17 (1940):
117-122, 194-198, 240-245, 290-292.

Pt. 1 is an author listing of 64 items, the largest
portion of which are unpublished theses (a few dissertations included). Pt. 2 consists of abstracts
of the majority of the unpublished studies. Pt. 3
is "Summary and Comments."

G319. "DISSERTATSIY po germanskoy i romanskoy filologii i metodike
prepodavnya inostrannykh yazykov, zashchishchennye v [1950/
1951-1960]" Inostrannye yazyki v shkole, 1952-1961. Title
varies. Irregular.

Lists theses and dissertations defended in U.S.S.R.
institutions on the Germanic and Romance languages
and the methodology of foreign language teaching.

G320. WINGARD, Peter. "Theses and Dissertations." English Language Teaching (London) 22 (1968): 277-279.

A select list of theses and dissertations completed in the Manchester University Department of Education between 1964 and 1967 which deal with English as a second language. Arranged chronologically.

Music Education

G321. MUSIC EDUCATORS NATIONAL CONFERENCE. Committee on Bibliography of Research Projects and Theses. Bibliography of Research Studies in Music Education, 1932-1948. Revised ed. Prepared by William S. Larson, Chicago: 1949. 119 p.

First edition, covering the years 1932-1944, was prepared by Arnold M. Small for the Committee on Research in Music Education, reorganized in 1944 under the name Committee on Bibliography of Research Projects and Theses, and was published by the State University of Iowa in 1944.

Contains over 1,600 theses and dissertations "which make a contribution to the teaching of music." Arranged by state, then institution. Extensive topical index.

_____ _____ Supplement. 1949. 4 p.

Prepared as an inset. Contains approximately 350 additional titles.

Continued by:

G322. LARSON, William S. "Bibliography of Research Studies in Music Education, 1949-1956." Journal of Research in Music Education 5 (1957): 61-225.

Incorporates titles from Item G321 and its supplement, which appeared in Music Educators Journal 37 (1949/1950)-43 (1956/1957).

Lists about 2,000 completed theses and dissertations from 75 institutions "which make a contribution to the teaching of music," arranged by state, university, and then author. Includes items not in main list. Topical index.

G323. WORTHINGTON, Richard A. _A Review of Doctoral Dissertations in Music Education_. Ann Arbor, Mich.: University Microfilms, 1957. 581 p. (Ed.D. Dissertation, University of Illinois, 1956)

> An analytic review of 391 dissertations completed from 1940 to 1954 submitted by candidates majoring in music education or by students interested in the area of music education.

G324. "CRITIQUES." _In_ Council for Research in Music Education. _Bulletin_, no. 1 (1963)-   . Semiannual.

> Extensive evaluations of three to ten dissertations in each number.

G325. BORG, Earl R. _A Codified Bibliography of Music Education Research at the Master's Level in Selected Institutions_. Ann Arbor: University Microfilms, 1964. 2 vols. (Ph.D., Northwestern University)

> Vol. 2 contains an extensive listing of theses from selected institutions of the North Central Association of Colleges and Universities, arranged by institution. Covers the years 1936-1962. The codification provides such information as educational level of the subjects of the data, research procedure, sources of data, size of sampling, intent of project, use for data, and topic (subject or area) of research. Classified index. Appendixes include an author index, list of unexamined studies, and bibliography of studies at the master's and doctoral level related to experimental and testing research.

G326. "THESES and Dissertations Submitted to Colorado Colleges and Universities [1963-1967]" _Colorado Journal of Research in Music Education_ 1 (1964)-4 (1968). Annual. Spring issue.

> Alphabetical lists by author. Entry gives degree and institution. In first two lists several of the items are analyzed in "Reviews," which follows the list.

G327. GORDON, Roderick D. "Doctoral Dissertations in Music and Music Education, 1957-1963." _Journal of Research in Music_

Education 12 (1964): 7-112.

> An alphabetical author listing. Includes material
> from fields other than music education, such as
> acoustics, psychology, tests and measurements, as
> well as historical musicology, if relevant. Some
> pre-1957 items omitted from Item G322 are included,
> as are some foreign dissertations. Topical index.

> Supplemented by:

G328. _____ "Doctoral Dissertations in Music and Music Education
[1963/1964-   ]" Journal of Research in Music Education
13 (1965)-   . Annual.

> An alphabetical author listing.

> Cumulated in:

G329. _____ "Doctoral Dissertations in Music and Music Education,
1963-1967." Journal of Research in Music Education 16 (1968):
83-216.

> Continued by:

_____ "Doctoral Dissertations in Music and Music Education,
1968-1971." Journal of Research in Music Education 20
(1972): 2-190.

> Includes dissertations previously omitted, as well
> as those reported incompletely or inaccurately.
> Parenthetical notes indicate languages, format, or
> instruments. Author listing with topical index.

G330. MATHISON, Curtis. "A Bibliography of Research on the Evaluation of Music Teacher Education Programs." Journal of
Research in Music Education 19 (1971): 106-114.

> Contains an "Annotated Bibliography of Disserta-
> tions" (p. 106-113), which includes all pertinent
> items found in Dissertation Abstracts, vols. 26
> (1966)-30 (1969), classified under "Music" and
> "Education."

Reading

G331. BETTS, Emmett A. and Thelma M. Betts. An Index to Professional Literature on Reading and Related Topics (to January 1, 1943). New York: American Book Co., 1945. 137 p.

Lists 8,278 references in an alphabetical arrangement. Theses and dissertations from many universities are included.

G332. SUMMERS, Edward G. "Dissertations in College Reading: 1918 to October 1960." Journal of Reading 4 (1961): 268-271.

Chronological listing of 61 dissertations on reading among college students completed at American institutions.

G333. _____ "Doctoral Dissertation Research in Elementary and Secondary Reading: 1958-1959 and 1960." Journal of Reading 5 (1962): 232-244.

A classified listing of 111 items reported in Dissertation Abstracts for the 1958-1960 period.

Continued by:

G334. _____ "Doctoral Dissertation Research in Reading Reported for [1961-1970]" Journal of Reading 6 (1963)-14 (1970/1971).

Annotated author listings of studies reported in Dissertation Abstracts. Covers elementary, secondary, and college reading.

Supplemented by:

G335. SUMMERS, Edward G. and others. "Doctoral Dissertations in Secondary Reading [1966-1968]" Journal of Reading 12 (1969): 627-654, 681-696; 13 (1970): 597-602, 638-642.

Abstracts of dissertations located in Dissertation Abstracts. Entry gives adviser and purchase information.

G336. DURRELL, Donald D. and Helen A. Murphy. "Boston University Research in Elementary School Reading, 1933-1963." Journal of Education 146 (Dec. 1963): 1-53.

Abstracts of 497 theses and dissertations completed

at Boston University for the Ed.M. and Ed.D. brought together by subject. The items abstracted are arranged alphabetically by author immediately following each section.

Continued by:

G337. CHAMBERS, J. Richard and Roselmina Indrisano. "Boston University Research in Elementary School Reading (1963-1969) and Language Arts (1927-1969)." Journal of Education 154 (April 1972): 3-68.

Follows same format as Item G336 and represents the work of approximately 600 students. A final section lists theses and dissertations not included in the body of the work.

G338. U.S. Office of Education. Research in Reading at the Primary Level; An Annotated Bibliography. By Doris V. Gunderson. Washington: 1963. 114 p. (Its Bulletin, 1963, no. 42)

Summaries of research from 1955 to 1960, approximately half of which are theses and dissertations. In two parts: (1) "Summary of Research in Teaching of Primary Reading," and (2) "Studies in the Teaching of Primary Reading." Each is subdivided into major topics. Pt. 2 lists the abstracts of the studies within each topic, giving the purpose and the conclusions.

G339. FAY, Leo C., Weldon G. Bradtmueller, and Edward G. Summers. Doctoral Studies in Reading, 1919 through 1960. Bloomington, Ind.: Indiana University, Bureau of Education Studies and Testing, 1964. 80 p. (Indiana University. School of Education. Bulletin, vol. 40, no. 4)

A classified listing of 701 dissertations completed within the period 1919-1961. Bibliography is preceded by a summary statement of the items included in each category. Author index.

G340. SUMMERS, Edward G. Recent Doctoral Dissertation Research in Reading. Bloomington, Ind.: ERIC Clearinghouse on Retrieval of Information and Evaluation of Reading, 1967. 214 p. (ERIC/CRIER Reading Review Series, vol. 1, Bibliography,

no. 2)

ED 012 693.

Lists 379 completed dissertations in the areas of preschool, elementary, secondary, college, and adult reading from 1960 and reported in Dissertation Abstracts 21 (1960)-26 (1966). Entry includes abstract which indicates procedure, design, and conclusion of the study.

Continued by:

G341. _____ _____ Supplement 1. Bloomington, Ind.: ERIC Clearinghouse on Retrieval of Information and Evaluation of Reading, 1969. 178 p. (ERIC/CRIER Reading Review Series Bibliography, no. 14)

ED 028 055.

Abstracts of 344 dissertations listed in Dissertation Abstracts 27 (1966) and 28 (1968) in the areas of preschool, elementary, secondary, college, and adult reading. Abstract gives procedures, design, and conclusion. Entry gives adviser. Indexed by author, subject, and grade level in Indexes to ERIC/CRIER Basic References.

Continued by:

G342. LONGSTREET, Wilma and Edward G. Summers. Recent Doctoral Dissertation Research in Reading, Supplement 2. Bloomington, Ind.: ERIC Clearinghouse on Retrieval of Information and Evaluation of Reading, 1970. 103 p. (Reading Review Series Bibliography, no. 24)

ED 035 793.

An alphabetical author listing of abstracts of 192 dissertations in preschool, elementary, secondary, college, and adult reading found in Dissertation Abstracts 29 (July 1968–June 1969). Abstracts are based on information found therein and include procedure, design, and conclusion. Entry gives publication information.

G343. DUKER, Sam. Individualized Reading: An Annotated Bibliography.

Metuchen, N.J.: Scarecrow Press, 1968. 209 p.

Supersedes his "Master's Studies in Individualized Reading" in Elementary English 40 (1963): 280-282.

The subject index provides separate listings for 24 dissertations and for 123 theses.

Continued and supplemented by:

G344. _____ "Master's Studies in Individualized Reading II." Elementary English 47 (1970): 656-660.

Represents 90 theses completed since 1961 and 25 pre-1961 theses omitted from the earlier list.

G345. PI LAMBDA THETA. Lambda Chapter. Annotated List of Ph.D. Dissertations in Reading, 1916-1969. Chicago: University of Chicago, Dept. of Education, 1970. 20 p.

An annotated author listing of 72 dissertations completed at the University of Chicago on topics related to reading and the teaching of reading.

G346. FAY, Leo C. and Ivan J. Quandt. "Doctoral Research in Reading and Language Arts at Indiana University." Viewpoints 47 (1971): 101-180.

Summaries of 114 dissertations completed at Indiana University in the English language arts between 1941 and 1970. The items are arranged by topic and for each are given the age of the subjects studied, type of research approach used, and topic. Index of authors by year of dissertation.

Religious Education

G347. NATIONAL COUNCIL OF THE CHURCHES OF CHRIST OF THE UNITED STATES OF AMERICA. Bureau of Research and Survey. Selected Doctoral Theses in Religious Education [no. 1 (1933)-10 (1942)] Chicago: 1933-1943. Title varies. Annual.

Nos. 1 (1933)-6 (1938) include theses as well as dissertations. In two parts, an alphabetical author listing of abstracts and a listing by institution.

Entry gives publication information.

G348. "ABSTRACTS of Doctoral Dissertations in Religious Education."
Religious Education 38 (1943)-   . Title varies. Irregular.

A classified list appearing in one issue of most
years, presenting short abstracts of selected dissertations completed in the previous academic year
(1973 list is for 1970/1971) for the Ph.D., Ed.D.,
Th.D., S.T.D., D.Div. degrees. Selection is made
from Dissertation Abstracts. Entry gives reference
to Dissertation Abstracts.

G349. EELLS, Walter C. "American Doctoral Dissertations on Religion Written by Women in the Nineteenth Century." Religious
Education 52 (1957): 204-205.

Eleven dissertations are listed. The earliest is
1888. Entry indicates previous degrees (institution and dates) and publication information.

G350. NATIONAL CONFERENCE OF CHRISTIANS AND JEWS. Dissertations
and Theses in Religion and Public Education; A Partial
Listing. Compiled by Elizabeth D. Norris for the Religion
and Public Education Committee, Commission on Religious
Organization, The National Conference on Christians and Jews.
New York: 1958. 6 p.

A classified listing of studies completed or underway.

G351. DROUIN, Edmund G. The School Question; A Bibliography on
Church-State Relationships in American Education, 1940-1960.
Washington: Catholic University of America Press, 1963.
261 p.

Contains over 140 theses and dissertations, which
are listed in a separate section under each of the
major topics.

G352. LITTLE, Lawrence C. Religion and Public Education: A Bibliography. Pittsburgh: University of Pittsburgh, School of
Education, Program in Religious Education, 1966. 203 p.

Contains (1) an alphabetical author listing of dissertations indicating the type of degree and refer-

ence to <u>Dissertation Abstracts</u> (p. 42-57); and (2)
an alphabetical author listing of bachelor of divinity and masters' theses (p. 58-81). Covers the
period to 1964.

G353. WHEATON COLLEGE. Library. <u>Graduate Theses in Christian</u>
<u>Education Written at Wheaton College, 1938-1970</u>. Wheaton,
Ill.: 1970? 27 p.

An alphabetical author listing of masters' theses.

Safety Education

G354. SCHOR, Gene. "Research in Safety Education." <u>Safety Educa-</u>
<u>tion</u> 21 (Feb. 1942): 254-257.

Covers the period 1927-1941, listing 80 studies.
Theses and dissertations are listed separately.

G355. NEW YORK UNIVERSITY. Division of General Education. Center
for Safety Education. <u>Research Studies in Safety Education:</u>
<u>Research on the Doctoral Level or Equivalent Level and</u>
<u>Research Needs in Safety Education</u>. New York: 1948. ?

G356. YOST, Charles P. <u>An Analysis of Graduate Theses in School</u>
<u>Safety in the United States from 1925 to 1950</u>. Ann Arbor,
Mich.: University Microfilms, 1957. 459 p. (Ph.D. Dissertation, University of Pittsburgh, 1956)

Alphabetical listing of 298 theses and dissertations,
p. 235-254.

Science and Mathematics Education

G357. EELLS, Walter C. "American Doctoral Dissertations on Scientific and Mathematical Education in Foreign Countries."
<u>Science Education</u> 43 (1959): 274-275.

Thirty-three items written from 1905 to 1955.

G358. SUMMERS, Edward G. "Elementary and Secondary Science and
Mathematics Dissertations Reported in 1962." <u>School Science</u>

and Mathematics 63 (1963): 733-738.

In part continues Item G371.

Lists 85 titles reported in Dissertation Abstracts arranged by elementary and secondary levels under major areas of science and mathematics.

Continued by:

G359. "DOCTORAL Dissertation Research in Science and Mathematics Reported for [1964-   ]" School Science and Mathematics 67 (1967)-   . Title varies. Annual.

Continues Item G366.

Lists dissertations reported in Dissertation Abstracts related to science and mathematics. Arranged by elementary, secondary, teacher education, and college levels under the headings science and mathematics.

Biology

G360. "UNPUBLISHED Masters Theses." American Biology Teacher 11 (1949): 129-130.

Eighteen theses selected from a list which the National Association for Research in Science Teaching was compiling, including "unpublished theses or other manuscripts dealing with science teaching." Theses in this selection cover the period 1929-1940.

Chemistry

G361. BESKOV, C. D. "Dissertatsiy po metodike prepodavannya khimii (za period s 1953 po 1959 g.)." Khimiya v shkole, 1960, no. 2: 92-94, no. 3: 86-92.

A chronologically arranged annotated listing of 21 dissertations on the teaching of chemistry.

Mathematics

G362. EELLS, Walter C. "American Doctoral Dissertations on Mathematics and Astronomy Written by Women in the Nineteenth Century." Mathematics Teacher 50 (1957): 374-376.

A listing of 11 women, with their birth and death dates and bibliographical data on their dissertations.

G363. SUMMERS, Edward G. "A Bibliography of Doctoral Dissertations Completed in Elementary and Secondary Mathematics from 1918 to 1952." School Science and Mathematics 61 (1961): 323-335.

Lists 267 dissertations completed in American institutions arranged by broad topics under the headings secondary and elementary.

G364. SUMMERS, Edward G. and James E. Stochl. "A Bibliography of Doctoral Dissertations Completed in Elementary and Secondary Mathematics from 1950 to 1960." School Science and Mathematics 61 (1961): 431-439.

Lists 143 dissertations completed in American institutions, arranged by broad topic under headings elementary (through grade six) and secondary.

G365. KHORUNOV, R. KH. "Dissertatsionnye rabaty po nachertatel'noy geometrii i grafike (1937-1960 gg.)." In Voprosy nachertatel'noy geometrii i. inz. grafiki, p. 161-172. Tashkent: 1963. (Tashkent. Institut inzhenerov zheleznodorozhnogo transporta. Sbornik trudov, vyp. 26)

Lists approximately 250 studies completed in the U.S.S.R.

G366. SUMMERS, Edward G. and Hubrig, Billie. "Doctoral Dissertation Research in Mathematics Reported for 1963." School Science and Mathematics 65 (1965): 505-528.

Abstracts of dissertations reported in Dissertation Abstracts arranged under the headings elementary, secondary, teacher education, and college levels. Abstracts provide major problem and conclusions. Entry gives adviser.

G367. SUYDAM, Marilyn N. and J. Fred Weaver. "Research on Mathematics Education (K-12) Reported in [1970-]" Journal for Research in Mathematics Education 2 (1971)- . Annual.

> A separate section of "Dissertation Abstracts" lists dissertations completed in American institutions since 1968. Arranged alphabetically by author. Entry gives descriptive note.

Physics

G368. "DISSERTATSIY zashchishchennye v 1954-1962 gg." Fizika v shkole, 1963, no. 1: 110-112.

> A chronological listing of 69 studies on methods of teaching physics.

Science

G369. NATIONAL ASSOCIATION FOR RESEARCH IN SCIENCE TEACHING. Committee on Research in Science Teaching. "General Science Bibliography: Unpublished Titles Arranged by Subjects and Authors, 1928-1940." Science Education 32 (1948): 183-185.

_____ "A Partial Bibliography of Theses and Dissertations." Science Education 33 (1949): 176-179.

_____ "Reviews of Unpublished Investigations of General Science." Science Education 34 (1950): 188-191.

> Primarily masters' theses. The first two lists are compiled from Item G4. The first listing gives the name of the author only; list two is by school and gives the author's name only; list three is an author listing with full bibliographic information and includes 20 items not previously reported.

G370. GOOSSEN, Carl V. and Edward G. Summers. "Bibliography of Doctoral Dissertations Reported in Elementary and Secondary Science from 1918 to 1952." School Science and Mathematics 62 (1962): 99-110.

> A classified list of 216 dissertations from American universities. Arranged under major headings: secondary, elementary, and unspecified as to level.

Continued by:

G371. SUMMERS, Edward G. and Ronald W. Mitchell. "Doctoral Research in Elementary and Secondary Science, 1952 to 1961." School Science and Mathematics 63 (1963): 27-37.

Continued by Item G358.

A topical listing of 183 dissertations reported in Dissertation Abstracts, arranged under the headings secondary and elementary.

Secondary Education

G372. "CURRENT Research in the Field of Secondary Education." Journal of Secondary Education 14 (1939)-23 (Feb. 1948).

A series of one to three reviews in each issue of significant research in secondary education. Nearly all are theses or dissertations, most of them done in California. Entry gives a report and evaluation.

G373. "THESES Written on School Assemblies." In National Association of Secondary School Principals. Bulletin 30 (1946): 224-227.

Part of "The Assembly Program in the Secondary Schools," under the direction of C. C. Harvey.

Lists 70 unpublished theses written at all graduate schools of education between 1925 and 1946 on the aims, organization, and practices of school assemblies in secondary schools.

G374. EELLS, Walter C. "American Doctoral Dissertations on Secondary Education in Foreign Countries." In National Association of Secondary School Principals. Bulletin 40 (1956): 166-175.

Geographical listing of 121 dissertations from 23 American universities from 1904. Represents work on 31 countries, with Canada having the largest number, followed by China and India.

G375. PARKER, Franklin. The American High School; A Bibliography of 424 Doctoral Dissertations. Austin, Tex.: 1959. 30 p.

Alphabetical listing covering the period 1904-1959.

G376. _____ Doctoral Dissertations Pertainins to the History of High School Education. Austin, Tex.: 1959. 4 p.

Alphabetical author list of 42 American dissertations covering the period 1904-1959.

G377. _____ "American Doctoral Dissertations Pertaining to the History of the Junior High School." Paedagogica Historica 1 (1961): 392-393.

Lists seven dissertations completed to 1958.

G378. _____ "Fifty Years of the Junior High School; Preface to a Bibliography of 131 Doctoral Dissertations." In National Association of Secondary School Principals. Bulletin 46 (1962): 435-445.

Also appeared as a separate in 1961.

Preceded by a discussion of the history of the junior high school. Alphabetical author list.

G379. _____ "The American High School: A Bibliography of 422 Doctoral Dissertations." Illinois State University Journal 29, no. 1 (1966): 9-31.

An alphabetical author listing, covering the period 1918-1959.

G380. McGLASSON, Maurice A. and Vernon D. Pace. Junior High School and Middle School Education; Indiana University Research. Bloomington, Ind.: Indiana University, School of Education, 1971.

"Doctoral Theses Reviewed" (p. 126-129) is an alpha-betical author listing of the approximately 55 dis-sertations analyzed, representing work done at Ind-iana University between 1953 and 1970.

Social Sciences

G381. "SPISOK dissertatsiy po metodike istorii i obshchestvovede-
niya zashchishchennykh [1945-1968 gg.]" Prepodavanie istorii
v shkole, 1954, vyp. 2: 125-128; 1957, vyp. 2: 116-119; 1969,
vyp. 1: 122-125.

> Lists in 1954 and 1957 cover 1945-1956; 1969 list
> covers 1957-1968.

> Alphabetical author listing of studies completed
> in the U.S.S.R.

> Translated by:

G382. HANKIN, Robert. "List of Dissertations on Methods in History and Social Sciences Defended between 1957 and 1968."
Soviet Education, 1954, no. 2: 125-128; 1957, no. 2: 116-
119; 1969, no. 1: 53-64.

G383. EELLS, Walter C. "Doctoral Theses on Social Studies in
Foreign Countries." Social Education 20 (1956): 23-26, 28.

> An arrangement of 82 American dissertations by
> region and country. Covers the period 1913-1954.

G384. KING, James H. A Critical Analysis of Experimental Doctoral
Research in Teaching Secondary School Social Studies, 1941-
1957. 193 p. (D.Ed. Dissertation, University of Colorado,
1959)

> Cites approximately 150 dissertations completed
> between 1940 and 1958. "Published Doctoral Disser-
> tations," p. 177; "Unpublished Doctoral Disserta-
> tions," p. 178-184; "Abstracts of Doctoral Disser-
> tations," p. 184-193. Last listing indicates
> location of abstract.

G385. McPHIE, Walter E. Dissertations in Social Studies Education;
A Comprehensive Guide. Washington: National Council for the
Social Studies, 1964. 99 p. (National Council for the
Social Studies. Research Bulletin, no. 2)

> An enlarged listing of what originally appeared as
> pt. 2 of his Factors in the Use and Value of Disser-

tations in Social Studies Education, 1934-1957 (Ph.
D. Dissertation, Stanford University, 1959).

A classified listing of 566 dissertations completed
between 1934 and 1962 (some for 1963). Entry gives
publication information and includes a summary of
the study. Author and subject indexes.

Continued by:

G386. GROSS, Richard E. and Leonardo De La Cruz. Social Studies
Dissertations, 1963-1969. Boulder, Colo.: ERIC Clearinghouse for Social Studies/Social Science Education, 1971.
285 p.

ED 054 999.

Abstracts of 216 American dissertations listed
under curriculum, instruction, cognition and learning, teacher education and teacher evaluation, and
general, and subdivided under each by elementary,
secondary, college, and general. Subject and
author indexes.

Teacher Education

G387. "DOCTORAL Studies on the Education of Teachers and Administrators [1950/1951-1965/1966]" Journal of Teacher Education
3 (1952)-19 (1968). Title varies. Annual.

None published in vol. 18 (1967).

This listing of American and Canadian dissertations
is carried in the section "With the Researchers."
That portion dealing with administrators begins with
the listing for 1956/1957 in vol. 9 (1958). Arranged
by such subjects as provision and administration of
teacher education, education of administrators, pre-
service and in-service education.

G388. EELLS, Walter C. "American Doctoral Dissertations on Teacher
Education in Foreign Countries." Journal of Teacher Education 6 (1955): 301-304.

Lists 82 dissertations written at American institutions since 1904, including works on teacher organi-

zations, welfare, and working conditions. Arranged geographically.

G389. PARKER, Franklin. "Bibliography of Doctoral Dissertations in Teacher Education." Teacher Education 24, no. 2 (1961): 1-39.

Whole number; also appeared as a separate in 1959.

An alphabetical author listing of studies completed in the United States in the period 1904-1959. Subject index.

G390. _____ "Doctoral Dissertations Pertaining to the History of Teacher Education." Paedagogica Historica 3 (1963): 203-204.

Previously published in 1959.

An alphabetical author listing of 26 dissertations completed in American institutions from 1912 to 1959, primarily on teacher education in the United States.

G391. "ABSTRACTS of Doctoral Dissertations Completed by Research Assistants in the Teacher Education Research Project (under the Direction of Joseph C. Bledsoe), University of Georgia, 1965-1968." Journal of Research and Development in Education 2 (Fall 1968): 87-114.

Dissertations submitted at the University of Georgia College of Education for the Ed.D.

Vocabulary Studies

G392. CAVANAUGH, Mildred R. A Survey of Unpublished Reading Vocabulary Studies from the First to the Sixth Grade. Philadelphia: Temple University, 1938. 345 p. (M.E. Thesis, Temple University)

The 61 theses analyzed in the study are listed on p. 241-247. These cover the period 1926 through 1936.

G393. CURTIS, Francis D. Investigations of Vocabulary in Textbooks of Science for Secondary Schools. Boston: Ginn, 1938. 127 p.

"Bibliography of the Unpublished Investigations
Incorporated in This Book" (p. 121-127) lists 66
graduate student studies (mostly masters') completed
at the University of Michigan Graduate School from
1931 through 1937.

G394. DALE, Edgar. Bibliography of Vocabulary Studies. Columbus:
Ohio State University, Bureau of Educational Research, 1949.
101 p.

A revision of the 1939 edition, which did not include dissertations and theses.

Includes titles of all unpublished theses and dissertations in the field from the U.S. Office of
Education file (which is incomplete from 1943) and
from the Ohio State University file of abstracts of
work completed at other universities, up to July
1948.

Arranged by subject. Entry gives publication
information. Author index.

Vocational Education

G395. IOWA. State University of Science and Technology, Ames.
Titles of Master's Theses Accepted at Iowa State College in
the Departments of Vocational Education, Home Economics
Education and Industrial Arts, 1921-June, 1932. Ames: 1932.
20 p.

Supersedes 1931 edition.

Approximately 220 theses arranged chronologically
under such broad topics as administration and supervision of rural education, agricultural education,
industrial education, vocational guidance.

G396. HUNTER, William L. Annotated List of Graduate Theses to
1933 and Dissertations in Industrial Arts Education Accepted
by Institutions of Higher Learning in Iowa. Ames, Iowa: Iowa
State College, 1933. 13 p.

Alphabetical author listing of 80 theses and dissertations in industrial arts education and in vocational-
industrial education completed at the State University

of Iowa (Iowa City) and the Iowa State University (Ames).

G397. MANUAL ARTS CONFERENCE. Special Research Committee. Annotated List of 800 Graduate Theses and Dissertations in Industrial-Arts Education and Vocational-Industrial Education Accepted in Institutions of Higher Learning in the United States, 1892-1933. Compiled for the Twenty-fourth Manual Arts Conference, 1933. Ames, Iowa: Iowa State College Industrial Arts Dept., 1933. 89 p.

> An alphabetical author listing. Not all items are annotated.

G398. GEORGE PEABODY COLLEGE FOR TEACHERS, Nashville, Tenn. Department of Industrial Education. Master's Theses on Industrial Subjects. Nashville: 1934. 24 p.

> An alphabetical listing of theses done at Peabody to 1933. Includes theses from other departments related to Smith-Hughes work, industrial subjects, and those dealing with teaching methods applicable to industrial arts.

> "Supplement" (p. 13-24) covers the period 1934-1935 and includes both theses and dissertations.

G399. HUNTER, William L. Abstracts of Graduate Theses and Dissertations in Industrial Arts Education and Vocational-Industrial Education Accepted by Institutions of Higher Learning in Pennsylvania, 1921-33. Ames, Iowa: Iowa State College, Industrial Arts Department, 1934. 16 p.

> An alphabetical author listing of 52 studies completed at the Universities of Temple, Pittsburgh, Pennsylvania, and Pennsylvania State. Entry gives purpose, procedure, and findings of the study. Topical index.

G400. _____ Theses Pertaining to Industrial Arts Education, Iowa State College, 1922-1935. Ames, Iowa: Iowa State College, 1935. 18 p.

> An annotated author listing of 106 theses completed at Iowa State University.

G401. BAWDEN, William T. <u>Annotated Bibliography of Master's Theses and Theses Problems. Department of Industrial Education from 1938-1943</u>. Pittsburg, Kans.: Kansas State Teachers College, 1945. 21 p.

Lists 49 studies chronologically. Author index.

G402. U.S. Office of Education. Vocational Education Division. <u>Research in Industrial Education: Summaries of Studies, 1930-1955</u>. Washington: U.S. Government Printing Office, 1957. 527 p. (<u>Its</u> Bulletin, no. 264)

Represents the material in American Vocational Association, <u>Summaries of Studies in Industrial Education</u> (1949) covering the period January 30, 1930, to September 1948; the 1953 supplement, covering the period September 1948 to September 1950; and studies covering the period August 31, 1950, to August 31, 1955.

A classified listing of 3,801 studies, primarily theses and dissertations. Many are annotated.

Continued by:

G403. STRONG, Merle E. <u>Research in Industrial Education; Summaries of Studies, 1956-1959, with Subject Index to Studies Listed in Research in Industrial Education--Summaries of Studies, 1930-1955</u>. Washington: U.S. Office of Education, 1961. 148 p. (U.S. Office of Education. Vocational Division. Bulletin, no. 293; Trade and Industrial Education Series, no. 72)

In three parts: (1) "Summaries of Studies, 1956-59," grouped into "Doctoral Studies" (p. 1-37), "Masters Studies" (p. 37-113), and "Staff Studies"; (2) "Authors of Doctoral Studies, 1930-55"; (3) "Subject Index." Entry indicates purpose of the study, source of data, method of study, and findings and conclusions. Subject index includes summaries of studies, 1930-1959.

Continued by:

G404. _____ <u>Research in Industrial Education; Summaries of Studies, 1960-61</u>. Washington: U.S. Office of Education, 1962. 34 p. (U.S. Office of Education. Vocational Division. Bulletin, no. 299; Trade and Industrial Education Series,

no. 75)

> In three parts: (1) "Doctoral Studies" (p. 1-13),
> (2) "Master's Studies" (p. 14-30), (3) "Staff
> Studies" (p. 31-32). Entry indicates purpose of
> study, findings, and conclusions. Subject index.

G405. LARSON, Milton E. and Melvin E. Johnson. "Recently Completed Doctoral Research in Industrial Education." Journal of Industrial Teacher Education 5 (Fall 1967): 56-63; 5 (Winter 1968): 48-55; 5 (Spring 1968): 58-64; 5 (Summer 1968): 71-76; 6 (Summer 1969): 61-86; 7 (Fall 1969): 53-74.

> An alphabetical author listing of 188 American
> dissertations completed between June 1, 1966, and
> September 15, 1968. Abstract includes purpose and
> conclusions.

G406. RUT, N. A. "Dissertatsiy po trudovomy i proizvodstvennomy obucheniyu." Shkola i proizvodstvo, 1967, no. 5: 53-62.

> Lists 60 dissertations completed between 1945 and
> July 1965 in the U.S.S.R.

G407. WEIR, E. Lee. "The Researcher's Index." Man/Society/Technology 38 (Nov./Dec. 1968)- . Title varies.

> Abstracts of dissertations located in Dissertation
> Abstracts International dealing with industrial arts
> and technical and vocational education.

H. Fine Arts

Art

General

H1. FESTSCHRIFT für Adolph Goldschmidt zum 60. Geburtstag am 15 Januar 1923. Leipzig: E. A. Seeman, 1923. 148 p.

Includes "Bibliographie der Doktordissertationen" (p. 143-148), listing dissertations done at the Universities of Halle and Berlin for which Gold-schmidt acted as adviser. Arranged chronological-ly. Includes publication information.

H2. "THESES and Dissertations: Fine Arts and Allied Fields." Parnassus 2 (May 1930): 44-45.

Theses and dissertations in progress in several U.S. institutions. Arranged by institution, giving degree and "year in which the work is to be pre-sented."

H3. HISS, Priscilla and Roberta Fansler. Research in Fine Arts in the Colleges and Universities of the United States. New York: Carnegie Corporation, 1934. 223 p.

Includes a selected "List of Masters' Essays and Doctors' Theses Written in the Colleges and Univer-sities of the U.S. between the Years 1875 and 1932" in art and archaeology, arranged by school (p. 181-197). Also contains a "Table of Graduate Theses in the Field of Art and Archaeology" (p. 198-207).

H4. REUTERSWÄRD, Oscar. Sex konsthistoriska disputationer.

Stockholm: A. Bonnier, 1945. 197 p.

> Bibliographic essays on studies done in Sweden,
> which deal with dissertations separately. Index
> of authors.

H5. "CHECKLIST of Graduate Theses in the Fine Arts Presented in
American Universities, 1940-1948." Marsyas 5 (1947/1949):
123-128.

> Lists theses and dissertations by schools. Includes
> only Harvard, Iowa State, Johns Hopkins, New York
> University, Ohio State, Ohio, Smith, Wellesley, Yale,
> Chicago, and Princeton.

H6. GOWANS, Alan. "...Report on Pending Ph.D. Theses in Art
History." College Art Journal 10 (Winter 1950/1951): 162-
166; 11 (Winter 1951/1952): 127-130; 12 (Fall 1952): 62-64.

> A classified listing of work in progress and com-
> pleted. Entry gives institution, title, date of sub-
> mission or proposed submission, and occasional one
> to two sentence explanation by author of the disser-
> tation. First report includes only American institu-
> tions; second includes England and Holland; third
> includes Courtauld Institute, University of London,
> and University of Rome.

H7. WESTERN ART ASSOCIATION. Study Committee No. 4, Policies
and Research Committee. Graduate Theses Titles, 1946-1952.
Compiled by Marjorie D. Campbell. Cedar Falls, Iowa: 1952.
19 p.

> Records 520 theses and dissertations completed or
> in progress during the period 1946-1952, at 35 of
> the 125 institutions within the Western Arts area.
> Also included are research papers in support of
> creative projects. The studies are organized into
> three general groupings: art education, art history,
> and fine arts; under each, works are listed by type
> of degree, state, school, and author's name.

H8. "HOCHSCHULEN und Forschungsinstitute." Kunstchronik 6
(1953)-   . Annual.

Consists primarily of German language dissertations.
Arranged by country, subdivided by city and institution. Under institution, completed work and work-
in-progress are listed separately.

H9.   GÖTTINGEN. Universität. Seminar für Handwerkswesen. <u>Bib-
liographie des Handwerks; Verzeichnis der Dissertationen</u>.
Leipzig: 1955-   . Irregular.

Issued as <u>Bibliographie des Handwerks: Gruppe D</u>:
<u>Dissertationen</u>.

Volume covering 1885-1908 published 1960; 1918-
1961 published 1961; 1933-1944 (edited by Marianne
Kidery) published 1956; 1945-1952 (edited by Gerhard Kämpf) published 1955; 1953-1959 published
1962.

Classified listings of German, Austrian, and German
language Swiss dissertations. Includes all academic faculties. Covers such areas as history, economics, organization. Author and subject index in
each volume.

H10. LINDSAY, Kenneth C. <u>The Harpur Index of Master's Theses in
Art Written at American Institutions of Higher Learning</u>.
Endicott, N.Y.: Harpur College, 1957. 5 Microcards.

A chronological listing of 2,168 unpublished theses
in art written between 1876 and 1953 from 76 report-
ing American institutions. Index of theses dealing
with historical subjects.

H11. "THESES et travaux des dernières années dans les universités
allemandes; Table par époques et par sujets." <u>Gazette des
beaux-arts</u> , ser. 6, vol. 51 (March 1958): suppl. p. 13-16.

Dissertations completed or in progress, arranged by
subject or period. Entry indicates if in progress.

H12. SOUTH DAKOTA. State College of Agriculture and Mechanic
Arts, Brookings. Graduate Printing Management. <u>Theses in
Graphic Arts and Related Fields, 1930-1960; A List of Theses
Prepared at Institutions of Higher Learning in the Past 30
Years</u>. Brookings: 1961. 21 p.

A chronological listing of approximately 150 theses.
Some are abstracted.

H13. "DISSERTATIONS in Progress." Art Journal 22 (1963): 168-169.

A "tentative and incomplete list of doctoral dissertations in the history of art," altogether about 200,
arranged according to the five contributing institutions, Princeton, Columbia, Harvard, Yale, and New
York University.

H14. "TRAVAUX en cours." L'Information d'histoire de l'art 9
(1964)-13 (1968). Annual.

Lists theses and dissertations in progress in French
institutions. Arranged under such topics as prehistory, Egyptology, ancient art and archaeology,
Middle Ages, modern and contemporary art. Under
each topic theses and dissertations are listed separately. Entry gives adviser.

H15. WAGNER-RIEGER, Renate. Auszüge aus kunsthistorischen Dissertationen österreichischer Hochschulen seit 1956. Wien:
Gesellschaft für Vergleichende Kunstforschung, 1966. 86 p.
(Mitteilungen der Gesellschaft für Vergleichende Kunstforschung in Wien, 16/17)

Abstracts of approximately 50 dissertations, arranged
chronologically under institution and faculty. Entry
gives publication information.

Individual Institutions

H16. "VERZEICHNIS der an der Universität Basel fertiggestellten
Dissertationen, 1938-1945." Phoebus 1 (1946): 47-48.

A chronological listing of 14 dissertations. Entry
gives publication information.

H17. "LISTE de thèses et mémoires soutenues pendant l'année
académique [1957-1959] à l'Université catholique de Louvain."
Gazette des beaux arts, ser. 6, vol. 54, suppl. Dec. 1959,
p. 23; ser. 6, vol. 55, suppl. April 1960, p. 19.

Ser. 6, vol. 54 lists the 1957/1958 studies and
ser. 6, vol. 55 lists the 1958/1959 studies.

Arranged by type of degree.

H18. "LES THÈSES de l'Institute of Fine Arts de l'Université de
New York 1946–1957; Table par époques et par sujets."
Gazette des beaux-arts, ser. 6, vol. 51 (Jan. 1958): suppl.
p. 13–16.

Lists theses and dissertations.

H19. NEW YORK. University. Institute of Fine Arts. Alumni
Association. A Listing of Theses Accepted by the Institute
of Fine Arts, New York University, 1924–1966. New York:
1966. 76 p.

Supersedes listing and abstracts of theses and dissertations in Item H20 and Item H21.

Contains 510 theses and dissertations. Section 1
lists theses by author. Section 2 arranged by
subject categories.

Continued by:

H20. "THESES Accepted at the Institute of Fine Arts, New York
University [June 1941/Feb. 1942–   ]" Marsyas 2 (1942)–
. Title varies. Irregular.

Vols. 2 (1942)–5 (1947/1949) carry abstracts of
theses and dissertations for the period 1941/1942–
1947/1948; from vol. 6 theses are listed.

Theses and dissertations are in separate lists.

H21. "SUMMARIES of Dissertations Submitted at the Institute of
Fine Arts, New York University." Marsyas 10 (1960/1961)–
. Irregular.

Continues Item H19.

Dissertations arranged by broad historical eras.

H22. ERLANDE-BRANDENBOURG, A. "Relevé des thèses restées inédites

sur l'archéologie et l'histoire de l'art d'après la table
generale des 'positions de thèses' récemment publiée."
Gazette des beaux-arts, ser. 6, vol. 70 (Oct. 1967): suppl.
p. 18-20.

    A chronological list of approximately 125 theses
    completed at l'École des chartes, Paris, covering
    the period 1850-1966.

H23. "THÈSES soutenues à l'École du Louvre [1928/1929-   ]"
Musées de France 1 (1929)-   . Annual.

    None published 1939-February 1945.

    Alphabetical author listing. Entry gives adviser.

H24. PARIS. École du Louvre. Positions des thèses soutenues par
les anciens élèves de l'École du Louvre pour obtenir le diplôme de l'École du Louvre. Paris: 1956. 2 vols.

    Supersedes annual listings in Item H25.

    Vol. 1 covers 1911-1944; vol. 2 covers 1944-1952.

    Abstracts of theses arranged chronologically. Each
    volume has a separate subject index.

    Continued by:

        Positions des thèses soutenues par les élèves agréés
de 1945 à 1953 et des mémoires présentés par les élèves
libres de 1948 à 1953 pour obtenir le diplôme supérieur et
le diplôme simple de l'École du Louvre. Paris: 1954. 159 p.

        Positions des thèses soutenues par les élèves agréés
de 1953 à 1959 et des mémoires présentés par les élèves
libres de 1953 à 1959 pour obtenir le diplôme supérieur et
le diplôme simple de l'Ecole du Louvre. Paris: 1959. 213 p.

    Abstracts of theses listed alphabetically by author.
    Subject index.

H25. "RÉSUMÉS des thèses [1928/1929-   ]" Musées de France 1
(1929)-   . Annual.

    None published 1939-February 1945.

Abstracts of selected dissertations completed at the
École du Louvre.

H26.   "LES THÈSES et mémoires de l'École du Louvre, 1886-1953."
Gazette des beaux-arts, ser. 6, vol. 49 (Feb. 1957): suppl.
p. 113-123.

Intended as a special index to Item H24.

Arranged by period and subdivided by subject. Entry
indicates if work has been published in whole or in
part.

Continued by:

H27.   "THÈSES et mémoires de l'École du Louvre 1953-1959." Gazette
des beaux-arts, ser. 6, vol. 56 (Sept. 1960): suppl. p. 19-
20.

Arranged under subject or period.

Dance

H28.   GOODE, Elizabeth. Dance Research Completed in the Colleges
and Universities of the United States. New York: 1946. 63
(M.A. Thesis, New York University)

Arranged by broad subject, then chronologically.
Primarily masters' theses, some doctors', from 11
institutions. Entry gives annotation when seen
by compiler. Indexes of authors and of kinds of
dance.

H29.   LOCKHART, A. "Recent Studies in Dance." Journal of Health,
Physical Education, Recreation 23 (Nov. 1952): 23, 59.

A selected list of completed theses and dissertations from 60 American institutions. Includes work
done from about 1942 to 1952. Contains a general
analysis of subjects covered.

H30.   AMERICAN ASSOCIATION FOR HEALTH, PHYSICAL EDUCATION, AND
RECREATION. National Section on Dance. Compilation on Dance
Research, 1901-1964. Edited by Esther E. Pease. Washington

1964. 52 p.

Supersedes earlier listings by the Research Committee of the National Section on Dance, Dance Research, pt. 1 (1955) and pt. 2 (1958); Focus on Dance I (1960) and II (1962); and "Dance Research and Theses" in its Dance Research; Reference Materials with Suggestions for Research, edited by Virginia Moomaw (1958).

An alphabetical listing of 704 American masters' theses, problems and projects, and dissertations completed within the period 1901-1963. A broad topical classification indicates area of research. Symbols indicate availability of the items.

Supplemented by:

H31. AMERICAN ASSOCIATION FOR HEALTH, PHYSICAL EDUCATION, AND RECREATION. Dance Division. Research in Dance I. Washington: 1968. 45 p.

In addition to providing separate listings of theses and dissertations, lists graduate projects, reports, and postgraduate research projects. There is a section of research related to dance. Altogether 266 items are listed. Subject index.

H32. "MASTERS Theses and Doctoral Dissertations." In Folk Dance Guide, 15th annual ed., p. 56-59. Edited by Paul Schwartz. New York: Carlton Press, 1965.

Supersedes listings in previous editions.

A cumulative listing of theses and dissertations completed in U.S. institutions from 1929.

Music

H33. "DISSERTATIONEN [1921-1938]" Jahrbuch der Musikbibliothek Peters 28 (1921)-44 (1938). Leipzig: 1922-1939. Annual.

Appears as pt. 10 in the "Verzeichnis der in allen Kulturländern im Jahre...erschienenen Bücher und Schriften über Musik."

Listings of German, Austrian, and German language
Swiss dissertations. Arranged by institution.
Entry gives publication information.

Continued by:

H34. "VERZEICHNIS aller im Berichtsjahr...bei der deutschen
Bücherei in Leipzig registrierten musikwissenschaftlichen
Dissertationen und Habilitationsschriften." Compiled by
Ortrun Landmann. Deutsches Jahrbuch der Musikwissenschaft
[1957-   ] Leipzig: Peters, 1958-   . Annual.

Alphabetical author listing, concentrating on East
German institutions. Entry gives publication information.

H35. STRUNK, William O. State and Resources of Musicology in the
United States; A Survey Made for the American Council of
Learned Societies. Washington: American Council of Learned
Societies, 1932. 76 p. (American Council of Learned
Societies Bulletin, no. 19)

"Some Theses Bearing Directly or Indirectly on
Music, Accepted at American Universities since
1919" (p. 43-51) lists approximately 175 theses
and dissertations by institution. Entry gives
degree and date.

H36. "GRADUATE Theses Related Directly or Indirectly to Musicol-
ogy Accepted in the United States, 1932-1938." In American
Council of Learned Societies. Committee on Musicology. A
Report on Publication and Research in Musicology and Allied
Fields in the United States, 1932-1938, p. 57-74. Washing-
ton: 1938.

Theses and dissertations, some from fields other
than music, arranged under institution. Entry
gives publishing information.

H37. "GRADUATE Theses Accepted." In A Bibliography of Periodical
Literature in Musicology and Allied Fields and a Record of
Graduate Theses Accepted, no. 1 (Oct. 1, 1938-Sept. 30, 1939),
p. 126-135. Washington: American Council of Learned Societies, Committee on Musicology, 1940.

Listing of theses and dissertations appears in

no. 1 only and covers the period October 1938 to
September 1939. Includes some in fields other
than music, such as English, psychology, library
service. Arranged by department. Entry gives
publication information.

H38. KLEMENT, Alfred von. Die Heimatlieder der Sudetendeutschen.
Mit einem Anhang: Die volkskundlichen Dissertationen 1908-
1940 des Seminars für deutsche Volkskunde 1933-1940 der
Deutschen Karls-Universität in Prag. Prag: Universitäts-
buchhandlung J. G. Calve, 1940. 11 p.

"Die volkskundlichen Dissertationen," p. 6-7.

H39. "DISSERTATIONS [1947/1948-   ]" Musica Disciplina 2
(1948)-   . Irregular.

Lists American dissertations and European theses
and dissertations alphabetically by author.

H40. "IM JAHRE...angenommene musikwissenschaftliche Dissertation-
en." Die Musikforschung 2 (1949)-   . Annual.

An annual listing (sometimes more frequently) of
dissertations completed in Germany, Austria, and
Switzerland, arranged by institution. With vol.
18 (1965) the journal has also included a special
section reviewing selected dissertations.

H41. REFARDT, Edgar. "Schweizerische musikwissenschaftliche
Hochschulschriften." In Schweizerische Musikforschende
Gesellschaft. Mitteilungsblatt 19 (July 1953): 4-9.

Two separate chronological listings, dissertations
and habilitations. Covers the period 1901-1952,
inclusive.

H42. "DODATEK: Prace doktorskie i magisterskie z zakresu musykol-
ogii wykonane na uniwersytetach polskich w latach 1917-1954."
In Michałowski, Kornel. Bibliografia polskiego piśmiennict-
wa muzycznego, p. 215-226. Wyd. 1. Cracow: Polskie Wydawn.
Muzyczne, 1955. (Materiały do bibliografil muzyki polskiej,
t. 3)

Lists 187 theses and dissertations, arranged by

institution.

_____ _____ Supplementa za lata 1955-1963 i uzupłnienia za lata poprzednie, p. 217-226. Wyd. 1. Cracow: Polskie Wydawn. Muzyczne, 1964. (Materiały do bibliografil muzyki polskiej, t.4)

H43. NORTHWESTERN UNIVERSITY, Evanston, Ill. School of Music. Bibliography of Research, School of Music, Northwestern University: Theses, Projects, Dissertations. Edited by Hazel B. Morgan. Evanston: 1958. 47 p.

An alphabetical listing of 939 studies from the first granting of advanced degrees through January 1958. These represent either (1) theses for certain majors at the master's level, (2) dissertations for the degrees of Ph.D. and Ed.D., or (3) series of projects for the degree of D.Mus. Entry indicates if it is a score. Detailed classified index. There is a listing of "Studies in Progress" (p. 46-47).

H44. TAYLOR, Laurence. "Research for the Flute: A List of Theses. Instrumentalist 14 (1960): 58-60.

Includes items listed in his earlier bibliography in Instrumentalist 9 (1954).

An alphabetical author listing of 32 theses and dissertations related to the flute, including items on flutists and the teaching of woodwinds. Covers the period from 1939.

H45. FRICKL, Jobst P. "Verzeichnis der von Karl Gustav Fellerer betreuten Dissertationen." In Festschrift Karl Gustav Fellerer zum sechzigesten Geburtstag am 7. Juli 1962, überreicht von Freunden und Schülern. Regensburg: G. Bosse, 1962. 593 p.

Lists approximately 75 dissertations, representing work completed at the Universities of Münster (Westfalen), Freiberg (Switzerland), and Cologne. Entry gives publication information.

H46. LINDER, Kerstin. "Förteckning över trebetygsuppsatser och licentiatavhandlinger." Svensk tidskrift för musikforsk-

<u>ning</u> 44 (1962): 67-72.

An alphabetical author listing of theses covering the period 1933 through 1962. Entry gives publication information.

H47. "THESES and Dissertations Related to Hymnody." <u>Hymn</u> 14 (1963): 8, 21, 57; 15 (1964): 94; 16 (1965): 94.

Lists of theses and dissertations completed at American institutions, arranged alphabetically by author. Includes studies completed prior to 1963.

H48. DOE, Paul. "Register of Theses in Music." <u>R.M.A. Research Chronicle</u>, no. 3, p. 1-25. Taunton: Barnicotts, Ltd., for the Royal Musical Association, 1963.

Appeared as a separate.

A classified listing of 265 theses and dissertations, completed or in progress in British universities, covering the period from about 1938. Includes studies from faculties other than music if they have a substantial musical content or relevance. European music is treated separately from British music and is arranged chronologically by subject. Other groupings consist of "non-European music" and acoustics.

Continued by:

_____ _____ "Amendments and Additions." <u>R.M.A. Research Chronicle</u>, no. 4-   . Taunton: Barnicotts, Ltd., for the Royal Musical Association, 1964-   . Irregular.

H49. SCHAAL, Richard. <u>Verzeichnis deutschsprachiger musikwissenschaftlicher Dissertationen, 1861-1960</u>. Kassel: Bärenreiter, 1963. 167 p. (Musikwissenschaftliche Arbeiten, Nr. 19)

An alphabetical author listing of 2,819 German language music dissertations. Publication information provided. Subject index.

Supplemented by:

H50.   WESSELY, Othmar.   "Ergänzungen zur Bibliographie der deutsch-
       sprachigen musikwissenschaftlichen Hochschulschriften."   Die
       Musikforschung 20 (1967): 57-61.

           An alphabetical author listing of 63 dissertations
           not included in the Schaal list.   Entry gives pub-
           lication information.

H51.   "PRACE doktorskiez Zakresu muzykologii przgotowywane w
       Polsce."   Musyka 9, nr. 1-2 (1964): 153.

           Lists approximately 30 dissertations arranged by
           institution.

H52.   TEXAS MUSIC EDUCATORS ASSOCIATION.   A Bibliography of Mas-
       ter's Theses and Doctoral Dissertations in Music Completed
       at Texas Colleges and Universities, 1919-1962.   Houston:
       1964.   77 p.

           Theses and dissertations arranged chronologically
           under schools.   Subject and author indexes.

H53.   "DISSERTATIONS."   Current Musicology, no. 1 (1964)-   .
       Semiannual.

           None included in no. 8 (1969) and no. 14 (1972).

           Abstracts of dissertations completed in American
           institutions.

H54.   UNIVERSITY MICROFILMS, Ann Arbor, Mich.   Doctoral Disserta-
       tions: Music, 1949-1964.   Ann Arbor: 1964.   2 vols.

           A sales catalog of approximately 700 American and
           Canadian dissertations available from University
           Microfilms on film or by Xerox copy.   One volume
           is by subject and the other by date of acquisition
           by University Microfilms.   The institution in
           which the work was done is not identified.   Entry
           gives abstract and purchasing information.

H55.   "DISSERTATIONS from Abroad."   Current Musicology, no. 2
       (1965)-6 (1968).   Semiannual.

           Lists theses, dissertations, and Habilitations-

schriften completed or in progress in non-American
institutions. Arranged by institution.

H56. GILLIS, Frank and Alan P. Merriam. Ethnomusicology and Folk
Music: An International Bibliography of Dissertations and
Theses. Middletown, Conn.: Published for the Society for
Ethnomusicology by the Wesleyan University Press, 1966. 148
p. (Special Series in Ethnomusicology, vol. 1)

Supersedes the bibliographies of theses and dissertations published in Ethnomusicology 4 (1960): 21-
35 and 6 (1962): 191-214.

An annotated alphabetical listing of 873 items
completed or in process. Includes a wide variety
of items which the compilers felt had a relevance
to music, such as the humanities and social science,
as well as other areas of science, the education of
youth and children in non-Western music, the sociology and psychology of music, etc. Institutional
and subject indexes.

H57. HARTLEY, Kenneth R. Bibliography of Theses and Dissertations
in Sacred Music. Detroit: Information Coordinators, 1966.
127 p. (Detroit Studies in Music Bibliography, 9)

Lists 1,525 theses and dissertations arranged by
institution. Index of biography, index to the works
of individual composers, and author and subject
indexes.

H58. "DOKTORATY." Musyka 11, nr. 1 (1966): 102.

Dissertations in musicology and ethnomusicology
completed in Polish universities in 1965.

H59. "VERZEICHNIS der seit 1945 an den österreichischen Universitäten approbierten musikwissenschaftlichen Dissertationen."
Österreichische Musikzeitschrift 21 (1966): 555-559.

Approximately 175 dissertations completed through
1965 arranged chronologically under university
and institute. Includes work done in faculties
other than music.

H60. "CURRENT Bibliography and Discography." Ethnomusicology 11, no. 1 (1967)-   .

> A regularly appearing separate section of completed theses and dissertations. Includes work done in departments other than music and also some done outside the United States. Entry carries an occasional note indicating relevance.

H61. "REGISTER of Theses on Musical Subjects Accepted for Higher Degrees and Research on Musical Subjects in Progress for Higher Degrees at Australian and New Zealand Universities." Studies in Music (Australia) 1 (1967)-   . Annual.

> Vol. 1 (1967): 102-107 is a classified listing of 54 theses and dissertations completed between 1927 and 1967.

> Two separate listings, (1) theses and dissertations completed and (2) those in progress. Both listings are grouped by genre of music, i.e. European and non-European, and by period.

H62. McCREDIE, Andrew D. "International Research Synopsis." Miscellanea Musicologica; Adelaide Studies in Musicology 3 (1968): 258-285.

> Abstracts of dissertations and research papers in European languages other than English.

H63. DE LERMA, Dominique-Rene. A Selective List of Masters' Theses in Musicology. Compiled for the American Musicological Society. Bloomington, Ind.: Denia Press, 1970. 42 p.

> An alphabetical author listing of 257 theses submitted at 36 institutions. Entry gives publication information, contents of the theses, and topical notes. Index of proper names and index of topics.

H64. ADKINS, Cecil. Doctoral Dissertations in Musicology. 5th ed. Philadelphia: American Musicological Society, 1971. 203 p.

> Preliminary edition compiled by H. T. David for Music Teachers National Association and American Musicological Society (1951). First edition by

the Joint Committee of the Music Teachers National
Association and the American Musicological Society
(1952). Helen Hewitt compiled the 2nd to 4th editions (1957, 1961, 1965). This edition supersedes
previous editions and also the supplements to those
two editions which appeared in the American Musicological Society Journal (1954, 1955, 1956, 1958,
1959, 1969) and the American Music Teacher (1953,
1954, 1955, 1956, 1959). Supersedes also for doctoral dissertations Item H35, Item H36, and Item
H37. Includes those dissertations closely related
to musicology listed in Item G321.

A topical listing of 1,917 American and Canadian
dissertations complete or in progress covering the
period through July 1970. Broader in scope than
earlier editions to include items of use in musicological research. Some dissertations in music education included, if they are historical in nature.
Bibliographic data on published dissertations
omitted from this listing.

Continued in part by:

H65.   _____ "American Doctoral Dissertations in Musicology: Supplement [1968-   ]" In American Musicological Society.
Journal 22 (1969)-   . Annual.

Arranged by period and classified under subjects
within each period. Subject and author indexes.

H66.   _____ "Musicological Works in Progress." Acta Musicologica
44 (1972)-   . Annual.

Continues in part Item H64.

An international register (excluding American) of
dissertations and some theses in progress, as well
as other major musicological projects. The entries
are classified under broad chronological period.
Subject and author indexes.

H67.   RAHN, Douglas J. "Masters' Theses in Musicology." Current
Musicology, no. 12 (1971): 7-37.

Lists theses accepted by American university graduate departments of music between July 1965 and

June 1970. Does not include pedagogical and Doctor
of Musical Arts theses. Arranged by historical period
and such subjects as instruments, ethnomusicology,
and theory; subdivided by institution.

H68. "FORSKNING." In Svenskt musikhistoriskt archiv. Bulletin
7 (1971): 42-47.

Swedish theses and dissertations completed or in
progress in 1970 and 1971. Arranged under institution.

H69. JENNINGS, John M. "New Zealand Music Research." Current
Musicology, no. 14 (1972): 70-76.

Lists 15 theses and one dissertation completed in
New Zealand institutions up to 1970, which deal
with subjects of immediate concern to New Zealand.
Arranged by subject, with analysis following each
section.

Theatre

General

H70. AMERICAN EDUCATIONAL THEATRE ASSOCIATION. Committee on
Research. Bibliography on Theatre and Drama in American
Colleges and Universities, 1937-1947. Iowa City, Iowa:
Speech Association of America, State University of Iowa,
1949. 124 p.

Also appeared as Speech Monographs , vol. 16, no. 3
(Nov. 1949). Supersedes earlier edition by Samuel
Selden, Research in Drama and Theatre in the Universities and Colleges of the United States, 1937-1942
(1944).

The majority of the items are theses and dissertations, including production theses. Classified
arrangement. Entry gives adviser and publication
information. Institutional and author indexes.

H71. JOHNSON, Albert E. "Doctoral Projects in Progress in Theatre
Arts [1948-   ]" Educational Theatre Journal 1 (1949)-   .

Annual. May issue.

In two parts: (1) a geographical listing subdivided by theatre practice and history and studies of dramatic literature under which Great Britain and the United States are further subdivided by period, and (2) a classified listing by period or subject, including creative, film, educational theatre, theory, and case study. Entry gives adviser and expected date of completion.

H72. KLAIN, J. M. "Graduate Projects in Progress in Theatre Arts [1948/1949-1951]" Educational Theatre Journal 1 (1949): 86-94; 2 (1950): 163-175; 3 (1951): 156-172; 4 (1952): 158-169. Title varies.

Compiled under the auspices of the American Educational Theatre Association Research Committee.

Lists theses and dissertations in progress in American institutions. A classified listing arranged under drama, the theatre as a means of communication, the theatre in its social function, and related means of communication. Entry gives expected date of completion and adviser.

H73. KNOWER, Franklin H. "Graduate Theses in Theatre [1949-1961]" Educational Theatre Journal 3 (1951)-15 (1963). Title varies. Annual. May issue.

Items also appear in Item L138.

A classified listing of theses and dissertations completed in American institutions.

H74. SCHWANBECK, Gisela. Bibliographie der deutschsprachigen Hochschulschriften zur Theaterwissenschaft von 1885 bis 1952. Berlin: Gesellschaft für Theatergeschichte, 1956. 563 p. (Gesellschaft für Theatergeschichte, e.V. Berlin. Schriften, Bd. 58)

A classified list of 3,309 dissertations. Author and catchword index.

H75. STRATMAN, Carl J. "Unpublished Dissertations in the History and Theory of Tragedy [1889/1957-1959]" Bulletin of

Bibliography and Magazine Notes 22 (1958/1959): 161-164, 190-192, 214-216, 237-240; 23 (1960/1962): 15-20, 162-165, 187-192.

Five parts and two addenda.

Lists 859 dissertations and theses from over 100 universities in the United States, Canada, England, Scotland, Wales, Ireland, and South Africa. Addenda have 397 additional titles and bring the work through 1959. Subject arrangement: first by country, then period, then individual authors treated.

H76. CHALAUPKA, Christl. "Austrian Theses on Theatre Research." Theatre Research 2 (1960): 37-43.

Classified list of dissertations covering the period 1953 to 1958. Most of items represent work done at the Institut für Theaterwissenschaft of the University of Vienna. Others from Graz and Innsbruck.

H77. CHEVALLEY, Sylvie. "Recherches théâtrales; Thèses de doctorat soutenues et en préparation dans les universités de France, 1944-1959." Theatre Research 2 (1960): 99-108, 141-162.

A classified listing of 434 titles, 136 of which were already complete.

H78. WILCKE, Joachim. "Berliner theaterwissenschaftliche Dissertationen, 1953-1959." Maske und Kothurn 7 (1961): 368-369.

An alphabetical author listing of the 30 dissertations completed in the Freie Universität (Berlin) Theaterwissenschaftliche Institute.

H79. ROJEK, Hans J. Bibliographie der deutschsprachigen Hochschulschriften zur Theaterwissenschaft von 1953 bis 1960. Berlin: Selbstverlag der Gesellschaft für Theatergeschichte, 1962. 170 p. (Schriften der Gesellschaft für Theatergeschichte, Bd. 61)

Lists 769 dissertations and Habilitationsschriften, including Austrian and Swiss. Theatre is broadly defined to include film ,opera, ballet, marionettes,

censorship, etc. Sociology and economics, as they
affect theatre, are also included. Arranged as
follows: pt. A: general topical listing; pt. B: by
place; pt. C: historical-geographic. Author index
and index of people, subjects, and places.

H80. LITTO, Fredric M. American Dissertations on the Drama and
the Theatre; A Bibliography. Kent, Ohio: Kent State University Press, 1969. 519 p.

A modified author listing of 4,565 dissertations
"on subjects related to theatre and drama completed
in all academic departments of United States and
Canadian universities through 1965." It includes
studies which contain primary or secondary level
information about the theatrical performing arts
(drama, the legitimate stage, opera, film, radio
and television, dance, and popular entertainments).
Author index, permuted title (KWIC) index, and a
subject index which incorporates geographical and
chronological features.

H81. "WIENER theaterwissenschaftliche Dissertationen bei Heinz
Kindermann." Maske und Kothurn 16 (1970): 282-319.

An alphabetical listing of the dissertations (with
their tables of contents) completed at the University of Vienna to May 1970 with Professor Heinz
Kindermann as first or second reader. Entry gives
date.

Supplemented by:

_____ "Mai 1970 bis ende August, 1971." Maske und
Kothurn 17 (1971): 132-164.

Abstracts of dissertations.

H82. SCHERER, Colette. "Thèses (état, université, 3e cycle) et
mémoires (maîtrises et diplômes d'études supérieures) en
depôt à la Bibliothèque de l'Institut d'études théâtrales
au 1. 1. 1971." Revue d'histoire du théâtre 24 (1972):
81-101.

Lists approximately 250 items. In two parts: (1)
studies deposited in the Institute Library and (2)
studies by those enrolled in the Institute. In

each part the studies are listed under subject.

H83. MIKHAIL, E. H. <u>Dissertations on Anglo-Irish Drama; A Bibliography of Studies</u>. Totowa, N.J.: Rowman and Littlefield, 1973. 73 p.

Lists more than 500 dissertations on 24 dramatists. The studies were completed between 1870 and 1970 in universities in Great Britain, Ireland, the United States, Germany, France, and Canada. Arranged by dramatist. Author and institutional indexes.

Special Subjects

Medieval Drama

H84. STRATMAN, Carl J. <u>Bibliography of Medieval Drama</u>. Berkeley: University of California Press, 1954. 423 p.

Covers the drama of medieval Europe. Lists more than 200 unpublished theses and dissertations in separate groupings under each subject.

Renaissance Drama

H85. "RESEARCH Projects." <u>Research Opportunities in Renaissance Drama</u>, no. 1 (1955)-   . Title varies. Annual.

This publication represents the Modern Language Association Conference on Research Opportunities in Renaissance Drama annual report. No. 7 was issued as a supplement to <u>Renaissance Drama</u>, vol. 7 (1964).

Includes a substantial number of theses and dissertations in progress. International in coverage. Entry gives description of the study.

Restoration and 18th Century Drama

H86. "DISSERTATIONS of Interest and Value." <u>Restoration and 18th</u>

Century Theatre Research 2 (May 1963): 37-38.

    Lists 12 American dissertations completed in the
period 1927-1958.

H87. STRATMAN, Carl J. "Theses and Dissertations in Restoration
and 18th Century Theatre." Restoration and 18th Century
Theatre Research 2 (Nov. 1963): 20-45.

    Lists 361 studies (136 dissertations, 209 theses,
ten B.Litt. theses, and six honors theses) completed
between 1897 and 1962 in the United States, Canada,
and Great Britain. Arranged alphabetically by topic.
Author index.

    Supplemented and continued by:

H88. PERRIN, Michel P. "Theses and Dissertations in Restoration
and 18th Century Theatre: Further Addenda." Restoration and
18th Century Theatre Research 7 (May 1968): 1-6.

    Lists 81 theses and dissertations which were not
included in Item H87 and brings the basic listing
up to 1965. In two groups, British and Irish
universities and Canadian universities.

H89. VERNON, P. F. "Theses and Dissertations in Restoration and
18th Century Theatre: Addenda." Restoration and 18th Century Theatre Research 6 (May 1967): 55-56.

    Supplements Item H87.

    An alphabetical listing of theses and dissertations
completed through 1966 and available at the University of London, which were not included in Item H87.

Places

Berlin

H90. THEATERWISSENSCHAFT in Berlin. Beschreibende Bibliographie
der am Theaterwissenschaftlichen Institute unter Hans
Knudsen entstandenen Dissertationen (Frederich-Wilhelms-
Universität 1945 und Freie Universität Berlin 1949-1966).

Berlin: Colloquium Verlag, 1966. 141 p.

Abstracts of 77 dissertations arranged chronologically. In large part the dissertations concern the
area of the history of theatre in Berlin in the
nineteenth and twentieth centuries. Author and
subject indexes.

France

H91. SCHERER, Jacques. "La Sorbonne et le théâtre; Thèses sur le
théâtre française." Revue d'histoire du théâtre 12 (1960):
38-39.

A listing of dissertations defended at the University of Paris in 1957 and 1958 for the Doctorat ès
lettres. Some entries are annotated.

United States

H92. HAMER, Clifford E. "American Theatre History: A Geographical
Index. Educational Theatre Journal 1 (1949): 164-194.

Includes a large number of unpublished theses and
dissertations on theatre history in American cities,
states, and the District of Columbia.

H93. BROCKETT, O. G. "The Theatre of the Southern United States
from the Beginnings through 1865: A Bibliographical Essay."
Theatre Research 3 (1960): 163-174.

Pt. 5, "Doctoral Dissertations" (p. 172-173), lists
13 dissertations and includes brief descriptive
notes.

H94. STRATMAN, Carl J. "The New York Stage: A Checklist of Unpublished Dissertations and Theses." Bulletin of Bibliography and Magazine Notes 24 (1963): 41-44.

A subject listing of 125 theses and dissertations
completed between 1955 and 1961 in American institutions.

J. History

General

J1.   MULLER, Frederik, & Co., Amsterdam. <u>Catalogus dissertation-</u>
<u>um et orationum historicarum et antiquariarum.</u> <u>Defensarum</u>
<u>et habitarum ab a. 1650 usque ad 1851 in academiis Germaniae,</u>
<u>etc. praesertim Neerlandiae.</u> <u>Quae venales prostant apud</u>
<u>Fredericum Muller...</u> Amstelodami: 1851. 16 p.

    A dealer's catalog of 441 items. In two parts, (1)
quarto and (2) octavo.

J2.   <u>LIST of Doctoral Dissertations in History in Progress in the</u>
<u>United States</u> [1901-   ] Title varies. Irregular.

    Compiler until 1935 was John Franklin Jameson.

    Annual lists for 1902-1911 published as separates
by the Carnegie Institution of Washington Division
of Historical Research. (The 1909 list includes
dissertations completed 1897-1909, except for Columbia University, which covers from 1884, and Harvard University, from 1876.) List for 1912 in
<u>History Teachers' Magazine</u> 4 (Jan. 1913): 8-15;
1913-1917 in <u>American Historical Review</u> 19 (1914)-
23 (1918), Jan. issue; 1918-1938 published as separates by Carnegie Institution of Washington Division
of Historical Research; 1939-1940 issued as supplements to <u>American Historical Review</u> 45 (1940)-46
(1941), April issue, and include work in Canadian
universities; 1941 published as American Historical
Association <u>Annual Report 1941</u> (1943), vol. 3, and
includes work in Canadian universities; no list
published for 1942-1946, 1948; 1947 compiled by
Lowell Ragatz and published by American Historical
Association (1947); 1949-1952 not published; from
1952 issued triennially by American Historical

Association (1958-1966 include dissertations completed).

Dissertations are arranged by historical period or geographical area. Once listed items do not reappear in later issues. Author and subject indexes.

J3. "UNIVERSITY Research [1911/1918-1927/1928]" History, n.s. 4 (1919)-14 (1929).

Theses and dissertations in history in Great Britain. N.s. vol. 4 (1919) covers the period 1911-1919; vols. 5 (1920)-13 (1928) are annual lists; vol. 14 (1929) is a cumulative author index to the previous listings. Arranged by institution and subdivided by level of degree. Entry gives publication information.

Continued by:

J4. LONDON. University. Institute of Historical Research. "Historical Research for University Degrees in the United Kingdom [1928/1929-1930/1931]" In its Bulletin 7 (1929/1930): 173-179; 8 (1930/1931): 171-177; 9 (1931/1932): 181-188.

Completed theses and dissertations, listed separately under institution. Entry gives adviser and publication information, if published as a book.

Continued by:

J5. _____ Historical Research for University Degrees in the United Kingdom [1931/1932-   ] London: 1933-   . (Its Bulletin. Theses Supplement, no. 1-   ) Annual.

Nos. 1-14 issued irregularly; beginning with no. 15 (1954), issued in May.

Nos. 1-14 contain theses and dissertations in two parts: (1) theses completed, (2) theses in progress; nos. 15-21 arranged by university; nos. 22 (1961)-
     arranged by chronological periods and regions. Theses in geography with historical interest are also included. Each part has an author index and there is a subject index for completed theses.

J6. "LISTE des mémoires de maîtrise d'histoire soutenues...dans
les facultés des lettres et sciences humaines [1944-   ]"
Revue historique 200 (1948)-   . Title varies. Irregular.

   Coverage for nos. 200 (1948)-237 (1967) represents
   work done in the facultés des lettres; no. 210
   (1953) covers history, economics, and human geography; nos. 228 (1962), 230 (1963), 238 (1967), and
   240 (1968) represent work done in the facultés des
   lettres and sciences humaines. No. 200 (1948) includes work done in 1944-1947.

   Theses in the historical sciences completed in French
   universities. Arranged by university.

J7. "DIPLÔMES ès sciences (mention histoire et géographie)
[1947/1948-   ] Annales du Midi 6 (1948/1949)-   . Annual.

   Lists theses completed in the Universities of Toulouse, Bordeaux, Aix-Marseilles, and Nice in separate institutional listings. Coverage for each
   institution varies.

J8. "RESEARCH Work [1950-   ]" Historical Studies; Australia
and New Zealand 4 (1950)-   . Annual. 1950-1963 in Nov.
issue; 1964-   in Oct. issue.

   Australian dissertations completed from July 1953
   to 1956 not included. Listing in vol. 7 (1955/1957),
   for 1956, includes only in-progress portion of
   Australian work, as well as New Zealand theses and
   dissertations completed and in progress.

   Theses and dissertations in Australian and New
   Zealand universities, arranged under the categories
   "Theses Completed," "Theses Commenced," and "Theses
   Abandoned," then by university.

J9. "PERECHEN' dissertatsiy, avtoram kotorykh prisuzhdena
uchenaya stepen' kandidata istoricheskikh nauk [1952-1957]"
Voprosy istorii, 1953, vyp. 8: 176-189; 1954, vyp. 6: 182-
190, vyp. 8: 182-190; 1955, vyp. 9: 173-176, vyp. 11: 198-
201; 1958, vyp. 1: 203-213, vyp. 4: 201-209. Title varies.

   A listing of theses defended in the U.S.S.R., arranged by historical eras.

Supplemented by:

J10. "SPISOK tem doktorskikh dissertatsiy utverzhdennykh v [1952-1960]" <u>Voprosy istorii</u>, 1954, vyp. 12: 173; 1961, vyp. 3: 177-181. Title varies.

List in 1954 covers 1952-1954; 1961 list covers period 1954-1960.

A listing of dissertations completed in the U.S.S.R., arranged by year of defense and subdivided by historical period.

J11. "DISSERTATSIY, zashchishchennye v Institute istorii AN SSSR v [1953-1955]" <u>In</u> Akademiya nauk SSSR. Institut istorii. <u>Doklady i soobshcheniya</u>, 1954, vyp. 1: 133-134; 1955, vyp. 7: 103-108; 1956, vyp. 10: 106-107.

Separate listings of dissertations and theses. Each list is subdivided into (1) history of the U.S.S.R. and (2) general history.

J12. "POST-GRADUATE Theses in History, Political Science, etc. [sic] Held by Australian Universities." <u>Historical Studies: Australia and New Zealand</u> 7 (1955/1957): 348-358.

A list of theses and dissertations held by Australian libraries or departments together with a select list of theses and dissertations in other fields which might be of interest to the historian. Arranged by (1) Australia, (2) Pacific and Asian, and (3) "Other Theses in History and Political Science," and then by institution. No inclusive dates given but list goes back to about 1910.

J13. "DISSERTATSIY po novoy i noveyshey istorii zashcheshchennye v 1956-1960 godakh." <u>Novaya i noveyshaya istoriya</u>, 1958, vyp. 1: 193-195; 1961, vyp. 1: 169-170, vyp. 2: 179-180.

Lists approximately 260 U.S.S.R. theses and dissertations in two parts, 1956-1957 and 1957-1960. Each separates theses and dissertations. The 1957-1960 listing is arranged by subject and/or country (primarily East European).

J14. "THÈSES de doctorat soutenues en 1957-58-59." In Société des professeurs d'histoire et de geographie de l'enseignement public. Bulletin 49 (1959): 517-518.

Dissertations completed in French universities. Does not include the Sorbonne. Arranged by institution.

J15. GT. BRIT. Colonial Social Science Research Council. Committee on History and Administration. List of Theses in Colonial History and Administrative Subjects. 1960. 10 p. ??

J16. "THESES Presented [1956/1961-   ]" Quarterly Review of Historical Studies (Calcutta) 1 (1961)-   . Irregular.

Abstracts of dissertations completed in Indian universities.

J17. DEUTSCHE Dissertationen zur Zeitgeschichte [1945/1948-   ] Auswahlbibliographie. Berlin: Deutsches Institut für Zeitgeschichte, 1965-   . Irregular.

A selected bibliography of dissertations on contemporary topics completed in East and West German institutions. Arranged alphabetically by author. Entry gives publication information. Key word index in three parts: (1) German Democratic Republic, (2) West Berlin, and (3) West Germany. Author indexed under institution.

J18. "DOCTORAL Dissertations in History Recently Completed in the United States [1963-   ]" In American Historical Association. Annual Report [1964-   ] Washington: Smithsonian Institution Press, 1965-   . Annual.

In part continues Item J2.

Appears in vol. 1, "Proceedings."

Arranged by country or region, subdivided by historical period or by topic.

J19. KUEHL, Warren F. Dissertations in History; An Index to Dissertations Completed in History Departments of United States and Canadian Universities, 1873-1960. Lexington: University of Kentucky Press, 1965. 249 p.

Alphabetical author listing of 7,695 dissertations
which have been written in formally organized departments of history during the period 1873-1960. A
numerical summary indicates the year in which each
institution gave the first degree in history and
the distribution of degrees by periods. Subject
index.

_____ _____, 1961-1970. 1972. 238 p.

Lists 5,884 dissertations completed in the period
1961-June 1970 and items not included in main work.
Subject index.

J20. LÜCKE, Peter R. Sowjetzonale Hochschulschriften aus dem
Gebiet der Geschichte, 1946-1963. Hrsg. vom Bundesminister-
ium für Gesamtdeutsche Fragen. Bonn: 1965. 98 p.

Supersedes the listing of dissertations and Habilitationsschriften in Albrecht Timm, Das Fach Geschichte
in Forschung und Lehre in der Sowjetischen Besat-
zungszone von 1945 bis 1955, p. 41, 95-99 (1957).

A listing of 731 doctoral dissertations and Habilitationsschriften arranged by year and then by institution. In addition to the Philosophy Faculty,
covers relevant items from the Faculties of Economics,
Law, Education, and the Faculty of Journalism of the
Karl Marx University in Leipzig, as well as from
collections from other institutions in the Soviet
Zone. Author index.

J21. ÖSTERREICHISCHE historische Bibliographie. Austrian Historical Bibliography [1965-   ] Annual.

Covers dissertations submitted at Austrian universities on the history of Austria and, if published in
Austria, of other countries. Arranged by region and
country. Does not include pre-history. Includes
a separate list of the titles of 1965 dissertations
for the state examination of the Institut für Österreichische Geschichtsforschung. Author index.

J22. CANADA. Public Archives. Register of Post-Graduate Dissertations in Progress in History and Related Subjects. Reper-

toire des thèses en cours portant sur des sujets d'histoire
et autres sujets connexes [no. 1 (1966)-   ] Ottawa: Canadian Historical Association, 1966-   . Annual.

Continues and expands Item J63.

A listing of theses and dissertations in progress
in Canadian universities. In addition to including
all theses and dissertations in preparation in
Candaian departments of history, contains work being
done in other departments, e.g. political science,
economics, geography, if it involves historical
research or is of value in Canadian studies. Attempts
also to include non-Canadian research on Canadian
history, government, and politics. Studies are
arranged under broad chronological and geographical
headings and subdivided chronologically. Entry gives
degree sought, year work was begun, and adviser. In
some instances there is an indication if the work
was completed, discontinued, or changed. Author
index.

J23.   "INVENTORY of Doctoral Dissertations in Progress." In Society for Spanish and Portuguese Historical Studies. Newsletter
1 (1969)-   . Three times per year.

Arranged by institution. Entry gives adviser.

Individual Institutions

J24.   "LISTS of Subjects of Theses by Cambridge University Students
Working for the Ph.D. or M.Litt. Degrees in the Faculty of
History [1927/1928-1954/1955]" Cambridge Historical Journal
2, no. 2 (1926/1928)-11 [1953/1958). Three times per year.

Vol. 10, no. 2 to vol. 11 carry "A Select List of
Theses on Historical Subjects in Faculties of the
University Other than That of History."

An alphabetical author listing, giving title and
college.

J25.   IOWA. University. Abstracts in History from Dissertations
for the Degree of Doctor of Philosophy as Accepted by the
Graduate College of the State University of Iowa [1922-1942]
Iowa City: 1932-1943. 5 vols. (Its Studies in the Social
Sciences, vol. 10, nos. 2, 3, 4; vol. 11, nos. 3, 4)

Number covering the period 1939-1942 reprinted from University of Iowa <u>Doctoral Dissertations, Abstracts and References</u>, vol. 3, Series on Aims and Progress of Research, no. 72: 83-228.

Each number contains about 15 abstracts.

J26. LAVOYE, Madeleine. "Catalogue des thèses d'histoire defendues à l'Université de Liège de 1890 à 1936." <u>In Annuaire de la Commission communale de l'Histoire de l'ancien pays de Liège, 1937</u>, p. 301-305. Liège: Vaillant-Carmanne, 1937. ?

J27. "SUMMARIES of Theses." <u>In</u> London. University. Institute of Historical Research. <u>Bulletin</u> 1 (1923/1924)-   . Semiannual.

Long abstracts of theses and dissertations presented to the Institute.

J28. MADRID. Universidad. Facultad de Filosofía y Letras. <u>Sumarios y extractos de las teses doctorales...en la sección de historia</u> [1939-1947] Madrid: 1954-1955. 2 vols.

First volume covers the period 1939-1944; second volume 1944-1947.

A chronological listing of 105 abstracts. Entry gives adviser. Title and author indexes.

J29. SCHLEBECKER, John T. "List of Master's Theses in the Field of History Prepared at Montana State University, Missoula, 1915-1954." <u>Montana: The Magazine of Western History</u> 6 (Jan. 1956): 61-63.

Arranged by geographical area.

J30. "UNIVERSITÉ de Montréal. Faculté des lettres. Liste des thèses présentées à l'Institut d'histoire (1947-1965)." <u>Revue d'histoire de l'Amérique française</u> 20 (1966/1967): 515-521.

Lists 79 theses and 23 dissertations in separate chronological listings.

J31. OHIO. State University, Columbus. <u>Roster of Doctors of</u>

Philosophy in History at the Ohio State University, 1925-1951. Columbus: 1952. 7 p.

A chronological listing.

J32. TRUDEL, Marcel. "Thèses d'histoire soutenues à l'Université d'Ottawa, 1965-1967." Revue d'histoire de l'Amérique française 22 (1968): 24.

A chronological listing.

Separate lists of theses for 1965/1966 and 1966/1967.

J33. PARIS. École des chartes. Positions des thèses soutenues pour obtenir le diplôme d'archiviste-paléographe. Table générale, 1949-1966. Paris: 1967. 255 p.

Lists 1,625 dissertations chronologically. Entry gives publication information. Author and subject indexes.

J34. TREGONNING, K. G. "Higher Degree Theses." In his Malaysian Historical Sources, p. 77. Singapore: University of Singapore, Department of History, 1962.

A listing of theses and dissertations prepared at the University of Singapore.

J35. "SUJETS de thèses de doctorat déposés à la Sorbonne [1953-]" In Société des professeurs d'histoire et de géographie de l'enseignement public. Bulletin 46 (1956)- . Title varies. Irregular.

Completed dissertations listed in two parts, history and geography.

J36. CUMBERLAND, Charles. Classified List of Master of Arts Dissertations in History, 1895-1940, Inclusive. Austin: University of Texas, 1941. 63 p.

Geographical arrangement of 985 theses completed at the University of Texas. In two parts, (1) the United States and (2) Texas. Each is subdivided by subject.

J37. FASCICULI historici [1958-] Warszawa: 1968- .

Abstracts in Russian, French, or English.

Selected abstracts of dissertations for the doctorate and habilitations completed in the University
of Warsaw Faculty of History. No. 1 (1968) contains
a chronological listing of dissertations completed
since 1958. Abstracts in nos. 2 (1969)-   bear no
reference to year in which number is issued. Entry
gives adviser.

J38. UNIVERSITY Studies in History [vol. 1-   ] Nedlands: University of Western Australia Press, 1934-   . Title varies.
Annual.

None issued for 1935-1937 and 1939-1952.

Abstracts of theses completed in the University of
Western Australia Departments of History and of
Economics.

Military History

J39. MAHON, John K. "Doctoral Dissertations on Military History."
Military Affairs 17 (1953): 140-142.

Approximately 100 studies in progress.

J40. ROBERTSON, James I., Jr. "Graduate Writings on the Civil
War." Civil War History 5 (1959): 145-155.

A subject listing of 212 theses and dissertations
from 54 cooperating institutions.

J41. U.S. Department of the Army. Army Library. Theses and
Dissertations in the Holdings of the Army Library, A List
of Titles. 3d rev. ed. Washington: 1966. 101 p. (Its
Special Bibliography, no. 20)

Incorporates items included in the earlier lists
published in 1957 and in 1961.

A classified compilation of 836 items. Includes
material on the social sciences, science and technology, earth sciences, psychology, the humanities,
foreign relations, and international law.

J42. MILLET, Allan R. and B. Franklin Cooling III. <u>Doctoral Dissertations in Military Affairs; A Bibliography</u>. Manhattan, Kans.: Kansas State University Library, 1972. 153 p. (Kansas State University Library Bibliography Series, no. 10)

> In large part supersedes Item J39.
>
> Dissertations in English, primarily representing studies completed in the United States, with many from Great Britain and the Commonwealth, covering approximately the period from 1900 through 1970. Entries indicate whether published and the department in which done, if other than history. Excludes works devoted to theoretical discussions of international affairs and the factors or causes leading to war. Pt. 1: "Studies of World Military Affairs" (largely chronological); pt. 2: "Military Affairs of the United States"; pt. 3: "Studies of War and the Military."
>
> Continued by:

J43. _____ "Doctoral Dissertations in Military History [Supplement 1-   ]" <u>Military Affairs</u> 37 (1973)-   . Annual.

> Vol. 37 (1973) includes dissertations completed in the period 1969 through 1972. Same coverage and same arrangement as in main work.

Places

Africa

J44. LONDON. University. Institute of Historical Research. "Historical Theses on African Subjects Completed in Great Britain." <u>African Studies Bulletin</u> 4 (Oct. 1961): 1-9.

> A geographical listing of theses and dissertations. Reference is made to published abstracts.

Asia

General

J45. "CURRENT Research in South-East Asian History." Journal of
      Southeast Asian History 2 (Oct. 1961): 83-90.

      An international listing, with varying coverage
      among and in countries, including many theses and
      dissertations completed and in progress. Listed
      by country and institutions.

J46. CASE, Margaret H. South Asian History, 1750-1950; A Guide
      to Periodicals, Dissertations and Newspapers. Princeton,
      N.J.: Princeton University Press, 1968. 561 p.

      Pt. 2 (p. 387-436) is a classified list of approx-
      imately 650 dissertations on the modern history of
      the India-Pakistan subcontinent. Includes disser-
      tations accepted through 1965. Institutional index.

China

J47. CHENG CHIH HSÜEH, Mu-cha, Formosa. She hui k'o hsüeh tzu
      liao chung hsin. Kuo fu ssu hsiang tzu liao mu lu. Taipei:
      1972. 6, 96 p.

      "Bibliography of Works on Dr. Sun Yat-sen, and
      Catalogue of Doctoral Dissertations & Masters'
      Theses." (Title, p. 4 of cover)

      Lists theses and dissertations completed at Cheng
      Che University (p. 57-96). Arranged by department
      and includes work in education, political science,
      journalism, and foreign affairs. Entry gives
      adviser and date.

India

J48. RECENT Researches. Editor: Panchanand Misra. Bhagalpur,
      India: Bhagalpur University, Post Graduate Department of
      History, Research Centre, 1971-   . Irregular.

First issue contains long summaries of unpublished dissertations, completed at Indian universities, of interest to historians of India but not necessarily earned in departments of history.

Austria

General

J49. EPSTEIN, Fritz T. "Austrian Dissertations in the Library of Congress." <u>Austrian History News Letter</u>, no. 1 (1960): 56-57.

A listing of microfilms of typewritten Austrian dissertations acquired by the Library of Congress.

J50. "RECENTLY Completed Dissertations at the Universities of Vienna, Graz, and Innsbruck." <u>Austrian History News Letter</u>, no. 3 (1962): 136-137.

Supplements lists in Item J59 and Item J61.

J51. "DOCTORAL Dissertations in the United States." <u>Austrian History News Letter</u>, no. 1 (1960)-4 (1963). Title varies.

Each number of this publication lists dissertations completed and in progress. Arranged by historical periods.

J52. "AUSTRIAN Doctoral Dissertations on the History of Austria." <u>Austrian History Yearbook</u> 1 (1965)- . Title varies. Annual.

Divided into those already completed and those in progress. Each grouping is arranged by historical period.

J53. "DOCTORAL Dissertations in the United States and Canada." <u>Austrian History Yearbook</u> 1 (1965)- . Annual

Divided into those already completed and those in progress. Each grouping is arranged by historical period. The list in vol. 1 is retrospective.

J54. "A PARTIAL List of British Doctoral Dissertations." Austrian History Yearbook 4/5 (1968/1969): 432-433.

> In two sections, "Dissertations Already Completed," which is retrospective, and "Doctoral Dissertations in Progress in 1966."

J55. EPSTEIN, Fritz T. "The History of Austria in United States and Canadian Dissertations." Austrian History Yearbook 6/7 (1970/1971): 221-238.

> A topical arrangement of the dissertations in Item J20 which pertain to Austrian history. Indicates if published.

Historical Period

1648-

J56. "NEW Doctoral Dissertations Dealing with Austrian History from 1648 to the Present in Progress at the Universities of Vienna and Graz." Austrian History News Letter, no. 3 (1962): 135-136.

> Supplements listing in item J57.
>
> Entry gives adviser.

1648-1848

J57. "DISSERTATIONS in Progress at the University of Vienna Dealing with Austrian History from 1648-1848." Austrian History News Letter, no. 2 (1961): 74-76.

> Entry gives adviser.

J58. RECHBERGER, Walther. "Austrian Doctoral Dissertations Dealing with Austrian History from 1648 to 1790." Austrian History News Letter, no. 3 (1962): 89-135.

> Dissertations written under the supervision of the Faculties of Philosophy, Law, Theology, and Medicine in the Universitites of Vienna, Graz, and Innsbruck.

Arranged by historical period.

J59.   _____ "Austrian Doctoral Dissertations Dealing with Austrian History from 1790 to 1848." _Austrian History News Letter_, no. 2 (1961): 42-74.

All dissertations written under the supervision of the Faculties of Philosophy, Law, Theology, and Medicine in the Universities of Vienna, Graz, and Innsbruck. Dissertations dealing with the Revolution of 1848 are excluded as they are in Item J60.

1848-1918

J60.   RECHBERGER, Walther. "Austrian Doctoral Dissertations Dealing with the Problems of the Habsburg Monarchy from 1848 to 1918." _Austrian History News Letter_, no. 1 (1960): 3-55.

A classified bibliography of dissertations accepted by the University of Vienna during 1918-1960, by the University of Graz during 1918-1960, by the Philosophy Faculty of the University of Innsbruck during 1918-1937, and by all the faculties of the University of Innsbruck during 1947-1960.

Supplemented by:

J61.   "NEW Doctoral Dissertations Dealing with the Problems of the Habsburg Monarchy from 1848 to 1918 in Progress at the University of Vienna." _Austrian History News Letter_, no. 2 (1961): 77-78.

J62.   "COMPLETED Austrian Doctoral Dissertations Dealing with the Problems of the Habsburg Monarchy from 1848 to 1918." _Austrian History News Letter_, no. 2 (1961): 79-82.

Supplements Item J60.

J63.   "DOCTORAL Dissertations Dealing with the Problems of the Habsburg Monarchy from 1848 to 1918 in Progress at the University of Graz." _Austrian History News Letter_, no. 2 (1961): 78-79.

Entry gives adviser.

Vienna

J64. WOHLRAB-WEINZETTE, Hertha. "Dissertationen zur Geschichte Wiens, 1956-1960." Wiener Geschichtsblätter 21 (1966): 65-70.

   Covers such areas as biography, political history, social history, economics, cultural history, art history.

   _____ "1961-1965." Wiener Geschichtsblätter 25 (1970): 94-96, 118-112.

   Includes approximately 120 additional dissertations.

Canada

General

J65. "GRADUATE Theses in Canadian History and Related Subjects [1927-1965]" Canadian Historical Review 8 (1927)-46 (1965). Title varies. Annual. Usually Sept. issue.

   Lists Canadian and non-Canadian theses and dissertations in progress and recently completed. Includes such related subjects as Canadian external relations, economics, government, political science, law, geography, and selected historical items which bear indirectly rather than directly on Canadian history. In two parts: (1) theses for the doctor's degree; (2) theses for the master's degree. Entry gives previous degrees (institution and date) and, if completed, the date.

J66. "THÈSES en préparation [1964/1965-   ]" Revue d'histoire de l'Amérique française 19 (1965/1966)-   . Title varies. Irregular.

   Vol. 27 (1973): 471-475 lists only theses and dissertations in progress at the University of Laval.

   Theses and dissertations on French-Canadian history in progress in Canadian universities. Includes English language titles. Entry gives degree sought.

British Columbia

J67. WOODWARD, Frances. Theses on British Columbia History and Related Subjects in the Library of the University of British Columbia. Revised and enlarged. Vancouver: University of British Columbia Library, 1971. 57 p. (University of British Columbia Library. Reference Publication, no. 35)

> First edition 1969.

> Theses and dissertations completed in Canadian and American universities. Section 1, "Theses on British Columbia History and Related Subjects Completed at the University of British Columbia," is arranged alphabetically under departments, excluding business administration, social work, and community and regional planning. Section 2, "Theses on British Collumbia History and Related Subjects Completed at Other Universities, Held by the Library of the University of British Columbia," is an alphabetical author list. Author index.

France

General

J68. "LE DIPLÔME d'études supérieures à la Faculté des lettres et sciences humaines de Toulouse [1958-1961]" Annales historiques de la Revolution française 31 (1958): 301-303; 32 (1960): 262-365; 35 (1963): 382-384.

> Vol. 35 (1963) covers 1960 and 1961.

> Bibliographic essays on theses on the 18th century and on the French Revolution.

J69. GUSEV, V. V. "Dissertatsiy sovetskikh issledovateley po istorii Frantsii." Frantsuzskiy ezhegodnik, 1961: 518-526.

> Lists approximately 225 U.S.S.R. theses and dissertations arranged under medieval history, modern history, and current history.

Eastern France

J70. "FACULTÉ des lettres de Nancy; Liste de diplômes d'études supérieures d'histoire et de géographie intéressant l'est de la France [1945/1950-1951]" <u>Annales de l'est</u>, sér. 5, vol. 1 (1950): 151-153; sér. 5, vol. 2 (1951): 329.

Série 5, vol. 1 (1950) covers theses completed in the period 1945-1950, arranged under medieval history, geography, and rural life. Série 5, vol. 2 (1951) is an alphabetical author listing covering 1951.

Northern France

J71. "TRAVAUX et recherches d'histoire régionale [1949/1950-   ]" <u>Revue du nord</u> 34 (1952)-   . Annual.

Carries a separate listing of the theses and disser-tations completed in history and archaeology in the University of Lille Faculty of Letters.

Provence

J72. "THÈSES, diplômes, mémoires soutenus devant les facultés de droit et des lettres d'Aix au cours des années [1951/1954-1955/1956]" <u>Provence historique</u> 5 (1955): 93-96; 7 (1957): 228-231.

Vol. 5 covers 1951-1954; vol. 7, 1955-1956.

Theses and dissertations arranged under historical periods and human geography.

Germany

J73. MILATZ, Alfred and Thilo Vogelsang. <u>Hochschulschriften zur neueren deutschen Geschichte; Eine Bibliographie</u>. 1. Aus-gabe: 1945-1955. Im Auftrage der Kommission für Geschichte des Parlamentarismus und der Politischen Parteien sowie des Instituts für Zeitgeschichte. Bonn: Selbstverlag der Kommis-sion für Geschichte des Parlamentarismus und der Politischen Parteien, 1956. 142 p.

Theses and dissertations dealing with all aspects of German life, completed or in progress in German and non-German universities. Section 1 is an alphabetical listing of 1,925 completed studies. Section 2 lists 400 works in progress. Subject index.

Great Britain-East Anglia

J74. BAKER, Gillian. East Anglian History--Theses Completed. Norwich: University of East Anglia, Centre of East Anglian Studies, 1972. 23 p.

Lists approximately 205 theses and dissertations completed through 1971 on Norfolk, Suffolk, Essex, Cambridgeshire, Huntingdonshire, the Soke of Peterborough, and the Lincolnshire Fens. International in scope. In three parts: (1) medieval up to 1500, (2) modern, (3) general subjects.

Ireland

J75. "RESEARCH on Irish History in Irish Universities [1937/1938-]" Irish Historical Studies 1 (1938/1939)-   . Title varies. Annual. March issue.

Lists theses and dissertations on Irish historical subjects or on subjects having a distinct bearing on Irish history. In two parts: (1) completed, (2) in progress; further subdivided by historical periods. Entry gives adviser.

Latin America

General

J76. "DOCTORAL Dissertations on Latin American Topics, 1954-1955." Hispanic American Historical Review 35 (1955): 221-270; 36 (1956): 348-380.

Abstracts of dissertations accepted in U. S. universities during the previous year. Some in fields other than history.

J77. CHAFFEE, Wilber, Jr. and Honor M. Griffin. <u>Dissertations on Latin America by U.S. Historians, 1960-1970; A Bibliography.</u> Austin, Tex.: University of Texas, Institute of Latin American Studies, 1973. 62 p. (University of Texas, Institute of Latin American Studies, Guides and Bibliographies Series, 7)

    Approximately 450 dissertations arranged by country. Entry indicates availability.

Mexico

J78. MEIER, Matt S. "Dissertations." <u>Journal of Mexican American History</u> 1 (1971): 170-190.

    An alphabetical author listing of selected theses and dissertations "holding promise of containing historical materials" and excluding those purely educational and sociological. With few exceptions all were completed at U.S. institutions.

J79. RAAT, William D. "Two Decades of Unpublished Doctoral Dissertations on Mexico, 1950-70." <u>In</u> Greenleaf, Richard E. and Michael C. Meyer. <u>Research in Mexican History</u>, p. 197-211. Compiled for the Committee on Mexican Studies, Conference on Latin American History. Lincoln, Neb.: University of Nebraska Press, 1973.

    A listing of approximately 225 dissertations completed or in progress at American institutions. Arranged under historical periods from colonial to the contemporary period (1940 to the present).

Netherlands

J80. MAATSCHAPPIJ DER NEDERLANDSCHE LETTERKUNDE, Leiden. Commissie van geschied- en oudheidkunde. <u>Register van academische dissertatien en oratien betreffende de geschiedenis des vaderlands, aanhangsel op het Repertorium van verhandelingen en bijdragen, bijeengebragt en systematisch geschikt door de Commissie van geschied- en oudheidkunde van de Maatschappij der Nederlandsche letterkunde.</u> Leiden: E. J. Brill, 1866. 104 p.

    A classified bibliography of 1,601 dissertations.

_____ _____ <u>Supplement</u>. Leiden: E. J. Brill, 1882. 47 p.

Supplements main volume, bringing the coverage to
1880. Includes items omitted from main volume.

New Zealand

J81. RODGERS, Margaret D. <u>Theses on the History of New Zealand</u>.
North Palmerston, N.Z.: Massey University, 1968-1972. 4 pts.
(Massey University, Library Series, nos. 1-4)

Vol. 1 edited with K. A. Pickens.

Lists theses and dissertations completed or in progress in universities in New Zealand and in Great
Britain, Canada, and the United States. In four
parts: (1) biographical studies; (2) political history; (3) social history; and (4) economic, agricultural, and industrial history. Pt. 1 is arranged
by biographee and pts. 2-4 are classified. Entry
gives location of copies. Pts. 1-4 have separate
author indexes. Pts. 2-4 have separate subject
indexes.

Slavic and U.S.S.R.

General

J82. RUSSIA (1923-   U.S.S.R.) Upravlenie prepodavaniya obshchestvennykh nauk. <u>Spisok tem dissertatsiy, zashchishchennykh na soiskanie uchenoi stepeni kandidata istoricheskikh
nauk po razdelu "Istoriia Kommunistcheskoi Partii Sovetskogo
Soiuza"</u> (za 1949-1953 gg.) Moskva: 1953. 59 p. ?

J83. "SPISOK tem dissertatsiy zashchishchennykh v [1952-1957] na
soiskanie uchenoy stepeni kandidata istorichskikh nauk po
rasdelu 'Historiya kommunisticheskoy partii Sovetskogo
Soyuza.'" <u>Vestnik vysshey shkoly</u>, 1953, vyp. 11: 54-56,
vyp. 7: 58-60; 1954, vyp. 1: 55-62; 1955, vyp. 1: 56-63,
vyp. 7: 60-64; 1956, vyp. 2: 58-64, vyp. 10: 60-63; 1957,
vyp. 3: 93-96, vyp. 4: 94-96; 1958, vyp. 2: 94.

A listing of theses defended in the U.S.S.R. Each
year's work is arranged under time periods. Entry

indicates the time period covered by the study.

J84. "DISSERTATIONEN und Habilitationen auf den Gebieten der Slawistik und osteuropäischen Geschichte angenommen an den Universitäten der DDR [1956/1957-1962/1963]" Zeitschrift für Slawistik 2 (1957)-9 (1964). Irregular. Usually in Nr. 2.

None in vols. 7 (1962) and 8 (1963); only vol. 9 (1964) includes Habilitationen.

Arranged alphabetically by author. Entry gives publication information.

J85. AKADEMIYA NAUK SSSR. Institut istorii. SSSR v period Velkoy Otechestvennoi voyny, 1941-1945 gg; Ukazatel' dissertatsiy i avtorferatov. Sost. G. A. Kumanev. Moskva: 1961. 41 p.

Lists approximately 500 theses and dissertations completed in Russian institutions through September 1960. The dissertations are listed alphabetically by author and the theses are in a classified arrangement, under such topics as economics, transportation, culture. Abstracts are provided.

Tadzhikistan

J86. KHOLDZHURAEV, Khabibullo K. Dissertatsiy istorikov po materialam Tadzhikistana. Referativnyi ukazatel'. Red. M. I. Irkaev. Dushanbe: 1970. 281 p.

A classified listing of 12 dissertations and 130 theses on Tadzhik topics completed in the period 1947-1969. Includes studies from institutions outside Tadzhikistan. In two parts: (1) Communist Party and (2) the history of the Tadzhik people. Entry carries an abstract. Author index.

Tatar Republic

J87. TAGOROV, R. Sh. "Bibliograficheskiy ukazatel' doktorskikh i kandidatskikh dissertatsiy." Kommunist Tatarii, 1958, vyp. 9: 90-93.

Theses and dissertations on the history of the Tatar Republic, defended in the period 1939-1957.

Ukraine

J88. "SPISOK dissertatsiĭ pro revolyutsiyu 1905-1907 rr. na Ukraĭni (krim tykh, shcho zakhyshchals' v Instytuti istoriĭ AN URSR)." In Revolyutsiya 1905-1907 rr. na Ukraĭni, p. 317-318. Kyĭv: 1955. (Akademiya nauk URSR, Kiev. Instytut istorii. Naukovi zapysky, T. 6)

An alphabetical author listing of 23 dissertations.

United States

General

J89. STEWART, William J. The Era of Franklin D. Roosevelt; A Selected Bibliography of Periodical and Dissertation Literature, 1945-1966. Hyde Park, N.Y.: National Archives and Records Service, The Franklin D. Roosevelt Library, 1967. 175 p.

An annotated bibliography covering the period 1945-1966. Divided into four major sections: Franklin D. Roosevelt; New Deal; World War II; and archives, bibliography, and historiography. The dissertations included represent work done at American institutions. Author and subject indexes.

J90. UNIVERSITY MICROFILMS, Ann Arbor, Mich. A Bibliography of Doctoral Research on the Civil War and the Reconstruction Era. Ann Arbor: 1971. 35 p.

An alphabetical author list of more than 300 dissertations accepted at American universities and published by University Microfilms during the period 1938-1970. Entry includes reference to Dissertation Abstracts International and University Microfilms purchase order number.

California

J91. BLEICH, Pamela A. "A Study of Graduate Research in Califor-
      nia History in California Colleges and Universities." Cali-
      fornia Historical Society Quarterly 43 (1964): 231-245, 331-
      343; 44 (1965): 35-49, 139-163, 237-250; 45 (1966): 149-161.

      An examination of 743 theses and dissertations com-
      pleted in the period 1899 to 1959 at 16 California
      colleges and universities in history, social studies,
      or social science departments. Theses and disserta-
      tions from 1902 to 1959 found at the various insti-
      tutions are listed separately by institution and are
      annotated.

Kansas

J92. SOCOLOFSKY, Homer E. Kansas History in Graduate Study; A
      Bibliography of Theses and Dissertations. Revision. Topeka:
      Kansas State Historical Society, 1970. 58 p.

      First edition published as Kansas Association of
      Teachers of History and Related Fields, Bibliography
      of Theses and Dissertations Pertaining to Kansas
      History, edited by Homer E. Socolofsky (1958). A
      slightly expanded edition appeared as Homer E.
      Socolofsky, Kansas History in Graduate Study (1959).

      A classified bibliography of 1,617 items, including
      bachelor of divinity theses, masters' theses, and
      dissertations. Lists some items from institutions
      outside Kansas. Includes such areas as agriculture,
      education, Eisenhower, political and social history,
      the military, and transportation. Author index.

Kentucky

J93. MALLALIEU, William C. "List of Master of Arts Theses on
      Kentucky History in the University of Louisville Library."
      Filson Club Historical Quarterly 18 (1944): 109-111.

      Listed under two headings: general Kentucky history
      and Louisville history. Most done in the University
      of Louisville's Department of History and Political
      Science; a few in other departments.

Maryland

J94. BROWN, Dorothy M. and Richard R. Duncan. "Masters Theses and Doctoral Dissertations in Maryland History." Maryland Historical Magazine 63 (1968): 412-419; 64 (1969): 65-73, 161-168.

Earlier listings covering only 1951-1953 were published in Maryland Historical Magazine 48 (March 1953): 64; 50 (March 1954): 53.

An alphabetical listing of 125 dissertations and 240 theses in the fields of history, political science, economics, education, and library science completed in American institutions.

Michigan

J95. "MICHIGAN Bibliography [1947-   ]" Michigan History 32 (1948)-   . Annual.

None in vol. 48 (1964).

Carries a separate section on unpublished materials, which consists in large part of theses and dissertations submitted to Michigan institutions.

J96. CHAVIS, John. A Brief Survey of Theses in Michigan History. Rev. ed. Detroit: Detroit Historical Society, 1959. 20 p.

First issued in 1956.

An author listing of theses and dissertations completed at the Michigan universities of Detroit, Michigan State, Western Michigan, and the University of Michigan, as well as at the Universities of Chicago, Northwestern, Columbia, Western Ontario, Toledo, and Illinois.

Minnesota

J97. OSTREM, Walter M. A Bibliography of Theses on Minnesota History, including Theses on Subjects Relating to Minnesota History. Mankato, Minn.: 1966. 104 p.

Lists 693 items, including undergraduate papers as
well as theses and dissertations. Approximately half
of items are annotated. Also includes research completed at non-Minnesota institutions. Location in
the Minnesota Historical Collection is indicated.
Subject index.

Mississippi

J98. BETTERSWORTH, John K. Mississippi Theses, 1928-1952; A
Checklist of Graduate Theses Dealing with Mississippi Done
at State Institutions of Higher Learning. State College,
Miss.: Mississippi State College, Social Science Research
Center, 1953. 19 p. (Mississippi. State College. Social
Science Research Center. Bibliographical Series, no. 1)

An alphabetical author list of theses written at
the University of Mississippi, Mississippi State
College, and Mississippi Southern College.

Continued by:

J99. "A BIBLIOGRAPHY of Theses and Dissertations Relating to
Mississippi [1953-   ]" Journal of Mississippi History 16
(1956)-   . Annual.

Separate alphabetical author listings of theses and
dissertations (1) completed or (2) in progress.
Includes work from institutions outside Mississippi.
Items not incorporated in previous listings are
added when known. Entry gives status of work.

Missouri

J100. "GRADUATE Theses Relating to Missouri [1935/1936-   ]"
Missouri Historical Review 32 (1938)-   . Annual.

Lists theses and dissertations completed in Missouri
colleges and universities. Coverage for each institution is as follows: University of Missouri, 1935/
1936-   in vol. 32 (1938)-   ; St. Louis University, 1935/1936-   in vol. 32 (1938)-   ; Washington University, 1935/1936-   in vol. 32 (1938)-
    ; University of Kansas City, 1940/1941-1963/1964
in vol. 37 (1942)-59 (1964/1965); Northeast Missouri

State Teachers College, 1949/1950–   in vol. 46
(1951)–   ; Lincoln University, 1959–   in vol.
55 (1960/1961)–   ; Central Missouri State College,
1963/1964–   in vol. 59 (1964/1965)–   ; Southeast
Missouri State College, 1971–   in vol. 66 (1971/
1972)–   ; Southwest Missouri State College, 1971–
    in vol. 66 (1971/1972)–   . Generally, the
listings for each school are regular.

St. Louis

J101. THROEN, Selwyn K. <u>A Guide to Resources on the History of
St. Louis</u>. St. Louis: Washington University, Institute for
Urban and Regional Studies, 1971. 1 vol. (various pagings)
(Washington University Institute for Urban and Regional
Studies. Working Paper INS 9)

Section 3, "Dissertations Relating to St. Louis,"
lists 476 American theses and dissertations alphabetically by author. The subject index separates the
references to the theses and dissertations under
each term.

New Jersey

J102. HOULROYD, Magdalena. <u>Master's Theses in New Jersey History</u>:
<u>Glassboro State College, 1952–1967; An Annotated Bibliogra-
phy</u>. Glassboro, N.J.: Glassboro State College, Savitz
Library, 1968. Unpaged.

An alphabetical author listing of 46 unpublished
theses submitted to the College in the areas of
New Jersey local history and/or social and educational history, or economic conditions. Index.

New York

J103. DUNN, James T. <u>Masters' Theses and Doctoral Dissertations
on New York History, 1870–1954</u>. Revised. Cooperstown,
N.Y.: State Historical Association, 1955. 20 p.

Reprinted from <u>New York History</u> 36 (1955): 233–251,
which represented a cumulation and augmentation of
previously published lists of "Masters' Theses and

Doctoral Dissertations in New York History" that appeared in New York History 33 (1952): 232-236, 356-358.

Listed alphabetically by author under the granting university.

J104. CORNELL UNIVERSITY. Collection of Regional History. List of Theses Written at Cornell Relating Directly or Indirectly to the History of New York State. Compiled by the Collection of Regional History and University Archives. Ithaca, N.Y.: 1956. 73 p.

An alphabetical author listing of approximately 1,900 theses and dissertations completed between 1870 and 1953. Covers all aspects of New York, including the natural and physical sciences.

Ohio

J105. "CHECK-LIST of Major Research-in-Progress and Completed Masters and Doctors Degrees in Topics Relating to Ohio [Aug. 1959/July 1960-   ]" Ohio History 60 (1960)-   . Title varies. Annual.

In vols. 60 (1960)-80 (1971) theses and dissertations are carried separately in the annual bibliographic survey. Checklist in vol. 78 (1969) does not include section on theses and dissertations. Checklist not published in vols. 79 (1970)-80 (1971).

Approximately half of the research-in-progress is theses and dissertations and is arranged by chronological eras. Theses and dissertations are listed alphabetically by author and represent work done in Ohio institutions.

Oregon

J106. "HISTORICAL Theses on Oregon." Oregon Historical Quarterly 41 (1940): 236.

Lists 16 theses completed between 1923 and 1939 at the University of Oregon and Oregon State University.

Pennsylvania

J107. BOUMANN, Roland M. "Dissertations on Pennsylvania History, 1886-1971: A Bibliography." In Pennsylvania Historical Association. Journal 39 (1972): 72-114.

Lists 726 dissertations completed in American institutions under historical periods, education, and religion.

The Southeast

J108. KIDDER, Frederick E. and Allen D. Bushong. "A Tentative Bibliography of Doctoral Dissertations Relating to Latin American Contacts with the Southeast Accepted by United States Colleges and Universities through 1955/56." Southeastern Latin Americanist 2 (March 1959): 23.

An alphabetical author list of 33 American dissertations, covering the period 1917-1955.

Tennessee

J109. "WRITINGS in Tennessee History." East Tennessee Historical Society Publications 2 (1930)-   . Annual. Irregular.

No listings in vols. 20, 33, 36, 37.

Carries a separate listing of theses and dissertations.

Texas

J110. CARROLL, Horace B. and Milton R. Gutsch. "A Check List of Theses and Dissertations in Texas History Produced in the Department of History of the University of Texas, 1893-1951." Southwestern Historical Quarterly 56 (July 1952/April 1953): 59-101, 254-309, 417-454, 507-542.

Also appeared as Horace B. Carroll and Milton R. Gutsch, Texas History Theses (1955).

Alphabetical author listing of 470 studies. Descriptive information on maps, illustrations, and contents.

Continued by:

J111. CARROLL, Horace B. "Texas Collection." Southwestern Historical Quarterly 56 (1952): 316-317; 57 (1954): 393-395; 58
(1955): 442-443; 59 (1955): 230-233; 61 (1958): 413-415; 62
(1959): 547.

> Carries separate lists of theses and dissertations
> in Texas history completed at the University of Texas
> from June 1952 through May 1958. Includes work done
> in departments other than history.

J112. ELLIOTT, Claude. Theses on Texas History; A Check List of
Theses and Dissertations in Texas History Produced in the
Departments of History of Eighteen Texas Graduate Schools
and Thirty-Three Graduate Schools outside of Texas, 1907-
1952. Austin: Texas State Historical Association, 1955.
280 p.

> Also appeared as "A Check List of Theses and Disser-
> tations in Texas History, 1907-1952" in Southwestern
> Historical Quarterly 57 (1954): 336-388, 475-505;
> 58 (1955): 98-142, 249-288, 372-404, 489-522.

> An alphabetical annotated list of 652 theses and
> dissertations. Entry includes notes for illustra-
> tions, etc. Author and analytical subject index.

Utah

J113. "UTAH, the Mormons and the West." Utah Historical Quarterly
23 (1954/1955): 75-85, 279-284; 25 (1957): 163-169; 27
(1959): 85-100, 169-190.

> Contents: vol. 23 (1954): 75-85: "A Check List of
> Theses at the University of Utah"; vol. 23 (1955):
> 279-284: "A Check List of Theses at the Brigham
> Young University"; vol. 25 (1957): 163-169: "A Check
> List of Theses at the Utah State Agricultural Col-
> lege"; vol. 27 (1959): 85-100, 169-190: "Selections
> from A Bibliography of Theses and Dissertations con-
> cerning Utah or the Mormons Written outside the
> State of Utah," by Ida-Marie C. Logan (based on her
> master's thesis, Utah State Agricultural College,

1956).

The check lists contain theses and dissertations on
all subjects relating to the people or the area.
Each part is an alphabetical author list. The listing
in vol. 27 (1959) indicates institution and year.
Copies of items recorded are available at the University of Utah Library.

Virginia

J114. DUNCAN, Richard R. and Dorothy M. Brown. "Theses and Dissertations in Virginia History: A Bibliography." <u>Virginia
Magazine of History and Biography</u> 79 (1971): 55-109.

Approximately 1,100 theses and dissertations arranged
alphabetically under historical period, Black history,
education, and religion. Includes materials in the
fields of education, economics, political science,
agriculture, etc. Listing contains items up to
1970 but, in the main, goes only to 1968. In cases
of some major universities, only dissertations are
included.

K. Home Economics

General

K1.   U.S. Office of Education. <u>Titles of Completed Research</u>
<u>from Home Economics Departments in American Colleges and</u>
<u>Universities, 1918 to 1923</u>. Washington: U.S. Government
Printing Office, 1924. 14 p. (<u>Its</u> Home Economics Circular,
no. 18, June 1924)

    Theses and dissertations listed separately under
    institutions. Also covers economics and sociology,
    as related to family, aesthetics, home economics
    education, household engineering. Entry gives
    publication information.

K2.   U.S. Bureau of Home Economics. <u>Titles of Unpublished</u>
<u>Theses in the Field of Home Economics Completed during the</u>
<u>Years 1924-1931</u>. Compiled by Hazel E. Munsell and Edith
Evers. Washington: 1932. 73 p.

    _____ _____, <u>1931-1933</u>. Compiled by Hazel E. Munsell and
Edith Evers. Washington: 1933. 24 p.

    _____ _____, <u>1933-1935</u>. Compiled by Edith Evers and Hazel
E. Munsell. Washington: 1935. 26 p.

    Classified bibliographies of theses and a few dis-
    sertations.

K3.   <u>NOTES on Graduate Studies and Research in Home Economics and</u>
<u>Home Economics Education</u> [1934/1936-1939/1940] Washington:
1936-1940. Title varies. Annual.

    Number for 1934/1936 prepared by the Association of
    Land-Grant Colleges and Universities, Home Economics
    Section, Research Committee; 1936/1937 compiled by

Hazel E. Munsell; 1937/1938-1939/1940 compiled at
the U.S. Office of Education. Lists for 1934/1936,
1936/1937, 1938/1939, 1939/1940 issued by the U.S.
Department of Agriculture Office of Experiment
Stations.

Classified bibliography of abstracts of graduate
studies and research completed or in progress,
arranged under broad topics. Topics include foods,
physiology of nutrition, diet, textiles and clothing, the house, family economics, institutional
management, home economics education. Entry indicates if completed or in progress.

K4. TITLES of Theses; Home Economics and Related Fields [1942/
1946-1967/1968] Washington: 1946-1969. Title varies.
Annual.

Volumes for 1942/1946-1951/1952 issued by the U.S.
Bureau of Human Nutrition and Home Economics; 1952/
1953-1961/1962 by the U.S. Agricultural Research
Service; 1962/1963-1967/1968 by the American Home
Economics Association and reprinted from Journal of
Home Economics 56 (1964)-61 (1969) (Item K7).

Theses and dissertations completed in U.S. institutions arranged in a subject classification including
arts and crafts, child development, clothing and
textiles, family economics and management, family
life, housing and equipment, institution management, nutrition and food, home economics education.
Includes an author index and, since 1948/1949 issue,
a list of graduates receiving masters' degrees
without theses.

K5. "THESES: Doctoral Theses Related to Home Economics [1947-
1950/1951]" Journal of Home Economics 41 (1949): 513-518,
569-571; 42 (1950): 729-731; 43 (1951): 711-712. Title
varies. Annual.

Abstracts of dissertations completed in American
universities. Arranged under such areas as education, foods and nutrition, textiles. Entry gives
publication information.

Continued by:

K6. "ABSTRACTS of Doctoral Theses Related to Home Economics

[1951/1952-1961/1962]" <u>Journal of Home Economics</u> 45 (1953)-55 (1963). Annual.

Items selected from Item K4.

Abstracts by home economists and by others in related fields. Arranged under subjects, such as education, family economics, institution management.

K7. "TITLES of Theses: Home Economics and Related Fields [1961/1962-1967/1969]" <u>Journal of Home Economics</u> 55 (1963)-61 (1969). Title varies. Annual.

A classified listing of theses and dissertations arranged under such subjects as art, food and nutrition, home economics education, textiles and clothing. Author index.

Continued by:

K8. AMERICAN HOME ECONOMICS ASSOCIATION. <u>Titles of Dissertations and Theses Completed in Home Economics</u> [1968/1969-   ] Washington: 1970-   . Annual.

Classified listing of theses and dissertations completed in American institutions. Under each subject dissertations precede theses. Author index.

Special Subjects

Art, Housing, and Furnishings

K9. SHEARER, Jane K. <u>Research Related to Design, Housing and Equipment, Home Furnishings, and Interior Design, 1942-1965</u>. Washington: American Home Economics Association, 1966. 94 p.

Compiled from Item K4.

A classified list, primarily of theses, arranged chronologically under subject. Index of selected cross-references and author index.

K10. AMERICAN HOME ECONOMICS ASSOCIATION. <u>Art, Housing, Furnish-</u>

ings, and Equipment [1966-   ] Washington: 1967-   .
(Home Economics Research Abstracts, series 4) Annual.

Abstracts of theses and dissertations completed in
American institutions, arranged under broad topics.
Author index.

Communication

K11.   AMERICAN HOME ECONOMICS ASSOCIATION. Home Economics Communication: Home Economics Education [1966-   ] Washington:
1967-   . (Home Economics Research Abstracts, series 5)
Title varies. Annual.

Abstracts of theses and dissertations completed in
American institutions, arranged by broad topics
under home economics communication and home economics
education. Topics include audience and communication
analysis, media use and public relations administration, evaluation, methods and materials, and program
planning. Author index.

Family Economics-Home Management

K12.   DAVIS, Jean and Ruth Deacon. Selected Bibliography of Theses
and Research in Family Economics and Home Management. Prepared for the American Home Economics Association, Family
Economics--Home Management Section. Washington: American
Home Economics Association, 1961. 67 p.

Supersedes Elizabeth Weigand, Selected Bibliography
of Theses and Research in Family Economics, Home
Economics and Related Areas (1954) and the 1955,
1957, and 1959 supplements.

A classified listing of approximately 500 items,
the largest part being theses and dissertations,
completed in American universities.

Continued by:

K13.   MANNING, Sarah L. and Marilyn Dunsing. Selected Bibliography of Theses and Research in Family Economics and Home
Management: 1965 Supplement. Washington: 1965. 54 p.

Supersedes Ruth Deacon and Marilyn Dunsing, <u>Selected Bibliography of Theses and Research in Family Economics: 1963 Supplement</u> (1963).

A classified listing of approximately 500 studies. Author index.

K14. <u>JOURNAL of Family Economics--Home Management</u> [1 (1962)-5 (1966)] Washington: American Home Economics Association, Family Economics--Home Management Section, 1962-1966. Annual.

Each number consists of abstracts of unpublished research in family economics and home economics, primarily theses and dissertations.

Continued by:

K15. AMERICAN HOME ECONOMICS ASSOCIATION. <u>Family Economics-- Home Management</u> [1966-   ] Washington: 1967-   . (Home Economics Research Abstracts, no. 1) Annual.

Abstracts of theses and dissertations completed in American institutions, arranged under broad topics. Topics include home management, human resources, homemaker rehabilitation, teaching, consumer ecology, consumer education, and studies of low-income house- holds. Author index.

Family Relations-Child Development

K16. AMERICAN HOME ECONOMICS ASSOCIATION. <u>Family Relations and Child Development</u> [1966-   ] Washington: 1967-   . (Home Economics Research Abstracts, no. 6)

Abstracts of selected theses and dissertations com- pleted in American graduate schools of home economics. Arranged under family relations, child development, international studies, and miscellaneous. The sec- tions for family relations and child development are classified. Author index.

Food and Nutrition

K17. AMERICAN HOME ECONOMICS ASSOCIATION. <u>Food and Nutrition</u>

[1968-   ] Washington: 1969-   . (Home Economics Research
Abstracts, series 7) Annual.

Abstracts of theses and dissertations completed in
American institutions, arranged under broad topics.
Topics include food habits and nutritional status,
food quality, nutrition and metabolism, and nutrition
education and history. Author index.

Institutional Administration

K18. AMERICAN HOME ECONOMICS ASSOCIATION. Institutional Administration [1966-   ] Washington: 1967-   . (Home Economics
Research Abstracts, no. 2) Annual.

Abstracts of theses and dissertations completed in
American institutions arranged under broad topics.
Topics include educational techniques and training
programs, facilities design, personnel and management attitudes. Author index.

Textiles and Clothing

K19. AMERICAN HOME ECONOMICS ASSOCIATION. Textiles and Clothing
[1966-   ] Washington: 1967-   . (Home Economics
Research Abstracts, series 3) Annual.

Abstracts of theses and dissertations completed in
American institutions, arranged under broad topics.
Topics include teaching, textiles, consumer aspects,
sociology, psychology, and history. Author index.

L. Languages and Literature

General

L1. MULLER, Frederik, & Co., Amsterdam. <u>Catalogus dissertationum</u>
<u>et orationum argumenti litterarii et biographici, defensarum</u>
<u>et habitarum ab a. 1650 usque ad 1851 in academiis Germaniae,</u>
<u>etc. praesertim Neerlandiae. Quae venales prostant apud</u>
<u>Fredericum Muller.</u> Amstelodami: 1851. 12 p.

> A dealer's catalog of 337 items. In two parts, (1)
> quarto and (2) octavo.

L2. BOEKEREN, W. van, bookseller, Groningen. <u>Catalogus litterar-</u>
<u>ium dissertationum, quaestionum academicarum et orationum</u>
<u>quae veneunt Groningen.</u> Groningen: 1853. 16 p.

> Lists 504 dissertations. In two parts, (1) quarto
> and (2) octavo. Items are listed alphabetically by
> author in each part.

L3. MOURIER, Athénaïs and Nicolas F. Deltour. <u>Notice sur le</u>
<u>doctorat ès lettres, suivie du Catalogue et l'analyse des</u>
<u>thèses françaises et latines admises par les facultés des</u>
<u>lettres depuis 1810, avec index et table alphabétique des</u>
<u>docteurs.</u> 4. éd. Paris: Delalain frères, 1880. 442 p.

> Reprinted in 1969.
>
> First edition (1852) and 2nd edition (1855) by
> Mourier; 3rd edition (1869) by Mourier and Deltour.
>
> A chronological listing, subdivided by university.
> Entry identifies the author and indicates the major
> divisions and ideas in the dissertation. Subject
> and author indexes.

Continued by:

L4.   RECUEIL Mourier-Deltour. Catalogue et analyse des thèses
       latines et françaises admises par les facultés des lettres
       avec index et table alphabétique des docteurs [année scho-
       laire 1880/1881-1901/1902] Paris: Delalain frères, 1882-
       1902. 22 vols. Title varies. Annual.

           Follows same pattern as main work. Each volume has
           subject and author indexes.

L5.   PICARD, firm, Paris. Répertoire des thèses de doctorat ès
       lettres d'occasion. Paris: 1898. 80 p.

           Price list of 2,000 published theses. Some items
           have brief descriptive notes.

L6.   MAIRE, Albert. Répertoire alphabétique des thèses de docto-
       rat ès lettres des universités françaises, 1810-1900, avec
       table chronologique par université et table detaillée des
       matières. Paris: A. Picard, 1903. 226 p.

           An alphabetical author listing of 2,182 disserta-
           tions. Entry gives institution if not the University
           of Paris, publication information, and indicates
           dissertations which were not accepted.

L7.   "DOCTORAL Dissertations [1923-1959]" Progress of Medieval
       and Renaissance Studies in the United States and Canada
       Bulletin, no. 1 (1923)-25 (1960). Annual through 1933.
       Irregular.

           No. 1 (1923) lists theses and dissertations com-
           pleted and in progress for 1923; nos. 1-14 include
           medieval studies only.

           To no. 23 (1955) dissertations in progress and
           completed were listed separately. Later listings
           are arranged by broad field, e.g. arts, English
           language and literature, Romance language and lit-
           erature. Nos. 1 (1923)-10 (1932) contain only
           American dissertations. Entry gives publishing
           information.

L8.   COLUMBIA UNIVERSITY. Department of English and Comparative

Literature. Doctoral Dissertations of the Department of English and Comparative Literature of Columbia University, 1899-1929. New York: 1929. 7 p.

In two parts: (1) a chronological list of dissertations appearing in the Columbia University Studies in English and Comparative Literature; (2) dissertations not published by the Columbia University Press, indicating publication information. Covers the period 1899-1929.

L9.   GUIGE, Albert. La Faculté des lettres de l'Université de Paris, depuis sa fondation (17 mars 1808) jusqu'au 1er janvier 1935. Paris: Librairie Felix Alcan, 1935. 371 p.

"Liste des thèses de doctorat ès lettres depuis le 14 fevrier 1810 jusqu'au 1er janvier 1935" (p. 57-184); "Liste des thèses de doctorat d'université du 30 mai 1899 au 1er janvier 1935" (p. 207-232). Each is listed in chronological order. Author index.

L10.   WORK in Progress in the Modern Humanities [1938-1942] London: Modern Humanities Research Association, 1938-1943. (Modern Humanities Research Association. Bulletin, nos. 16A, 17A, 18A, 19A, 20A)

Issue for 1940 is supplement to 1939; 1941 a cumulative supplement to 1939; 1942 complete in itself.

Includes work in progress throughout the world, of dissertation standard only. Arranged by broad linguistic area (English studies, Romance studies, Germanic studies, and Slavonic studies), then subdivided into smaller subjects. Nos. 17A-19A report on works discontinued, works completed, and works not included in new issue because of lack of information on current status.

Continued by:

L11.   "RESEARCH in Progress in the Modern Languages and Literatures [1948-1960]" In Modern Language Association. Publications 63 (1948)-75 (1960). Annual through vol. 67 (1952); biennial for vols. 69 (1954)-75 (1960). April issue, 1950-1958; May issue, 1960.

About one-third are doctoral dissertations. World-

wide in coverage. Detailed classification, mainly
by language. Each list includes a report on the
status of previously listed items. Entry gives
statement of subject. "Subject Index" and "Index
of Researchers" in vol. 63; "Index of Researchers,"
vols. 64-67.

L12. SMITH, Albert H. and Arthur T. Hatto. A List of English,
Scandinavian and German Theses in the University of London.
London: University College, 1939. 40 p. (London Mediaeval
Studies. Monograph no. 2)

Lists 403 theses and dissertations submitted at the
University of London from 1906 to 1938. Subjects
include Old and Middle English language and literature, English philology, English literature, Scandinavian and German philology, Old and Middle High
German, modern German, and Dutch.

L13. VAN CAMP, Eliza L. Bibliography of Masters' Theses Accepted
by English Departments in Texas. Huntsville, Tex.: Sam
Houston State Teachers College, 1939. 226 p.

An annotated bibliography covering the period through
1938. Arranged alphabetically by author under the
school. In three parts, the University of Texas,
other state colleges, and independent colleges.

L14. LEBEL, Maurice. Thèses présentées à la Faculté des lettres
de l'Université Laval, 1940-1947. Québec: Chez l'auteur,
1947. 15 p.

Also appears in Culture 13 (1947): 67-75.

Lists 61 theses and dissertations, primarily in
literature.

L15. "LISTE des thèses de lettres soutenues devant les universités
françaises (Paris et province) [1948/1949-1956]" In Paris.
Université. Annales 20 (1950)-27 (1957). Title varies.
Annual.

Edited by Araxie Torossian.

Lists dissertations submitted to French universities.
Arranged by institution, subdivided by type of

doctorate.

L16. EELLS, Walter C. "American Doctoral Theses on Modern Languages Written by Women in the Nineteenth Century." Modern Language Journal 41 (1957): 209-211.

An analysis and listing of 34 items, all known to have been written by women in the 19th century. Entry gives year of bachelor's degree, birth and death dates, and publication information.

L17. DASSONVILLE, Michel. "Répertoire des thèses présentées à la Faculté des lettres de l'Université Laval, 1946-1956." Culture 20 (1959): 195-220.

Alphabetical list of 174 theses and dissertations. Pt. A: "Maîtrise ès arts"; pt. B: "Doctorat l'université"; pt. C: "Doctorat ès lettres." Subject index.

L18. "FINNISH Theses and Dissertations in Modern Languages and Literatures; Work in Progress: Academic Year [1963/1964-   ]" Neuphilologische Mitteilungen 65 (1964)-   . Annual.

Items are arranged alphabetically under English, French, and German.

L19. "FÖRTECKNING över ämnen för licentiat- och doktorsavhandlingar i litteraturhistoria." Samlaren 85 (1964): 223-233.

Theses and dissertations accepted in Swedish institutions from 1935 through 1964. Arranged chronologically under institution.

L20. SACKETT, S. J. "Masters' Theses in Literature Presented at American Colleges and Universities, July 1, 1964-June 30, 1965." In Fort Hays Kansas State College. Language and Literature Series, no. 7 (1966): 89-165.

An alphabetical author listing of 895 theses. Subject index and index of authors and titles.

L21. LUKENBILL, Willis B. A Working Bibliography of American Doctoral Dissertations in Children's and Adolescents' Literature, 1930-1971. Champaign, Ill.: University of Illinois, Graduate School of Library Science, 1972. 56 p. (University of Illinois Graduate Library School. Occasional Papers, no. 103)

> Following a bibliographic essay, covering such areas as education, history, and literary criticism, there is an alphabetical author listing of dissertations.

African Literature

L22. SCHMIDT, Nancy J. "Bibliography of American Doctoral Dissertations on African Literature." Research in African Literature 1 (1970): 62-65.

> An alphabetical author listing of about 35 dissertations, covering the period 1923 through 1969. Entry indicates if an abstract is available.

Anglo-American Literature

General

L23. VERZEICHNIS der an der Universität Leipzig erschienenen Dissertationen und Fakultätschriften auf englischen Gebiet. Leipzig: Seele, 1900. 7 p.

> A chronological list covering 1875-1900.

L24. "NEUE Dissertationen." Anglia: Beiblatt 43 (1932)-55 (1944). Irregular.

> Alphabetical author listings of dissertations completed in German universities and of German language Swiss dissertations.

L25. "BIBLIOGRAPHIE der an deutschen und österreichischen Universitäten [1939/1951-1952/1955] angenommenen anglistischen Dissertationen." Anglia: Zeitschrift für englische Philologie 70 (1952): 454-460; 71 (1953): 127, 249-256, 376, 498; 74 (1956): 385-412.

> A list in five parts and a supplement, arranged

chronologically by university, of German and Austrian
dissertations which had not yet appeared in the
Jahresverzeichnis der deutschen Hochschulschriften
(Item B36). Only last name is given for printed
dissertations; for others full information is given,
including adviser and location of dissertation. In
vol. 74, covering the period 1952-1955, all are
arranged in one list, with no mention of publication.

L26. MUMMENDEY, Richard. Language and Literature of the Anglo-
Saxon Nations as Presented in German Doctoral Dissertations,
1885-1950: A Bibliography. Bonn: H. Bouvier; Charlottesville, Va.: Bibliographical Society of the University of
Virginia, 1954. 200 p.

Added title page in German.

Lists 2,989 dissertations on Anglistics completed
in German universities. Includes Strasbourg up to
1918 and the Austrian universities from 1938 to 1945.
In three major groups: (1) linguistics, subdivided
by subject; (2) literary science; and (3) theatrical
science, subdivided by historical period. Author
and subject index.

L27. EELLS, Walter C. "American Doctoral Dissertations on English
Written by Women in the Nineteenth Century." In College
Language Association. Journal 2 (Sept. 1958): 25-33.

An alphabetical listing of 48 of the 228 known
doctoral dissertations by women during 1885-1900.
Gives institution and date of bachelor's degree
and publishing information.

L28. A DIRECTORY of Dissertations on English Produced by Indian
Scholars. Published on behalf of the Indian Association
for English Studies. Bombay: Orient Longmans, 1967. 15 p.

An alphabetical author list. Only English language
items included. Also lists work other than the doctoral dissertation, if taken after the M.A., and work
done outside India by Indian students. Entry indicates published title.

L29. McNAMEE, Lawrence E. Dissertations in English and American
Literature; Theses Accepted by American, British and German

Universities, 1865-1964. New York: Bowker, 1968. 1,124 p.

_____ _____ Supplement One: Theses Accepted 1964-1968.
New York: Bowker, 1969. 450 p.

> Approximately 19,000 dissertations arranged in 35
> chapters, reflecting time, period, and subject,
> each classified. Provides code number for univer-
> sity. A cross index of authors acts as a subject
> index. Alphabetical index of authors of disserta-
> tions.

L30. KUSHWAHA, Mahesh S. English Research in India. Lucknow:
Swastika Publications, 1972. 101 p.

> Issued as vol. 1.

> A retrospective listing of 1,233 dissertations and
> M.Litt. theses completed and in progress on English
> (including American literature, Indian writing in
> English, etc.) in Indian universities and institutes.
> Arranged by institution, subdivided by (1) completed
> and (2) in progress. An appendix lists "Doctoral
> Dissertations in Other Subjects Relating to English
> Language and Literature." Subject index.

American Literature

L31. LEISY, Ernest E. "Materials for Investigations in American
Literature: A Bibliography of Dissertations, Articles, Research in Progress, and Collections of Americana." Studies
in Philology 23 (1926): 90-115; 24 (1927): 480-483.

> Two sections in vol. 23 (1926) list dissertations:
> "A. Doctoral Dissertations" (p. 90-93) contains a
> subject-arranged list of completed dissertations
> dating from 1897, giving publishing information if
> known; "C. Dissertations in Progress" (p. 96-97)
> gives proposed title, author, and institution.
> List in vol. 24 (1927) contains addenda and errata
> to that in vol. 23.

> Continued by:

L32. _____ "Dissertations and Americana." In Foerster, Norman,
ed. The Reinterpretation of American Literature, p. 237-271.

New York: Harcourt, Brace, 1928.

> Lists completed dissertations (p. 237-244) and dissertations in progress (p. 248-251). Each list subdivided according to general topics and individual writers, then alphabetically listed by title. Covers work from beginning of the 20th century, on American literature.

L33. "RESEARCH in Progress." American Literature 1 (1929)- .
Quarterly.

> Lists dissertations in progress. Early volumes include dissertations completed and theses in progress. In three parts: (1) "Dissertations on Individual Authors," listing items alphabetically by author treated; (2) "Dissertations on Topics of a General Nature": (3) "Other [Non-Doctoral] Research in Progress."

> Continued and supplemented by:

L34. LEISY, Ernest E. and Jay B. Hubbell. "Doctoral Dissertations in American Literature." American Literature 4 (1933): 419-465.

> Also reprinted as a separate by Duke University, 1933.

> Lists 406 dissertations in two parts: dissertations completed, giving author's address and publishing information if known; and dissertations in progress, giving subject as announced. Both sections are arranged by era, then by author treated or "general topics." Includes U.S., Canadian, French, and German dissertations.

> Continued by:

L35. LEARY, Lewis. "Doctoral Dissertations in American Literature, 1933-1948." American Literature 20 (1948): 169-230.

> Also reprinted as a separate by Duke University, 1948.

> Contains 1,142 dissertations, including those announced in Item L33, March 1933 to March 1948,

plus additional titles and corrections that have
been reported. Encompasses work in departments
other than English, including American speech, if
item deals with an American of letters or a literary movement or form. Divided according to (1)
dissertations on individual authors and (2) those
on general topics. Entry indicates department, if
other than English. Some German and French items
are included.

L36. BALLA-CAYARD, L. "German Dissertations on American Literature Accepted between 1900 and 1945." <u>American Literature</u>
24 (1952): 384-388.

A chronological listing of approximately 75 dissertations and Habilitationsschriften compiled from
the official catalogs of German universities. Entry
gives publication information.

Continued by:

L37. MARBURG. Universität. English Seminar. "German Dissertations on American Literature between 1945 and 1952." <u>Amer-
ican Literature</u> 24 (1952): 288-290.

A chronological listing of approximately 30 dissertations.

L38. HIBLER, Leo, Karl Brunner, and Herbert Koziol. "Austrian
Dissertations on American Literature." <u>American Literature</u>
24 (Jan. 1953): 543-547.

Work completed or in progress at the Universities
of Vienna, Innsbruck, and Graz. For each institution, the material is listed in two parts: (1) dissertations completed, arranged by date of acceptance;
and (2) dissertations in progress, arranged alphabetically by student.

L39. CANTRELL, Clyde H. and Walton R. Patrick. <u>Southern Literary
Culture; A Bibliography of Masters' and Doctors' Theses.</u>
Tuscaloosa, Ala.: University of Alabama Press, 1955. 124 p.

Lists and locates 2,529 theses and dissertations
relating to the literary history of the South, regardless of academic department. Covers work done in 150

graduate schools throughout America to the end of
1948. Arranged alphabetically by author, with
department given and often a brief note to clarify
subject. A subject index includes authors, newspaper and periodical titles, literary forms, as
well as subjects.

L40. WOODRESS, James L. <u>Dissertations in American Literature</u>,
<u>1891-1955</u>. Newly revised and enlarged with the assistance
of Marian Koritz. Durham, N.C.: Duke University Press, 1968.
185 p.

First edition 1957. Second edition 1962.

An alphabetical subject listing of 4,631 dissertations, completed and in progress. International
in coverage. Entry gives publication information.
If not written in an English department, the discipline is indicated. Author index.

L41. JONES, Lawrence J. "Canadian Theses and Dissertations on
American Literature: 1947-1968 Checklist." <u>Serif</u> 8 (March
1971): 8-17.

Approximately 225 items are listed under studies of
individual authors, general studies, and comparative
studies.

L42. HOWARD, Patsy C. <u>Theses in American Literature, 1894-1970</u>.
Ann Arbor, Mich.: Pierian Press, 1973. 307 p.

Lists 7,000 bachelors' and masters' theses under
individual authors as subjects. International in
coverage; however, most of the items are American,
Canadian, or British. Title and personal name
index and author index.

Australian Literature

L43. "RESEARCH in Progress in Australian Literature." <u>Australian
Literary Studies</u> 2 (1956)-   . With vol. 5 (1972), every
two years.

An international listing, consisting in largest
part of theses and dissertations in progress, though

some of the items listed indicate that they have been completed. Arranged by institution.

Canadian Literature

L44. KLINCK, Carl F. "Theses [1959-1970]" _Canadian Literature_, no. 3 (1960)-no. 49 (1971). Irregular.

> Lists theses and dissertations completed in Canadian institutions. Nos. 3 (1960)-40 (1969) include both English-Canadian and French-Canadian works in two separate lists. No. 49 (1971), covering 1969 and 1970, lists only English-Canadian theses and dissertations. French-Canadian items for 1969 are listed in Item L117. Entry gives adviser.

> Continued by:

L45. REGISTER of Post-Graduate Theses in Canadian Literature: English and English-French Comparative [no. 13 (1971)-14 (1972)] London, Ontario: 1972-1973. Annual.

> List for 1972 includes work in progress.

> Alphabetical author listings of English language theses and dissertations completed in Canadian universities.

> Supplemented and continued by:

L46. "POST-GRADUATE Theses in Canadian Literature: English and English-French Comparative [1971-   ]" _Journal of Canadian Fiction_ 1 (1972)-   . Annual.

> List in vol. 1 (1972) edited by Carl F. Klinck.

> Lists theses and dissertations completed or in progress in Canadian universities. In three parts: (1) completed, (2) in preparation, and (3) held over from previous lists. Entry gives adviser.

English Literature

L47. ALTICK, Richard D. and William R. Matthews. _Guide to Doc-_

toral Dissertations in Victorian Literature, 1886-1958. Urbana, Ill.: University of Illinois Press, 1960. 119 p.

Contains 2,105 completed dissertations from the U.S., Austria, Switzerland (through 1958), France (through 1957), the United Kingdom and Germany (through 1956) on the literature of Great Britain from about 1837 to 1900. The studies are classed by general topic or by author treated, with cross references and an author index.

L48. "MIDDLE English Research in Progress [1963/1964-   ]" Neuphilologische Mitteilungen 65 (1964)-   . Annual.

A subject listing, including a substantial number of dissertations. International in scope. Does not include Old English, Chaucer, or late Tudor studies. Entry gives aspect of topic.

L49. "OLD English Research in Progress [1964/1965-   ]" Neuphilologische Mitteilungen 66 (1965)-   .

A subject listing of works in progress or complete but not yet in print. Includes a substantial number of dissertations and some other graduate research. International in coverage.

L50. HOWARD, Patsy C. Theses in English Literature, 1894-1970. Ann Arbor, Mich.: Pierian Press, 1973. 387 p.

Lists 9,000 bachelors' and masters' theses under individual authors as subjects. International in coverage; however, most of the items listed are American, Canadian, and British. Title and name index and index of thesis authors.

Classical Studies

L51. FOCK, Gustav, firm, booksellers, Leipzig. Catalogus dissertationum philologicarum classicarum. Editio II. Verzeichnis von etwa 27400 Abhandlungen aus dem Gesamtgebiete der klassischen Philologie und Altertumskunde. Zusammengestellt von der Zentralstelle für Dissertationen und Programme der Buchhandlung Gustav Fock... 2. Aufl. Leipzig: 1910. 652 p.

First edition 1894.

Continued and supplemented by:

_____ Catalogus dissertationum philologicarum classicarum.
Editio III. Erläuterungsschriften zu den griechischen und
lateinischen Schriftstellern, enthaltend du Literatur aus
den Jahren 1911-1936 und eine Auswahl früher erscheinener
Schriften_. Zusammengestellt von der Zentralstelle für
Dissertationen und Programme der Buchhandlung Gustav Fock...
Leipzig: 1937. 176 p.

Both editions reprinted in 1963.

A book dealer's catalog that includes dissertations
and programs. Editio II includes approximately 27,400
items and Editio III, covering the period 1911-1937,
as well as selected earlier publications, includes
5,836 items. Brief bibliographic data which do not
include institutional affiliation. Arranged by
Greek authors, Latin authors, and classified subject.
Editio II includes an author index.

L52. SCHLICHER, J. J. "Doctors' Dissertations in the Classics
[1900-1911]" Classical Journal 1 (1906): 233-239; 2 (1907):
177-179; 3 (1908): 198-199; 4 (1909): 180-181; 5 (1910):
133-134; 6 (1911): 373-374; 7 (1912): 187-188.

Completed dissertations arranged by university.
Entry gives publication information.

L53. "DOCTORS of Philosophy in Classical Philology and Classical
Archaeology of Harvard University, 1875-1909." Harvard
Studies in Classical Philology 21 (1910): 161-167.

A chronological listing.

L54. "SUMMARIES of Dissertations for the Degree of Ph.D. [1910/
1911-   ]" Harvard Studies in Classical Philology 22
(1911)-   . Annual. None published in vols. 29 (1918)-
32 (1921).

"Summaries of all doctoral dissertations accepted
by the Department of Classics of Harvard University
and by Radcliffe, in Classical Philology, in Classical Archaeology, and in Medieval and Patristic Greek,
and in Medieval and Patristic Latin..."

L55. SCHONACK, Wilhelm. Ein Jahrhundert berliner philologischer
Dissertationen, (1810-1910); Mit ein historisch-kritischen
Einleitung. Wolfenbüttel: J. Zwissler, 1914. 231 p.

    University of Berlin dissertations in the area of
classical philology, including works in related and
auxiliary subjects. Altogether about 1,500 items.
Classified listing.

L56. "LISTE des mémoires de diplômes d'études supérieures agréés
par la Faculté des lettres de Paris [1930/1934-1950]" Revue
des études latines (Paris) 12 (1934)-28 (1950). Annual.

    Vol. 12 (1934) listing covers the years 1930-1934.
No lists published in vols. 19 (1941)-22 (1944) and
27 (1949).

    An alphabetical author listing.

L57. "RESEARCH in Classical Studies for University Degrees in
Great Britain and Ireland [1951-   ]" In London. University. Institute of Classical Studies. Bulletin, no. 1, pt. 2
(1954)-   . Annual.

    Includes ancient history and archaeology. Section A
lists work in progress above the M.A. arranged by
institution; section B lists work completed, including the M.A., arranged by institution.

L58. "THESES in Progress [1966/1967-   ]" Agon, no. 1 (1967)-
. Annual.

    Dissertations in classical studies in progress at
American universities. Includes literature and
drama; philology; paleography; numismatics; Greek
history; Roman history; art and archaeology; myth-
ology and religion; philosophy and science. Entry
indicates expected date of completion.

L59. THOMPSON, Lawrence S. A Bibliography of American Doctoral
Dissertations in Classical Studies and Related Fields.
Hamden, Conn.: Shoestring Press, 1968. 250 p.

    A bibliography of American dissertations in the
broad area of classical studies and related fields
from the beginning of graduate study in North America

through 1964 and including some items from 1965.
All aspects of the culture of Greece and Rome, from
pre-historic Greece and Italy to 500 A.D. New
Testament dissertations have been included only if
the subject matter appears to be useful for cultural,
textual, or linguistic study. Christian literature,
Greek and Latin, has been included, unless it has
been exegetical or theological. In two parts: an
alphabetical author listing and a subject, title,
and topographical index. In some cases, entry gives
publication information or location of an abstract.
Includes indexes of Greek and Latin words.

Comparative Literature

L60. ROSENBERG, Ralph P. "Doctoral Dissertations." Romanic
Review 36 (1945): 194-199.

Lists studies in French and German literature in
two parts, "Doctoral Dissertations" and "Works in
Progress." International in scope. Covers the
period 1897-1943. Entry gives publication information.

L61. "SOUTENANCES de thèses récentes." Revue de littérature comparée 18 (1938)-28 (1954). Irregular.

Dissertations submitted to the University of Paris.
Vols. 18 (1938) and 19 (1939) list American dissertations.

L62. "TRAVAUX en cours." Revue de littérature comparée 15 (1935)-
28 (1954). Quarterly. Irregular.

Appears in one to four issues of each yearly volume.
Beginning in vol. 15 (1935) are lists of theses in
comparative literature (primarily but not exclusively
French-oriented). Most are works submitted to the
Faculté des lettres de Paris or l'Institut de literature comparée, Sorbonne, but other institutions are
occasionally included.

In vol. 28 (1954) "Travaux en cours" contains one
list of theses from England and one of those from
Geneva. In vol. 30 (1956) there are two lists,
"Travaux universitaires," giving English, Austrian,

and Swiss theses.

Folklore

L63. "DOCTORAL Dissertations." In International Arthurian Society. Bibliographical Bulletin 3 (1951)- . Annual.

Pt. 4 of the bibliographical report of the American Branch, covering the United States and Canada.

L64. RÖHRICH, Lutz. Bibliographie volkskundlicher Dissertationen an deutschen Universitäten 1945-1950. Als Manuskript hrsg. von der Württembergischen Landesstelle für Volkskunde. Stuttgart: 1951. 18 p.

A classified listing of 214 dissertations.

L65. THOMPSON, Harold W. "Folklore in the Schools; Theses on Folklore, Albany State College and Cornell University." New York Folklore Quarterly 8 (1952): 230-232.

Alphabetical author lists of (1) "Masters' Theses, Albany," (2) "Masters' Theses and Essays, Cornell," (3) "Doctoral Theses, Cornell." Largely on New York folklore, but contains other studies on folklore as well. Covers the period 1935-1951.

_____ "Additional List of Theses; Albany and Cornell." New York Folklore Quarterly 9 (1953): 55-56.

Supplements earlier list with theses primarily from S.U.N.Y.-Albany. Extends period covered from 1934 to 1952.

L66. MEL'TS, M. IA. "Bibliografiya avtoreferatov dissertatsiy po problemam narodnogo poĕticheskogo tvorchestva [1949/1955-1956] Russkiy fol'klor 1 (1956): 313-346; 2 (1957): 363-373.

Vol. 1 (1956) covers 1949-1955.

Classified listings of 505 theses and dissertations. Author and national group indexes.

L67. KROLIKOWSKA, Elżbieta. "Problematyka folklorystyczna w etno-
graficznych pracach magisterskich." In Lodz, Poland. Museum
Archeologiczne i Etnograficzne. Prace i materialy. Seria
ethnograficzna 14 (1970): 207-212.

A listing of 69 theses completed in Polish universities between 1946 and 1969.

Germanic Languages and Literature

L68. "BIBLIOGRAPHY: Americana Germanica [1951-1966]" American
German Review 8 (1941/1942)-33 (1966/1967). Title varies.
Annual.

Contains a section of "...Research in Progress and
Unpublished Studies." Lists American theses and
dissertations completed and in progress of German
interest and German dissertations of American interest. Contents vary and lists sometimes carry abstracts and publication information.

L69. "DOCTOR of Philosophy: A List of Those Who Have Taken the
Doctorate in the Department of German at the Ohio State
University during the Chairmanship of Professor M. Blake-
more Evans (1911-1945)." Monatshefte 37 (1945): 204-205.

An alphabetical listing of 22 items.

L70. "DOCTORAL Degrees Granted [1945/1946-   ]" Monatshefte 38
(1946)-   . Annual. Title varies.

No lists in vols. 39 (1947)-41 (1949).

American and Canadian dissertations arranged by
university. Entry gives adviser.

L71. "DISSERTATIONS in Progress." Monatshefte 41 (1949): 52-55.

Alphabetical author listing of work being done at
American universities. Entry gives adviser.

L72. FISCHER, Hanns. "Neue Forschungen zur deutschen Dichtung
des späten Mittelalters (1230-1500)" Deutsche Vierteljahre-
schrift für Literaturwissenschaft und Geistesgeschichte 31

(1957): 342-345.

Lists approximately 90 German and Austrian dissertations completed in the period 1945-1955 on the
poetry of the late Middle Ages.

L73. WERNER, Julius. "Bibliographie deutschsprachiger Hochschulschriften zur deutsche Literatur von der Aufklärung bis zur
bürgerlichen Revolution 1848/49, die in den Jahren 1945 bis
1953 erschienen sind." Weimarer Beiträge 3 (1957): 134-183.

Lists 617 German language dissertations arranged by
(1) literary history and works dealing with an individual theme, and (2) individuals as subjects. Entry
gives publication information. Author index.

L74. BERLIN. Freie Universität. Germanisches Seminar. Verzeichnis der im Entstehen begriffen Dissertationen aus dem Gebiete
der deutsche Sprache und Literatur [Liste 1 (Feb. 25, 1958)-
] Berlin: 1958-   . Annual.

Classified international listing of work in progress
in Germanic language and linguistics. Section B
notes dissertations previously listed and now complete.

L75. HILL, Claude and Ralph Ley. The Drama of German Expressionism: A German-English Bibliography. Chapel Hill: University
of North Carolina Press, 1960. 211 p. (University of North
Carolina Studies in Germanic Languages and Literatures, no.
28)

Pt. 1: "Drama of German Expressionism in General."
Pt. 2: individual dramatists. Section of books and
dissertations included in each chapter. Within
this, German and American dissertations are listed
separately. Covers the period to January 1, 1958,
except that German dissertations are not covered
after January 1, 1957.

L76. DEPREZ, Ada. "Licentiaatwerken en doctoraten im verband met
de literatuurwetenschap of de Nederlandse literatuurstudie;
Systematisch overzicht van de aan de Belgische universiteiten
voorgelegde werken (1934-1964)." Studia germanica gandensia
7 (1965): 141-215.

A classified listing of 862 theses and dissertations.

Author index.

L77. "DISSERTATIONS in Progress [as of May 31, 1966]" <u>Monatshefte</u>
58 (1966): 258-267.

A classified listing of 351 items from 56 universities in the United States, Canada, Australia, New
Zealand, and South Africa. Entry gives expected
date of completion.

_____ "June 1967." <u>Monatshefte</u> 59 (1967): 255-262.

Updates basic list, indicating revisions and drops.

Hebrew Literature

L78. "GRADUATE Degrees Conferred; Recipients of the Master of
Hebrew Literature...Recipients of the Doctor of Hebrew
Literature Degree, and the Subjects of Their Theses." <u>In</u>
Yeshiva University. Bernard Revel Graduate School. <u>Cata-
logue, 1953-1954</u>, p. 87-91. New York: 1953.

Cumulates listings which appeared annually in the
catalogs since 1943.

The first doctorates were awarded in 1929. However,
the formal program did not begin until 1942. Entries
indicate earlier degrees taken.

Hindi Literature

L79. SINGH, Uday B. <u>Hindī ke svīkrta sodhaprabandha</u>. Delhi:
1963. 524 p.

Supersedes 1959 edition.

In Hindi.

A chronological listing of 539 dissertations. Includes some studies from non-Indian institutions,
the titles of which have been translated into Hindi.
Institutional index, subdivided chronologically,
and subject index.

Language and Linguistics

L80. "AMERICAN Doctoral Degrees Granted in the Field of Modern
Languages [1921/1922-   ]" <u>Modern Language Journal</u> 7
(1922/1923)-   . Title varies. Usually March issue.

No lists in vols. 15 (1930)-19 (1934); these years
are covered in 21 (Jan., Feb. 1937) and 22 (Jan.,
Feb., March 1938); no list in 26 (1942)-32 (1948),
34 (1950), 36 (1952), 50 (1966), and 54 (1970), but
information for years since 1948 is carried in the
subsequent volume. Vol. 57 (Nov. 1973) carries a
supplement to 1971/1972 listing. Beginning with
vol. 35 (1951) includes Canadian universities.

Arranged by language or topic, e.g. comparative
literature, foreign language, education, linguistics.
Entry gives adviser.

L81. "THESES for the Year [1936-   ] in English and Modern Foreign Languages Accepted in the Colleges and Universities of
the South Atlantic States." <u>South Atlantic Bulletin</u> 2
(1936)-   . Vols. 2-13 in Oct. issue; vol. 14-   in Nov.
issue.

Lists theses and dissertations arranged by university and language department. Entry gives adviser.

L82. RUSSELL, H. K. "Theses in English and Modern Foreign Lan-
guages Accepted in the Colleges of North Carolina, South
Carolina, Georgia, Florida, and Alabama, 1917-1937." <u>South
Atlantic Bulletin</u> 4, no. 1 (April 1938): suppl., 15 p.

Alphabetical author listing of theses and some dissertations arranged by university and department.

L83. FAIRON, E. "Thèses relatives à la toponymie et à la dialectologie présentées pour l'obtention des grades de Licence ou
Docteur en philologie et lettres aux universités belges
(1920-1943)." <u>In</u> Belgium. Commission royale de toponymie
et de dialectologie. <u>Bulletin</u> 17 (1943): 175-192.   ?

L84. "THESES Accepted in the Universities of Great Britain and
Ireland during the Calendar Year [1950-1956]" <u>Year's Work
in Modern Language Studies</u> 12 (1950)-18 (1956). Title varies.

Annual.

Theses and dissertations classified by language.

L85. "ABSTRACTS of Dissertations." Linguistics, no. 9 (1964)-20 (1966). Irregular.

Each number contains 15 to 20 abstracts of American dissertations, beginning with those completed in 1962.

L86. HORNUNG, Herwig. "Verzeichnis der Dissertationen, die unter der Leitung von Eberhard Kranzmayer seit 1950 an der Wiener Universität entstanden sind (abgeschlossen Dezember 1966)." In Mundart und Geschichte; E. Kranzmayer zu seinem 70. Geburtstag. Am 15 Mai 1967, Appendix, p. 13-19. Graz: Böhlau, 1967.

An alphabetical author listing of 128 dissertations. Subject index.

L87. RUTHERFORD, Phillip R. A Bibliography of American Doctoral Dissertations in Linguistics, 1900-1964. Washington: Center for Applied Linguistics, 1968. 139 p.

Supersedes Amy E. Shaughnessy, Dissertations in Linguistics, 1957-1964 (1965).

Lists 1,733 items, arranged alphabetically by author. Some items included if only somewhat linguistic in nature. Topical and analytical index.

Continued by:

L88. "DISSERTATIONS in Linguistics." In Linguistic Society of America. Bulletin, no. 45: 16-29.

Lists dissertations completed in American institutions in the period 1965-1970. Arranged by institution.

L89. CIUTI. "Lijst van de scripties; Liste de thèses; Bibliographie der diplomarbeiten [1967/1968-1968/1969]" Linguistica Antverpiensia (Antwerp) 2 (1968): 508-517; 3 (1969): 319-328. ?

Lists theses completed in the affiliated institutions of higher education.

L90. "THESES and Dissertations within the SCMLA Region [1970-   ]" South Central Bulletin 37 (1972)-   . Annual.

Vol. 37 (1972) includes work completed in 1970 and 1971.

Lists theses and dissertations completed within the region of the South-Central Modern Language Association. Arranged by language and under language subdivided into (1) general and (2) authors and works. Entry gives adviser.

Philippine Literature

L91. FLORENTINO, Alberto S. "A Bibliography of Unpublished Graduate Theses on Philippine Literature." In his Midcentury Guide to Philippine Literature in English, p. 45-53. Manila: Filipiniana Publishers, 1963.

Lists 83 theses and three dissertations completed from 1938 to 1962 in Philippine institutions. Arranged by authors as subjects and by the various literary forms, then chronologically.

Philology

L92. MULLER, Frederik, & Co., Amsterdam. Catalogus dissertationum et orationum philologicarum, defensarum et habitarum ab a. 1650 usque ad 1851 in academiis Germaniae, etc., praesertim Neerlandiae. Quae venales prostant apud Fredericum Muller. Amstelodami: 1851. 11 p.

A dealer's catalog listing 284 items. In two parts, (1) quarto and (2) octavo.

L93. VARNHAGEN, Hermann. Systematisches Verzeichnis der Programm- abhandlungen, Dissertationen und Habilitationsschriften aus dem Gebiete der romanischen und englischen Philologie sowie der allgemeinen Sprach- und Litteraturwissenschaft und der Pädagogik und Methodik. 2. vollst. umgearb. Aufl. Besorgt von Johannes Martin. Leipzig: Koch, 1893. 296 p.

First edition in 1877, also published as a supplement
to Bernhard Schmitz, Encyclopädie des philologischen
Studiums der neueren Sprachen, hauptsächlich der
französischen und englischen.

Includes approximately 4,000 dissertations. Primarily
German, but also includes Swedish, Swiss, French,
Italian, Danish, and other dissertations. Pt. 1:
linguistic philology and literature in general; pt.
2: Romance philology; pt. 3: English philology; pt.
4: pedagogics and methodology. Entry gives title
in original language. Author index.

L94. "TESIS doctorales sobre filología española." Revista de
filología española 6 (1919): 312-313.

A list of dissertations taken from Item L100.

L95. VOLKOV, S. S. "Novy trudy po filologii (obzor dissertatsiy
zashchishchennye v 1960-1961 gg. na filologich facul'tete)."
In Leningrad. Universitet. Vestnik, vyp. 2: Seriya istorii,
yazyka i literatury 27, no. 8 (1962): 137-145.

An analysis and abstracts of U.S.S.R. theses and
dissertations.

L96. "TEZE de doctorat în filologie sustinute în anii [1966/1967-
1968]" Limba Romînă 17 (1968): 271-275; 18 (1969): 339-343.

Dissertations defended at Romanian institutions
arranged by institution and faculty. Listing for
1968 includes abstracts. Entry gives adviser.

L97. WATHELET-WILLEM, Jeanne. "Recension des mémoires présentés
à la Section de philologie romane de l'Université de Liège
depuis sa fondation, 1891-1962." Marche romaine 13 (1963):
3-32, 141.

A chronological listing of 555 theses and a separate
listing of studies for the doctorate. Author index
and an analytical classified index which is arranged
by historical period and further subdivided into such
areas as syntax, morphology, genres and literary
themes, esthetics, and cultural influences.

L98. "VERZEICHNIS der literatur-wissenschaftlichen Dissertationen an österreichischen Hochschulen, Studienjahr [1969/1970-]" _Sprachkunst_ 1970- . Annual.

> Covers German, English, Romance, Slavic, and classical philology. Arranged by field. Entry gives adviser. Some items carry abstracts.

Romance Languages and Literature

General

L99. GERIG, John L. "Advanced Degrees and Doctoral Dissertations in the Romance Languages at the Johns Hopkins University: A Survey and Bibliography." _Romanic Review_ 8 (1917): 328-340.

> Two lists: "Doctoral Dissertations" and "Essays Offered for the M.A. Degree." Arranged chronologically from first such degrees. Entry gives publication information.

L100. _____ "Doctoral Dissertations in Romance Languages at Harvard University: A Survey and Bibliography." _Romanic Review_ 10 (1919): 67-78.

> Arranged chronologically, beginning with first dissertations in the field at Harvard. Entry gives publication information.

L101. _____ "Doctoral Dissertations in the Romance Languages at Yale University: A Survey and Bibliography." _Romanic Review_ 11 (1920): 70-75.

> Arranged chronologically, from first such degrees issued. Entry gives publication information.

L102. _____ "Doctoral Dissertations in the Romance Languages at Columbia University: A Survey and Bibliography." _Romanic Review_ 12 (1921): 73-79.

> Arranged chronologically from first such degrees issued. Entry gives publication information.

L103. MERRILL, Ray M. American Doctoral Dissertations in the
Romance Field, 1876-1926. New York: Columbia University
Press, 1927. 87 p.

Lists 521 titles from 30 institutions, of which 183
were unpublished. An author listing covering items
from the beginnings of work in this field in America,
including some from other fields which would be
useful to workers in Romance languages. Entry gives
publication information. Romance authors' and
topical index.

L104. "DIE ROMANTISCHEN Dissertationen; Seit 1945 an deutschen
Universitäten angenommene, nicht im Druck erschienene
Doktorarbeiten." Romantisches Jahrbuch 4 (1951): 43-51.

Dissertations completed or in progress in German
universities. In two parts: (1) an alphabetical
listing under the year of completion from 1945 to
1954; (2) a list of titles (no authors) of work in
progress arranged by institution.

L105. "ROMANISTICHE Habilitationsschriften und Dissertationen
[1947-   ]" Romantisches Jahrbuch 5 (1952)-   . Title
varies. Annual.

Dissertations and Habilitationsschriften completed
or in progress in German and Austrian institutions.
Separate listings of (1) completed Habilitationsschriften, (2) completed dissertations, (3) Habilitationsschriften in progress, (4) dissertations in
progress. Each list arranged by country and university. In progress lists give the title only (no
author).

L106. FLASCHE, Hans. Die Sprachen und Literaturen der Romanen im
Spiegel der deutschen Universitätsschriften, 1885-1950; Eine
Bibliographie. Bonn: Bouvier, 1958. 299 p. (Bonner Bei-
träge zur Bibliotheks- und Bücherkunde, Bd. 3)

In German, French, and English.

Also published as Romance Languages and Literatures
as Presented in German Doctoral Dissertations, 1885-
1950; A Bibliography.

Lists 4,030 dissertations completed in German

universities (including Strasbourg up to 1918 and
the universities in Austria from 1938 to 1945) in
Romance studies and other fields, i.e. philosophy,
comparative literature, English studies, and German
studies, which contain material relating to Romance
studies. Divided into linguistics and literary
science. Under linguistics the items are classified
under broad subject groupings and under literary
science they are grouped by historical period. In
both sections the items are listed by author or
writer dealt with. Name and subject indexes.

L107. "MÉMOIRES de diplômes d'études supérieures soutenus devant
la Faculté des lettres de Strasbourg (langue et littératures
romanes) 1945-1960." In Strasbourg. Université. Centre
de philologie et de littératures romaines. Programme de
l'année..., fasc. 5: 93-99. Strasbourg: Université de
Strasbourg, Faculté des lettres, 1960. ?

Entry gives adviser.

Continued by:

L108. "DIPLÔMES d'études supérieures soutenus depuis juin 1960."
In Strasbourg. Université. Centre de philologie et de
littératures romaines. Programme de l'année..., fasc. 7:
53-54. Strasbourg: Université de Strasbourg, Faculté des
lettres, 1962. ?

Entry gives adviser.

Continued by:

L109. "THÈSES et diplômes achevés, soutenus à la fin de l'année
1961-1962 et au cours de l'année 1962-1963." In Strasbourg.
Université. Centre de philologie et de littératures
romaines. Programme de l'année..., fasc. 8: 50-51. Strasbourg: Université de Strasbourg, Faculté des lettres,
1963. ?

Entry gives adviser.

French Literature

L110. "LES THÈSES de lettres à Paris depuis 1939." Revue d'histoire littéraire de la France 48 (1948): 110-112.

Chronological listing of approximately 50 theses in
modern French literature submitted to the University
of Paris Faculté des lettres from January 1939 to
July 1947. Entry gives publication information.

L111. "LES SUJETS de thèses à Paris." Revue d'histoire littéraire
de la France 48 (1948): 183-190, 285-288, 372-380.

Lists subjects of dissertations for the doctorate
in letters and the University doctorate in modern
French literature completed at the University of
Paris since 1939.

L112. "THÈSES de littérature française Université de Londres,
1951." In Association internationale des études françaises.
Cahiers, no. 2 (Mai 1952): 111.

Lists nine completed items.

L113. "THÈSES allemandes." Revue d'histoire littéraire de la
France 66 (1966): 358-359.

Lists dissertations in progress, arranged by institution. Entry gives title only.

L114. "DISSERTATIONS in Progress." French Review 37 (1963)-
Annual. Oct. issue.

Dissertations reported in major American universities on subjects in French language and literature.
Arrangement is by subject, with literature category
subdivided according to time period, then author.
Abandonments, changes, and completions are noted.
With vol. 44 (1970) a separate classified list gives
dissertations completed and defended in previous
academic year.

French Canadian Literature

L115. MARION, Séraphin. "À la conquête du haut savoir." Revue de
l'Université d'Ottawa 15 (1945): 446-470.

Contains separate listings of theses and dissertations dealing with French Canada, representing work done in Canadian institutions. Most of the items are in the fields of history, literature, and folklore.

L116. "THÈSES de doctorat et de D.E.S. présentées à l'Université Laval de Montreal et d'Ottawa [1961-   ]" Livres et auteurs quebeçois 1961-   . Annual.

Lists only those theses and dissertations written in French. Arranged by institution, subdivided by type of degree. Entry carries a descriptive note.

L117. NAAMAN, Antoine. Guide bibliographique des thèses littéraires canadiennes de 1921 à 1969. Montreal: Cosmos, 1970. 338 p.

Lists 2,851 theses and dissertations completed or in progress by Canadians in Canadian institutions and in institutions outside Canada. Arranged in three major parts: pt. 1: "Thèses en lettres canadiennes anglaises et françaises"; pt. 2: "Thèses en lettres françaises et de langue françaises"; pt. 3: "Thèses en lettres anciennes et étrangères (echantillonnage)." Each part divided by subject and by authors as subjects. Entry gives publication information. Key word analytical subject index, index of authors and thesis advisers, and an index of authors as subjects.

Continued by:

L118. BRODEUR, Léo A. and Antoine Naaman. "Thèses contemporaines de littérature canadienne en française." Journal of Canadian Fiction 1 (1972): 79-86.

Lists approximately 500 theses and dissertations completed in Canadian universities in the period 1969 through 1971. In three parts: (1) general subjects, (2) comparative studies, and (3) authors.

L119. LEMIRE, Maurice and Kenneth Landry. Répertoire des specialistes de littérature canadienne-française. Québec: Université Laval, 1971.

"Thèses de littérature canadienne-française (1923-

1970)" (p. 37-66) lists approximately 450 theses
and dissertations, completed or in progress in
Canadian universities, alphabetically by author.
Entry gives adviser.

Hispanic Literature

L120. "DISSERTATIONS in the Hispanic Languages and Literatures..."
Hispania 18 (1935)-   . Title varies. Annual. May issue
since 1942.

First list, May 1935, contained completed works from
1915 at U.S. institutions. It was arranged by years,
then alphabetically by author, with subject index
following. Early listings included completed M.A.
theses and Ph.D. dissertations in progress and completed. With vol. 33 (1950) coverage was broadened
to include all Hispanic studies rather than only
Latin American, and narrowed to include only doctoral
dissertations completed and in progress. In vol.
37 (1954) the retrospective listing of all Hispanic
subjects was completed. Vol. 37 (1954): 185-202
contains a subject index of all dissertations listed
since 1935. Arrangement is alphabetical by author.
Entry gives adviser and publishing information.
Currently each list includes doctoral dissertations
in U.S. and Canadian institutions completed and in
progress during the previous year.

L121. MAPES, E. K. "Bibliografía de theses sobre literatura iberoamericana preparadas en las universidades de Iberoamérica."
Revista iberoamericana 6 (1943): 203-206.

Includes all theses completed and dissertations
completed and in progress in the universities of
Puerto Rico, Havana, Buenos Aires, and Mexico.
Separate lists of theses, dissertations, and dissertations in progress.

L122. JOHNSON, Harvey L. "Doctoral Dissertations Written in the
United States on Latin American Languages and Literature and
Related Topics." In Symposium on the Languages and Litera-
tures of Spanish America and Brazil, University of Texas,
1956. Proceedings, p. 51-62. Austin: University of Texas,
Department of Romance Studies and the Institute of Latin-
American Studies, 1957. 62 p. (Texas. University.

Institute of Latin American Studies. Latin American Studies, 15)

Lists approximately 275 dissertations by country.

L123. CASTILLO, Homero. "La literatura chilena en los Estados Unidos de América." Anales de la Universidad de Chile 113 (1959): 83-128.

Lists 25 dissertations completed or in progress and 28 completed theses (p. 99-101). Addendum lists five additional dissertations in progress.

L124. _____ "La literatura hispanoamericana en las tesis de los Estados Unidos." Anales de la Universidad de Chile 119 (1961): 131-141.

An alphabetical listing of 238 dissertations completed to 1959, inclusive. Entry includes dissertation adviser. Index of persons as subjects, institutions where work was done, advisers, and countries treated in the studies.

Continued and supplemented by:

L125. LARSON, Ross F. "La literatura hispanoamericana en las tesis doctorales de los Estados Unidos." Anales de la Universidad de Chile 123 (1965): 157-170.

An alphabetical listing of 128 dissertations completed in the period 1909 to 1963, incorporating material not included in Castillo's work. Entry gives adviser. Index of persons as subjects, institutions where work was done, advisers, and countries treated in the studies.

L126. CHATHAM, James R. and Enrique Ruiz-Fornells. Dissertations in Hispanic Languages and Literatures; An Index of Dissertations Completed in the United States and Canada, 1876-1966. Lexington, Ky.: University Press of Kentucky, 1970. 120 p.

A classified list covering comparative literature and applied linguistics, as well as the work done in Romance language departments. Dissertations dealing entirely with the indigenous non-Romance

languages of the Iberian Peninsula and Latin America
have been excluded. Includes reference to the abstract series of the institution where completed,
Library of Congress card number, and variant publication title. General index of subjects, authors as
subjects, and authors of dissertations.

L127. ZUBATSKY, David S. "An International Guide of Completed
Theses and Dissertations in the Hispanic Languages and Literature." Hispania 55 (1972): 293-302.

A bibliography of lists or abstracts of unpublished
theses and dissertations in the fields of Romance
and/or Hispanic languages and literature. Institutions arranged by country or geographical region,
subject covering the theses of a given country, and
theses of individual institutions which have significant concentrations in the field.

Italian Literature

L128. MARRARO, Howard R. "Doctoral Dissertations in Italian Accepted by Romance Language Departments in American Universities, 1876-1950." Bulletin of Bibliography and Magazine
Notes 20 (1951): 94-99.

Supersedes his "Doctoral Dissertations in Italian
Accepted by American Universities, 1934-1948."
Italica 26 (1949): 289-293.

An analysis and listing of 152 dissertations. Arranged chronologically under institution. (First
Ph.D. was granted by a Romance language department
in 1876.) Entry gives publication information.

Slavic and East European Languages and Literature

General

L129. ARONSON, Howard. "American Doctoral Dissertations in the
Fields of Slavic and East European Languages and Literatures."
The Slavic and East European Journal 7 (1963): 1-8, 449-450.

Attempts to complement Dossick's <u>Doctoral Research
on Russia and the Soviet Union</u> (Item C112) by excluding items found in Dossick, unless they deal
with languages other than Russian.

Lists 139 dissertations covering the period 1921-
1962. Main part arranged chronologically under
language.

L130. DADE, I. "Dissertationen und Hausarbeiten zu Frage der
deutsch-slavischen literarischen Wechselbeziehungen." <u>Zeit-
schrift für Slawistik</u> 7 (1962): 46-59.

A classified listing of 184 studies covering the
period 1945 through 1960 completed in institutes of
Slavic studies in the D.D.R. Entry indicates level
of study. Author and subject index.

L131. MAGNER, Thomas F. <u>Soviet Dissertations for Advanced Degrees
in Russian Literature and Slavic Linguistics, 1934-1962</u>.
University Park, Pa.: Pennsylvania State University, Department of Slavic Languages, 1966. 100 p.

Transliterated.

A classified bibliography of 1,313 dissertations in
Russian literature and Balto-Slavic linguistics,
completed for the Kandidat nauk and the Doktor nauk
degrees. Frequently indicates location. Index of
writers as subjects.

Estonian Language and Literature

L132. VAHER, M. <u>Eesti rahvaluule ja kirjanduse olal 1948-1965
aastani kaitstud diplomitööd</u>. Tartu: 1968. 114 p.

A classified listing of 276 abstracts of theses
completed in Estonian institutions. Author index.

L133. ALVRE, Paul, V. Kingisepp, and A. Veski. <u>Soome-Ugri keelte
kateedri ja Eesti keele kateedri tööd, 1947-1969. Biblio-
graafia</u>. Tartu: 1970. 165 p.

In Estonian and Russian.

In two parts, (1) Finnish-Ugaritic and (2) Estonian.
Under each, theses and dissertations are arranged
chronologically in separate listings. Author and
subject index.

Russian Literature

L134. "KANDIDATSKIE dissertatsiy po istorii, teorii i metodike
sovetskoy literatury, zashchishchennye v 1953 gody." Literatura v shkole, 1954, no. 5: 83-84.

Lists 97 theses under (1) philology and (2) pedagogy.

Speech

L135. KNOWER, Franklin H. "Graduate Theses. An Index of Graduate
Work in the Field of Speech from 1902 to 1934." Speech
Monographs 2 (1935): 1-49.

Records 685 theses and dissertations. Arranged by
institution with theses and dissertations listed
separately and chronologically under the institution. Subject index.

Continued by:

L136. _____ "Graduate Theses: An Index of Graduate Work in Speech
and Cognate Fields [1935-1968]" Speech Monographs 3 (1936)-
26 (1969). Annual. From vol. 19 (1952) in Aug. issue.

Vol. 3 (1936) includes retrospective lists of theses
and dissertations for institutions not included in
Item L135.

Includes theses and dissertations completed in
American speech departments in the areas of speech,
dramatic art, radio, television, film, speech pathology, and audiology. Arranged by institution,
then by type of degree. Subject index.

Continued by:

L137. BIBLIOGRAPHIC Annual in Speech Communication [1970-   ]
New York: Speech Communication Association, 1971-   .

Annual.

Lists American works as follows: (1) "Doctoral Dissertations in Speech Communication: Work in Progress [1970-   ]" arranged under the headings forensics, instructional development, interpersonal and small group interaction, interpretation, mass communication, public address, rhetorical and communications theory. Entry gives expected date of completion. (2) "Abstracts of Doctoral Dissertations in the Field of Speech Communication [1969-   ]" under forensics, instructional development, interpersonal and small group interaction, interpretation, mass communication, public address, rhetorical and communication theory, speech sciences and theatre. (3) "Graduate Theses and Dissertation Titles: An Index of Graduate Research in Speech Communication [1969/1970-   ]" Arranged by institutions subdivided into separate thesis and dissertation listings. First number covers the period 1968 and 1969. Title index.

L138. KNOWER, Franklin H. "Graduate Theses; A Combined Index of Reports of Graduate Work in the Field of Speech and Dramatic Art, 1902-1944." Speech Monographs 12 (1945): 9-29.

A classified subject index to the 2,526 theses listed annually in Speech Monographs 2 (1935)-12 (1945), representing work completed in American institutions.

L139. "ABSTRACTS of Dissertations in the Field of Speech." Speech Monographs 13 (1946)-36 (1969). Title varies. Annual.

Through vol. 21 (1954) includes abstracts of theses and dissertations. With vol. 22 (1955) carries only dissertations. Arranged by broad subject, such as public address, theatre, speech and hearing disorders, speech education.

L140. GETCHELL, Charles M. "Southern Graduate Study in Speech and Theatre..." Southern Speech Journal 15 (1949/1950): 222-229, 297-306; 16 (1950/1951): 218-227; 18 (1952/1953): 125-131; 20 (1954/1955): 332-344.

Theses and dissertations completed between 1932 and 1954. Vol. 15 covers the period 1932-1940 and 1941-

1950 and is a classified listing of 235 studies
arranged chronologically under such subjects as
public address, radio, speech, education, speech
science, theatre, and interpretation. Vol. 16
(containing 91 studies for 1950), vol. 18 (containing 87 studies for 1951), and vol. 20 (containing
93 studies for 1952-1954) use the same arrangement
as main listing.

L141. "DOCTORAL Dissertations in Speech: Work in Progress [1951-
1969]" Speech Monographs 18 (1951)-36 (1969). Annual.

Continued by Item L137.

No list in vol. 27 (1960).

Classified listing including such topics as public
address, theatre, speech and hearing disorders, fun-
damentals of speech, speech education, film, radio,
and television. These are subdivided by the first
principal word in the title (except for studies of
individual orators and playwrights). Items previously listed are not repeated.

L142. SPEECH ASSOCIATION OF AMERICA. Abstracts of Master's Theses
in Speech and Dramatic Art, 1953. Iowa City, Iowa: 1954.
43 p.

Represents a selection of theses completed in American institutions in 1953. No department submitted
more than ten items and departments granting less
than 20 masters' degrees generally submitted fewer
than ten for inclusion. Arranged under broad subjects.

L143. GRAY, Giles W. "Doctoral Dissertations in Areas Contiguous
to Speech." Speech Monographs 24 (1957): 299-308.

Studies for the Ph.D. and Ed.D. of interest in the
field of speech written at institutions which do
not confer doctorates in speech, covering the period
from about 1912 to 1946. Arranged by subject.

L144. MULGRAVE, Dorothy I., Clark S. Marlor, and Elmer E. Baker.
Bibliography of Speech and Allied Areas, 1950-1960. Philadelphia: Chilton Co., 1962. 184 p.

A selective classified bibliography of dissertations
and books in speech and drama and other fields of
research in which the subject matter relates directly
to these subjects. This includes anatomy, education,
fine arts, history, journalism, literature, physiology,
and psychology. Under each topic, dissertations are
listed separately. Provides reference to abstracts
and summaries.

L145. KRUGER, Arthur N. A Classified Bibliography of Argumenta-
tion and Debate. New York: Scarecrow Press, 1964. 400 p.

A classified bibliography, organized in 21 sections,
of research done in the United States in the twentieth
century. Each section contains a separate listing
of theses and dissertations. Author index.

L146. "PARTIAL List of Academic Theses on Rate-Controlled Speech."
Journal of Communication 18 (Sept. 1968): on covers, 3 p.

Dissertations and theses in two separate lists,
covering the period 1939-1967. Entries for dissertations include reference to available summaries.

Individual Authors

Baudelaire

L147. CARGO, Robert T. "Répertoire de thèses de maîtrise améri-
canes sur Baudelaire (1912-1966)." Bulletin Baudelaire,
no. 2 (1967): 1-7.

Alphabetical arrangement of 97 theses.

Clemens

L148. SELBY, Paul O. Theses on Mark Twain, 1910-1967. Kirksville,
Mo.: Northwest Missouri State College, Missouriana Library,
1969. 44 p.

A chronological listing of theses and dissertations.

Conrad

L149. BOJARSKI, Edmund A. and Henry T. Bojarski. "Joseph Conrad: A Bibliography of Masters Theses and Doctoral Dissertations, 1917-1963." Bulletin of Bibliography and Magazine Notes 26 (1969): 61-66, 79-83.

> An alphabetical listing of 336 unpublished studies, covering the graduate schools in the United States, Great Britain and Ireland, Canada, New Zealand, Poland, South Africa, France, and Germany. Some entries include references to abstracts.

Fitzgerald

L150. BRYER, Jackson R. "F. Scott Fitzgerald and His Critics: A Bibliographical Record. Pt. V: Graduate Research." Bulletin of Bibliography and Magazine Notes 23 (1962): 206-208.

> In two parts: "A. Doctoral Dissertations"; "B. Masters Essays at American Institutions."

Kafka

L151. JONAS, Klaus W. "Die Hochschulschriften über Franz Kafka und sein Werk." Philobiblon 12 (1968): 194-203.

> A chronological international listing of 89 theses and dissertations covering the period 1941 through 1967, including some 1967 studies in progress. Entry indicates contents. Author and subject indexes and index to Kafka's writings as a subject.

Lawrence

L152. CRUMP, G. B. "Doctoral Dissertations on D. H. Lawrence, 1931-1969: A Bibliography." D. H. Lawrence Review 3 (1970): 80-86.

> An international listing of approximately 110 dissertations arranged alphabetically by author.

> Supplemented by:

L153. GARMON, Gerald M. "Doctoral Dissertations on D. H. Lawrence: Bibliographical Addenda." D. H. Lawrence Review 5 (1972): 170-173.

>An international listing of 39 dissertations arranged alphabetically by author. Entry gives publication information.

L154. GARMON, Gerald and others. "Theses on D. H. Lawrence: 1913-1972: A Bibliography with Addenda of Senior Theses and Works in Progress." D. H. Lawrence Review 6 (1973): 217-230.

>An alphabetical author listing of approximately 115 theses, mostly American with some Canadian and English. The addenda (p. 228-230) list approximately 20 honors papers and two works in progress.

Melville

L155. MYERSON, Joel and Arthur H. Miller. Melville Dissertations; An Annotated Directory. Philadelphia: Melville Society of America, 1972. 57 p.

>Supersedes Tyrus Hillway and Hershel Parker, Directory of Melville Dissertations (1962) and Tyrus Hillway, Dissertations on Herman Melville (1953).

>A chronological listing of 248 dissertations. Lists separately 41 dissertations in progress, with institution and expected date of completion. International in coverage. Entry gives publication information. Author index.

Shakespeare

L156. "DISSERTATION Digest." Shakespeare Newsletter 4 (1954)- . Irregular.

>Abstracts of dissertations completed at American universities. Vols. 4 (1954)-7 (1957) include a separate listing of dissertations in progress.

L157. "SHAKESPEAREAN Work in Progress [1965-   ]" In Shakespearean Research and Opportunities; The Report of the Modern

Language Association of America Conference, no. 1-
Riverside, Calif.: University of California, 1965-
Annual.

>An alphabetical author listing which includes Amer-
>ican and European dissertations recently completed
>or in progress in American universities. Most items
>are annotated and include expected completion date.
>Subject index.

Shaw

L158. "SHAVIANA--Dissertations." Shaw Review 2, no. 2 (Sept.
1958)- . Irregular.

>Pt. 4 of "A Continuing Checklist of Shaviana,"
>which is an annotated list of completed American--
>and some foreign--dissertations.

Spenser

L159. STEPHENS, Robert F. A Check List of Masters' Theses on
Edmund Spenser. Charlottesville, Va.: Bibliographical
Society of the University of Virginia, 1950. 16 p.

>A chronological listing of 178 theses completed at
>American institutions from 1902 through November
>1949. Author index.

Steinbeck

L160. HAYASHI, Teksumaro. John Steinbeck: A Guide to Doctoral
Dissertations; A Collection of Doctoral Abstracts (1946-
1969). Muncie, Ind.: Ball State University, 1971. 32 p.
(Steinbeck Monograph Series, no. 1)

>Supersedes his earlier lists, "John Steinbeck: A .
>Checklist of Ph.D. Dissertations (1946-1967)" in
>Serif, December 1968, p. 30-31; Who's Who in Stein-
>beck Studies (1969), p. 4-5, and (1970), p. 3-5;
>and John Steinbeck: A Concise Bibliography (1930-
>1965) (1967), which also lists a few theses.

>Reprints of the abstracts of 16 dissertations which

appeared in <u>Dissertation Abstracts</u>, arranged chronologically.

Thoreau

L161. HARDING, Walter R. <u>A Thoreau Handbook</u>. New York: New York
University Press, 1959. 229 p.

A discussion of all Thoreau scholarship, with a
particular effort made to include all American
doctoral dissertations and theses. Lists separately authors and institutions of all dissertations
and theses (p. ix).

Unamuno

L162. SEDWICK, Frank. "Theses on Miguel de Unamuno at North American Universities (to February 1955)." <u>Kentucky Foreign
Language Quarterly</u> 3 (1956): 192-196.

Approximately 60 senior and masters' theses and
dissertations completed or in progress from 1920.
Arranged by institution.

L163. "TESIS y tesinas." <u>In</u> Salamanca. Universidad. Facultad de
Filosofía y Letras. Catedra Miguel de Unamuno. <u>Cuadernos
de la Catedra Miguel de Unamuno</u> 18 (1968)-   . Annual.
Irregular.

An international listing of theses and dissertations
completed or in progress. Entry gives adviser.

Vega Carpio

L164. POESSE, Walter. "Disertaciones lopescas: una compilacion."
<u>Hispanófila</u> 6 (1963): 77-89; 9 (1966): 1-6.

An international classified listing of 125 theses
and dissertations (a large portion being work completed in the United States). Organized by (1)
critical editions, (2) aspects of his dramatic works,
(3) non-dramatic works, and (4) relevant studies

for students of Lope de Vega. Entry gives location
of reviews and publication information.

Wordsworth

L165. HENLEY, Elton F. <u>A Check List of Masters' Theses in the
United States on William Wordsworth</u>. Charlottesville, Va.:
The Bibliographical Society of the University of Virginia,
1962. 29 p.

A chronological list of 381 theses completed from
1887 through 1959. List obtained from schools
offering graduate work in English. Author and subject indexes.

M. Law

General

M1.   MULLER, Frederik, & Co., Amsterdam. <u>Catalogus dissertation-</u>
<u>um et orationum juridicarum, defensarum et habitarum ab a.</u>
<u>1650 usque ad 1851 in academiis Germaniae, etc. praesertim</u>
<u>Neerlandiae. Quae venales prostant apud Fredericum Muller</u>
<u>...</u> Amstelodami: 1851. 110 p.

    A dealer's catalog of 3,813 dissertations. Arranged
alphabetically by author.

M2.   BOEKEREN, W. van, bookseller, Groningen. <u>Catalogus juridi-</u>
<u>carum dissertationum, quaestionum academicarum, orationum</u>
<u>etc. quae veneunt Groningen</u>. Groningen: 1853. 62 p.

    Lists 2,288 dissertations in two parts, (1) quarto
and (2) octavo. Items are listed alphabetically
by author in each part.

M3.   FONTAINE DE RESBECQ, Adolphe C. T. <u>Notice sur le doctorat</u>
<u>en droit, avec un tableau de l'enseignement et des études</u>
<u>dans les neuf facultés de droit, et une analyse chrono-</u>
<u>gique des lois, statuts, décrets, règlements et circulaires</u>
<u>relatifs à cet enseignement, de 1791 à 1857; suivie de la</u>
<u>liste générale des docteurs admis depuis 1806 jusqu'à 1857</u>
<u>et du catalogue raisonné des thèses soutenues de 1851 à</u>
<u>1857</u>. Paris: A. Durand, 1857.

    In two parts: (1) list of successful candidates cov-
ering 1806 to 1850; (2) from 1851 to 1857, indicating
subject of dissertation. Both parts arranged chronologically, subdivided by institution. Author index.

M4.   MULLER, Frederik, & Co., Amsterdam. <u>Catalogus dissertation-</u>

um et orationum juridicarum defensarum et habitarum ab a.
1600 usque ad 1866 in academiis Neerlandiae, Germaniae et
Sueciae, quae venales prostant apud Fredericum Muller...
Accedunt duo indices prior rerum, altera locorum corp. juris,
cet., curante E. J. van Lier. Amstelodami: 1867. 264 p.

> A dealer's catalog of 10,148 dissertations listed
> alphabetically by author, approximately half of
> which are in the area of law. Subject and place
> index.

M5.   AMSTERDAM. Universiteit. Faculteit der Rechtsgeleerdheid.
De academische rechtsliteratuur van Amsterdam, 1787-1887.
Amsterdam: C. A. Spin, 1887. 32 p.

> Approximately 600 theses arranged alphabetically by
> author under year.

> Continued by:

_____ De academische rechtsliteratuur van Amsterdam. 1e
vervolg, 1887-1892. Amsterdam: 1893. 23 p.

> Records 93 dissertations arranged alphabetically
> by author under year.

M6.   MULLER, Frederik, & Co., Amsterdam. Catalogus plus quam
10,000 dissertationum et orationum juridicarum defensarum et
habitarum ab a. 1600 usque ad 1878 in academiis Neerlandiae,
Germaniae, Sueciae etc., quae venales prostant apud Fredericum Muller & Co....Accedunt duo indices. Prior rerum,
altera locorum corp. juris, cet. Amstelodami: 1879. 256 p.

> Supplementum: 12 p. at end.

> A dealer's catalog with the items listed alphabeti-
> cally by author. Subject and place indexes.

M7.   BURGERSDIJK, firm, booksellers, Leyden. (1898. Burgersdijk
& Niermans). Thèses de droit soutenues aux universités des
Pays-Bas 1700-1898, avec table des matières. Leyden: Bur-
gersdijk & Niermans, 1898. 151 p.

> Cover title: Catalogus dissertationum iuridicarum
> defensarum in academiis Neerlandiae 1700-1898.

> A sales catalog. Entries listed alphabetically by

author. Subject index.

M8.   RÉPERTOIRE des thèses de droit soutenues dans les facultés
françaises, period [1910/1911-1912/1913] Paris: Librairie
centrale des facultés, 1911-1913. 3 vols. Annual.

A chronological listing. Arranged alphabetically
by author under each academic year. Each part
(academic year) has a subject index.

M9.   LA PLATA. Universidad Nacional. Biblioteca. Catálogo de
la colección de tesis jurídicas arreglada según clasifica-
ción decimal. Buenos Aires: Impr. de Coni Hermanos, 1914.
101 p.

A record of holdings. Includes items from the
Universities of Buenos Aires, Córdoba, Lima, La Plata,
Montevideo, Mexico, Panama, Santiago de Chile, Tucu-
mán. Subject and author indexes.

M10.   NOSKE, Robert, firm, publishers and printers, Borna-Leipzig.
Dreitausend juristische Dissertationen im eigener Buchdruck-
erei hergestellt. Leipzig-Borna: 1927. 167 p.

A dealer's catalog of approximately 4,800 dissertations completed since 1901. Classified under such
areas as municipal law, foreign law, business law,
canon law.

M11.   PARIS. Université. Faculté de droit et des sciences économiques. Répertoire des thèses de droit comparé soutenues
dans les facultés de droit de province pendant les années
1900 à 1929. Paris: Les Presses universitaire de Paris,
1929. 32 p. (Its Bulletin de documentation législative
et sociale, 22) ?

M12.   _____ Bibliothèque. Catalogue des thèses de droit soute-
nues devant les facultés de France [1 (1933)-5 (1937)]
Paris: Recueil Sirey (société anonyme), 1934-1938. 5 vols.
Annual.

Alphabetical author lists of dissertations defended
in French university faculties of law. Vols. 3
(1935)-5 (1937) include dissertations on legal topics, such as industrial law, administrative law, and

legal history, completed in faculties of letters.
Subject index.

M13. GOMEZ C., Arturo. "Lista de memorias de prueba recibidas en
la Biblioteca de la Escuela de Derecho de la Universidad de
Chile, durante el año 1942." In Chile. Universidad, Santiago. Facultad de Ciencias Jurídicas y Sociales. Anales 9
(1943): 171-181.

An alphabetical author listing. Includes items
from other Chilean institutions and some earlier
than 1942.

M14. LONDON. University. Institute of Advanced Legal Studies.
List of Current Legal Research Topics; Being Topics Forming
the Subject of Research by Students for Degrees in the
United Kingdom. London: 1950-   . Title varies. Annual.

Prepared in cooperation with the Society of Public
Teachers of Law.

An alphabetical author listing of theses and dissertations in progress on legal subjects in universities
in the United Kingdom. Entry gives institution,
degree sought, and title or topic of the study.

M15. _____ List of Legal Research Topics Completed and Approved
since About 1935. London: 1961. 27 p.

Prepared in cooperation with the Society of Public
Teachers of Law.

First edition 1954.

Lists approximately 500 degrees of the United Kingdom and those Commonwealth degrees which have been
notified. Classified arrangement covering such areas
as legal history, international law, public law,
private law, conflict of laws, other systems of law.

_____ _____ Supplement 1961-July 1966. London: 1966. 16 p.

Lists approximately 250 items.

M16. "NÓMINA de las obras y memorias de prueba ingresadas a la
Biblioteca de la Escuela de Derecho de Santiago durante los

años [1952-1957] classificadas por seminario." In Chile.
Universidad, Santiago. Facultad de Ciencias Jurídicas y
Sociales. Anales, época 3, vols. 1 (1952)-4 (1957). Annual.

A record of accessions of theses received from
other institutions, primarily Chilean, arranged
by year of accession. Items may have been completed prior to year of accession.

M17. AMERICAN BAR FOUNDATION. Index to Legal Theses and Research
Projects [1953/1954-1963/1964] Chicago: 1954-1965. (Its
Publication, no. 1-11) Annual. Title varies.

Sometimes referred to as "Little Green Book."

No. 1 in two parts. Pt. 1, "List of Unpublished
Legal Theses in American Law Schools," is a retrospective subject listing of 1,928 LL.M., S.J.D.,
J.D., M.A. and Ph.D. theses and dissertations in
the libraries and files of accredited American law
schools. Entry indicates degree, date, and institution. Pt. 2, "List of Current Legal Research
Projects in American Law Schools," includes work
in progress for advanced degrees. Publication no.
1, Supplement A, lists 187 theses and dissertations
accepted for the academic year 1953-54. Publication no. 1, Supplement B, "Graduate Degrees in Law,
1954-55" (1955), lists 137 theses and dissertations
arranged by subject. Publication no. 1, Supplement
C, "Graduate Degrees in Law, 1955-56," lists 142
theses and dissertations arranged by subject. (Supplements A, B, and C represent Publication nos. 2-4.)
Publication no. 9 (1962), covering 1960-61, contains
sections for "Graduate Theses in Law" and "Graduate
Theses in Related Fields," which represents dissertations in departments other than law. Publication no. 11 (1965), covering 1963-64, includes
British theses and dissertations. Author index
beginning with no. 5.

M18. "THESES concernant l'histoire du droit et des institutions
[1961/1962-   ]" Revue historique du droit français et
étranger 41 (1963)-   . Annual.

Vol. 41 (1963) covers 1961 and 1962.

Vols. 41 (1963)-49 (1971) cover the University of
Paris only.

An alphabetical author listing of dissertations completed in French universities.

M19. RAKHLEVSKIY, Vladislav A. <u>Bibliograficheskiy spravochnik dissertatsiy na iskanie uchennoy stepeni kandidata i doktora yuridicheskikh nauk</u>. Dushanve: Irfoe, 1965. 540 p.

A classified listing of approximately 3,000 U.S.S.R. theses and dissertations, roughly from the period 1940. Arranged under such areas as administrative law, criminology, criminal law, the history of the state and law. Under each subject theses and dissertations are listed separately. Entry gives location of a copy.

M20. KÖBLER, Gerhard. <u>Bibliographie der deutschen Hochschulschriften zur Rechtsgeschichte (1945-1964)</u>. Göttingen: Musterschmidt, 1969. 170 p.

Lists approximately 2,000 items, primarily dissertations. Arranged under historical period. Author and subject indexes.

M21. RAWENGEL, Lisolette. "Westdeutsche Dissertationen über das Recht in der DDR." <u>Deutschland Archiv</u> 3 (1970): 832-843.

A classified list of 145 dissertations completed between 1951 and 1969 (most represent work done 1960-1969). Includes such areas as civil, family, and economic law; agricultural law; labor and community law; public law; international law. Entry gives publication information. Author index.

Individual Institutions

M22. BONN. Universität. Rechts- und Staatswissenschaftliche Fakultät. <u>Jahrbuch der Dissertation</u> [1 (1952/1953)-8 (1960 /1961)] Bonn: 1954-1962. Annual.

Vol. 1 (1952/1953) issued by the Rechts- und Staatswissenschaftliche Fakultät Abteilung für Gesellschafts- und Wirtschaftswissenschaften and covers only studies completed in that department.

Abstracts of dissertations arranged under area, as

history of law, criminology, public and canon law.
Entry gives biographical note and adviser. Author
index.

M23. "THÈSES de l'École nationale des chartes soutenues par les
élèves de la promotion [1961/1962-   ]" Revue historique
de droit français et étranger 41 (1963)-   . Title varies.
Irregular.

Vol. 41 (1963) covers 1961 and 1962.

An alphabetical author listing.

M24. LE FORT, Charles G. Catalogue des thèses soutenues devant
la Faculté de droit de Genève de 1821 à 1877. Genève: 1878.
32 p. ?

M25. REHFOUS, Louis. Université de Genève, Faculté de droit,
1896-1914. Genève: Georg, 1914. 31 p.

Lists "Dissertations [1896-1914]" (p. 24-27), which
is a chronological listing of approximately 40 dissertations.

M26. GIESSEN. Universität. Juristische Fakultät. Auszüge aus
den der Juristischen Fakultät der Universität Giessen
vorgelegten Dissertationen. Giessen: 1922-1929. 6 vols.
Irregular.

Vols. 1-2 include dissertations approved in 1921;
vol. 6 covers the period 1919-1921.

Abstracts of dissertations covering the period
1919-1927. Entry gives adviser. Author index.

M27. ZAVALA CORDERO, Jaime. "Lista de los títulos de tesis de
los graduados en la Facultad de Ciencias Jurídicas y Sociales, lapso de 1940-1957." In Guatemala (City). Universidad de San Carlos. Facultad de Ciencias Jurídicas y
Sociales. Revista 6 (1959): 189-208. ?

M28. WEIDLICH, Christoph. Vollständiges Verzeichniss aller auf
dem Königl. preuss. Friedrich-Universität zu Halle seit
ihrer Stiftung bis auf den heutigen Tag herausgekommener

juristischen Disputationen und Programmen, mit einigen lit-
terarischen Anmerkungen. Nebst beigefügter Succession aller
Rechtsgelehrten dieser berühmten Universität, und deren
kurzgefasste Biographien. Als ein Beytrag zur Gelehrten-
Geschichte der Friedrichs-Universität Halle. Halle: J. C.
Hendel, 1789. 151, 74 p.

> A chronological listing covering the period 1690-
> 1789, arranged by praeses. Entry indicates the
> respondent.

M29. LIMA. Universidad de San Marcos. Facultad de Derecho y
Ciencias Políticas. Catálogo de tesis de la Facultad de
Derecho. Lima: 1944. 149 p.

> A classified bibliography of theses and disserta-
> tions in all aspects of law: civil, penal, labor,
> administrative, industrial, international, etc.

M30. PARIS. Université. Faculté de droit et des sciences économiques. Répertoire des thèses de droit comparé soutenues à
la Faculté de droit de Paris pendant les années 1900 à 1930.
Paris: Les Presses universitaires de France, 1931. 70 p.
(Its Bulletin de documentation législative et sociale, 23)

> A classified listing of approximately 1,050 disser-
> tations. In two parts: (1) general studies and com-
> parative law, subdivided into such subjects as penal,
> family, constitutional law; (2) legislation in other
> countries, arranged by country and subdivided into
> private and public law.

M31. "CHRONIQUE méridionale." Revue historique du droit français
et étranger 41 (1963): 166-169.

> A chronological listing, covering the period 1944-
> 1962, of dissertations on the history of law and
> on economic organizations completed at the Univer-
> sity of Toulouse.

Special Subjects

Administrative Law

M32. RUTZ, Walter. Bibliographie der Dissertationen im Staats-

und Verwaltungsrecht 1945-1960. Berlin: Duncker & Humblot, 1965. 210 p.

A classified bibliography of approximately 3,200 German language dissertations arranged under (1) public law, general; (2) German constitutional law; (3) constitutional law, general; (4) constitutional law, special; and (5) foreign constitutional law. Entries give faculty in which the degree was taken and the date of acceptance. Author index.

Business Law

M33. DISSERTATIONEN über kartellrechtliche und weltberwerbstheo-retische Probleme 1949 ff. 6. Ausg. Berlin: 1970. 148 p.

Subject list of about 1,500 German dissertations.

M34. MUELLER, Charles E. "Lawyers' Guide to the Economic Litera-ture on Competition and Monopoly: An Introduction to the Doctorate Dissertations." Antitrust Law and Economic Review 5 (Summer 1972): 83-100; 6 (Fall 1972): 67-94; 6 (Winter 1972): 85-106.

A classified listing of dissertations covering the period 1958-1969. Divided into industry and ana-lytical studies.

International Law

M35. "PROEFSCHRIFTEN over internationaal rechtelijke onderwerpen verdedigd aan Nederlandsche universiteiten." In Vereeniging voor Volkenbond en Vrede. Vredes- en volkenbondstentoonstel-ling...van 7 Februari tot 6 Maart 1930..., p. 147-158. The Hague: 1930. ?

M36. SCHLOCHAUER, Hans-Jürgen. "Völkerrechtliche Dissertationen aus der Zeit von 1919 bis 1931 auf Grund amtlichen Materials und gütiger Aüskunfte." Zeitschrift für Völkerrecht 16 (1931/1932): 487-517; 17 (1933): 113-138.

Also published as a separate, Deutsche völkerrecht-liche Dissertationen, 1919-1932 (1933).

A classified bibliography of 917 German and Austrian dissertations on international law covering its history, the state, the Versailles agreement, and war.

Continued by:

M37. MENZEL, Eberhard. Die völkerrechtlichen Dissertationen, 1933-1939. Berlin: Duncker und Humblot, 1941. 64 p.

Supplement to Zeitschrift für Völkerrecht 25 (1941).

Lists 585 dissertations completed in German universities. Entry includes publication information.

Continued by:

M38. _____ "Die völkerrechtlichen Dissertationen an den westdeutschen Universitäten 1945-1957." In Deutsche Gesellschaft für Völkerrecht. Berichte, Hefte 2 (1958). 145 p.

Also published as a separate.

A classified listing of about 500 dissertations, listed under (1) the nature and substance of international law; (2) history of international law and of diplomacy; (3) international law themes; (4) international organizations; (5) international law in regions; and (6) war and the law of neutrality. Author index.

Continued by:

M39. RAUSCHNING, Dietrich. "Die deutschen völkerrechtlichen Dissertationen 1958-1964." Jahrbuch für internationales Recht 12 (1965): 599-629.

Lists 374 dissertations completed in West German institutions. Arranged under such subjects as history of international law, law of war and neutrality, law of international economics. Author index.

Roman Law

M40. CAES, Lucien and Roger Henrion. Collectio bibliographica

<u>operum ad ius romanum pertinentium</u>. Bruxelles: Office inter-
national de librairie, 1949-1960.

Series II: Theses. Vol. 1: "Theses Galliae...sci-
licet theses prelo impressas, quarum auctores gradum
doctoris iuris aut litterarum in Facultatibus Galliae
consecuti sunt ab ineunte saeculo XIXe ad annum 1948"
(1949), 447 p.; vol. 2: "Theses Germaniae, 1885-
1958" (1960), 216 p.

Each volume contains an alphabetical author list
and carries a separate analytical index. German
volume contains both dissertations and Habilitationsschriften.

N. Library and Information Services

General

N1. "THESES and Dissertations Accepted by Graduate Library
     Schools [1928-   ]" Library Quarterly 3 (1933)-   . Title
     varies. Irregular.

>   Vol. 3 (1933): 267-291 lists theses and disserta-
>   tions completed June 1928-June 1932; vol. 17 (1947):
>   43-57 lists theses and dissertations completed July
>   1938-June 1945; lists in vols. 20 (1950)-30 (1960)
>   published annually in October issue.

>   An alphabetical author listing of theses and disser-
>   tations completed in American library schools ar-
>   ranged under institution.

N2. "ABSTRACTS of Theses Presented to Library Schools by Students
     Majoring in Cataloging [1935-1939]" In American Library
     Association. Division of Cataloging and Classification.
     Catalogers' and Classifiers' Yearbook, no. 5 (1935)-9 (1939).
     Annual.

>   Alphabetical author listings.

N3. "LIBRARY Schools--Theses [1936-   ]" Library Literature,
     1936/1939-   .

>   Lists theses and dissertations completed at Ameri-
>   can institutions. To 1958 some were annotated else-
>   where in the same volume. Entry gives publication
>   information.

N4. WITMER, Eleanor M. "School Library Studies and Research."
     Library Quarterly 6 (1936): 382-403.

The section on "Recent Studies" (p. 395-401) lists
approximately 100 items on school libraries, the
majority of which are theses. Arranged under broad
topic. Covers the period 1930-1935.

N5. "THESES in A.L.A. Library." In American Library Association.
Bulletin 33 (1939): 773, 814.

An alphabetical listing of approximately 30 theses
prepared through A.L.A. grants-in-aid. Entry gives
publication information.

N6. PURDY, G. Flint. "Research and Experimentation." College
and Research Libraries 1 (1940): 372-375.

A classified list of research work completed and in
progress in libraries and library schools throughout the U.S. The level of each study is not speci-
fied but most are said to be theses.

N7. HOFFMAN, Hester. The Graduate Thesis in Library Science.
Chicago: 1941. 161 p. (M.A. Thesis, University of Chicago)

"The Doctor's Thesis List of Titles and Contents"
(p. 70-71) contains the 24 theses completed at the
University of Chicago through June 1940. "Appendix
II: Alphabetical Index, Arranged for Each School,
of the Authors and Titles of Theses" (p. 120-161)
lists theses for the period 1927 to 1940 completed
in American institutions.

N8. "PRZEGLĄD prac kandydackich i doktorskich z zakresu biblio-
tekoznawstwa i bibliografii w Związku Radzieckim w latach
1938-1946." Bibliotekarz 15 (1948): 189-190.

Alphabetical author listing of 41 theses and dissertations on bibliography and library science completed in Leningrad and Moscow in the period 1938-1946.

N9. "GRADUATE Studies in College and Research Librarianship
[1947-1948]" College and Research Libraries 9 (1948): 175;
10 (1949): 256-257.

Mainly theses, some dissertations in vol. 10 (1949),
arranged by institution. Entry indicates where

abstracted.

N10. COLE, Dorothy E. "Library School Studies [1951-1955]" <u>College and Research Libraries</u> 13 (1952): 359-363; 15 (1954): 61-63; 17 (1956): 236-238.

 A classified list of completed theses of interest to college and research libraries. Primarily theses with a few dissertations.

N11. "SPISOK dissertatsiy po bibliotekobedeniyu, bibliografii i istorii knigi." <u>Bibliotekar</u>, 1952, no. 4: 44-46.

 Annotated author listing of 36 theses completed in the period 1947 through October 1951 in institutions in Moscow and Leningrad.

N12. FRAREY, Carlyle J. and Sarah R. Reed. "Studies in Progress." <u>College and Research Libraries</u> 13 (1952): 362-363.

 Consists largely of theses and dissertations. Arranged under topic. Entry gives degree sought.

N13. MAURIN, Raissa B. "Dissertations in the Field of Library Science Defended in the U.S.S.R. during the Period 1948-1951." <u>In her A Survey of Soviet Literature in Library Science, 1948-1952</u>, p. 138-142. Washington: Catholic University of America, 1954. (M.S.L.S. Thesis, Catholic University of America)

 An annotated list of 15 dissertations.

N14. HOVE, Julien van. <u>Inventaire des mémoires présentés aux écoles de bibliothécaires de Belgique.</u> Bruxelles: Commission belge de bibliographie, 1957. 86 p. (Bibliographie belgica, 25)

 Title also in Dutch.

 Contains separate lists of dissertations and of theses of the library section of the Institut d'études sociales de l'état, Brussells, 1920-1956; Middelbare School voor Opleiding van Bibliotheek-, Archief-, en Museumpersoneel, Antwerp, 1942-1956; Cours supérieurs pour bibliothécaires, Liège, 1943-

1955; École provinciale de bibliothécaire, Brabant,
1945-1956; Vrije Middelbare Bibliotheekschool,
Antwerp, 1951-1954. Author and subject indexes.

N15. DANTON, J. Periam. "Doctoral Study in Librarianship in the
United States." College and Research Libraries 20 (1959):
435-453, 458.

An analysis of the subject, including an alphabetical list of all dissertations completed in the five
U.S. institutions which at the time offered Ph.D.'s
in "Doctoral Dissertations in Librarianship, 1930-
1959" (p. 450-453, 458).

Continued by:

N16. MERRITT, Le Roy C. "Doctoral Study in Librarianship--A Supplement." College and Research Libraries 23 (1962): 539-
540.

Lists 44 titles of dissertations awarded from July
1, 1959, through June 30, 1962.

N17. U.S. Office of Education. Library Services Branch. Library
Research in Progress [no. 1 (Oct. 1959)-14 (Sept. 1964)]
Washington: 1959-1964. Irregular.

Classified listing consisting in large part of theses
and dissertations. Entry gives purpose, scope and
methodology, expected duration, and cooperating
groups. Author and subject indexes.

N18. SOUTHEASTERN LIBRARY ASSOCIATION. Historical Committee.
"Graduate Studies Relating to Library Service, Accepted by
Institutions of Higher Education in the Southeast." South-
eastern Librarian 10 (Spring 1960): 12-44.

A classified listing of 595 theses and masters'
papers, covering the period through 1958.

N19. COHEN, Nathan M., Barbara Denison, and Jessie C. Boehlert.
Library Science Dissertations, 1925-60; An Annotated Biblio-
graphy of Doctoral Studies. Washington: U.S. Dept. of
Health, Education, and Welfare, Office of Education, U.S.
Government Printing Office, 1963. 120 p. (U.S. Office of

Education. Bulletin 1963, no. 38)

>An annotated bibliography of 224 dissertations.
>Dissertations completed in departments other than
>library science are included if they deal with a
>topic central to librarianship. Arranged in eight
>subject groupings. Entries are arranged chronolo-
>gically in each group. Author and subject indexes.

N20. <u>DAS BUCH- und Bibliothekswesen im Spiegel der Jahresverzeichnisse der deutschen Hochschulschriften, 1885-1961; Eine Bib-
liographie</u>. Jena: Gesellschaftswissenschaftliche Beratungs-
stelle der Universitätsbibliothek Jena, 1964. 50 p. (Bibliographische Mitteilungen der Universitätsbibliothek Jena,
Nr. 6)

>A classified bibliography of 769 dissertations and
>Habilitationsschriften on the development and cur-
>rent status of the book, the book trade and publish-
>ing, and libraries. Includes such topics as the
>social function of books, the psychology of reading
>and writing. Institutional, author, and subject
>indexes.

N21. HARRIS, Michael H. <u>A Guide to Research in American Library
History</u>. Metuchen, N. J.: Scarecrow Press, 1968. 186 p.

>An annotated bibliography of graduate research in
>American library history, incorporating approximate-
>ly 500 theses and dissertations completed through
>1965.

N22. "DOCTORAL Dissertation Topics Accepted in Library and Information Science." <u>Journal of Education for Librarianship</u> 9,
no. 2 (Fall 1968)-   . Quarterly.

>An alphabetical listing of dissertations in progress
>in American institutions. Entry gives title, date
>of acceptance of the topic, and adviser. Vol. 9,
>no. 2 (Fall 1968) includes the dissertations in pro-
>gress from the Universities of Chicago and Illinois
>only.

N23. REID-SMITH, Edward R. "A Select Catalogue of Unpublished
Theses, Dissertations and Essays Presented for British Qual-
ifications, of Some Interest to Librarians." <u>Research in</u>

Librarianship 9 (1968): 67-78.

An alphabetical author list of 139 studies (excluding bibliographies concerned purely with aspects of librarianship) presented for the Fellowship of the Library Association, for the doctorate, master's degree, diploma, or certificate at British universities. Covers the period 1948-1967. Index to names and subjects.

N24.   KRUGER, J. A.   "Research for Theses and Dissertations in Library Science at South African Universities up to 1967." South African Libraries 35 (1968): 95-99.

In English and Afrikaans.

Contains 29 studies arranged in two parts: completed and current research. Each part subdivided into dissertations and theses. Entry gives publication and review information.

N25.   ANDERTON, Ray L. and Joseph L. Mapes.   Doctoral Research in Library Media; Completed and Underway.   Boulder, Colo.: University of Colorado, School of Education, 1970.   78 p.

Lists 709 dissertations from 98 institutions. Covers such areas as audio-literary, visual literary, library media, computers in education, projected materials, and television.

N26.   AARON, Shirley L.   "A Review of Selected Studies in School Librarianship, 1967-1971: Part I."   School Libraries 21 (1972): 29-46.

Examines 58 completed dissertations, which are cited in the bibliography.

N27.   EYMAN, David H.   Doctoral Dissertations in Library Science; Titles Accepted by Accredited Library Schools, 1930-1972. Ann Arbor, Mich.: Xerox University Microfilms, 1973.   17 p.

Supersedes University Microfilms, Ann Arbor, Mich., Dissertations in Library Science, 1951-1966 (1966).

An alphabetical author listing of 469 studies completed in American graduate library schools.   Institutional and subject index.

Individual Institutions

N28. BIRMINGHAM, Mary A. Survey of Theses Submitted by Candidates for the Master of Science in Library Science Degree, Catholic University, 1950-1966. Washington: 1966. 321 p. (M.S. Thesis, Catholic University of America)

> Supersedes "Library School Theses." Catholic Library World 22 (1951): 201-206, and James J. Kortendick, "Master's Theses in Library Science at Catholic University of America." DC Libraries 23 (April 1952): 3-12.

> An alphabetical author listing of 880 theses. Entry gives adviser. Subject index and separate lists of items dealing with the history or survey of libraries, American imprints, Catholic imprints, indexing, bio-bibliographies, etc.

N29. CHICAGO. University. Graduate Library School. Dissertations, Theses, and Papers of the School, 1930-1945; A Bibliography. Compiled by Dorothy Charles. Chicago: 1946. 32 p.

> _____ _____ Supplement, 1945-1947. Chicago: 1947. 2 p.

> A subject listing of studies submitted as part of the degree requirements.

N30. DERBYSHIRE, Ruth. Masters Essays, Columbia University School of Library Service. New York: Columbia University School of Library Service, 1967. 30 p.

> Supersedes "Graduate Theses Accepted by Library Schools in the United States, 1950-1951. Supplement." Library Quarterly 22 (1952): 36-37.

> Lists 429 theses covering the period 1928 through 1951, when the thesis requirement for the degree was in effect. Field studies are not included. Arranged under broad subjects. Author index.

N31. FLORIDA. State University, Tallahassee. Library School.

Theses, Studies and Papers Done in the Library School, 1948-1958. Tallahassee: 1958. 13 p.

Supersedes 1955 listing and 1956 and 1957 supplements.

An alphabetical author listing of approximately 250 items. Entry indicates if a thesis or a paper.

N32. LONDON. University. School of Librarianship and Archives. Cumulated List of Bibliographies and Theses Accepted for Part II of the University of London Diplomas in Librarianship and Archives in the Post-War Years 1946-1960. London: 1961. 37 p. (Its Occasional Publications, no. 10)

Lists for the pre-war years are included in the School's Occasional Publications, nos. 1 and 3.

Lists 299 items under 24 broad headings. A substantial portion of the entries are in the areas of literature and history.

_____ _____, 1961-1962. London: 1963. 9 p. (Its Occasional Publications, no. 12)

A topical listing of 55 items. Index of proper names.

_____ _____, 1963-1967. London: 1968. 14 p. (Its Occasional Publications, no. 14)

Lists 122 items under such topics as manuscripts, printing and publishing, psychology, religion, geography. Index of proper names.

N33. LOZANO RIVERA, Uriel. Resúmenes de tesis presentadas por los candidatos al título de licenciado en bibliotecología de 1960 a 1966. Medellín, Colombia: Editorial Universidad de Antioquia, 1967. 109 p.

An alphabetical author listing of 71 thesis abstracts completed in the Escuela Interamericano de Bibliotecología, Universidad de Antioquia. Entry gives adviser. Subject and author indexes.

Continued by:

_____ Resúmenes de tesis presentadas por los candidatos al título de licenciado en bibliotecología de 1967 a junio de

<u>1969</u>. Medellin, Colombia: Editorial Universidad de Antio-
quia, 1969. 38 p. (Universidad de Antioquia. Escuela
Interamericana de Bibliotecología. Publicaciones. Ser. Bib-
liografias, no. 29)

An alphabetical author listing of 31 theses. Entry
gives adviser. Subject and author indexes.

N34. CHALIFOUX, Jean-Pierre. <u>Bio-bibliographies et bibliographies; Liste des travaux bibliographiques des étudiants en
bibliothéconomie de l'Université de Montréal</u>. Montréal:
Ministère des affaires culturelles, 1970. 60 p.

Lists theses completed between 1938 and 1960. In
two parts: an alphabetical listing by the subject
of the bio-bibliography (approximately 500 items)
and a title listing of approximately 50 bibliographies. Entry indicates availability of a microfilm
copy. Author index.

N35. "UNPUBLISHED Masters' Theses in the School of Library Science, University of North Carolina, 1953-1957." <u>North Carolina Libraries</u> 16 (1958): 54-56.

The master's program began in 1953.

N36. "THESES Completed, 1961-1962." <u>North Carolina Libraries</u> 21
(Fall 1962): 25.

Theses completed at the University of North Carolina
School of Library Science.

N37. NORTH DAKOTA. University. College of Education. "Master's
Theses on School Libraries Available at the University Libra-
ry, University of North Dakota." <u>College of Education
Record</u> 41 (Dec. 1955): 45.

Thirteen theses written between 1931 and 1955 at
the University of North Dakota.

N38. OHIO. State University, Kent. School of Library Science.
<u>Master's Theses and Master's Research Papers Accepted, 1966-
1970</u>. 75 p.

An alphabetical author listing of approximately 160
items. Chronological and subject indexes.

P. Medical Sciences

General

P1. HEFFTER, Johann K. <u>Museum disputatorum physico-medicum tri-</u>
<u>partitum.</u> Zittaviae Lusatorum: Apud J. J. Schoepsium, 1756-
1764. 2 vols.

> Lists 18,498 European theses of the 16th through
> 18th centuries. In each volume the theses are enter-
> ed under the praeses. Subject and respondent indexes.

P2. BALDINGER, Ernst G. "Verzeichnis semiotischer akademischer
Schriften." <u>Neues Magazin vor Aerzte</u> 13 (1791): 246-275.

> A classified listing of which a substantial number
> are dissertations. Entered under the praeses.
> Entry gives respondent.

P3. _____ <u>Litteratura universa materiae medicae, alimentariae,</u>
<u>toxicologiae, pharmaciae, et therapiae generalis, medicae</u>
<u>atque chirurgicae, potissimum academica.</u> Marburgi: In
officina nova libraria Academiae, 1793. 359 p.

> A revised and enlarged edition of his earlier <u>Cata-</u>
> <u>logus dissertationum quae medicamentorum historiam...</u>
> (1768).

> A classified listing under (1) medical sciences,
> subdivided under prognosis and treatment, and (2)
> pharmacy, subdivided under mineral and botanic.
> Entry is by praeses and gives respondent.

P4. SCHWEICKHARD, Christian L. <u>Tentamen catalogi rationalis</u>
<u>dissertationum ad artem obstetriciam spectantium ab anno</u>
<u>1515 ad nostra usque tempora.</u> Francofurti a. Moenum: Georg

Ludov. Macklot, 1795. 232 p.

An index to 1,174 dissertations listed in other sources, covering the period 1515 to 1792, arranged chronologically. Subject and name indexes.

P5. SCRWEICKHARD, Christian L. [i.e. Schweickhard] Tentamen catalogi rationalis dissertationum ad medicinam forensem et politiam medicam spectantium ab anno MDLXIX ad nostra usque tempora. Francofurti a. Moenum: Georg Ludov. Macklot, 1796. 156 p.

Index to 616 dissertations covering the period 1569-1795. Arranged chronologically. Subject and name indexes.

P6. DOERING, Sebastian J. L. Critisches Repertorium der auf in- und ausländischen höhern Lehranstalten vom Jahre 1781 bis 1800 herausgekommenen Probe- und Einladungsschriften aus dem Gebiete der Arzneygelahrtheit und Naturkunde. Erste Abtheilung, enthaltend das Verzeichniss der Schriften von 1781 bis 1790. Herborn: Hohe-Schulbuchhandlung, 1803. 412 p.

A classified listing, of which 2,794 items are theses. Entry gives abstract and critical notes. Author index and subject indexes in both Latin and German.

P7. HOLTROP, Leonardus S. A. Bibliotheca medico-chirurgica et pharmaceutico-chemica, sive catalogus alphabeticus omnium librorum, dissertationum etc. ad anatomiam, artem medicam, chirurgicum, obstetriciam, pharmaceuticam, chemicam, botanicum, physicomedicam et veterinariam pertinentium, et in Belgio ab anno 1790 ad annum 1840 editorum, cum separatim tum in diariis criticis et actis societatum; accedunt: 1. Index systematicus latinus. 2. Index belgico-latinus. 3. Index alphabeticus nomunum eorum qui versiones dederunt, vel aliorum opera annotationibus suis illustraverunt. The Hague: C. Fuhri, 1842. 427, 199 p.

Title page in Dutch and Latin.

An alphabetical author listing. Dissertation items are identified.

P8. FRÄNKEL, Gottlob H. F. Bibliotheca medicinae militaris et navalis... I. Inaugural-Abhandlungen. Thesen. Programme.

Glogau: Mosche, 1876. 68 p.

Band 1 all published.

An alphabetical listing (either by praeses, respondent, or author) of approximately 1,300 studies. Entry gives type of academic exercise, respondent, and publication information. Subject index.

P9. PETROV, Nikolaĭ P. Bibliograficheskiy ukazatel' russkikh dissertatsiy po meditsine i veterinarii. Index bibliographique des thèses concernant la médecine et l'art vétérinaire présentées à l'Académie de médecine et aux universités russes. S" 1860 po 1-e iyunya 1892 g. Vklyuchitel' no. 2. Dopolnennoe izd. S.-Peterburg": Tip. Departamenta Udelov", 1892. 101 p.

Lists 2,287 Russian dissertations under medical fields such as physiology, pharmacy, veterinary medicine. Indexes of Russian and non-Russian works.

_____ Dopolnenie k"bibliograficheskomy ukazalyu russkikh' dissertatsiy po meditsine, farmatsii i veterinarii, izdanie 1892 goda. S.-Peterburg": Tipo-lit. I. A. Frolova, 1896. 42 p.

Covers the period 1893-1895 and lists an additional 1,025 items alphabetically by author.

_____ Vtoroe dopolnenie k"bibliograficheskomy ukazatelyu russkikh" dissertatsiy po meditsine, farmatsii v veterinarii izdaniya 1892 goda. S.-Peterburg": Izd. N. I. Petrova, 1898. 82 p.

Covers the period 1896-1898 and lists an additional 617 items.

P10. ROYAL COLLEGE OF SURGEONS OF LONDON. Library. Catalogue of Russian Medical Dissertations and Other Works Collected by Theodore Maxwell, M.D., B.Sc., of Woolwich and Presented by Him to the Royal College of Surgeons of England. London: 1892. 32 p.

An alphabetical author listing of approximately 750 items, mainly dissertations for the doctor of medicine in the Imperial Military Academy of St. Petersburg. Titles are translated into English, but original language is indicated.

P11. RICKER, Karl L., firm, bookseller, St. Petersburg. Ukazatel' meditsinskoy literatury; Spisok dissertatsiy, imeyushchikhsya v knizhhom magazine. St. Petersburg: 1904. 146 p.

A bookseller's catalog listing 2,305 items under medical fields such as anatomy, physiology and physiological chemistry, surgery, pharmacy, hygiene. Author index.

_____ Prilozhenne; Spisok dissertatsiy, vyshedskikh za 1904-11 gg. 23 p.

Supersedes listing for 1904-1907 (1908).

P12. LOEB, Fritz. "Deutsche neurologische Universitätsschriften [1906/1907-1907/1908]" Zentralblatt für Nervenheilkunde und Psychiatrie 31 (1908): 483-488; 32 (1909): 652-658. Title varies. Annual.

Each list cites approximately 125 dissertations under institution.

P13. _____ "[Verzeichnis der an den] schweizer Universitäten [1906/1907-1907/1908] erschienen einschlägigen Schriften." Zentralblatt für Nervenheilkunde und Psychiatrie 31 (1908): 408; 32 (1909): 303-304. Annual.

Alphabetical author listings.

P14. "VERZEICHNIS der im Universitäts-Jahr [1906/1907-1907/1908] an den französischen Universitäten erschienen Schriften, die sich auf Neurologie und Psychiatrie beziehen." Zentralblatt für Nervenheilkunde und Psychiatrie 31 (1908): 404-408; 32 (1909): 298-303. Annual.

Each list cites approximately 100 dissertations under institution.

P15. WICKERSHEIMER, Ernest. "Les Thèses françaises d'histoire de la médecine de 1904 à 1909." Janus 16 (1911): 53-65.

Also issued as a separate.

Contains 194 theses which deal in some part with the history of medical sciences, completed in the medical faculties of French universities. Includes

law, pharmacy, and literature. Arranged by period
or topic.

P16. ANDERSON, Peter J. Notes on Academic Theses, with a Bibliography of Duncan Liddell. Aberdeen: Printed for the University of Aberdeen, 1912. 52 p. (Aberdeen University Studies,
no. 58)

Contains the following: (1) A table of "Theses of
Aberdeen University" (p. 17-23). Covers the period
1616-1732. Entry gives date, praeses, title, number of candidates, and location. (2) "Theses:
Liddell Acting as Praeses" (p. 33-42). Contains 82
theses completed at the institutions with which he
was associated.

P17. HULL, Callie and Clarence J. West. "Doctorates in Medical
Sciences Conferred by American Universities, 1922-1923,
1923-1924, 1924-1925." Archives of Pathology and Laboratory
Medicine 1 (1926): 259-262.

Lists 160 dissertations under the headings anatomy,
bacteriology, pathology, and physiology, subdivided
by academic year and institution under each heading.

P18. SONNENSCHEIN, Curt. Verzeichnis in Deutschland erschienener
neuerer Dissertationen und Habilitationsschriften aus dem
Gebiet der Tropenmedizin und Tropenhygiene, Auslandsmedizin
und deren Grenzgebieten (1930-1938). Leipzig: Barth, 1940.
63 p.

An alphabetical author listing of 753 entries.
Entry gives publication information. Subject index.

P19. KOCHERGIN, Ivan G. Doktorskie dissertatsiy po meditsine za
1941-1945: Kratkoe soderzhanie 450 doktorskikh dissertatsiy.
Medgiz: 1947-1949. 2 vols.

Abstracts of 450 Russian dissertations completed in
the period 1941-1945. Arranged by general medical
fields, e.g. gynecology, psychiatry, urology. The
table of contents in each volume acts as an index.

P20. LIETUVOS TSR medicinos moksio kandidato laipsniui igyti
apgintu disertaciju sarašas. Vilna: 1950. 4 p. ?

P21. GRMEK, Mirko D. <u>Inauguralne disertacije hrvatskih, srpskih i slovenačkih liječnika</u>. Zagreb: Jugoslavenska Akademija Znanosti i Umjetnosti, 1951. 97-258 p.

A chronological listing of 356 dissertationc covering 1660-1865. Author index.

P22. JULIUS, W. "Dissertationen und Habilitationsschriften...aus dem Gebiete der Tuberkulose und der Erkrankungen der Thoraxorgane, 1943-1952." <u>Zeitschrift für Tuberkulose</u> 103 (1953): 89-135.

A classified listing of completed German and German language Swiss studies, including veterinary medicine. Entry gives publication information. Author index.

_____ _____ [1. Fortsetzung-7. Fortsetzung] <u>Zeitschrift für Tuberkulose</u> 106 (1955): 37-44, 95-102; 108 (1956): 348-359; 109 (1956): 301-304; 110 (1957/1958): 103-105; 113 (1959): 71-82; 115 (1960/1961): 93-102. Title varies.

Fortsetzung 1 lists only additional items for the 1949-1952 period.

Continues main listing for studies completed through 1960. Author index.

P23. <u>NIHON igaku hakashi roku</u>. Tokyo: Chūō Igakusha, 1954. 1,037 p.

A directory of Japanese doctors of medicine, covering the period 1881-1958. Arranged alphabetically. Title index.

P24. GUSEVA, I. C. and V. A. Sorokina. "Annotatsiy kandidatskikh i doktorskikh dissertatsiy po organizatsii i istorii zdravookhraneniya i sanitarnoy statistike, zashchishchennykh v 1952-1953 gg." <u>Sovetskoe zdravookhranenie</u> 13, no. 1 (1954): 57-61.

Alphabetical author listing of 237 abstracts of theses and dissertations.

P25. VASILENKO, L. D. and Z. I. Umidovoy. <u>Referaty dissertatsiy uchenykh Uzbekskoy SSR (meditsina)</u>. Tashkent: Gos. izd-vo Uzbekskoy SSR, 1954. 280 p.

Abstracts of approximately 60 dissertations in medicine defended at medical institutions in the Uzbek
SSR during the period 1917-1953. Arranged by medical fields, subdivided by institution.

P26. JULIUS, W. "Dissertationen und Habilitationsschriften [1945/
1952-   ] Zentralblatt für Chirurgie 79 (1954)-   . Title
varies. Annual.

Vol. 79 (1954): 44-45, 74-76, 109-115, 173-174, 193-
204, 239-246, 283-290, 336-346, 389-398, 420-426,
466-476, 635-636, 694-697, 725-729, 904-911, 946-
958 covers 1945-1952.

Dissertations on surgery and related fields completed
in German institutions, listed under such subjects
as nervous systems, neck, heart, head.

P27. VAIL, Vitaliy S. Bibliografiya otechestvennykh dissertatsiy
po pediatrii, detskim infektsiyam, istorii pediatrii i organizatsii detskogo zdravookhraneniya za 150 let (1804-1954 gg.).
Stalinabad: 1955. 148 p.

Lists approximately 2,700 theses and dissertations.
In two parts, (1) pre-1917, arranged chronologically,
and (2) post-1917, separate alphabetical author
listings of theses and dissertations.

_____ _____ Suppl. 1. 1957. ?

_____ _____ Suppl. 2. 1960. 72 p. ?

P28. "DISSERTATSIY, zashchishchennye v meditsinskikh institutakh
Ukrainya v 1955 gody." Vrachebnoe delo, 1955, no. 7: 683-
686, no. 8: 775-778, no. 9: 907-910, no. 10: 1,019-1,022,
no. 11: 1,129-1,132. Title varies in pieces.

Annotated listing of 67 theses and dissertations
defended in the Dnepropetrovskiy, Kiev, and Kharkhov
medical institutes.

P29. SADILOVA, N. M. Dissertatsiy i monografii russkikh uchenykh
XV-XIX vv. po meditsine na inostrannykh yazykakh. Leningrad:
1956-1957. 2 vols. ?

P30. MOSCOW. Institut organizatsii zdravookhraneniya i istorii
meditsiny. Otdel nauchnoy meditsinskoy informatsii. Dissertatsiy na stepen' doktora i kandidata meditsinskikh nauk;
Bibliografiya za 1956 god. Pod. red. S. M. Bagdasar'yana.
Moskva: 1957. 2 pts. in 1 vol.

A classified listing of 104 dissertations and 1,232
candidate theses completed in U.S.S.R. institutions.

P31. GUTAUSKAS, V. and V. Simkūnas. "Lietuvos TSR medicinos ir
farmacijos mokslo darbuotojų disertacyų apgintu iki 1957.
Spalio 1 a. sąrašas." Sveikatos apsauga, 1957, nr. 11: 51-
57. ?

P32. LIETUVOS TSR MOKSLŲ AKADEMIJA, Vilna. Centrinė biblioteka.
Medicinos daktarų disertacijos, apgintos arba pripažintoes
Vilniaus Universitete 1793-1842 metais; Bibliografine
rodykle. Sudarė A. Bielinis. Vilnius: 1958. 131 p.

Lists 180 titles in Latin with short titles in
Lithuanian and Russian.

P33. LITVINOVA, E. V. and A. V. Chaklin. "Obzor dissertatsiy po
onkologii, zashchishchennykh za period s 1947 po 1954 g."
Voprosy onkologii 4 (1958): 113-119, 365-368.

Abstracts of approximately 100 U.S.S.R. theses and
dissertations on cancer submitted between 1947 and
1954.

P34. RASULOV, M. YA. and U. S. Vayl'. Dissertatsiy uchenykh
Tadzhikistana po meditsine i biologi; Kratkie referat. Stalinabad: 1959. 271 p.

Abstracts of 20 dissertations and 123 theses completed by Tadzhiks between 1938 and 1958. Arranged
chronologically. Author index.

Continued by:

P35. _____ Dissertatsiy uchenykh Tadzhikistana po meditsinie.
Dop. 1. Dushanbe: 1968. 311 p. (Dushanbinskii Institut
Epidemiologii i gigieny. Publikatsiya, no. 38)

An annotated listing of 108 theses and dissertations

completed between 1964 and 1967.

P36.   TIKOVA, T. C.   "Dissertatsiy po gigine truda, fiziologii truda i smezhnym distsilplinam (1958-1959)." Kratkiy obzor gigina i sanitariya, 1960, no. 11: 111-114.

Lists 80 studies.

P37.   AL'TSHULER, N. S.   "Bibliografiya doktorskikh i kandidatskikh dissertatsiy po epidemiologii, profilaktike i organizatsii bor'by s tuberkulezom (1888-1959 gg.)." In Moscow. Moskovskiy nauchno-issledovatel'skiy institut tuberkuleza. Sbornik po obmenu opytom raboty protivotuberkuleznykh uchrezhdeniy RSFSR, vyp. 2 (1960): 173-189.

Lists approximately 200 theses and dissertations completed in the U.S.S.R.

P38.   ALIEVA, A. V.   "Dissertatsiy po istorii meditsiny i zdravookhraneniya, zashchishchennye s 1934 po 1958 g." Sovetskoe zdravookhranenie 19, no. 5 (1960): 73-81.

Alphabetical author listing of 263 U.S.S.R. theses and dissertations.

Continued in part by:

P39.   PRANOVA, L. C.   "Dissertatsiy po sanitarnoy statistike, zashchishchennye na soiskanie uchenoy stepeni kandidata meditsinskikh nauk v 1945-1962 gg." Sovetskoe zdravookhranenie 25, no. 10 (1966): 62-72.

A chronological listing of 263 theses completed in the U.S.S.R.

P40.   NEVSKIY, V. A.   "Otechestvennye dissertatsiy po venerologii i dermatologii v XVIII i pervoy poloviny XIX veka (1736-1850)." Vestnik dermatologii i venerologii 34, no. 9 (1960): 61-68.

A chronological listing of 76 Russian dissertations. The titles are given in the language in which originally written and translated into Russian.   Entry gives place where completed.

P41. VASIL'EV, T. V. "Doktorskie i kandidatskie dissertatsiy po
voprosam dermatologii, venerologii i smezhnym naukam, zashchishchennye za 40 let Sovetskoy vlasti, 1917-1957." Vestnik
dermatologii i venerologii 34 (1960), vyp. 2: 87-95, vyp. 3:
88-93, vyp. 4: 84-91, vyp. 5: 81-89, vyp. 6: 86-93, vyp. 7:
88-94.

A list of approximately 1,400 U.S.S.R. theses and
dissertations listed under major topics.

P42. NESTERENKO, A. I. and M. I. Kamenskaya. "Dissertatsiy po
khirurgii i voprosom smezhnykh spetsial' nostey, zashchishchennye v [1957/1958-1961/1962]" Vestnik khirurgii 84 (1960),
vyp. 2: 154-158; 85 (1960), vyp. 10: 153-159; 88 (1962),
vyp. 6: 132-140; 89 (1962), vyp. 7: 156-158, vyp. 8: 151-
157; 90 (1963), vyp. 4: 152-158; 93 (1964), vyp. 8: 142-145,
vyp. 9: 148-151; 95 (1965), vyp. 6: 143-151; 96 (1965), vyp.
5: 136-141, 143-151; 97 (1967), vyp. 7: 132-138.

A classified listing of dissertations completed in
the U.S.S.R. Covers such areas as anesthesiology,
shock, trauma.

P43. "DISSERTATSIY po grippy." Voprosy virusologii 5, no. 1
(1960): 118-120.

A chronological listing of 80 dissertations completed in the U.S.S.R. between 1943 and 1951.

_____ Voprosy virusologii 8, no. 1 (1963): 122-123.

Lists 23 dissertations completed between 1957 and
1961.

P44. AKADEMIYA MEDITSINSKIKH NAUK SSSR, Moscow. Otdel nauchnoy
meditsinskoy informatsii. Dissertatsiy na stepen' doktora
i kandidata meditsinskikh nauk, zashchishchennye v 1951-
1955 gg. Pod. red. S. M. Bagdasar'yana. Moskva: 1961-
1964. 3 vols.

Separate classified listings of 5,546 theses and
603 dissertations in medicine defended in the
U.S.S.R. during 1951-1955. Author indexes for
doctorates and for candidates.

P45. "DISSERTATSIY po antibiotikam s 1959 g. po fevral' 1962 g."

Antibiotiki 7 (1962): 1,120-1,126.

Separate listings of five dissertations and 129 theses. Each list arranged alphabetically by author.

P46. SAPIN, M. R. "Dissertatsiy po anatomii, gistologii i embriologii, vypolnennye [1960-   ]" Arkhiv anatomii gistologii i embriologii 43 (1962)-   . Annual.

An alphabetical author listing of theses and dissertations defended in the U.S.S.R.

P47. BUKHANSTSEVA, G. I. "Avtoreferat dissertatsiy po sotsial'noy gigine, organizatsii zdravookhraneniiya, sanitarnoy statistike i istorii meditsiny [1958/1961-   ]" Sovetskoe zdravookhranenie 21 (1962)-   . Title varies.

Vol. 21, vyp. 12 (1962): 74-77 covers 1958-1961; 29, vyp. 11 (1970): 64-75 covers 1961-1965; 30, vyp. 4 (1971): 79-88 covers 1966-1968; 30, vyp. 6 (1971): 72-76 covers 1969; from 31 (1972), covering 1970, the list is annual.

Lists theses and dissertations defended in the U.S.S.R.

P48. "DISSERTATION Listings, 1960-1961." Training School Bulletin 59 (1962): 59-62.

A classified list of completed American dissertations relevant to the field of mental retardation. Includes such topics as pharmacology, physiology, psychology, and speech.

P49. HUU, Nguyen and Vu van Nguyen. "Médecine et sciences affiliées." Bulletin analytique des travaux scientifiques publiés au Viet-Nam [1 (1942-1962), section 1] Saigon: 1963. 160 p.

Whole number.

Issued by the Vietnam Centre nationale de la recherche scientifique.

A classified listing, a substantial number of which are dissertations (état and université) presented

to the faculties of medicine at Hanoi and Saigon.
Includes such areas as anatomy and physical anthropology, diseases, medical chemistry and pharmacy,
public health, history of medicine. Author index.

P50. NAUMENKO, V. G. "Dissertatsiy po problemam sudebnoy meditsiny za 1960-1962 gg." Sudebno-meditsinskaya ekspertiza
6, no. 4 (1963): 54-56.

Alphabetical author listing of 31 theses and dissertations completed in the U.S.S.R.

P51. BELMONTE ROMÁN, Lucía. Tesis existentes en la Biblioteca de
la Facultad de Medicina. Bogotá: Univ. Nacional de Colombia,
Centro de Bibliografía y Documentación, 1964. 200 p. ?

P52. DVINYANINOV, Leonid I. Fiziologiia patologiia zheludochno-
kishechnogo trakta; Referaty dissertatsiy otechestvennykh
avtorov s 1765 po 1917 g. i bibliograficheskiy ukazatel'
dissertatsiy s 1918 po 1964 g. Moskva: Nauka, 1966. 266 p.

Pt. 1 is a classified listing of U.S.S.R. dissertations, covering the period 1765 to 1917; pt. 2
covers the period 1918-1964. In pt. 1 the entry
carries an abstract and indicates location. Author
and subject indexes.

P53. "SPISOK otechestvennyukh dissertatsiy po nevrolatologii psikhiatrii i smezhnym distsplinam, postulivskikh v gosudarst-
vennyyu tsentralnuyu nauchnyyu meditsinskyyu biblioteky po
[1967-   ]" Zhurnal nevropathologii i psikhiatrii imeni
S. S. Korsakova 69 (1967)-   . Annual.

Separate lists of theses and dissertations defended
in the U.S.S.R.

P54. "DISSERTATSIY po antibiotikam s fevraly 1962 g. po sentyabr'
1967 g." Antibiotiki 13 (1968), no. 9: 853-859, no. 10:
952-957.

Lists 247 theses and dissertations completed in the
U.S.S.R.

P55. "SPISOK avtoreferatov dissertatsiy po stomatologii i smezh-

nym distsiplinam, postupivshikh v GTSNMB v [1968-   ]"
<u>Stomatologiia</u> (Moskva) 48 (1969)-   . Annual.

Lists in separate listings theses and dissertations
received by the Gosudarstvennaya nauchnaya meditsinskaya biblioteka (Moscow).

P56. WOŹNIEWSKI, Zbigniew. <u>Rozprawy na stopień doktora medycyny</u>
<u>polskich wydziałów lekarskich; Okres miedzywojenny</u>. Warszawa:
Państwowy Zakład Wydawn Lekarskich, 1969. 106 p.

An alphabetical author listing of 533 dissertations.
Entry gives previous degrees and dates, adviser,
and availability and location of copies. Index to
adviser with bibliographical sketch. Subject index.

P57. DRAGUNIENES, T. <u>Lietuvos medicinos mokslu darktaru ir kandi-</u>
<u>datu disertacyu sarašas (1898-1968)</u>. N.p.: 1970. ?

P58. DIETHELM, Oskar. <u>Medical Dissertations of Psychiatric In-</u>
<u>terest Printed before 1750</u>. New York: Karger, 1971. 209 p.

"List of Dissertations" (p. 161-211) is an alphabetical author listing of 1,100 dissertations arranged
by respondent. Entry gives location of copies.
Index of praeses.

P59. "DOKTORSKIE dissertatsiy po khirurgii, postulivshie v Gosudarstvennuyu tsentral'nuyu nauchnyu meditsinskuyu biblioteky [1972-   ] <u>Khirurgiia</u> 48 (1972)-   . Irregular.

Lists dissertations in surgery received by the
Gosudarstvennaya nauchnaya meditsinskaya biblioteka
(Moscow).

P60. "THESES and Dissertations." <u>Physical Therapy</u> 52 (1972): 58-
79.

A retrospective listing of theses and dissertations
completed in American institutions to 1970. Arranged
under such areas as amputation, arthritis, gout,
physiology, spinal injuries.

_____ [1970-   ]" <u>Physical Therapy</u> 53 (1973)-   .
Annual.

Vol. 53 (1973) covers 1970 and 1971.

Follows same arrangement as main work.

Individual Institutions

P61. MUNGALINSKIY, P. "Bibliografiya dissertatsiy Azerbaydzhan-
skogo meditsinskogo instituta za 25 let." In Akademiya nauk
Azerbaydzhanskoy SSR, Baku. Izvestiya, 1945, vyp. 12: 84-103.

A listing of studies accepted at the Institute in
the period 1920-1945.

P62. IASHKOV, P. Z. Dissertatsiy, zashchishchennye nauchnymi
rabotnikami Kazakhskogo gosudarstvennogo meditsinskogo instituta s 1935 po 1953. Alma-Ata: 1953. 48 p.

Separate alphabetical author lists of 32 dissertations
and 194 theses defended by the staff of the Alma-
Atinskiy meditsinskiy institut between 1935 and 1953.
Chronological index.

P63. ALMA-ATINSKIY MEDITSINSKIY INSTITUT. Nauchno-meditsinskaya
biblioteka. Bibliograficheskiy ukazatel' nauchnykh rabot
sotrudnikov Alma-Atinskogo gosudarstvennogo meditsinskogo
instituta, 1957-1969. Red. koll. S. R. Karynbaev. Alma-Ata:
Nauka, 1971. 563 p.

Lists 6,872 theses and dissertations defended by the
staff of the Institute. Classified under general
science, public health and medical sciences, related
sciences, and other sciences. Under each subject,
theses and dissertations are listed separately.
Entry gives location of an abstract. Subject index.

P64. AFANAS'EVA, A. V. "Perechen' doktorskikh i kandidatskikh
dissertatsiy, zashchishchennykh nauchnymi rabotnikami Astra-
khanskogo gosudarstvennogo meditsinskogo instituta za 1918-
1957 gg." In Astrakhanskiy gosudarstvennyy meditsinskiy
institut. Trudy 13 (1957): suppl. 34 p.

Lists the approximately 100 theses and dissertations
defended by the staff of the Institute.

P65.   ABIEV, G. S. and G. G. Mirzoyan. <u>Dissertatsiy zashchishchen-</u>
<u>nye v Azerbaydzhanskom gosudarstvennom meditsinskom institute</u>
<u>imeni N. Narimanova s 1922 po 1960 god</u>. Baku: 1961. 71 p.

Dissertations defended at the Institute.

P66.   BAHIA, Brazil (State). Universidade. Faculdade de Medicina.
<u>Catalogo de thesis</u>. Compiled by Pedro Rodrigues Guimarães.
Bahia: 1910. 304 p.   ??

P67.   HUSNER, Fritz. <u>Verzeichnis der Basler Medizinischen Univer-</u>
<u>sitätsschriften von 1575-1829</u>. Basel: 1942. 137 p.

Issued as a separate in <u>Festschrift für Dr. J.</u>
<u>Brodbeck-Sandreuter, 18. Juni 1942</u>.

A chronological listing of 1,631 dissertations
arranged by praeses. Entry gives name of respondent and his place of residence. Author and subject
indexes.

P68.   BERLIN. Universität. Medizinische Fakultät. <u>Jahrbuch der</u>
<u>Dissertationen der Medizinischen Fakultät der Friedrich-</u>
<u>Wilhelms-Universität zu Berlin</u> [1922/1923-1929/1930] Berlin:
Ebering, 1923-1930. 8 vols.

Abstracts of dissertations. Entry gives brief
biographical note and adviser.

P69.   BERN. Universität. Medizinische Fakultät. <u>Auszüge aus</u>
<u>den Inauguraldissertationen der Medizinischen Fakultät der</u>
<u>Universität Bern</u> [1920/1921-   ] Bern: Grunau, 1921-   .
Annual.

Abstracts of published dissertations. Entry gives
brief biographical information.

P70.   BONN. Universität. Medizinische Fakultät. <u>Jahrbuch der</u>
<u>Dissertationen</u> [1 (1951)-8 (1957/1959)] Bonn: 1952-1960.
Annual.

Abstracts of dissertations in the medical sciences,
including medicine, pharmacy, and dentistry, arranged
under specialization. Entry gives biographical and
academic data and adviser.

P71. BORDEAUX. Université. Faculté de médecine et de pharmacie. Catalogue complet des thèses de doctorat de la Faculté de médecine de Bordeaux, depuis sa fondation (1878) jusqu'en juillet 1902...suivi...de la Liste complète des thèses de pharmacie. Bordeaux: Robin, 1903. 48 p.

A subject list of 1,765 dissertations in medicine and 39 theses and dissertations in pharmacy. Author index.

P72. BUENOS AIRES. Universidad Nacional. Facultad de Ciencias Médicas. Biblioteca. Catálogo de la Colección de Tesis, 1827-1917. Buenos Aires: A. Flaiban, 1918. 492 p.

Represents 3,652 theses presented to the Faculty of Medical Sciences. (Some are not available at the Library.) Arranged chronologically, with an author index, a classified arrangement, and an analytical index.

P73. CLERMONT-FERRAND, France. Université. Faculté mixte de médecine et de pharmacie. Catalogue décennial des thèses soutenues devant la Faculté, 1958-1965. Clermont-Ferrand: France Quercy-Auvergne, 1968. 62 p.

Set out by Jacques Archimbaud.

In two parts: (1) medicine and (2) pharmacy. Arranged chronologically under each. Separate author index. Subject index.

P74. "RELACIÓN de las tesis publicados y sostenidas por los alumnos de la Facultad de Medicina, para recibir el título de doctores, y fechas en que éstas se han expedido." Revista literaria (Bogotá) 5 (1894): 116-119.

An annotated list of 93 theses completed at the University of Colombia Faculty of Medicine.

P75. ZELIGMAN, S. B. Annotatsii dissertatsiy sotrudnikov instituta, 1930-1965. Donetsk: 1966. 679 p.

Abstracts of the theses or dissertations completed by members of the Donetsk Medical Institute. The 238 studies are listed under such fields as morphology, biological chemistry, physiology, pharmacology, hygiene. Author index.

P76. DNEPROPETROVSKIY MEDITSINSKIY INSTITUT. Sbornik referatov
dissertatsionnykh rabot, 1935-1937. Otvetstvennyy redaktor:
M. M. Trostanetskiy. Dnepropetrovsk: 1938. 322 p. (Dnepropetrovskiy meditsinskiy institut. Zbirnyk naukovo-doslid-
nykh robit, t. 5) ?

In Russian and Ukrainian.

P77. GRÜNFELD, Abraham. "Verzeichniss der von medicinischen Fac-
ultät zu Dorpat seit ihrer Grundung veröffentlichen Schriften.
In Kaiserliche Universität zu Dorpat. Pharmakologische Institut. Historische Studien, vol. 3, p. 1-76. Halle a. S.:
1893.

A chronological list of 1,363 items. Entry indicates publication information if in a journal.

P78. EDINBURGH. University. List of Graduates in Medicine in
the University of Edinburgh, from MDCCV to MDCCCLXVI [with
Titles of Their Theses] Edinburgh: 1867. 73 p.

Supersedes its Statuta solennia de doctoratus in
medicina gradu in Academia edinburgena capessando,
a facultate medica proposita, et in posterum,
jubente senata academico, observanda (1800).

A chronological listing. Name index.

P79. CATALOGUE of Old and Rare Books in Medicine, Surgery etc.
and of a Series of Medical Theses by Students from America
at Edinburgh University, 1760 to 1813. On sale by George
P. Johnston... Edinburgh: 1902.

Contains a list of 126 medical theses by students
from America (124 U.S. and two Canadian) completed
at Edinburgh University from 1760 to 1813. (The
collection was purchased by W. Osler and is now in
the Medical and Chirurgical Faculty of the State of
Maryland Library.)

P80. FRANKFURT AM MAIN. Universität. Medizinische Fakultät.
Dissertationen der Medizinischen Fakultät, Frankfurt am
Main [1919-1921] Frankfurt am Main: 1919-1922. Annual.

Abstracts of dissertations in medicine and dentistry completed in the Faculty. Arranged by such
fields as internal medicine, pathology, physiology,
dentistry. Entry gives adviser. Author index.

P81. NAUCK, Ernst T. Die Doktorpromotionen der Medizinischen
Fakultät Freiburg i. Br. Freiburg im Breisgau: E. Albert,
1958. 110 p. (Freiburger Wissenschafts- und Universitätsgeschichte. Beiträge. Heft 20)

Contains a chronological "Verzeichnis der Promotionen
von 1500-1885" (p. 37-66); a chronological listing
of dissertations of the Freiburg University medical
faculty for 1595-1783 (p. 66-67); and a chronological listing covering the period 1698-1785 of medical
dissertations completed at Freiburg University (p.
68-69).

P82. BATUNIN, Mikhail P. Doktorskie i kandidatskie dissertatsiy,
zashchishchennye v Gor'kovskom gosudarstvennom meditsinskom
institute im. S. M. Kirova, 1935-1949. Gor'kiy: 1949. 16 p.

Separate alphabetical author listings of 17 dissertations and 169 theses defended at the Gor'kovskiy
gosudarstvennyy meditsinskiy institut in the period
1935-1949.

P83. SCHÖNFELD, Walther H. P. Zur Geschichte der Medizinischen
Fakultät und zur Entwicklung von Lehre und Forschung in den
Haut- und Geschlechtskrankheiten und der Universität Greifswald. Greifswald: Bamberg, 1927. (Greifswalder Universi-
tätsreden, 23)

Contains Beilage 4: "Disputationes et Dissertationes
medicae von 1599-1811" (p. 49-58), a chronological
listing of 171 items which were located in the
University library. Entry gives notes relative to
the author and publication. Beilage 5: "Greifswalder
Doktorarbeiten aus dem Gebiete der Haut- und Geschlechtskrankheiten von 1817-1920" (p. 59-65), a
chronological listing of 200 items.

P84. HEIDELBERG: Universität. Medizinische Fakultät. Jahrbuch
[1922/1923] Heidelberg: 1923.

Abstracts of dissertations in medical fields.

P85. INSTITUTUL DE MEDICINĂ ŞI FARMACIE, Bucharest. Biblioteca
      Centrala. Serviciul de Documentare si Bibliografie. Bib-
      liografia lucrarilor de diplomă sustinute la I.M.F. Bucureşti
      in anii 1959-1963. Bucureşti: 1968. 337 p.

      Alphabetical author listing of 3,397 theses.

P86. JERUSALEM. Hebrew University. Hadassah School of Medicine.
      Abstracts of Theses [1963-   ] Jerusalem: 1965-
      Annual.

      In Hebrew. Abstracts in English.

      Abstracts of theses and dissertations, arranged by
      type of degree. Author and subject indexes.

P87. HEADLEE, William H. A Final Report on the Development of
      the Jinnah Postgraduate Medical Center, Karachi, Pakistan;
      A Project of International Cooperation between the Govern-
      ment of the United States of America and the Government of
      Pakistan for the Development of Postgraduate Medical Educa-
      tion and the Training of Medical Educators...and Indiana
      University. Indianapolis, Ind.: Indiana University Medical
      Center, School of Medicine, 1967.

      Appendix C, "Theses Completed by Candidates for the
      Master of Science Degree, Basic Medical Sciences
      Division" (p. 185-188), arranged under major: ana-
      tomy, biochemistry, microbiology, pathology, pharma-
      cology, and psychology. Appendix D, "Theses Com-
      pleted by Participants Programmed for Advanced
      Training in the United States Who Were Candidates
      for Advanced Degrees," lists dissertations.

P88. JINNAH POSTGRADUATE MEDICAL CENTER. Basic Medical Sciences
      Division. Thesis Summaries, 1961-1965. Karachi: 1968.
      155 p.

      Abstracts of 93 theses in anatomy, microbiology,
      pathology, and pharmacology, arranged by year.
      Author and subject index.

      _____ _____ 1966-1968. Karachi: 1969. 50 p.

      Continues earlier listing with an additional 37
      theses.

P89. GLOZMAN, O. S. "Dissertatsiy Kazakhskogo meditsinskogo instituta za 25 let (1931-1956)." Zdravookhranenie Kazakhstana,
1956, vyp. 4: 24-27.

Dissertations in public health defended at the
Institute.

P90. MUKHAMED'YAROV, G. F. "Bibliografiya dissertatsiy Kazansko-
go gosudarstvennogo meditsinskogo instituta za 30 let
sovetskoy vlasti (1917-1947)." In Kazanskiy gosudarstvennyy
meditsinskiy institut. Trudy 1 (1947): 253-268.

Lists dissertations completed in the Institute.

P91. KIEL. Universität. Medizinische Fakultät. Dissertationen
Medizinische Fakultät Inhaltsangaben [1959/1960-   ]
Kiel: 1960-   . Annual.

Abstracts of dissertations. Arranged under fields
such as anatomy, physiology, pathology, internal
medicine, surgery. Entry gives adviser. Author
and subject indexes.

P92. KISHINEVSKIY GOSUDARSTVENNYY MEDITSINSKIY INSTITUT.
Annoterovannyy ukazatel' dissertatsiy sotrudnikov KGMI
(1946-1970). Sost. L. I. Trofimova. Kishinev: Shtlinstsa,
1973. 234 p.

A classified listing of abstracts of 304 theses
and dissertations. Author index.

P93. ORNATSKIY, V. V., V. P. Zamyatin, and T. A. Solov'eva.
"Ukazatel' dissertatsiy, zashchishchennykh v GIDUVe, i
pechatnykh rabot, izdannykh institutom." In Leningrad.
Gosudarstvennyy institut usovershenstvovaniya vrachey. Sem'
desyat piat'let Leningradskogo gos. ordena Lenina instituta
usovershenstvovaniya vrachey im. S. M. Kirova, p. 351-379.
Leningrad: 1960.

Lists 574 theses and 178 dissertations completed
at the Institute. The main section covers the
period 1935-June 1960 with theses and dissertations
listed separately. A 1959/1960 list contains nine
dissertations and 55 candidate theses.

P94. LENINGRAD. Meditsinskiy institut (1st). <u>Ukazatel' disser-</u>
<u>tatsiy, zashchishchennykh v I Leningradskom meditsinskom</u>
<u>institute v 1935-1958 gg</u>. Sost. T. A. Nikiforooskaya i M.
N. Suprun. Leningrad: Gos. Izd-vo med. lit-ry, 1959. 85 p.

   Lists approximately 850 theses and dissertations
   under such subjects as the history of medicine,
   hygiene, ophthalmology, surgery, biochemistry.
   Author index.

P95. GUKOV, A. P. <u>Annotatsii dissertatsiy, zashchishchennykh v</u>
<u>Voenno-morskoy meditsinskoy akademii (1946-1950)</u>. Leningrad:
VMMA, 1953. 274 p. ?

P96. ROUSSET, Jean. <u>Les thèses médicales soutenues à Lyon aux</u>
<u>XVIIe et XVIIIe siècles et le Collège royal de chirurgie de</u>
<u>1774 à 1792</u>. Lyon: 1950. 141 p.

   Previously published in <u>Albums du crocodile</u>, 1949,
   no. 5-6; 1950, no. 1-3.

   Abstracts and descriptions of one thesis written in
   the 17th century and 11 written in the 18th century,
   along with detailed biographical information on the
   authors (p. 11-41). Entry gives location of thesis.

P97. LYONS. Université. Faculté mixte de médecine et de pharmacie. <u>Table de thèses de médecine, pharmacie, chirurgie</u>
<u>dentaire, et médecine veterinaire</u> [1877-   ] Lyon: 1877-
   . Title varies. Annual.

   In three parts: (1) medicine (including pharmacy),
   (2) dental surgery, (3) veterinary medicine. Subject index.

P98. MARBURG. Universität. Medizinische Fakultät. <u>Jahrbuch</u>
[1922/1923-1923/1924] Marburg: 1923-1924. Annual.

   Abstracts of completed dissertations. Arranged
   under (1) medicine and (2) dentistry.

P99. _____ <u>Jahrbuch der Dissertationen</u> [1953-   ] Marburg:
1955-   . Annual.

   Abstracts of dissertations, arranged under pharmacy,

medicine, and dentistry. Entry gives adviser.

P100. MINNESOTA. University. Graduate School. Mayo Foundation
for Medical Education and Research. Subjects of Theses
Submitted by Fellows in the Mayo Foundation for Medical
Education and Research Who Obtained Graduate Degrees in the
University of Minnesota from January, 1915, to July 1945.
Rochester, Minn.: 1945. 55 p.

> Lists approximately 1,100 items. Theses and dis-
> sertations are arranged chronologically under major.
> Research in progress is listed separately and is
> also arranged by major. Entry gives the degree and
> the minor field of study.

P101. MONTEVIDEO. Universidad. Facultad de Medicina. Bibliotheca. Tesis de doctorado y para optar a las cátedras
presentadas a la Facultad de Medicina, 1878-1902. Par Hebe
Bollini Folchi. Montevideo: 1962. 37 p.

> A chronological listing. Author and subject index.

P102. GERMAIN, Alexandre C. Les Anciennes thèses de l'École de
médecine de Montpellier, collations de grades et concours
professoraux. Montpellier: Boehm et fils, 1886. 196 p.

> Also appeared in l'Académie des sciences et lettres
> de Montpellier. Mémoires 7 (1886): 499-690.

> Three lists: "Les Thèses d'étudiants" (candidates
> for doctor of medicine from 1586 to end of 18th
> century), p. 11-65; "Les Thèses de professeurs"
> (candidates for vacant chairs from 1567 to end of
> 18th century), p. 66-182; "Documents complémentaires,"
> p. 182-196.

P103. ZAMKOVA, Zinaida N. Dissertatsiy, zashchishchennye v TSentral'nom institute usovershenstvovaniya vrachey: Annotiro-
vannyy ukazatel' 1935-1946. Pod red. B. V. Ogneva. Moskva:
1948. 100 p.

> A classified list of 446 theses and dissertations
> defended at the Institute. Entry gives publication
> information and an annotation. Author and subject
> indexes.

P104. TERNOVSKIY, V. N. Bibliografiya dissertatsiy Meditsinskogo
fakul'teta Moskovskogo universiteta. 2 izd. Moskva: Akademiya med. nauk SSSR, 1949. 63 p.

> First edition 1930.
>
> A chronological listing of approximately 900 dis-
> sertations, covering the period 1794-1922. Latin
> titles are translated into Russian. Author and
> subject indexes.

P105. MOSCOW. Vtoroy moskovskiy meditsinskiy institut. Doktorskie
dissertatsiy, vypoenennye za 1959-1965 gg; Kratkie annotatsiy.
Moskva: 1966. 119 p.

> An annotated listing of dissertations defended at
> the Institute. Entry gives adviser.

P106. NANTES. Université. Bibliothèque. Liste de thèses soutenues en cours de l'annee [1962-   ] Nantes: 1962-   .
Annual.

> Separate lists of (1) dissertations and (2) theses,
> each subdivided into pharmacy and medicine.

P107. PARIS. École de médecine. Tables chronologique et alpha-
bétiques des thèses in 8e soutenues à l'École de médecine de
Paris, au nombre de 406, depuis le 28 frimaire an VII, jus-
ques et compris le floréal an XII. Rédigées par P. Sué.
Paris: Méquignon, 1806. 80 p.

> A chronological listing. Author index.

P108. PARIS. Université. Faculté de médecine. Tables de thèses
soutenues devant la Faculté de médecine de Paris [1798-   ]
Paris: 1798-   . Annual.

> Cumulated lists covering 1798-1804 and for 1803-
> 1806 were included in the 1798-1816 cumulation;
> another cumulation covers 1816-1825.
>
> Lists completed dissertations. Includes separate
> listings for theses in radiology, theses completed
> by foreign students, and dissertations in veterinary
> medicine and dental surgery.

_____ Table general des thèses soutenues à la Faculté de
médecine de Paris. Paris: 18   ?

Edition for 1940 edited by A. Hahn.

Compilations of the annual listings.

P109. "KANDIDÁTSKÉ a doktorské disertační prace [1963-   ]"
Sbornik Lekarsky 69 (1967)-   . Annual.

Separate lists in Czech, Russian, and English.

Vol. 69 (1967) covers 1963 and 1964; vol. 71 (1969)
covers 1966 and 1967; from vol. 73 (1971), covering
1968, lists are annual.

Lists theses and dissertations completed at the
University of Charles (Prague) Faculty of Medicine.
Arranged by year with theses and dissertations
listed separately.

P110. GUELLIOT, Octave. Les Thèses de l'ancienne Faculté de
médecine de Reims. Reims: F. Michaud, 1889. 175 p.

"Liste des thèses originales soutenues à la Faculté
de medecine de Reims [1550-1793]" (p. 71-143) is a
classified listing of 280 theses. Entry gives name
of praeses and an abstract.

P111. ARIPOV, U. A. "Dissertatsiy na soiskanie uchenoy stepeni
kandidata meditsinskikh nauk, zashchishchennye v Samarkand-
skom meditsinskom institute s 1 YAnvarya 1959 po sentyabr'
1960 goda." Meditsinsku zhurnal Uzbekistana, 1961, no. 2:
71-74.

An annotated listing of 13 theses completed at the
Institute.

P112. SARATOVSKIY MEDITSINSKIY INSTITUT. Bibliografiia dissertatsiy, zashchishchennykh v 1935-1958 gg. Sostavil Petr I.
Shamarin. Saratov: 1960. 232 p. (Its Trudy, t. 30)

Abstracts of approximately 300 theses and dissertations completed at the Institute. Subdivided by
level of degree under major medical fields and
listed chronologically.

P113. STRASBOURG. Université. Faculté de médecine. Tables générales des thèses soutenues à la Faculté de médecine de Strasbourg, pour la réception au doctorat, depuis de 19 vendémaire au VIII jusqu'au 31 décembre 1837. Strasbourg: 1840. ?

P114. WICKERSHEIMER, Ernest. "Les thèses non imprimées de la Faculté de médecine de Strasbourg, 1919-1922." Strasbourg médical 81, no. 14 (1923): cv-cviii.

Alphabetical author listing of approximately 160 dissertations. (These are not listed in Catalogue de thèses de doctorat soutenues devant les universités françaises.)

P115. TARTU. Ülikool. Teaduslik Raamatukogu. Tartu Ülikooli Arstiteaduskonnas 1892-1917 kaitstud väiterkirjad; Bibliograafia. Koostaja V. Leek. Tartu: 1965. 56 p.

In German or Russian.

A chronological listing of 291 theses and dissertations completed in the Faculty of Medicine. Subject indexes in Estonian and Russian. Author index.

P116. TÜBINGEN. Universität. Medizinische Fakultät. Jahrbuch der Auszüge aus den Dissertationen der Medizinischen Fakultät zu Tübingen [1 (1921/1922)-6 (1926/1927)] Tübingen: 1922-1927. Annual.

Vol. 1 (1921/1922) contains abstracts. Vols. 2 (1922/1923)-6 (1926/1927) are lists arranged into (1) medicine, subdivided by specialization, and (2) dentistry. Entry gives adviser.

P117. GASPARYAN, Aschot M. Dissertatsiy, zashchishchennye v meditsinskikh vuzakh i nauchno-issledovatel'skikh institutakh Ministerstva zdravookhraneniya Ukrainskoy SSR, 1935-1948: Bibliograficheskiy ukazatel'. Kiev: Gosmedizdat USSR, 1952. 128 p.

An alphabetical author listing of approximately 1,500 theses and dissertations defended in the medical institutions of education and research institutes of the Ukrainian Ministry of Public Health.

P118. VALLADOLID. Universidad. Cátedra de Anatomía. 25 tesis
doctorales, Facultad de Medicina de Valladolid, Cátedra de
Anatomía, prof. dr. Antonio Pérez Casas. Valladolid:
Facultad de Medicina de Valladolid, 1967. 125 p.

The conclusions of 25 studies completed under Antonio
Pérez Casas in the period 1960 through 1967.

P119. KOVEVA, Z. A. "Dissertatsiy zashchishchennye v institute
'Mikrob.'" Problemy osobo opasnykh infektsiy, 1968, no. 4:
224-230.

A chronological listing of 171 theses and dissertations completed between 1939 and 1968.

Dentistry

General

P120. "DISSERTATIONS." Dental Abstracts 1 (1956)-8 (1963).
Irregular.

Lists theses and dissertations accepted by dental
or graduate schools. International in coverage.

P121. SASSOUNI, Viken. 1964 Harvest of Orthodontic Theses, Compiled and Classified. Pittsburgh: University of Pittsburgh,
School of Dentistry, Orthodontic Dept., 1965. 64 p.

Theses completed in 1964. In four parts: (1) an
alphabetical listing by institution, (2) an alphabetical listing by author, (3) a subject index,
and (4) a section of one page abstracts.

P122. MINAS GERAES, Brazil. Universidade Federal. Faculdade de
Odontologia. Biblioteca. Bibliografia de teses apresenta-
das às faculdades de odontologia do Brasil. Pref. por
Luiza Penido de Rezende. Belo Horizonte: 1967. 1 vol.
(various pagings)

A classified bibliography (based upon the Dewey
decimal classification and A. Black's "Classification for Dental Literature") of theses approved by
Brazilian schools of dentistry. Subject, author,

and institutional indexes.

P123. LÖFGREN, A. B. "Swedish Doctoral Dissertations in Odontology, 1917-1970." Svensk tandläkare tidskrift 64 (1971): 12-39.

A chronological listing of 118 studies. Entry gives publication information. Author index.

Individual Institutions

P124. CÓRDOBA, Argentine Republic. Universidad Nacional. Facultad de Odontológia. Tesis odontológicas. Compiladas por Maria A. Morra y Helena E. Centeno. Córdoba: Univ. Nac. de Córdoba, Centro de Documentación, 1967. 21 p.

An alphabetical author listing of approximately 70 theses. Subject and chronological indexes.

P125. INDIANA. University. School of Dentistry. Library. Theses Catalogued, 1947 to Date. Indianapolis: 1960. 5 p.

Chronological listing of theses and dissertations.

_____ _____ Annual Supplement [1960-] Indianapolis: 1961- .

P126. MICHIGAN. University. School of Dentistry. Dental Library. Theses Available, 1932-1959. Ann Arbor: 1960. 23 p.

_____ _____ Supplements [1960/1961-] Irregular.

A chronological list of theses and dissertations.

P127. NORTHWESTERN UNIVERSITY, Evanston, Ill. Dental School, Chicago. Library. Completed Theses at Northwestern University Dental School Library. N.p.: 1950? 35 p.

Lists approximately 550 theses and dissertations.

_____ _____ Supplement [1 (1950/1951)-5 (1955)] Evanston: 1951-1955. Annual.

P128. "RESUMOS de teses, 1934-1967." In São Paulo, Brazil (City). Universidade. Faculdade de Odontologia. Seccão de Documentacão Odontológica. Bio-bibliografia do corpo docente da Faculdade de Odontologia, p. 81-186. São Paulo: 1969.

An alphabetical author listing of 320 theses.

Nursing

P129. "THESES in Professional Education." Education for Victory 3 (Jan. 20, 1945): 28.

Eight theses and dissertations (six in the field of nursing), with short abstracts, which are available in the U.S. Office of Education Library.

P130. CATHOLIC UNIVERSITY OF AMERICA. Library. Nursing Theses 1932-1961; An Alphabetical Listing and Keyword Index. Prepared by the Catholic University of America Libraries in cooperation with the School of Nursing, on the occasion of the 35th anniversary of the founding of the School of Nursing. Fred Blum, editor. Washington: 1970. 1 vol. (unpaged)

An alphabetical author listing of 975 theses accepted by the School of Nursing and its predecessor, the Division of Nursing. Entry gives religious order, if known. Key word index.

Ophthalmology and Optometry

P131. JALABERT, Adolphe and P. Chavernac. Catalogue général des thèses françaises d'ophtalmologie. Publié sous le direction du Dr. H. Truc. 2. éd. Montpellier: Delord-Boehm et Martial, 1904. 327 p.

First edition 1892.

In two parts, both chronological: (1) a listing by first letter of the author's last name and (2) a classified listing.

Continued by:

P132. THOMAS, Charles. "Répertoire méthodique des thèses françaises d'ophtalmologie soutenues [1904 à 1946]" <u>Archives</u>
<u>d'ophtalmologie</u>, n.s. 2 (1938): 481-496, 575-592; n.s. 7
(1947): 473-487.

N.s. 7 (1947), covering the period 1936-1946, was
compiled by Charles Thomas and Henriette Michel.

A classified listing of approximately 1,600 items,
including materials from veterinary medicine, pharmacy, and the other sciences if they relate to
ophthalmology. The classification has such major
headings as history, forensic medicine, and sports.

P133. LEVENE, J. R. "Bibliography of Visual Science Dissertations
and Theses: British Universities, 1957-1967." <u>American</u>
<u>Journal of Optometry and Archives of American Academy of</u>
<u>Optometry</u> 45 (1968): 613-616.

An alphabetical author listing of 73 theses and
dissertations.

Pharmacy

General

P134. DORVEAUX, Paul M. J. <u>Catalogue des thèses de pharmacie</u>
<u>soutenues en province depuis la création des écoles de phar-</u>
<u>macie jusqu'à nos jours (1803-1894), suivi d'un appendice</u>
<u>du "Catalogue des thèses soutenues devant l'École de pharma-</u>
<u>cie de Paris."</u> Paris: H. Welter, 1894. 117 p.

Theses in the pharmaceutical sciences completed in
French institutions of higher education in pharmacy
and medicine. Arranged chronologically under institution. Appendix (p. 91-95) covers the University
of Paris for the period 1890-1894, with some earlier
items omitted from Dorveaux listing for the University of Paris (Item P141). Entry gives brief biographical information. Author and subject indexes.

P135. "ANNOTATSII dissertatsiyna uchenye stepni doktora i kandidata farmatsevticheskikh nauk, zashchishchennyk [1952-
1965/1966]" <u>Farmatsiya</u> 1 (1952)-15 (1966). Title varies.
Annual.

Abstracts of theses and dissertations completed in
the U.S.S.R.

P136. AMERICAN ASSOCIATION OF COLLEGES OF PHARMACY. Committee on
Academic Resources. Bibliography of Theses and Dissertations
Relevant to Pharmacy Administration. Edited by David A.
Knapp. Silver Spring, Md.: American Association of Colleges
of Pharmacy, 1970. 65 p.

Supersedes the separate listings prepared by the
Committee for 1964, 1966, 1967, and 1968.

A classified bibliography of approximately 400 theses
and 350 dissertations completed from 1964 through
1968. The dissertations and some theses are annotated.

_____ _____ Section 5, April 1970. Silver Spring, Md.:
1970. 30 p.

In two parts: (1) "A Partially Annotated List of
Master's Theses" lists ten theses completed in
1969; and (2) "An Annotated List of Doctoral Dissertations" lists 113 items taken from Dissertation
Abstracts for 1969 and includes items for 1967
through 1969.

P137. CLERMONT-FERRAND, France. Bibliothèque de médecine et de
pharmacie. Catalogue des thèses de pharmacie soutenues
devant les universités de province [1 (1960/1967)-   ]
Clermont-Ferrand: 1970-   . Annual.

Edited by Jacques Archimbaud.

First volume covers the period 1960-1967.

Lists dissertations by institution, subdivided by
type of degree. Subject and author indexes.

P138. MENDITTO, Joseph. Drugs of Addiction and Non-Addiction;
Their Use and Abuse. A Comprehensive Bibliography, 1960-
1969. Troy, N.Y.: Whitston Publishing Company, 1970. 315 p.

Lists dissertations separately under such topics
as amphetamines and stimulants, marijuana, narcotic
trade, and narcotics.

P139. LUDWICKI, Henryk. <u>Prace habilitacyjne, doktorskie i mages-
terskie w zakresie nauk farmaceutycznych lata 1945-1968</u>.
Warsawa: Państwowy Zakład Wydawnictw Lekarskich, 1971. 302 p.

Theses, dissertations, and habilitacyjne completed
in Polish institutions. Arranged under major areas,
such as botanical pharmacy, organic chemistry, micro-
biology, and inorganic and analytic chemistry.
Under each area the studies are listed separately
under habilitacyjne, dissertations, or theses.
Subject index.

Individual Institutions

P140. NANCY. Université. <u>Catalogue des thèses soutenues devant
la Faculté de pharmacie de Nancy de 1873 à 1943</u>. Par Marie
Marchal. Nancy: G. Thomas, 1944. 48 p.

Lists approximately 250 dissertations chronologically by type of degree. Author and subject indexes.

P141. DORVEAUX, Paul M. J. <u>Catalogue des thèses soutenues devant
l'École de pharmacie de Paris, 1815-1889</u>. Paris: H. Welter,
1891. 74 p.

Coverage for the years 1890-1894 found on p. 91-95
of Item P134.

A chronological listing. Entry gives brief biographical note and publication information. Author
index.

Continued by:

P142. PARIS. Université. Faculté de pharmacie. Bibliothèque.
<u>Catalogue des thèses soutenues devant la Faculté de pharma-
cie de Paris de 1895 à 1959; de 1895 à 1940</u>. Par Gabriel
Garnier et Odette Barthélemy. 2. éd. rev. et augm. des
thèses soutenues de 1941 à 1959, par Suzanne Lavaud. Paris:
Person, 1960. 209 p.

First edition published 1941.

Lists 1,164 dissertations for the diplôme supérieur,
doctorat d'état, doctorat de l'université, diplôme
de pharmacien de 1re and 2e classe. Arranged by

year and then type of degree. Entry gives publication information. Author and subject index.

Continued by:

P143. _____ Catalogue des thèses soutenues devant la Faculté de pharmacie de Paris de 1960 à 1967, supplément à la 2e édition 1895-1959, par Suzanne Lavaud. Paris: Person, 1968. 100 p.

A chronological listing. Under each year the dissertations are subdivided by type of degree. Carries an addendum of dissertations completed between 1953 and 1959 not included in 1960 list (Item P142). Author and subject indexes.

P144. FLORÉN LOZANO, Luis. "Catálogo de tesis de farmacéuticos dominicanos, 1909/1910-1950/1951." In Santo Domingo. Universidad. Anales 21 (1956): 115-173.

An alphabetical author listing of approximately 300 theses. Entry gives the faculty in which the work was done.

P145. ZALAI, Károly and others. "Gyógyszészdoktori értekezések a Semmelweis Orvostudományi Egyetemen." Acta pharmaceutica hungarica 40 (1970): 255-279.

A chronological listing of 480 dissertations accepted between 1861 and 1970. Entry gives the institute in which the work was done and subject matter.

P146. _____ Gyógyszerésdoktori értekezések a Szegedi Orvostudományi Egyetemen." Acta pharmaceutica hungarica 42 (1972): 75-88.

A chronological listing of the 137 dissertations completed between 1921 and 1971.

Veterinary Medicine

General

P147. "ÉCOLES vétérinaire [1924-   ]" Recueil de médecine

vétérinaire 100 (1921)-   . Irregular.

Lists theses completed in French institutions.
Arranged by institution.

P148. "RELACION de tesis presentadas a las facultades de medicina
veterinaria de Buenos Aires, Caracas, Lima, Santiago, São
Paulo y Escuela Nacional de Agricultura [Peru]" In Lima.
Universidad de San Marcos. Facultad de Medicina Veterinaria. Contribución a la bibliografía veterinaria americana,
p. 21-47. Recopilada por Ramón Ponce Paz. Lima: 1951.

Theses are arranged by institution and cover the
years 1907-1951.

P149. ÅKESSON, Margareta. Veterinärmedicinska avhandlingar 1938-
1968. Stockholm: Kungl. Veterinärhögskolans Bibliotek, 1968.
42 p.

A chronological listing of 100 doctoral dissertations
in veterinary medicine accepted in Swedish institutions. Entry gives publication information. Institutional and author indexes.

P150. UTRECHT. Rijksuniversiteit. Bibliotheek. Lijst van 524
veterinaire proefschriften verschenen in 1967 en 1968.
Utrecht: 1969. 41 p. (Its Publikatie, nr. 8)

A classified listing including work done in Germany,
the Scandinavian countries, Greece, South Africa,
Finland, and Switzerland.

Individual Institutions

P151. BRÜNN. Vysoká škola zemědělská a lesnická. Fakulta veterinární. Index dissertationum Facultatis (Academiae) Medicinae Veterinariae Brunensis, 1945-1965. Sest Rudolf Böhm.
V Brně: 1965. 64-93, 218-377 p.

A classified listing of 2,379 theses, dissertations,
and habilitas submitted to the Veterinary Faculty.
Includes such areas as chemistry and toxicology,
pharmacology, parasitology, internal diseases, surgery and orthopedics, and judicial and public veterinary medicine. Subject index.

Special Groups

Aged

P152. MOORE, Julie L., Mort S. Tuchin, and James G. Birren. "A Bibliography of Doctoral Dissertations on Aging from American Institutions of Higher Education." Journal of Gerontology 26 (1971): 391-422.

> Lists 736 completed American dissertations classified under biological aspects, behavioral aspects, social aspects, health and health services, education (both adult and professional), and literary themes dealing with old age and death. Covers the period 1934-1969. Subject and author indexes.

> Continued by:

> MOORE, Julie L. and James E. Birren. "A Bibliography of Doctoral Dissertations on Aging from American Institutions of Higher Education [1969-   ]" Journal of Gerontology 27 (1972)-   . Annual.

> Vol. 27 (1972) covers dissertations completed 1969-1971. Includes items not found in previous list.

Blind

P153. AMERICAN FOUNDATION FOR THE BLIND. Doctors' Dissertations and Masters' Theses on the Visually Handicapped. New York: 1950. 30 p. (Library Series, no. 3)

> Based on the files of the American Foundation for the Blind; U.S. Office of Education, Bibliography of Research Studies in Education (1929-1942) (Item G4); and Item P154.

> Alphabetical author listing which provides information on publication and whether located in the American Foundation for the Blind Library.

P154. U.S. Office of Education. Vocational Education Division. Bibliography of Unpublished Research on the Blind, on File in University Libraries. Compiled under the auspices of the National Psychological Research Council for the Blind.

Washington: Federal Security Agency, Office of Vocational
Rehabilitation, 1950. 21 p. (Rehabilitation Service Series,
no. 109)

A record of 126 studies, nearly all theses and dissertations, resulting from a solicitation of 152
university libraries. Includes psychology, education, social work, and medicine and allied fields.

Speech and Hearing Disorders

General

P155. KNOWER, Franklin H. "Graduate Theses in Speech and Hearing
Disorders [1949-1955]" Journal of Speech and Hearing Disorders 15 (1950): 353-359; 16 (1951): 367-374; 18 (1953):
54-62; 19 (1954): 73-81; 20 (1955): 69-78; 21 (1956): 94-
100; 22 (1957): 104-112.

Completed theses and dissertations from U.S. institutions, listed under institution, then degree.
Subject index.

Continued by:

P156. _____ "Graduate Theses in Speech and Hearing Research [1956-
1957]" Journal of Speech and Hearing Research 1 (1958): 191-
198; 2 (1959): 91-98. Annual.

Theses and dissertations completed at American
universities. Arranged by institution and subdivided
into theses and dissertations. Subject index.

Continued by:

P157. _____ "Graduate Theses in Deafness, Speech and Hearing
[1958-1960]" DsH Abstracts 1 (1960/1961): 95-102, 383-390;
2 (1962): 279-288.

Three yearly lists. Theses and dissertations listed
separately by university. Subject index.

P158. GALLAUDET COLLEGE, Washington, D.C. Library. Doctoral
Dissertations Related to Deafness, Speech and Hearing.

Washington: 1972. 47, 8 p.

> In part supersedes <u>Doctors' Dissertations and Masters'</u>
> <u>Theses on Deafness and the Deaf Listed According to</u>
> <u>Subject Matter</u> (1960).

> An author listing of over 630 dissertations, covering
> the period from about 1900 to 1969. Includes some
> items from Great Britain. Author index.

P159. _____ <u>Masters Theses Relating to Deafness, Speech and Hear-</u>
<u>ing</u>. Washington: 1972. 45, 9 p.

> In part supersedes <u>Doctors' Dissertations and Masters'</u>
> <u>Theses on Deafness and the Deaf Listed According to</u>
> <u>Subject Matter</u> (1960).

> Lists over 325 items from American institutions
> covering the period 1897-1968. Author index.

Hearing

P160. BATCHELDER, Edith G. <u>An Annotated Checklist of Theses on</u>
<u>the Education of the Deaf in the Gallaudet College Library,</u>
<u>1912-1948</u>. Washington: Gallaudet College, 1948. 301 p.

> A subject arrangement of theses written in the
> Normal Training Department of the Columbia Institu-
> tion for the Deaf and by students of Gallaudet Col-
> lege.

P161. FLINT, Richard W. and others. "Doctors' Dissertations and
Masters' Theses on the Education of the Deaf, 1897-1955."
<u>American Annals of the Deaf</u> 100, no. 4 (1955).

> Whole issue.

> Supersedes M. M. Kerr, "Research on the Education
> of the Deaf." <u>American Annals of the Deaf</u> 93 (1948):
> 185-193.

> Separate author lists of 150 dissertations and 960
> theses completed in American institutions. Subject
> and institutional indexes for both theses and dis-
> sertations.

Continued by:

P162. "DOCTORAL Dissertations: Education of the Deaf [1956-   ]"
American Annals of the Deaf 101 (1956)-   . Title varies.
Annual.

Vols. 101 (1956)-115 (1970) list both theses and
dissertations.

An alphabetical author listing of dissertations
completed in American universities. Vols. 101 (1956)-
103 (1958) have subject indexes. Institutional index.

P163. DUKER, Sam. Listening Bibliography. 2d ed. New York:
Scarecrow Press, 1968. 316 p.

First edition published 1964.

Supersedes his "Master's Theses on Listening" in
Journal of Communication 12 (1962): 237-242, and
"Doctoral Dissertations on Listening" in Journal of
Communication 13 (1963): 111-117.

An annotated bibliography, a substantial portion of
which are theses and dissertations. The subject
index provides separate listings for theses and for
dissertations.

P164. UNIVERSITY MICROFILMS, Ann Arbor, Mich. A Bibliography of
Research Materials on the Deaf. Ann Arbor: University
Microfilms, 1970. 50 p.

Contains a separate classified listing of approximately 550 dissertations completed in American
institutions and available for purchase from University Microfilms (p. 27-49).

Speech

P165. LEUTENEGGER, Ralph R. "A Bibliography on Aphasia." Journal
of Speech and Hearing Disorders 16 (1951): 280-292.

Section on "Dissertations and Theses" (p. 292)
includes work accepted by U.S. institutions from
1932 through 1949. These items are on the speech

and hearing aspects of aphasia only.

P166. JOHNSON, Wendell and Ralph R. Leutenegger. <u>Stuttering in Children and Adults; Thirty Years of Research at the University of Iowa</u>. Minneapolis: University of Minnesota Press, 1955.

Contains "A Bibliography of University of Iowa Studies of Stuttering through 1954. Section I: Graduate Theses" (p. 447-452).

Lists 101 theses and 51 dissertations dealing with stuttering, those with portions dealing with stuttering, or those discussing handedness. Divided into theses and dissertations, then alphabetically by author. Earliest study listed is 1919.

Q. Philosophy

Q1. MULLER, Frederik, & Co., Amsterdam. Catalogus dissertationum
et orationum philosophicarum, defensarum et habitarum ab a.
1650 usque ad 1851 in academiis Germaniae, etc. praesertim
Neerlandiae. Quae venales prostant apud Fredericum Muller.
Amsterdam: 1851. 11 p.

   A dealer's catalog of 334 items. In two parts, (1)
   quarto and (2) octavo.

Q2. MADRID. Universidad. Facultad de Filosofía y Letras. Sum-
arios y extractos de las tesis doctorales, leídas desde 1940
a 1950 en las Secciones de Filosofía y Pedagogía. Madrid:
1953. 303 p.

   Separate chronological listings of abstracts of 37
   theses in philosophy and abstracts of 11 theses in
   education. Entry gives adviser. Title index.

Q3. "DISSERTATSII po filosofii, zashchishchennye v 1953-1954
godakh." Voprosy filosofii, 1955, no. 3: 197-211.

   Lists 488 items.

Q4. "DOCTORAL Dissertations [1956-   ]" Review of Metaphysics
10 (1956/1957)-   . Annual. Sept. no.

   List for 1956 appears in the December number.

   Canadian and American dissertations arranged by
   institution. Entry gives adviser.

Q5. FLASCHE, Hans and Utta Wawryznek. Materialen zur Begriffs-

geschichte; Eine Bibliographie deutscher Hochschulschriften
von 1900-1955. Bonn: Bouvier, 1960. 718 p. (Archiv für
Begriffsgeschichte; Bausteine zu einem historischen Wörter-
buch der Philosophie, Bd. 5)

> A subject listing of 9,491 German and Austrian dis-
> sertations and Habilitationsschriften. Includes
> material which concerns itself with the history of
> ideas, including literature, mythology, the law,
> the state, etc. Entry provides title, university,
> year in which item appears in the university year-
> book, and publication information. Index of authors
> as subjects and an author index.

Q6.   "LISTE de thèses de doctorat concernant la philosophie médiévale." In Société internationale pour l'étude de la philosophie médiévale. Bulletin de philosophie médiévale 2
(1960)-   . Annual.

> An international list of completed dissertations
> arranged by country, then alphabetically by author.
> Information is for current year or one or two pre-
> vious years. Source of citation is given.

Q7.   WALSH, Edward J. Philosophy and the History of Ideas; Dissertations in Progress, Canada and the United States
[1970-   ] Lakewood, N.J.: Georgian Court College,
1970-   . Title varies. Irregular.

> The dissertations are listed under such topics as
> aesthetics, anthropology, epistemology, method,
> nature, time and space, value theory, and philoso-
> phers. Entry gives the title or, if the exact
> title is not given, indicates the field or topic of
> research, institution, and expected date of com-
> pletion.

R. Psychology

General

R1. TINKER, Miles A. "Wundt's Doctorate Students and Their Theses, 1875-1920." American Journal of Psychology 44 (1932): 630-637.

In celebration of the 100th anniversary of Wilhelm Wundt's birth, this is a chronological list of the 186 theses written under him at the University of Leipzig. Most are on psychology, but many deal with philosophical subjects.

R2. GAMMELTOFT, S. A. "Danish Doctorate Theses on Psychiatry and Neurology (1835-1945)." Acta psychiatrica et neurologica Scandinavica (Copenhagen) 21 (1946): 281-305.

A discussion and analysis of the 84 dissertations submitted in this period. The largest number of items represents studies in clinical psychiatry, clinical neurology, and biochemistry. The dissertations are listed chronologically in the bibliography (p. 299-305). Entries include an English translation of the title.

R3. ØSTLYNGEN, Emil. Sammendrag av norske magistergradsavhandlinger i psykologi. Oslo: Skrivemaskinstua, 1947. 54 p.

Abstracts of 23 theses completed at the University of Oslo between 1928 and 1947 and published by the Norsk psykologforening.

R4. "CANADIAN Theses in Psychology [1948-1953]" Canadian Journal of Psychology 3 (1949)-8 (1954). Annual. March issue.

English and French.

Alphabetical author lists of dissertations and theses completed in Canadian universities.

Continued by:

R5.   "CANADIAN Theses in Psychology [1954-1955, 1958-1960]" Canadian Psychologist 4 (Jan. 1955): 4-7; 5 (June 1956): 5-9; new ser., 2a (1961): 113-124.

List in new ser., 2a (1961) is designated as Part 2.

Lists theses and dissertations completed in Canadian institutions. The 1954 and 1955 listings are arranged alphabetically by author and the entry gives the degree and institution. The listing for the period 1958-1960 contains theses only. It is arranged by institution and carries abstracts.

R6.   "UNPUBLISHED Theses." Psychological Abstracts 23 (1949)-28 (1954).

Listings of theses and dissertations, submitted by department chairmen of American universities, appear irregularly in two to four issues per year during the period covered. Date (usually previous year), degree, and institution are given.

R7.   ROHRACHER, H. "Scientific Work at the Psychological Department of the University of Vienna." Acta psychologica 8 (1952): 201-223; 13 (1957): 197-219. Title varies.

Vol. 8 list includes informal summaries of some researches being carried on, most of them for Ph.D.'s. Arranged by subject, with researcher's name given. List of publications by members of the Institute since 1945 at end. Vol. 13 list includes summaries of 22 dissertations selected from theses completed during the last five years.

R8.   UNIVERSITY MICROFILMS, Ann Arbor, Mich. Dissertations of the Sixties: Psychology. Ann Arbor: 1963. 50 p.

A subject listing of approximately 1,800 dissertations accepted by American universities in psycho-

logy and related areas and published by University
Microfilms. Entry indicates order number and cost.

Special Subjects

Child Psychology

R9.   U.S. Bureau of Human Nutrition and Home Economics. Child
Development; Summary of Titles of Theses Completed in Col-
leges and Universities of the United States, 1930 to 1949.
Washington: 1950. 33 p.

A classified listing of 457 theses and dissertations. Includes only those theses which are focused
primarily on the behavior and development of children, as judged from the titles.

R10. IOWA. University. Institute of Child Behavior and Development. Fifty Years of Research, 1917-1967. Iowa City: 1967.
189 p.

"Student Theses and Dissertations Accepted for Advanced Degrees in the Institute": p. 85-104. Dissertations and theses arranged alphabetically by
author in separate listings.

Educational Psychology

R11. "SUMMARIES of Researches Reported in Degree Theses." British
Journal of Educational Psychology 8 (1938)-41 (1971). Irregular.

Abstracts of theses and dissertations completed in
Great Britain.

R12. BLACKWELL, Annie M. "A List of Researches in Educational
Psychology and Teaching Method, Presented for Higher Degrees
of British Universities from 1918 to the Present Day."
British Journal of Educational Psychology 13 (1943): 153-
158; 14 (1944): 46-50, 99-105, 162-166; 15 (1945): 93-100.

Theses and dissertations completed in the universities of England, Scotland, Wales, and Eire are listed

according to Dewey decimal classification, with
cross references for subjects. Entries give degree,
institution, date, and publication information where
known.

R13. EELLS, Walter C. "American Doctoral Dissertations on Educational Psychology in Foreign Countries." Journal of Educational Psychology 47 (1956): 133-136.

Thirty-two dissertations arranged by region and
country. Entry indicates university and date.
Covers period 1884-1954.

R14. NEBRASKA. University. Teachers College. Department of
Educational Psychology and Measurements. General Index of
Theses, 1923-1958. Lincoln: University of Nebraska, 1958.
156 p.

Alphabetical listing of 323 abstracts of theses and
dissertations by students of the Department. Entry
gives adviser. Topical and chronological indexes.

Pastoral Psychology

R15. WILSON, Louis N. List of Papers in the Field of Religious
Psychology Presented at Clark University. Worcester, Mass.:
1911. 9 p. (Clark University. Library. Publications,
vol. 2, no. 8)

Separate lists of 16 theses and 22 dissertations.
Entry gives publication information.

R16. "DOCTORAL Dissertations in Pastoral Psychology." Pastoral
Psychology 12 (1962)-   . Annual. Jan. issue.

Vol. 11 (1961) has "Abstracts of Doctoral Dissertations in Pastoral Psychology," consisting of
seven dissertations completed in 1959/1960, compiled
by Helen F. Spaulding.

A subject listing of completed American dissertations
as reported by librarians of accredited theological
schools.

S. Sciences

General

S1. SCHWEICKHARD, Christian L. <u>Tentamen catalogi rationalis dissertationum ad anatomiam et physiologiam spectantium ab anno MDXXXIX, ad nostra usque tempora.</u> Tubingae: 1798. 444 p.

   A chronological listing of 3,328 dissertations. Entry cites reviews. Subject and author index.

S2. MULLER, Frederik, & Co., Amsterdam. <u>Catalogus dissertationum et orationum mathematicarum, astronomicarum et physicarum. Defensarum et habitarum ab a. 1650 usque ad 1851 in academiis Germaniae, etc. praesertim Neerlandiae. Quae venales prostant apud Fredericum Muller...</u> Amstelodami: 1851. 12 p.

   A dealer's catalog listing 339 items. In two parts, (1) quarto and (2) octavo.

S3. MAIRE, Albert. <u>Catalogue des thèses de sciences soutenues en France de 1810 à 1890 inclusivement.</u> Paris: H. Welter, 1892. (Bibliographie de thèses, no. 2)

   Chronological lists of dissertations in two parts: pt. 1, "Thèses de sciences de Paris"; pt. 2, "Thèses des universités de province," subdivided by university. Entry gives brief biographical data and publication information. Author and subject indexes.

S4. GRAF, J. H. "Verzeichnis der gedruckten mathematischen, astronomischen und physikalischen Doktor-Dissertationen der schweizerischen Hochschulen bis zum Jahre 1896." In Naturforschende Gesellschaft, Bern. <u>Mitteilungen,</u> 1897: 53-60.

Lists approximately 100 Swiss dissertations. Arranged by institution, and subdivided chronologically under mathematics, astronomy, and physics.

S5. "DOCTORATES Conferred in the Sciences by American Universities [1897/1898-1920/1921]" Science, n.s., vol. 8 (1898)- 42 (1915) (even numbered volumes only); 52 (1920); 55 (1922). Annual.

No lists published for 1915-1919.

Dissertations in the sciences listed by subject, then by institution. Includes tables of statistics on doctorates by institution and subject.

Partially reprinted and continued in:

S6. NATIONAL RESEARCH COUNCIL. Research Information Service. Doctorates Conferred in the Sciences by American Universities [1919/1920-1932/1933] Washington: 1920-1934. Title varies. (Its Reprint and Circular Series, nos. 12, 26, 42, 75, 80, 86, 91, 95, 101, 104, 105)

No lists published for 1922/1923, 1923/1924, 1924/ 1925. Lists for 1925/1926-1932/1933 edited by Callie Hull and Clarence J. West. Early lists are reprinted from Item S5 and Item B101. Only no. 42 (1921/1922 list) includes dissertations in the arts. Statistics for chemistry for these years were published in Item S53 and for the medical sciences in Item P17.

Dissertations arranged by broad subjects and alphabetically by author under institution.

S7. "DISSERTAZIONI accademiche delle università di Bonn, Greifswald, Halle, Heidelberg, Rostock, Tuebingen, Utrecht." In Accademia nazionale del Lincei, Rome. Rendiconti. Classe di scienze fisiche, matematiche et naturali, ser. 5, vol. 13, fasc. 1 (1904): 286-305.

Chronological listings under institutions, covering the period 1902-1903.

S8. CATALOGUS van proefschriften vervaardigd ter verkrijging van de graad van Doctor in één der natuurwetenschappen aan universiteiten of hoogescholen in Nederland in de jaren 1900-

1930. N.p.: 1931. 206 p. ?

S9.   "LISTE des thèses de sciences soutenues en France [1948/1949-
       1956]" In Paris. Université. Annales 20 (1950)-27 (1957).
       Title varies.

       Edited by Araxie Torossian.

       Lists dissertations submitted to French universities.
       Arranged by university, subdivided by type of docto-
       rate.

S10.   BLEDSOE, Barton. Master's Theses in Science, 1952. Washing-
       ton: Biblio Press, 1954. 252 p.

       First of a proposed annual subject list (no more
       published). Lists 5,588 theses from 138 American
       institutions, in pure and applied sciences. Insti-
       tutional index.

S11.   "DISSERTATSIY po istorii geologii, geografii, gornogo dela i
       metallurgii, zashchishchennye v 1944-1954 gg." In Akademiya
       nauk SSSR. Institut istorii estestvoznaniya i tekhniki.
       Trudy 3 (1955): 232-236.

       Two separate listings of four dissertations and 57
       theses completed in the U.S.S.R. between 1944 and
       1954.

S12.   FRENCH Bibliographical Digest. Series III. French Doctoral
       Theses. Sciences. No. 1. New York: French Cultural
       Services, 1955. 75 p.

       A classified listing of scientific theses accepted
       by French universities during 1951-1953. Arranged
       under biological sciences, earth sciences, physical
       sciences, and miscellaneous, with subdivisions under
       each. Subject index.

S13.   COLUMBIA UNIVERSITY. Libraries. Natural Sciences Libraries.
       Theses, 1954-1955. New York: 1956. 6 p. (Its Miscellaneous
       Publication no. 1)

       An alphabetical list of non-Columbia University
       doctoral theses in the fields of botany, geography,

geology, psychology, and zoology.

S14. MASTER Theses in the Pure and Applied Sciences Accepted by Colleges and Universities of the United States [vol. 1 (1955/1956)-   ] Lafayette, Ind.: Purdue University, Thermophysical Properties Research Center, 1957-   . Title varies. Annual.

Vol. 3, pt. 2 (1959) includes 2,846 dissertations for the 1956/1957 school year.

Arranged by disciplines such as astronomy, geology, metallurgy, and alphabetically by university under each discipline. Excludes mathematical and life sciences.

S15. EELLS, Walter C. "American Doctoral Dissertations on Science Written by Women in the Nineteenth Century." Science Education 41 (1957): 415-417.

Works of 38 women in the period 1877-1900. Contains biographical as well as bibliographic data. Entry gives publication information.

S16. U.S. Joint Publications Research Service. Dissertation [sic] for Degrees in Science and Engineering Defended at U.S.S.R. Higher Educational Institutions. New York: 1959. (Its JPRS L Series)

Translation of material from Knizhnaia Letopis'.

Lists approximately 200 items.

S17. DISSERTATIONS Presented for Degrees in Science and Engineering in Moscow in 1952. N.p.: 195? 110 p.

Lists 1,321 papers presented for doctors' or candidates' degrees at Moscow higher educational institutions. Information obtained from the Moscow daily newspaper Vechernaya Moskva during 1952. Arranged in nine broad classes by field, e.g. agriculture, biology, medical sciences, technical sciences. Under each field entries are divided into doctorates and candidates and arranged alphabetically.

S18. PANTELEEVA, A. A. "Dissertatsiy po geologii, mineralogii,

paleontologii i fizicheskoy geografii Karpat, zashchishchennye vo L'vovskom universitete (1947-1959)." Mineralogicheskiy sbornik, 1960, vyp. 14: 476-479.

A chronological listing of 38 dissertations on the
Carpathian mountains defended in Ukrainian institutions.

S19. "THESES." In Nova Scotia Research Foundation. Research
Record 1 (1947/1960): 56-63. Halifax, Nova Scotia: 1961.

Supersedes the listings in the Nova Scotia Research
Foundation Annual Report 6 (1952)-12 (1959).

Lists bachelors' and masters' theses and dissertations completed in American and Canadian institutions.

S20. PRAGUE. Státní technická knihovna. Disertace ve Státní
technické knihovně v Praze; Souborná bibliografie. Sest.
Jitka Kostková. Praha: 1966. 265 p. (Its Bibliografie,
sv. 91)

A classified listing of the 1,805 dissertations in
the Library, representing the pure and applied sciences. Largely Czech but includes material completed
outside Czechoslovakia as well. Author index.

S21. QUÉBEC (City). Université Laval. Centre de documentation.
Index des thèses de doctorat soutenues devant les universités françaises, 1959-1963. Sciences. Québec: 1967. 2 vols.

A record of approximately 5,200 thèses de doctorat
ès sciences from French universities, including
the Universities of Dakar and Algeria. Vol. 1:
subject index (keyed to title); vol. 2: alphabetical
author listing of dissertations with code employed
in vol. 1 for each item. Alphabetical list of
subjects used.

S22. "DISSERTATSIY po istorii estestvoznaniya i tekhnika, zashch-
ishchavshiesya v SSSR v 1943-1966 gg." Voprosy istorii
estestvoznaniya i tekhniki, no. 23 (1968): 138-146.

Lists approximately 300 theses and dissertations
under scientific discipline.

S23. BRITISH SOCIETY FOR THE HISTORY OF SCIENCE. <u>A List of Theses</u>
<u>and Dissertations in History of Science in British Universi-</u>
<u>ties in Progress or Recently Completed</u> [1970/1971-] Com-
piled by William H. Brock. London: 1970?- . Annual.

Listing for 1972/1973 supersedes previous lists for
work completed between 1971 and 1972.

Lists theses and dissertations. Arranged by type
of degree under institution, with completed work
preceding work in progress. Entry gives adviser.
Index of historical names.

S24. STUMPER, Robert. "L'Activité scientifique des Luxembourgeois
à l'étranger. Une siècle de doctorates universitaires."
<u>Letzeburger Land</u>, no. 14 (1970): 3⁄. ?

Individual Institutions

S25. BONN. Universität. Mathematisch-Naturwissenschaftliche
Fakultät. <u>Jahrbuch der Dissertationen</u> [1950/1951-1957/1959]
Bonn: 1952-1960. 5 vols.

Number for 1950/1951 includes a list of completed
dissertations from 1937 to 1950 (p. 1-20).

Abstracts of dissertations, arranged under disciplines, such as mathematics, astronomy, chemistry,
geography. Entry gives adviser. Author index.

S26. BUENOS AIRES. Universidad Nacional. Facultad de Ciencias
Exactas, Fisicas y Naturales. Biblioteca. <u>Catálogo de la</u>
<u>Biblioteca</u>. Buenos Aires: Impr. de la Universidad, 1930/
1931. 1,359 p. (Universidad de Buenos Aires. Facultad de
Ciencias Exactas, Fisicas y Naturales. Ser. A. Publicación no. 6)

"Tesis y proyectos finales de la Facultad de Ciencias
Exactas, Fisicas y Naturales": p. 1,033-1,108.

An alphabetical listing of material held by the
Library.

S27. CAIRO. Jāmi'at al-Qāhirah. Kullīyat al-'Ulūm. <u>al-Rasā'il</u>
<u>al-'ilmīyah</u> [1958-] Cairo: 1958- . Irregular.

Lists theses and dissertations completed in the College of Science.

S28. CHICAGO. University. Abstracts of Theses; Science Series, Ogden Graduate School of Science, Submitted to the Faculties of the Graduate Schools of the University of Chicago for the Degree of Doctor of Philosophy, June, 1922–June, 1932, with Abstracts of Some Theses Submitted at an Earlier Date. Chicago: University of Chicago Press, 1925–1934. 9 vols.

Includes the following fields: mathematics, physics, chemistry, geology and paleontology, geography, botany, zoology, anatomy, physical chemistry and pharmacy, hygiene and bacteriology, home economics. Arranged alphabetically by author under each department. Abstracts are given for unpublished theses; lists of theses published in full or in substance. Author index.

S29. GLASGOW. University. Summaries of Theses Approved for Higher Degrees in the Faculties of Science and Engineering during the Academical Year [1949/1950–] Glasgow: 1950– . Title varies. Annual, except for 1950/1951.

Abstracts of Ph.D. and Doctor of Science dissertations arranged under faculty and subdivided by general subjects.

S30. GÖTTINGEN. Universität. Mathematisch-Naturwissenschaftliche Fakultät. Jahrbuch der Mathematisch-Naturwissenschaftlichen Fakultät der Georg August-Universität zu Göttingen [1923–1924] Göttingen: W. F. Kaestner, 1924–1925. 2 vols.

Abstracts of dissertations.

S31. INDIAN INSTITUTE OF SCIENCE, Bangalore. Abstracts of Theses, 1970–1971. Bangalore: n.d. 71 p.

Dissertations arranged by faculty (science and engineering), subdivided by department. Author index.

S32. "ZASHCHITA dissertatsiy na Fiziko-matematicheskom fakul'tete L'vovskogo universiteta v 1948–1952 gg." In Lvöv. Universytet. Naukovi zapysky 22, vyp. 5 (1953): 125–127.

A chronological listing of 21 studies completed in
the Physics-Mathematics Faculty between 1948 and
1952. Entry gives the topic of the dissertation
and adviser.

S33. MICHIGAN. University. School of Natural Resources. Masters
Theses, 1928-1960. Ann Arbor: 1960. 33 p.

Supersedes previously published lists.

Arranged by areas within this school: conservation,
fisheries, forestry, wildlife management, wood
technology.

S34. MÜNSTER. Universität. Mathematisch-Naturwissenschaftliche
Fakultät. Dissertationen...in Referaten [1 (1952)-   ]
Münster: 1952-   . Annual.

Abstracts of dissertations. Entry gives department
and adviser.

S35. ESTANAVE, Eugène P. Revue décennale des thèses présentées
à la Faculté des sciences de Paris en vue du grade de docteur ès sciences, du 1er janvier 1891 au 31 décembre 1900.
Avec l'indication des périodiques contenant la plupart de
ces mémoires ou leurs analyses. Arcissur-Aube: L. Frémont,
1901. 114 p.

In part continues Item S3.

Lists 347 dissertations under (1) mathematical
science, (2) physical science, and (3) natural
sciences. The studies are listed chronologically
in each category. Entry gives brief biographical
information, publication information, and references to reviews or abstracts.

S36. LAVAUD, Suzanne. Catalogue des thèses de doctorat ès
sciences naturelles soutenues à Paris de 1891 à 1954. Paris:
Person, 1955. 257 p.

In part continues item S3.

A chronological listing of 1,181 dissertations in
the areas of zoology, botany, general biology, psychology, and their related fields. Entry gives

publication information. Author and subject
indexes.

S37. TOROSSIAN, Araxie. Catalogue des thèses de sciences phy-
siques (mention: physique et chimie) soutenues devant la
Faculté des sciences de l'Université de Paris de 1945 à 1960.
Paris: Person, 1964. 159 p.

An alphabetical author listing of 1,141 dissertations. Entry gives location of abstracts. Subject
index.

S38. "UNIVERSIDAD de Puerto Rico en Mayagüez, tesis de ciencias,
1969." Caribbean Journal of Science 10 (1970): 209-215.

Abstracts of theses for the master of science
degree in the area of the natural sciences. Arranged by department.

S39. STOREY, Margaret H. Stanford University Theses and Disser-
tations of Interest to Researchers in Natural History
(Systematics, Morphology, Ecology, etc.). Stanford, Calif:
Stanford University Natural History Museum, 1957. 58 p.
(Stanford University. Natural History Museum. Circular
no. 7)

Alphabetical author listing of approximately 600
items. Does not include experimental biology and
"hard rock geology." Entry indicates subject matter, such as botany, entomology, fishes, and gives
publication information.

S40. STOCKHOLM. Universitet. Wenner-Grens institut för experimentell biologi, fysiologisk kemi och ämnesomattningsforsk-
ning. Wenner-Grens institut, 1939-1959. Stockholm: 1959.
130 p.

Contains (1) research projects in progress in 1959
(p. 73-75); (2) a listing of dissertations defended
at the Institute during 1940-1959 (p. 128); and (3)
dissertations defended at the Karolinska Institut,
the University of Lund, and the Royal Institute of
Technology on work performed at the Institute
(p. 129).

Biology

S41. HJELT, Otto E. A. <u>Sveriges biologiska disputations- och program-litteratur, 1700-vårterminen 1910; Systematiskt ordnad</u>. Helsingfors: Finska litteratursällskapets tryckeri, 1911. 210 p. (Bidgrag till kännedom af Finlands natur och folk, h. 70, n: 01)

Lists approximately 2,200 Swedish and Finnish items. Arranged under such subjects as medicine and botany. Entry gives publication information.

S42. MURRAY, Margaret R. and Gertrude Kopeck. <u>A Bibliography of Research in Tissue Culture, 1884 to 1950; An Index to the Literature of the Living Cell Cultivated in Vitro</u>. New York: Academic Press, 1953. 2 vols.

Vol. 2, p. 1,585-1,586, lists approximately 50 theses and dissertations. International in coverage. Entry gives publication information or reference to an abstract.

S43. SHCHERBAKOVA, A. A. "Dissertatsiy po voprosam istorii biologicheskikh i sel'skokhozyaystvennykh nauk, zashchishchennye v SSSR v 1944-1953 gg." <u>In</u> Akademiya nauk SSSR. Institut istorii estestvoznaniya i tekhniki. <u>Trudy</u> 4 (1955): 400-403.

Lists two dissertations and 34 theses completed in the U.S.S.R. Theses are in a classified arrangement.

S44. KORNICKER, Louis S. "Bibliography of Ostracode Theses." <u>Micropaleontology</u> 3 (1957): 287-290.

An alphabetical author listing of 107 studies, most of them unpublished (some B.A. honors theses and dissertations), taken from Turner's <u>Bibliography of Geology Theses</u> (Item S97) and from <u>Dissertation Abstracts</u>, which were completed in American institutions.

S45. PONTIFICIA UNIVERSIDAD CATÓLICA JAVERIANA. Facultad de Bacteriología. <u>Tesis de grado</u>. Bogotá: 1958. 1 vol. (various pagings) ??

S46. "DISSERTATSIY zashchishchennye sotrudnikami doktorantanami i asperantami Gel'mintologicheskoy laboratorii AN SSSR so vremeni ee osnovaniia (1942)." In Akademiya nauk SSSR. Gel'mintologicheskaya laboratoriya. Trudy 10 (1960): 254-255.

Lists 20 theses and dissertations completed 1942-1960. Entry gives field of concentration.

S47. WYDALLIS, Elizabeth A. A Bibliography of Theses and Dissertations of the Ohio State University of Possible Interest to the Aquatic Biologist. Columbus, Ohio: Ohio State University, Ohio Comparative Fishing Unit, 1966. 59 p.

A listing of bachelors' and masters' theses and of dissertations arranged under broad topic. Includes material on insects, birds, mammals, pollution, geology, soils, limnology, higher plants, and conservation.

S48. GARSZCZYŃSKA, Bożena. "Bibliografia prac magisterskich, doktorskich i habilitacyjnych Wydziału biologii i nauki o ziemi (geografia) Uniwersytetu Mikołaja Kopernika zwiazanych z tematyką pomorską (1945-1967)." Rocznik Toruński 3 (1969): 187-206.

Separate alphabetical author listings of 202 theses, 15 dissertations, and one habilitacyjne. Entry gives major adviser. Publication information is provided for the dissertations. Author index.

Botany

S49. UTKIN, L. A., A. F. Gammerman, and V. A. Nevskiy. Bibliografiia po lekarstvennym rasteniyam: Ukazatel' otechestvennoy literatury. Rukopisi XVII-XIX vv. pechatnye izdaniya 1732-1954 gg. Moskva: 1957. 724 p.

Contains a separate listing of 299 Russian theses and dissertations (p. 618-639) for the period 1936-1954. Arranged chronologically.

S50. BANARAS HINDU UNIVERSITY. Abstracts of the Theses Accepted for the Doctorate Degree in Botany at Banares Hindu University [19 -] Banares, India: n.d.

Vol. 6 covers 1927-1965 and lists 30 dissertations chronologically.

Dissertations accepted by the Faculty of Science Department of Botany.

Chemistry

S51. BOLTON, Henry C. A Select Bibliography of Chemistry, 1492-1897; Section VIII: Academic Dissertations. Washington: Smithsonian Institution, 1901. 534 p. (Smithsonian Miscellaneous Collections, vol. 41, art. 3)

An alphabetical author listing of separately printed dissertations, especially those from France, Germany, Russia, and the United States. Does not include analytical chemistry. The Russian language items are listed separately but English translation is provided for the titles. The titles located in the U.S. Geological Survey Library and in the Library of Congress Smithsonian Deposit are identified. Subject index.

_____ A Select Bibliography of Chemistry, 1492-1902. Second Supplement. Washington: Smithsonian Institution, 1904. 462 p. (Smithsonian Miscellaneous Collections. Part of vol. 44)

Section VIII, "Academic Dissertations" (p. 230-396), supplements earlier volume. Subject index to whole volume.

S52. YALE UNIVERSITY. Graduate School. Doctors of Philosophy in Chemistry and Physiological Chemistry, 1866-1922. New Haven, Conn.: 1923. 19 p.

Earlier edition 1916.

Chronological listing of dissertations completed at Yale University, with reference to where published.

S53. HULL, Callie and Clarence J. West. "Doctorates Conferred in Chemistry by American Universities 1922/1923, 1923/1924, 1924/1925." Journal of Chemical Education 3 (1926): 77-99.

Lists dissertations by institution, subdivided by academic year.

S54. LENINGRAD. Tekhnologicheskiy institut. <u>Sbornik tezisov</u>
<u>dissertatsiy zashchishchennykh v LKhTI s 1935 po 1940 g</u>.
Leningrad: Gos. Nauchno-tekhnicheskoe Izd-vo Khimicheskoy
Literatury, 1941. 272 p.

> Abstracts of approximately 200 theses and disserta-
> tions defended at the Institute. Arranged under
> such subjects as inorganic chemistry; physical and
> colloidal chemistry; organic chemistry; mineral
> technology. Entry gives adviser.

S55. SILVERMAN, Alexander. <u>Research History of the Department of</u>
<u>Chemistry in the University of Pittsburgh</u>. Revised ed.
Pittsburgh, Pa.: 1946. 82 p.

> Contains a chronological list of "Master of Science
> Degrees Granted 1902-1945" (p. 69-75).

S56. "UNIVERSITY Chemical Research [1949-1964]" <u>Chemistry in</u>
<u>Canada</u> 1 (1949)-16 (1964). Title varies. Annual, usually
Dec. issue.

> Lists theses and dissertations completed in Canadian
> universities. Arranged by such fields as agricultural
> chemistry, biochemistry, chemical engineering, food
> chemistry; subdivided by institution, with theses and
> dissertations listed separately. Entry gives adviser.

S57. "PH.D. Theses in Chemistry and Chemical Engineering [1951]"
<u>Chemical and Engineering News</u> 29 (1951): 3,368, 3,470, 3,876,
4,003, 4,182, 4,184, 4,693, 5,163; 30 (1952): 178.

> Lists the work completed in 13 American universities.
> Arranged by institution. Entry gives adviser.

S58. AMERICAN CHEMICAL SOCIETY. Committee on Professional Training. <u>Titles of Theses Submitted for Doctoral Degrees in</u>
<u>Chemistry and Chemical Engineering at American Educational</u>
<u>Institutions, October 1, 1951, to September 30, 1952</u>. Wash-
ington: 1952. 55 p.

> In two parts: (1) chemistry, and (2) chemical engin-
> eering. Under each the theses are listed under
> institution. Entry gives adviser.

S59. _____ Directory of Graduate Research [1953-   ] Washington:
1953-   . Title varies. Biennial.

Lists American dissertations in (1) chemistry, (2)
chemical engineering, (3) biochemistry, (4) pharmaceutical and/or medical chemistry, subdivided by institution. Under each institution candidates completing
the doctorate are listed under the name of the adviser.

S60. MONTEVIDEO. Universidad. Facultad de Química y Farmacia.
Tesis de doctorado presentadas en la Facultad de Química y
Farmacia. Ordenadas y clasificadas por Marta Schoenberg de
Scheiner. Montevideo: 1954. 7 p.

Lists 32 items.

S61. "CHEMIE-Dissertations [1956-   ]" Chimia 11 (1957)-   .
Annual.

Dissertations in chemistry completed in Swiss institutions of higher education. Arranged by school and
subdivided by institution. Includes works in the
chemical sciences from other than institutes of
chemistry, such as pharmacy and veterinary medicine.

S62. BIBLIOGRAPHIE der Hochschulschriften zur Chemie: Ein systematisches Verzeichnis der an den Universitäten und Hochschulen der DDR, der BRD und Westberlins eingereichten
Dissertationen und Habilitationsschriften [1 (1957/1958)-
    ] Leipzig: Verlag für Buch- und Bibliothekswesen,
1960-   . Title varies. Semiannual.

Folge 1 covers 1957 and 1958.

A classified listing of dissertations covering all
aspects of chemistry, such as history, law, economics,
macromolecular, applied, and medical. Entry gives
publication information. Author index.

S63. LARSSON, Erik L. Kemiska institutionen i Lund: Lärare och
bibliografi, 1897-1956. Lund: 1958. 41 p.

"Dissertationer [och Licentiatavhandlingar]" (p. 36-
41) contains approximately 60 dissertations and 80
theses in separate listings.

S64. "PŘEHLED disertačních prací [1960/1961-   ]" Chemické
listy 54 (1960)-   . Irregular.

Theses and dissertations completed in Czech institutions of higher education are in separate lists.
Each arranged chronologically by date of defense.

S65. TURKEVICH, John. Chemistry in the Soviet Union. Princeton,
N.J.: Van Nostrand, 1965. 566 p.

Contains "Soviet Dissertations in Chemistry at
Soviet Universities" (p. 173-221) and "Soviet Dissertations in Chemistry at Soviet Institutes" (p.
222-278). Both contain studies for the candidacy
and the doctorate under major fields for the period
1930-1962. Titles are translated into English.

Ecology

S66. UNIVERSITY MICROFILMS, Ann Arbor, Mich. A Bibliography of
Doctoral Research on Ecology and the Environment. Ann Arbor:
1971. 92 p.

An alphabetical author listing of more than 900
dissertations accepted by American universities
and published by University Microfilms during the
period 1938-1970. Entry gives reference to
Dissertation Abstracts International and the University Microfilms order number.

Geography

General

S67. "MÉMOIRES de maîtrise présentés en [1923/1925-   ]" Annales
de géographie 35 (1926)-   . Title varies. Annual. Irregular.

Theses completed in French institutions arranged
by university.

S68. WHITTLESLEY, Derwent. "Dissertations in Geography Accepted
by Universities in the United States for the Degree of Ph.D.,

as of May, 1935." In Association of American Geographers.
Annals 25 (1935): 211-237.

A complete list compiled from information sent by
universities, covering the period from the turn of
the twentieth century. Arranged by geographical
region. Entry gives publication information.

Continued by:

S69. HEWES, Leslie. "Dissertations in Geography Accepted by
Universities in the United States and Canada for the Degree
of Ph.D., June, 1935, to June, 1946, and Those Currently in
Progress." In Association of American Geographers. Annals
36 (1946): 215-247.

Compiled from information received from universities
and from Doctoral Dissertations Accepted by American
Universities. In two parts, "Dissertations Accepted"
and "Titles under Investigation." Arranged by geographical region. Entry gives publication information and an occasional one-sentence explanatory note.
Author index.

Continued by:

S70. "RECENT Geography Dissertations and Theses Completed and in
Preparation [1946/1948-   ]" The Professional Geographer,
n.s. vol. 2 (1950)-   . Annual. Irregular. 1950-1960 in
March and Nov. issues; 1961-   in Nov. issue.

The 1950 and 1951 listings are retrospective to
1946.

Lists Canadian and American theses and dissertations.
In two parts: (1) "Ph.D. Dissertations Completed,"
which includes dissertations relating to geography
(especially Ed.D.) completed and in progress; (2)
"Masters' Theses Completed" and theses completed
other than in geography. Entry gives information on
availability and the location of abstracts.

S71. "DIE GEOGRAPHISCHEN Dissertationen der Universitäten Graz,
Innsbruck, Wien [1918-1943]" Geographischer Jahresbericht
aus Österreich 20 (1940)-21/22 (1943).

Vol. 20 (1940) covers 1918-1940, 21/22 covers 1940-1943.

Abstracts of completed dissertations in geography
and related fields. Geographical dissertations are
arranged chronologically by institution, followed
by a listing of dissertations of geographical interest.

Continued by:

S72. "ARBEITSBERICHTE [1943-   ]" Geographischer Jahresbericht
aus Österreich 23 (1943)-   . Title varies. Annual.

Lists dissertations completed in Austrian institutions of higher education in geography or of geographical interest. In two parts: (1) dissertations
in geography institutes and departments; (2) dissertations in other departments which are of geographical interest.

S73. ATWOOD, Wallace W. The Clark Graduate School of Geography:
Our First Twenty-Five Years. Worcester, Mass.: Clark University, 1946. 168 p.

On p. 91-161 theses and dissertations are recorded
chronologically. In two parts: (1) Doctors of
Philosophy, and (2) Masters of Arts. Entries for
the doctorates include previous degrees (institutions
and dates). Entry gives publication information.

S74. "DISSERTATSIY, zashchishchennye v uchenom sovete Geofizi-
cheskogo instituta AN SSSR v 1954 i 1955 gg." In Akademiya
nauk SSSR. Izvestiya: Seriya geograficheskaya i geofizi-
cheskaya, 1955, no. 3: 294-296.

An annotated listing of seven dissertations defended
at the Institute.

S75. "MÉMOIRES de diplômes d'études supérieures présentés depuis
1942 à l'Institut de géographie de la Faculté des lettres de
Montpellier." Revue de l'économie méridionale 6 (1958): 332.

A chronological listing of approximately 50 theses
completed through 1958. Entry gives publication
information.

S76. DARGENT, J. L. Bibliographie des thèses et mémoires géogra-
phiques belges, 1904-1953. 2e éd. Bruxelles: Commission

belge de bibliographie, 1959. 83 p. (Bibliographia belgica, 42)

First edition 1953.

The lists of mémoires have previously appeared in the Société d'études geographiques Bulletin and the Société royale belge de géographie Bulletin.

Lists 347 theses and dissertations for the licence and doctorate. Arranged by institution and then by type of degree. Entry gives publication information. Index.

S77. MATVEEV, G. P. "Dissertatsiy po geografii naseleniya i gorodam." Voprosy geografii 45 (1959): 267-269.

Lists 49 theses and dissertations completed in the U.S.S.R. between 1946 and 1956. In two parts: geography of population and cities.

S78. "THÈSES de géographie soutenues en [1961-   ] (thèses d'état, thèses d'université, thèses de 3e cycle)." Annales de géographie 72 (1963)-   . Annual.

Dissertations completed in French institutions. Arranged by institution, subdivided by type of degree taken.

S79. "LIST of Completed Theses Approved for Higher Degrees [1960-   ]" In Royal Geographical Society. New Geographical Literature and Maps, no. 25 (June 1963)-   . Title varies. Annual.

Theses and dissertations completed in Great Britain, arranged under the major regions of Great Britain, the continents, general geography, and cartography.

S80. "THESES in Geography [1963-   ]" New Zealand Geographer 19 (1963)-   . Semiannual. Oct. issue.

Appears separately in "Geographic Notebooks."

Lists (1) theses and (2) dissertations completed in New Zealand. Under each the studies are arranged by institution.

S81. "ABSTRACTS of Geography Theses Completed in West Pakistan
      Universities [1967-1968]" Pakistan Geography Review 22
      (1967): 52-53; 23 (1968): 54-56.

      Lists theses and dissertations.

S82. PENZ, Hugo. "Verzeichnis der von Univ.-Prof. Dr. Hans Kinzl
      betreuten Dissertation." In Festschrift für Hans Kinzl zum
      siebzigsten Geburtstag, p. 157-160. Innsbruck: Österreiche
      Kommissionsbuchhandlung, 1968. (Innsbruck. Universität.
      Alpenkunde Studien 1)

      A chronological listing of approximately 60 disser-
      tations. Entry gives publication information.

S83. BROWNING, Clyde E. A Bibliography of Dissertations in Geo-
      graphy, 1901 to 1969: American and Canadian Universities.
      Chapel Hill, N.C.: University of North Carolina, Dept. of
      Geography, 1970. 96 p. (North Carolina. University. Dept.
      of Geography. Studies in Geography, no. 1)

      Lists 1,582 dissertations in 22 subject categories.
      Broad regional index.

S84. RAY, William W. Urban Studies in Geography: A Bibliography
      of Dissertations and Theses in Geography, 1960-1970. Monti-
      cello, Ill.: 1971. 60 p. (Council of Planning Librarians
      Exchange Bibliography, no. 189)

      Records approximately 1,800 American and Canadian
      dissertations which deal with the geographical
      patterns of urban location and settlement; social,
      political, and economic considerations in the urban
      environment; and planning. Dissertations and theses
      in separate listings, each arranged alphabetically
      by author.

S85. CONFERENCE OF HEADS OF DEPARTMENTS OF GEOGRAPHY, Birkbeck
      College, London. 1972. List of Theses in Preparation
      1971/72 and of Theses Completed during 1972 in Departments
      of Geography in Universities in the British Isles. Compiled
      by Eila M. J. Campbell. London: Birkbeck College, Dept. of
      Geography, 1972. ?

S86. STUART, Merrill M. A Bibliography of Master's Theses in

Geography: American and Canadian Universities. Tualatin, Ore.: Geographic and Area Study Publications, 1973. 275 p.

Alphabetical author listing of 5,054 theses. Regional index.

Places

Asia

General

S87. SUKHWAL, B. L. A Bibliography of Theses and Dissertations in Geography on South Asia. Monticello, Ill.: 1973. 70 p. (Council of Planning Librarians Exchange Bibliography, no. 438)

A listing of approximately 900 unpublished theses and dissertations accepted in South Asian countries, the United States, the United Kingdom. (A few are from France and Germany.) The studies are arranged in a classified arrangement, which includes physical, urban, political, population, and settlement geography; social, cultural, and historical geography; general economic geography; and economic planning and development.

Pakistan

S88. "A LIST of Theses on Pakistan." Pakistan Geography Review 21 (July 1966): 57-60.

An international listing of approximately 125 theses and dissertations, under subjects such as climatology, geomorphology, historical geography, political geography, and agricultural geography.

Canada

S89. MEYER, W. C. Cumulative List of Theses on Canadian Geography. Liste des thèses sur la géographie du Canada. Ottawa: Dept. of Energy, Mines and Resources, Geographical Branch, 1966.

57 p. (Canada. Dept. of Energy, Mines and Resources.
Geographical Branch. Bibliographical Series/Série bibliographique, 34)

> Supersedes Canada. Department of Mines and Techni-
> cal Surveys. Geographical Branch. Cumulative List
> of Theses and Dissertations on Canadian Geography
> (1950) and later editions.

> Cumulative list of 797 Canadian and American bach-
> elors' and masters' theses and dissertations on
> Canadian geography, including titles accepted in
> 1965. Arranged by provinces and territories. Author
> and subject indexes.

S90. FRASER, J. Keith and Mary C. Hynes. List of Theses and Dissertations on Canadian Geography. Ottawa: Canada Dept. of
the Environment, 1972. 114 p. (Canada. Dept. of the Environment. Lands Directorate. Geographical Paper, no. 51)

> English and French.

> Supersedes editions published in 1954, 1958, 1964,
> and 1966.

> A listing of 2,418 completed studies covering up to
> and including the fall of 1971. Includes all bach-
> elors' and masters' theses and dissertations produced
> in Canadian geography departments which concern the
> geography of Canada and foreign areas and methodology,
> as well as theses and dissertations by Canadians at
> foreign institutions written in French or English.
> Does not include work in economics, history, or
> geology. Arranged by Canadian regions, followed by
> a section on foreign topics. Author and subject
> indexes.

Ontario

S91. ONTARIO. Department of Planning and Development. Community
Planning Branch. Geographic Theses; A Bibliography. Revised
copy. Toronto: 1958. 25 p.

> A bibliography of bachelors' and masters' theses
> and dissertations dealing in whole or in part with
> Ontario, completed at Toronto, McMaster, and
> Western Universities. In two parts: geographically

and by subject. Includes a separate listing of
theses written on subjects outside Ontario.

Quebec

S92. RAVENEAU, Jean. "Liste des thèses de maîtrise (1960-1971)
et mémoires de licence (1964-1971) présentés au Département
de géographie de l'Université Laval et concernant l'est du
Québec." Cahiers de géographie de Québec 16 (1972): 123-
129.

A classified listing of 160 theses.

France

S93. "DIPLÔMES d'études supérieures; Thèses de doctorat [1954-
]" Norois. Revue géographique de l'ouest 1 (1954)-
Annual.

Separate author listings of theses and dissertations
completed at the University of Rennes Institute of
Geography and in geography at the universities of
Caen and Poitiers.

Latin America

General

S94. GRIFFIN, Ernst C. and Clarence W. Minkel. A Bibliography of
Theses and Dissertations on Latin America by U.S. Geographers,
1960-1970. Washington: Pan American Institute of Geography
and History, U.S. National Section, 1970. 16 p. (Pan
American Institute of Geography and History. Special Publication, no. 2)

Completed theses and dissertations are arranged
by country. There is a separate alphabetical
listing of dissertations in progress.

Chile

S95. "MEMORIAS universitarias [proporcionan información que interese a la geografía en Chile]" In Chile. Universidad, Santiago. Instituto de Geografía. Informaciones geográficas 8 (1958): 75-96; 10 (1960): 97-109.

> Also includes work done at Chilean institutions other than the University of Chile. Arranged by university and faculty. Covers the period to 1958.

Geology

General

S96. "GEOLOGICAL Abstracts [1953-   ]" Canadian Mining Journal 74 (1953)-   . Annual. March issue, vols. 74 (1953)- 86 (1965).

> Abstracts of theses and dissertations completed in Canadian institutions.

S97. CHRONIC, Byron J. and Halka Chronic. Bibliography of Theses Written for Advanced Degrees in Geology and Related Sciences at Universities and Colleges in the United States and Canada through 1957. Boulder, Colo.: Pruett Press, 1958. 1 vol. (unpaged)

> An earlier preliminary compilation was prepared by Daniel S. Turner for the Petroleum Research Co., Bibliography of Geology Theses, Colleges and Universities of the United States (1954).

> Alphabetical author listing of 11,091 theses and dissertations prepared at United States and Canadian institutions through 1957. In addition to geology, topics include geophysics, geochemistry, geological and petroleum engineering, and mining and meteorology, if relevant. Index of geologic names and a general index.

> Continued by:

S98. _____ Bibliography of Theses in Geology, 1958-1963.

Washington: American Geological Institute, 1965. 1 vol.
(unpaged)

Alphabetical list of 5,886 theses and dissertations,
some of which were completed before 1958 but were
not recorded in the earlier list. This list gives
broader coverage, including geophysics; space science;
hydrology; biological and meteorological subjects
completed in earth science, geophysics, or geology
departments; engineering geology; and related subjects
in civil engineering. Many titles are annotated
parenthetically, to clarify age of rocks, location,
or some other feature. Index of geologic names.

Continued and supplemented by:

S99. WARD, Dederick C. <u>Bibliography of Theses in Geology, 1964</u>.
Washington: American Geological Institute, 1965. 33 p.

Published as a supplement to <u>Geoscience Abstracts</u>,
vol. 7, no. 12, pt. 1, p. 101-137 (December 1965).

Alphabetical author listing of 682 theses and dissertations conferred in 1964, and some not included
previously in Item S97 and Item S98. Index of
geologic names and a subject index.

Continued and supplemented by:

S100. WARD, Dederick C. and T. C. O'Callaghan. <u>Bibliography of
Theses in Geology, 1965-1966</u>. Washington: American Geological Institute, 1969. 255 p.

Contains Canadian theses and dissertations, including
those from 1964 which were not included in Item S99.
Arranged in 19 broad subject categories with an
extended subject index. Author index and an index of
geologic names, listing stratigraphic units covered
by the studies.

Continued by:

S101. WARD, Dederick C. <u>Bibliography of Theses in Geology, 1967-
1970</u>. Boulder, Colo.: Geological Society of America, 1973.
160, 274 p. (Geological Society of America. Special
Paper, 143)

Lists theses and dissertations completed in American and Canadian universities under such fields of interest as economic geology, geochemistry, geohydrology, soils. Includes some items not in previous listings. Subject and author indexes. Index of geologic names.

S102. PRETORIUS, D. A. List of Theses on Geological and Allied Subjects Submitted for Higher Education at South African Universities. Johannesburg: University of Witwatersrand, 1960. 75 p. (University of Witwatersrand. Economic Geology Research Unit, Information Circular, no. 2)

Lists 218 theses and 105 dissertations completed between 1919 and 1959. Based on a survey of theses and dissertations in the university libraries in South Africa. In three parts: (1) alphabetically by author, (2) by areas investigated, and (3) geological formations described, including areas outside South Africa. Contains a separate partial list of theses dealing with the geology of Southern, Central, and Eastern Africa submitted to overseas universities.

S103. MATTSON, Peter H. "Theses in Geological Sciences in the Caribbean; A List of Theses in Geological Sciences in Areas in the Caribbean, Submitted to United States and Canadian Universities and Colleges through 1957." Caribbean Journal of Science 2 (1962): 97-102.

Theses and dissertations arranged by place.

S104. HILLY, Jean. Répertoire général des sujets de thèses de géologie en cours d'étude au 1er mars 1965. Paris: Centre national de la recherche scientifique, Commission de géologie, paleontologie, et géologie appliquée, 1965. 134 p.

Records approximately 800 doctoral studies and theses. Pt. 1 lists theses by institution, faculty, and laboratory, and indicates the adviser. Pt. 2 consists of an index to geographical areas and a subject index.

S105. ROLFE, W. D. Ian. "Theses on Scottish Geology [1960/1968-]" Scottish Journal of Geology 6 (1970)- . Annual.

Listing in vol. 6 (1970) is a retrospective listing of approximately 200 dissertations completed in

Great Britain and Northern Ireland. Items omitted
in main list are included in later listings. Arranged under general, structural, and metamorphic
geology; geomorphology and hydrography; geophysics;
mineralogy, geochemistry, and petrology; geochron-
ology; paleontology.

S106. ETHERIDGE, Michael A. and Anthony J. Irving. <u>Theses in</u>
<u>Australian Universities, 1969-70: Abstracts.</u> Canberra: Aus-
tralian Government Publishing Service, 1972. 102 p. (Australia. Bureau of Mineral Resources, Geology and Geophysics.
Report no. 165)

Abstracts of bachelors' and masters' theses and
dissertations completed in Australian universities
in 1969 and 1970. Arranged by institution and
subdivided by year. Locality, subject, and stratigraphic name index and author index.

Individual Institutions

S107. COLUMBIA UNIVERSITY. Libraries. Geology Library. <u>M.A. and</u>
<u>Ph.D. Theses, 1946-1955.</u> New York: 1956. 16 p (<u>Its</u> Mis-
cellaneous Publication no. 2)

Separate listings of the theses and dissertations
completed at Columbia University. Entry gives
publication information.

S108. ILLINOIS. University. Department of Geology. <u>Chronological</u>
<u>List of Theses in Geology, University of Illinois, Urbana,</u>
<u>Illinois, 1904-1961.</u> Urbana: 1961. 29 p.

Lists 40 bachelors' honors, 332 masters' theses,
and 135 dissertations. Entry gives adviser.

S109. IOWA. University. Department of Geology. <u>Theses and Dis-</u>
<u>sertations of the Geology Department, State University of</u>
<u>Iowa, 1949-64, Inclusive.</u> Iowa City: 1964. 6 p.

Approximately 125 items arranged alphabetically by
author under year.

S110. MICHIGAN. University. Geology Department. <u>Theses Available</u>

in the Geology Department and University Library, June 1957.
Ann Arbor: n.d.   22 p.

> Theses and dissertations completed at the University
> of Michigan.

S111. TEXAS. University. Department of Geology. Graduate Degrees
in Geology, Coferred by the University of Texas from 1897 to
1956. Compiled by Ronald K. Deford. Austin: 1957.   23 p.

> Separate chronological listings of 352 theses and
> 21 dissertations. Entry gives adviser. Author
> index.

Places

Canada

Ontario

S112. KARROW, Paul F.   Bibliography of Theses on Ontario Geology,
Cambrian to Quaternary Inclusive.   N.p.: 1960.   11 p.
(Ontario. Dept. of Mines. Miscellaneous Paper, MP-1)

> An alphabetical list of 154 bachelors' and masters'
> theses and dissertations on post Precambrian geology
> completed in Canada and the United States prior to
> July 1959.

S113. GINN, R. M.   Bibliography of Theses on the Precambrian
Geology of Ontario.   Toronto: Ontario Dept. of Mines, 1961.
49 p.   (Ontario. Dept. of Mines. Miscellaneous Paper,
MP-2)

> An alphabetical list of 502 bachelors' and masters'
> theses and doctoral dissertations completed prior to
> September 1960 at Canadian and American universities.
> Entry indicates location of mining division.

United States

California

S114. JENNINGS, Charles W. and Rudolph G. Strand. <u>Index to Graduate Theses on California Geology to December 31, 1961</u>. San Francisco: 1963. 39 p. (California. Division of Mines and Geology. Special Report, 74)

> Approximately 1,200 theses and dissertations from 1892 to 1961, including work done outside California. Besides geology and paleontology, includes material from departments of geophysics, geochemistry, seismology, mining, and oceanography, as well as selected materials from soils science, geography, physics, engineering, and the natural sciences. Pt. 1 lists theses by specific areas; pt. 2 lists broad regional or topical studies. Author index.

Michigan

S115. KIRKBY, Edward A. <u>Index to Michigan Geologic Theses</u>. Lansing: Michigan Dept. of Conservation, Geological Survey Division, 1967. 33 p. (Michigan. Geological Survey. Circular 7)

> An alphabetical list of 387 theses and dissertations pertaining to Michigan and the surrounding Great Lakes. A few titles from adjacent states and Canada which may be useful in interpreting Michigan geology are also included. Subject index.

Montana

S116. BERG, Richard B. <u>Index of Graduate Theses on Montana Geology</u>. Butte: Montana College of Mineral Science and Technology, 1971. 48 p. (Montana. State Bureau of Mines and Geology. Special Publication, no. 53)

> Supersedes Montana State Bureau of Mines and Geology Special Publication no. 29 (1963) and no. 34 (1965).

> Lists 538 theses and dissertations completed in American and Canadian institutions up to 1969,

inclusive. In two parts: (1) an alphabetical author
listing and (2) a listing of selected items arranged
by subjects. Entry gives publication information.
Institutional index and index to localities by
plates.

Nevada

S117. WILSON, Roland V. <u>Bibliography of Graduate Theses on Nevada
Geology</u>. Reno: Mackay School of Mines, University of Nevada,
1965. 14 p., fold. map in pocket.

Supersedes an earlier listing compiled by Richard
Olsen in 1961.

An author listing of 301 theses and dissertations
completed in American institutions. Entries indicate
scale of maps. Topical index and "Index to Theses
Geologic Maps in Nevada," on which are located all
geologic maps that are parts of the theses or dissertations.

The Northwest

S118. "THESES Dealing with the Geology of Specific Areas." <u>North-
west Geology</u> 1 (1971)-   . Annual.

Supplements and continues Item S116.

Theses and dissertations dealing with the geology
of Wyoming, Montana, Oregon, and Washington and
completed at universities in the region. Vol. 1
(1971) includes 1968-1970 items. Arranged by
institution.

Oregon

S119. SCHLICKER, Herbert G. <u>Bibliography of Theses on Oregon
Geology</u>. Portland: 1959. 14 p. (Oregon Dept. of Geology
and Mineral Industries. Miscellaneous Paper, no. 7)

An alphabetical listing of 137 bachelors' and masters' theses and dissertations. Includes institutions outside Oregon. Provides publication

information. Index map indicates location of areas
covered in studies.

Utah

S120. CHILDERS, Barbara S. and Bernice Y. Smith. Abstracts of
Theses Concerning the Geology of Utah to 1966. Salt Lake
City: Utah Geological and Mineralogical Survey, 1970. 233 p.
(Utah. Geological and Mineralogical Survey. Bulletin 86)

An alphabetical author listing of abstracts of 572
theses and dissertations concerned with the geology
of Utah. Includes studies completed outside Utah.
Entry gives publication information. Author and
title index and subject and university indexes.

Geophysics

S121. TARBOX, George E. Bibliography of Graduate Theses on Geophysics in U.S. and Canadian Institutions. In Colorado
School of Mines. Quarterly 53, no. 1 (1958): 1-55.

Whole number of journal.

Theses from 46 institutions listed. "List of Theses
by Subject" gives publication information if known.
"List of Theses by School of Origin" arranged according to year and indicates if item is thesis or
dissertation. Also a "List of Theses by Author."
No theses on meteorology listed.

Mathematics

S122. VERZEICHNIS der seit 1850 an den deutschen Universitäten
erschienen Doctor-Dissertationen und Habilitationsschriften
aus den Reinen und Angewandten Mathematik. Herausgegeben
auf Grund des für die Deutsche Universitäts-Ausstellung in
Chicago erschienenen Verzeichnisses. München: C. Wolf &
Sohn, 1893. 35 p.

Lists approximately 1,200 items, arranged alphabetically under institution. Entry indicates if a
dissertation or Habilitationsschrift.

S123. ESTANAVE, Eugène P. Nomenclature des thèses de sciences mathématiques soutenues en France dans le courant du XIXe siècle devant les facultés des sciences de Paris et des départements. Paris: Gauthier-Villars, 1903. 44 p.

Lists 292 dissertations chronologically under institution for the period 1810-1900. Author index.

S124. "DOCTORATES in Mathematics Conferred by American Universities [1913/1914-1935]" American Mathematical Monthly 21 (1914); 24 (1917)-43 (1936). Annual.

Lists dissertations completed in American universities with mathematics as the major subject. Entry gives minor field.

S125. "SPISOK dissertatsiy, zashchishchennykh na zasedanii Uchenogo soveta Matematicheskogo instituta imeni V. A. Steklova Akademii nauk SSSR za 1937-1945." Uspekhi matematicheskikh nauk 1, no. 2 (1946): 202-204.

Listings of 18 dissertations and of 11 theses defended at the Akademiya nauk SSSR Matematicheskii institut between 1937 and 1945. Entry gives brief biographical information.

S126. NORTH CAROLINA. University. Institute of Statistics. A Record of Research [1 (July 1, 1948-June 30, 1951)-   ] Chapel Hill: 1951-   . Biennial.

Includes in a separate section brief abstracts of dissertations and theses recently completed at the Institute. Entry gives adviser.

S127. SUSHKEVICH, A. K. "Dissertatsiy po matematike v Khar'kovskom universitete za 1805-1917 gody." In Kharkov. Universytet. Matematychnyi viddi. Zapiski 24 (1956): 91-115.

Lists theses and dissertations.

S128. SQUIRE, William. "List of Doctoral Dissertations on Integrations and Integral Equations." In his Integration for Engineers and Scientists, p. 267-272. New York: American Elsevier Publishing Co., 1970.

Approximately 80 dissertations.

Physics

S129. ESTANAVE, Eugène P. Nomenclature des mémoires de physique expérimentale et de physique mathématique présentés en France dans le courant du XIXe siècle devant les facultés des sciences en vue du doctorat. 1903. 20 p. ?

S130. MARCKWORTH, M. Lois. Dissertations in Physics; An Indexed Bibliography of All Doctoral Theses Accepted by American Universities, 1861-1959. Compiled with the assistance of the staff of the Advanced Systems Development Division and Research Laboratories, International Business Machines Corp., San Jose, Calif. Stanford, Calif.: Stanford University Press, 1961. 803 p.

> Lists 8,216 dissertations from 97 institutions. In two parts. Pt. 1 is an alphabetical author listing, giving place where a copy may be secured or where major findings were published. Pt. 2 is a permutated index of significant words in the titles.

S131. "RÉPERTOIRE de thèses de physique soutenues...devant les facultés des sciences [1962-1963]" Annales de physique, ser. 13, vol. 7 (1963): 665-680; 9 (1964): 113-131.

> Arranged alphabetically under type of doctorate: (1) d'état ès sciences physique; (2) doctorats 3e cycle, doctorats d'université; (3) diplômes de docteur-ingénieur.

S132. NORTH CAROLINA. University. Department of Physics. Masters of Science, Masters of Arts, and Doctors of Philosophy in the Physics Dept., University of North Carolina at Chapel Hill. Chapel Hill: 1966. 22 p.

> A chronological listing covering the period 1908-1966. Entry gives adviser.

S133. "BIBLIOGRAPHY of U.S. Ph.D. Dissertations in Optical Atomic Spectroscopy (1957-1967)." In National Research Council. Committee on Line Spectra of the Elements. Research in Optical Spectroscopy; Present Status and Prospects, p. 25-31.

Washington: 1968. (National Research Council. Publication 1699)

A chronological listing of approximately 127 dissertations. Does not include dissertations involving
applications to problems in other fields. Entry
indicates content.

Water Resources

S134. FERGUSON, Stanley. Bibliography of Water-Related Theses and
Dissertations Written at the University of Texas at Austin,
1897-1970. Austin, Tex.: University of Texas, Center for
Research in Water Resources, 1970. 54 p. (Center for
Research in Water Resources. University of Texas at Austin.
CRWR-68)

A listing of approximately 1,000 studies arranged
chronologically under the department conferring
the degrees; within a given year there are separate
listings for theses and for dissertations. Includes
work done in such departments as aerospace engineering, business administration, electrical engineering, engineering mechanics, and architectural
engineering.

S135. IOWA. State University of Science and Technology, Ames.
Water Resources Research Institute. Books, Publications,
Project Completion Reports, M.S. and Ph.D. Theses; Research
Supported...under the Water Resources Research Act of 1964,
U.S. Public Law 88-379. Ames: 1970-   . Irregular.

A 1972 volume has also appeared.

Includes a separate listing of abstracts of completed theses and dissertations.

S136. DEANE, Mary. Theses on Water Submitted to Universities in
California through June 1969. Berkeley, Calif.: University
of California, Water Resources Center Archives, 1971. 152
p. (University of California. Water Resources Center
Archives. Archives Series Report, no. 22)

Supersedes Archives Series Report no. 2, Emily C.
Lumbard, Engineering, Economic, Social, and Legal
Aspects of Water: Theses Presented for Higher

Degrees, University of California, Berkeley, Davis, and Los Angeles, 1900-1957 (1958), and Archives Series Report no. 7, Gerald J. Giefer and others, Theses on Water Resources--Stanford University, California Institute of Technology and University of Southern California (1959).

An alphabetical author list of 1,686 theses and dissertations--and some baccalaureate theses from the California Institute of Technology--covering a broad interpretation of water to include groundwater geology, sedimentation, littoral drift, biological and environmental indicators of water quality, water administration, and water law. Covers the period from 1900.

S137. McCANN, James A. and Gail G. Smith. An Annotated Bibliography of the Masters Theses and Doctoral Dissertations on Water Resources and Their Uses, 1930-1970, University of Massachusetts, Amherst. Amherst, Mass.: University of Massachusetts, Massachusetts Water Resources Research Center, 1971. 43 p. (Massachusetts Cooperative Fishery Unit. Contribution no. 22)

Lists 302 studies completed at the University of Massachusetts on water resource related subjects, including economics, forestry, landscape architecture, entomology, etc. Entry carries an abstract. Subject index.

Zoology

S138. CRAMPTON, Henry E. The Department of Zoology of Columbia University, 1892-1942. New York: 1942. 84 p.

Dissertations completed in the Department listed chronologically, p. 68-74.

S139. LAWSON, William D. and Neil Hotchkiss. "[Theses and Dissertations Related to the Ecology and Management of Wildlife, 1934-1949]" Wildlife Review, no. 59 (1950). 62 p.

Whole number.

A classified listing of approximately 650 studies completed in American universities. Major headings include mammals, rodents, reptiles, vegetation, land and soils, water. Author and institutional indexes.

Continued and supplemented by:

S140. HOTCHKISS, Neil. "[Theses and Dissertations Related to the Ecology and Management of Wildlife. Supplement]" Wildlife Review, no. 63 (1951). 37 p.

Whole number.

Lists approximately 370 theses and dissertations, representing additions to the main listing, as well as work completed through 1950.

S141. COLUMBIA UNIVERSITY. Libraries. Zoology-Botany Library. Ph.D. Theses in Botany, 1900-1950. New York: 1952. 10 p. (Its Miscellaneous Publications, no. 1)

A chronological listing of approximately 170 dissertations completed at Columbia University. Entry gives publication information.

S142. AMERICAN ORNITHOLOGISTS' UNION. Committee on Research. "Unpublished Theses in Ornithology." Auk 71 (1954): 191-197.

An alphabetical listing of theses and dissertations from American and Canadian universities. Excludes any theses published even in part. Covers period from 1909 through 1951.

S143. SPORT FISHING INSTITUTE. Bibliography of Theses on Fishery Biology; A Compilation of Graduate Theses on Fishery Biology and Related Subjects. Edited by Robert M. Jenkins. Washington: 1959. 80 p.

Supersedes W. F. Carbine, Doctoral Dissertations on the Management and Ecology of Fisheries (U.S. Fish and Wildlife Service Special Scientific Report... Fisheries, no. 87) (1952) and its supplement, Harvey L. Moore, Doctoral Dissertations on the Management and Ecology of Fisheries, 1952-1955 (U.S. Fish and Wildlife Service Special Scientific Report...Fisheries, no. 272) (1959).

Lists 933 theses and 810 dissertations under general subjects.

_____ _____ First Supplement, 1959-1971. Edited by Robert G. Martin. Washington: 1972. 42 p.

A classified listing of 883 theses and 265 dissertations. Covers such subjects as commercial fisheries, diseases and parasites, embryology, life history-ecology, population dynamics, pollution, management.

S144. "MASTER'S Theses in Wildlife." Wildlife Review, no. 98 (1960): 66-76.

Abstracts of theses arranged under subject, covering the period 1956-1959. Index for number also carries these items.

S145. IOWA. State University of Science and Technology, Ames. Department of Zoology and Entomology. Theses from the Cooperative Wildlife and Fisheries Research Units, 1932 to September 1, 1965. Ames: 1965. 11 p.

Supersedes 1950 and 1960 editions.

In two parts: (1) approximately 70 theses and dissertations from the Wildlife Research Unit and (2) approximately 70 theses and dissertations from the Research Fisheries Unit. Represents work completed at the University and on file in the University Library.

S146. LOW, Jesse B. Master List of Publications, Theses and Dissertations from the Department of Wildlife Resources, Utah State University and the Utah Cooperative Wildlife Research Unit, 1936 to 1967. Logan: Utah State University, 1967. (Utah State University, Special Report, no. 11, 1967) ??

S147. MOORE, Julie L. Bibliography of Wildlife Theses; Bibliographie des thèses sauvage, 1900-1968. Los Angeles: Biological Information Service, 1970. 559 p.

A classified bibliography of 2,915 theses and dissertations on those species of birds and mammals within the United States and Canada which are

economically important, including game species, fur
species, and endangered species. Pt. 1 is devoted
to general topics; pt. 2 is arranged by taxonomic
groups of birds and mammals. Author, key word in
title, and subject indexes.

T. Social Sciences

General

T1. CHILE. Universidad, Santiago. Facultad de Ciencias Jurídicas y Sociales. "Lista de tesis de licenciatura apro- badas durante el año 1940." In its Anales 6 (1940): 203-211.

An alphabetical listing of 135 theses. Includes work done at other universities in Chile.

T2. CANADIAN RESEARCH COUNCIL IN THE SOCIAL SCIENCES. Report on Current Research in the Social Sciences in Canada, Feb. 1941. Toronto: 1941. 1 vol. (various pagings)

Classified list subdivided by institutions and schools. Includes theses and dissertations com- pleted and in progress with date of completion and probable completion.

T3. TOROSSIAN, Araxie. "Catalogue des thèses de lettres et de droit soutenues en 1945 devant les facultés de France." Bulletin analytique de documentation politique, économique et sociale contemporaine 2, no. 4 (July-Aug. 1947): 79-96.

Lists 411 dissertations by institution. Entry gives publication information. Analytical index.

T4. NATIONAL INSTITUTE OF ECONOMIC AND SOCIAL RESEARCH. Register of Research in the Social Sciences and Directory of Research Institutions [no. 5 (1947/1948)-13 (1956/1957)] London: Cambridge University Press, 1948-1956. Title varies. Annual.

Nos. 1 (1943)-4 (1946/1947) not available to the public.

A record of research in progress in Great Britain.
Includes only research related to the modern period
(since the industrial revolution). A classified
arrangement with dissertations listed separately by
institution at the end of each section or sub-sec-
tion. Dissertations are listed until completed.
Subject and author indexes.

T5.   "LISTS of Unpublished Theses Written by Graduates of Aus-
        tralian Universities [1949-1953]" In Australian Social
        Science Abstracts. Melbourne: Australian National Research
        Committee on Research in the Social Sciences, 1949-1954.

        Appears in nos. 8, 10, 12, 14, 16.

        Theses and dissertations in the various social sci-
        ences related to Australia, New Zealand, and their
        territories. Arranged by school and then department.

T6.   UNITED NATIONS EDUCATIONAL, SCIENTIFIC AND CULTURAL ORGANI-
        ZATION. Thèses de sciences sociales; Catalogue analytique
        international de thèses inédites de doctorat, 1940-1950.
        Theses in the Social Sciences; An International Analytical
        Catalogue of Unpublished Doctorate Theses, 1940-1950. Paris:
        1952. 236 p.

        Lists 3,215 unpublished dissertations from 23 par-
        ticipating nations, including Germany, divided into
        ten major classes and, within each subdivision, by
        original language. Titles translated into French
        or English. Entry indicates language in which dis-
        sertation was originally written. Subject, author,
        and geographical indexes and a table of languages.

T7.   KAUL, Jagan N. Dissertations in the Social Sciences by
        Indian Scholars. Ann Arbor, Mich.: 1955. 404 p. (Ph.D.
        Dissertation, University of Michigan)

        In addition to the bibliography of the 61 disserta-
        tions completed in American universities that were
        examined (p. 393-403), the study contains an alpha-
        betical author listing of 280 "Dissertations in
        Philosophy, Religion, Physical Sciences, Earth Sci-
        ences, Biological Sciences and Humanities by Indian
        Doctoral Students, 1933-1953" in the United States
        (p. 367-392). Entry gives subject area.

T8.   BIBLIOGRAPHY of Research in the Social Sciences in Australia
        [1954/1957-   ] Canberra: Social Science Research Council
        of Australia, 1958-   .

            Coverage for three year periods. Volumes published
            for 1954-1957 (1958), 1957-1960 (1961), and 1960-
            1963 (1966).

            In two parts, research and publications. Research
            section includes theses and dissertations. Entry
            indicates starting date and approximate date of
            completion, and the title of the study or a descrip-
            tion. Volumes for 1954-1957 and 1957-1960 are
            devoted exclusively to research in universities.
            Arranged by subject. Author index and an index of
            universities subdivided by subject.

T9.   HERRFAHRDT, Heinrich. "Amerikanische Staats- und Rechtsord-
        nung in deutschen juristischen Dissertationen." Jahrbuch
        für Amerikastudien 4 (1959): 96-106.

            Bibliographic essay on German dissertations completed
            between 1948 and 1958. Covers such areas as civil
            service, laissez-faire economics, pressure groups,
            independent regulatory agencies, elections, and juris-
            prudence.

T10.   BADGER, William V. [List of Recent Social Science Theses]
        Social Studies 52 (1961): 67-69.

            Lists 56 items completed in American institutions
            dealing wholly with social studies in elementary
            and secondary schools. No indication of level of
            degree. Covers the period 1956 to 1960.

T11.   "CHOIX de thèses intéressant les sciences sociales soutenues
        [1968-   ]" Revue française de sociologie 9 (1968)-   .
        Irregular.

            A classified listing of French theses and disserta-
            tions representing all university faculties. Includes
            such topics as art, communication, culture, criminol-
            ogy, demography, law and legislation, economics,
            education, psychology and social psychology, political
            sociology, labor. Entry gives faculty and committee
            chairman.

T12. "ABSTRACTS of Doctoral Dissertations in Government and Business." <u>American Economist</u> 11, no. 2 (Fall 1967): 101-117.

   Seventeen dissertations submitted to American institutions between 1965 and 1967.

T13. BUDAPEST. Magyar Közgazdaságtudományi Egyetem. Központi
Könyvtár. <u>Doktori értekezések a Marx Károly Közgazdaságtu-
domanyi Egyetemen [1958-1968]; Diplomamunkák, 1960-1968;
Bibliográfia.</u> Budapest: 1969. 273 p.

   Supersedes biennial numbers beginning 1958/1959.

   Pt. 1 lists 930 dissertations; pt. 2, 243 theses;
   pt. 3 is a classified arrangement.

T14. INDIAN COUNCIL OF SOCIAL SCIENCE RESEARCH. <u>Doctorates in
Social Sciences Awarded by Indian Universities</u> [1968-   ]
New Delhi: 1970-   . Irregular.

   Continues Item T17.

   Listing covering items completed in 1970 published
   in 1972.

   Arranged alphabetically by institution and institute.
   Each is further subdivided into six social science
   subject fields. Indexes for author, subject, and
   major adviser.

T15. "BIBLIOGRAPHY of Social Science Masters Theses Granted in
the California State College System, 1969-1970." <u>New
Scholar</u> 2 (1970): 260-271.

   Theses completed June 1969 through June 1970.
   Arranged by academic discipline, then alphabetically
   by author.

T16. INDIAN COUNCIL OF SOCIAL SCIENCE RESEARCH. <u>Doctoral Students
in Social Sciences</u> [1 (1969)-   ] Delhi: Inter-University
Board of India and Ceylon, 1971-   . Biannual.

   Vol. 1 lists 2,988 items.

   First volume is a register of students engaged in
   doctoral work in Indian universities as of September

30, 1969. Arranged by institution, subdivided by disciplines. Entry gives adviser. Author, adviser, and subject indexes.

T17. _____ Doctorates in Social Science Awarded by Indian Universities up to 1967. New Delhi: 1971. 401 p. (Its Publication, no. 23)

Continued by Item T14.

Lists 1,849 dissertations by broad areas under institution. Areas include economics, commerce and demography; administration and management; psychology and social psychology; sociology, anthropology, social work, and criminology; geography. Entry gives adviser. Author, adviser, and subject indexes.

T18. INDIAN Dissertation Abstracts [1 (1973)-   ] Bombay: Popular Prakashan, 1973-   . Quarterly.

Issued by the Indian Council of Social Science Research and the Inter-University Board of India.

Abstracts of dissertations in the social sciences arranged under fields such as economics and commerce, education, history, geography. Entry gives adviser. Author index.

Individual Institutions

T19. "BIBLIOGRAFIA de memorias para optar al grado de licenciado en ciencias jurídicas y sociales de la Universidad de Chile aprobadas durante el año [1952-1957]" In Chile. Universidad, Santiago. Facultad de Ciencias Jurídicas y Sociales. Anales, epoca 3, vol. 1 (1952)-4 (1957). Annual.

Abstracts of theses, arranged under seminar, such as private law, public law, penal and medical law.

T20. COLUMBIA UNIVERSITY. Faculty of Political Science. A Bibliography of the Faculty of Political Science of Columbia University, 1880-1930. New York: Columbia University Press, 1931. 366 p.

Supersedes Columbia University, A Catalogue of the

Publications of the Columbia Studies in History, Economics and Public Law, 1917 (1917).

Altogether lists over 600 doctoral dissertations written under the Faculty of Political Science. Pt. 1 (p. 315-341): "Studies in History, Economics and Public Law"; pt. 2 (p. 342-366): "Doctoral Dissertations Not Published in the Studies," arranged chronologically.

T21. FRANKFURT AM MAIN. Universität. Wirtschafts- und Sozialwissenschaftliche Fakultät. Dissertationen [1914/1922-1922/1928] Frankfurt am Main: 1922-1929. 2 vols.

Vol. 1 covers 1914-April 1922; vol. 2 covers April 1922-August 1928. Abstracts of unpublished dissertations, arranged chronologically.

T22. HUGHES, H. G. A. Theses in the Library of the University of London; A Selected List of Theses and Dissertations on Anthropology, Colonial History, Geography and Education, Available for Loan. N.p.: 1947. 10 p.

Lists approximately 170 theses and dissertations completed in the University between 1914 and 1947. Arranged under geographical area.

T23. MOSCOW. Akademiya obshchestvennykh nauk. Kandidatskie dissertatsiy, zashchishchennye v Akademii obshchestvennykh nauk pri Tsk KPSS. Moskva: 1951. 99 p.

A classified listing of theses defended at the Academy, largely in the social sciences.

_____ _____ 1951-31 dek. 1958 g. Moskva: 1958. ?

T24. NEW YORK. New School for Social Research. Graduate Faculty of Political and Social Sciences. Theses Topics for Master of Social Science and Doctor of Social Science, 1936-1947. New York: 1947. 11 p.

An alphabetical author listing of 104 theses and 17 dissertations.

T25. ROXAS, Aurora R. List of Graduates with Graduate Degrees

and the Titles of Their Theses. Quezon City: University of
the Philippines, Social Science Research Center, 1957. 108 p.

Lists 604 theses in the social sciences, mostly in
education, history, and anthropology, completed
from 1913 at the University of the Philippines. In
two sections: (1) roster of graduates and titles
arranged chronologically, and (2) subject listing.

T26. SALGADO, Cristobal. "Tesis que se conservan en Archivo de
la Secretaría de la Universidad Central para la consulta de
los alumnos." Revista de derecho y ciencias sociales (Quito.
Universidad Central. Facultad de Jurisprudencia y Ciencias
Sociales) 1 (May 1933): 98-106.

A chronological list, covering 1905 to 1933, of
dissertations for the doctorate and the Licenciado
completed in the Facultad de Jurisprudencia y
Ciencias Sociales.

Accounting

T27. "ACCOUNTING Theses." Accounting Review 12 (1937)-16 (1941).
Annual. Sept. issue.

Three sections in each list: "Theses Accepted for
the Ph.D. Degree, Year Ended June...," "Ph.D. Theses
in Progress as of June...," "Master's Theses Completed, Year Ended June..." Each section alphabetical by title.

T28. CLEVENGER, Earl. "Summary of Research in Bookkeeping."
Business Education World 19 (1939): 565-567, 633-636.

A selective alphabetical list of 89 theses (mainly
masters') dating from 1918, along with some periodical articles, chosen from all available in the
field. Some discussion and analysis appear in second
part.

T29. "ACCOUNTING Exchange." Accounting Review 16 (1941): 288-
296.

Lists theses and dissertations completed and works
in progress through June 1941. No date is given

for those completed prior to June 1941.

Continued by:

T30. "RESEARCH Projects in Accounting." <u>Accounting Review</u> 26 (1951)-35 (1960). Annual.

Vol. 26 (1951) lists 439 items, including all dissertations completed since 1941, dissertations in progress, and theses completed 1949-1950 and in progress; vol. 27 (1952) supplements this listing; vols. 28 (1953)-35 (1960) list only theses completed.

Items listed under broad subjects, such as theory, history, taxation, and law.

T31. "ABSTRACTS of Dissertations in Accounting." <u>Accounting Review</u> 30 (1955): 673-693; 31 (1956): 109-118, 444-453, 646-651; 33 (1958): 265-289; 34 (1959): 612-638; 35 (1960): 219-315.

Approximately 20 dissertation abstracts in each listing. Lists include dissertations completed prior to journal year. Entry summarizes the nature of the problem explored and the findings or conclusions.

T32. "DISSERTATSIY po voprosam ucheta i analiza khozyaystvennoy deyatel'nosti." <u>Bukhgalterskiy uchet</u>, 1956, no. 9: 51-55.

Annotated classified listing of 29 theses defended between 1954 and 1956.

T33. MYERS, John H. "Research Projects in Accounting, 1964." <u>Accounting Review</u> 39 (1964): 1,079-1,085.

Lists dissertations under broad subjects such as theory, control, systems, auditing, tax, and education. Entry gives expected completion date.

T34. "RESEARCH in Accounting [1966-   ]" <u>Accounting Review</u> 42 (1967)-   . Annual.

A classified bibliography with dissertations and faculty research. Includes theory, public practice, education, government, and eleemosynary subjects.

Advertising and Marketing

T35.   NATIONAL ASSOCIATION OF MARKETING TEACHERS. Committee on
Research Projects. List of Doctoral Theses in the Field of
Marketing and Advertising. N.p.: 1934. 9 p.

   Arranged by topics. Does not include agricultural
   marketing. Publication information provided.

T36.   BARTELS, Robert. "Research Completed in Colleges and Universities, 1952-1953." Journal of Marketing 17 (1952/1953): 80-
81, 316-320, 447; 18 (1954): 310-311.

   Includes a separate list of completed theses and
   dissertations arranged by university.

T37.   BARTELS, Robert. "Doctor's Dissertations and Master's
Theses in Marketing: To Be Completed by June 1954." Journal
of Marketing 18 (1953): 212-215.

   Arrangement of 114 theses and dissertations by
   topic, subdivided under each by type of degree.

T38.   NATIONAL SALES EXECUTIVES, INC., New York. Current List of
Unpublished Studies for Sales Executives and Specialists in
Marketing. Compiled and classified by J. S. Schiff. New
York: 1953. 40 p.

   A listing by subject of theses and dissertations
   completed at 32 U.S. institutions during 1951 and
   1952. Includes chapter headings of each work.

   _____ _____ 2d ed. New York: 1954. 31 p.

   Classified list of 204 theses and dissertations
   prepared in 1953. For each entry the chapter
   headings are given.

T39.   "DISSERTATSIY po voprosam ekonomiki i organizatsii torgovli
[1953-1963]" Sovetskaya torgovlya, 1954-1963. Title varies.
Annual.

   None in 1960, 1962, 1964.

   Annotated listings of theses and dissertations

completed in the U.S.S.R.

T40. NEW YORK UNIVERSITY. Graduate School of Business Administration. Bibliography of Graduate Theses in the Field of Marketing Written at U.S. College and Universities, 1950-1957. New York: 1957. 92 p.

> Based upon a questionnaire survey undertaken in connection with the President's Conference on Technical and Distribution Research for the Benefit of Small Business (1957).

> Theses and dissertations completed or in progress arranged by institution. No subject index but each item is classified by a code letter. Some annotated.

T41. "PH.D." Tide 32 (Nov. 8, 1957): 17.

> A selection of eight unpublished doctoral dissertations on marketing and advertising.

T42. ADVERTISING FEDERATION OF AMERICA. Bureau of Education and Research. Bibliography of Advertising and Marketing Theses for the Doctorate in United States Colleges and Universities, 1944-1959. By George T. Clarke. New York: Advertising Educational Foundation, 1961. 28 p.

> Lists 393 dissertations under such topics as advertising agencies, direct mail advertising, packaging, trademarks, warehousing.

T43. GOLDSTUCKER, Jac L. "Bibliography of Master's Theses in Retailing." Journal of Retailing 40 (Spring 1964): 30-38.

> Also appears in American Marketing Association, Committee on Teaching of Retailing, Newsletter for Collegiate Teachers in Retailing 6 (May 1962).

> Approximately 200 theses from 11 American universities, covering the period 1923 to 1961. Arranged chronologically under university.

Anthropology

T44. "SPISOK dissertatsiy, zashchishchennykh v Institute

ėtnografii AN SSSR v 1946-1952 gg." <u>Sovetskaya etnografiya</u>,
1952, no. 4: 232-234.

In two parts: doctoral dissertations listed alphabetically by author, and approximately 75 theses
arranged by geographical areas.

_____ "1953-1955 gg." <u>Sovetskaya etnografiya</u>, 1956, no. 1:
171-173.

Lists two dissertations and then approximately 70
theses by geographical areas.

_____ "1956-1960 gg." <u>Sovetskaya etnografiya</u>, 1961, no. 3:
138-139.

Lists eight dissertations and then approximately 35
theses by geographical area.

T45. "THÈSES et diplômes d'anthropologie physique à la Sorbonne."
<u>L'Anthropologie</u> 58 (1954): 152-153.

Nine theses and dissertations completed from 1945
to 1954.

T46. "ABSTRACTS of Ph.D. Dissertations, University of California
[1946/1949-1952/1953]" <u>In</u> Kroeber Anthropological Society.
<u>Papers</u>, no. 14 (Spring 1955): 93-103; no. 16 (Spring 1957):
77-91; no. 19 (Fall 1958): 103-106.

No. 14 (Spring 1955) covers 1946-1949; no. 16 (Spring
1957) includes a chronological listing of items
abstracted in no. 14 (Spring 1955).

Arranged under year.

T47. "DISSERTATIONS in Anthropology Submitted in Educational
Institutions of the World in Partial Fulfillment of Requirements for the Ph.D. or Equivalent." <u>In</u> Yearbook of Anthropology 1 (1955): 701-752.

An international listing of approximately 1,400
dissertations covering the period 1870-1954. Arranged chronologically under university. Entry
gives publication information.

Supplemented by:

T48. "PH.D. Dissertations in Anthropology." Current Anthropology 7 (1966): 606-627; 9 (1968): 590-606; 11 (1970): 234.

Vol. 11 (1970) lists corrections and also adds the University of Warsaw Center of African Studies.

Separate international retrospective listings of dissertations. Studies are coded to indicate whether in physical anthropology, prehistoric archaeology, social anthropology, or linguistics, and geographic area. Entry gives publication information. Institutional index in vol. 10 (1969): 261-264.

T49. "DISSERTATIONS in Anthropology: Titles of M.A. and Ph.D. Theses Accepted in the United States in the Academic Year [1955/1956-1956/1957]" In Kroeber Anthropological Society. Papers, no. 15 (Fall 1956): 111-116; no. 18 (Spring 1958): 87-93.

Arranged by institution.

T50. FÜRER-HAIMENDORF, Elizabeth von. An Anthropological Bibliography of South Asia. Paris: Mouton and Co., 1958.

"Dissertations for Higher Degrees" (p. 714-715) lists Western language dissertations completed between 1940 and 1954.

T51. SCHNEIDER, Jakob. Der Wein im Leben der Völker: Eine empirische Bibliographie deutschsprachiger Hochschulschriften über den globalen Weinbau mit seinen wechselseitigen beziehungen zwischen Natur, Technik und Wirtschaft in Deutschland, auf dem europäischen Kontinent und in der übrigen Welt; Als literaturkundlicher Handweiser zu Wissenschaft und Praxis im weinfach erstellt und dem deutschen Weinmuseum in Speyer zu seinem 50jährigen bestehen dargeboten. Neustadt an der Weinstrasse: D. Meininger, 1961. 64 p. (Weinblatt-Bücherei für die Berufstätigen im Weinfach, vol. 29)

A classified bibliography of 430 German language dissertations (includes Austrian and Swiss universities) on all aspects of wine and winemaking. Includes activities outside Germany. Entry gives

publication information. Author, subject, and
geographical indexes.

T52. "RECENT Ph.D. Dissertations in Anthropology." In American
Anthropological Association. Guide to Graduate Departments
of Anthropology [1963/1964-   ] Washington. Annual.

Volume for 1963/1964 covers the period 1959-1963.

An alphabetical author listing of dissertations
completed in American institutions. Entry indicates
major field.

T53. MIRANDA P., Jorge. "Tesis doctorales en antropología social
y cultural." América indígena 27 (1967): 363-382.

A retrospective alphabetical author listing of 275
dissertations, most of which represent work completed
in American institutions. Subject index.

T54. MONTEMAYOR, Felipe. 28 [i.e. Veintiocho] años de antropología: Tesis de la Escuela Nacional de Antropología e Historia
1944-1971. México: Instituto Nacional de Antropología e
Historia, 1971. 615 p.

Chronological listing of abstracts of 164 theses.
Abstract gives a brief description of the study and
a detailed summary of the conclusions. Entry gives
biographical information on the candidate, previous
academic work, and area of concentration. Subject,
place, and author indexes.

T55. "ABSTRACTS of Doctoral Dissertations in Anthropology [1969/
1970-   ]" In New Mexico. Eastern New Mexico University,
Paleo. Contributions in Anthropology 3, no. 1 (April 1971)-
. Annual.

Lists dissertations completed in American institutions
alphabetically under the divisions physical anthropology, archaeology and prehistory, ethnology and anthropological linguistics. Entry gives major adviser.
Author index.

Business and Economics

General

T56. TRAWEEK, Stella. <u>A Survey of University Business and Economic Research Reports: A Compilation of Faculty and Doctoral Research Projects in Business and Economics Completed or in Progress in University Schools of Business and Departments of Economics during the Academic Years 1957-1961</u>. Prepared for the Small Business Administration. Washington: U.S. Government Printing Office, 1961. 642 p.

> A classified listing of 3,298 studies completed or in progress in 320 universities. Includes sections on urban land, housing, real estate, agriculture, natural resources.

> Continued by:

T57. TEXAS. University. Bureau of Business Research. <u>A Survey of University Business and Economic Research Reports; A Compilation of Faculty and Doctoral Research Projects in Business and Economics Completed or in Progress in University Schools of Business and Departments of Economics during the Academic Years 1959 through 1963</u>. Prepared by Cynthia R. Bettinger and Charles T. Clark...for the Small Business Administration. Washington: U.S. Government Printing Office, 1963. 690 p.

> Classified listing of all faculty and doctoral research projects reported by 284 institutions completed during the academic years 1959/1960 and 1960/1961, as well as research to be completed during 1961/1962 and 1962/1963. Under each subdivision the studies are listed alphabetically by title, are briefly summarized, and give expected completion date. Author and subject indexes.

T58. MICHIGAN. State University, East Lansing. Bureau of Business and Economic Research. <u>Directory of Doctoral Degrees in Economics and Business in the Graduate School of Business Administration, Michigan State University, 1948-1965</u>. East Lansing: 1966. 29 p.

> A chronological listing. Entry gives publication information.

T59. "SWEDISH Dissertations in Economics and Business Administration [1968/1969-   ]" <u>Swedish Journal of Economics</u> 71 (1969)-   . Annual. Dec. issue.

    Abstracts of dissertations for the Licentiat degree. Includes some Finnish dissertations. Entry gives publication information.

T60. WASHINGTON (State). Department of Commerce and Economic Development. Business and Economic Research Division. <u>Directory of Graduate Thesis Studies from Washington State Business and Economics Schools, 1960-1968</u>. Olympia: 1969. 125 p.

    An alphabetical listing of theses. Entry indicates general subject of investigation. Classified topical index.

T61. WOOD, W. Donald, L. A. Kelly, and P. Kumar. <u>Canadian Graduate Theses 1919-1969; An Annotated Bibliography (Covering Economics, Business and Industrial Relations</u>). Kingston, Ontario: Queen's University, Industrial Relations Centre, 1970. 483 p. (Queen's University. Industrial Relations Centre. Bibliography Series, no. 4)

    Lists 2,494 theses and dissertations, classified under the place where the work was completed (Canada, the United States, and Great Britain). All Canadian theses and dissertations which deal with the subject are included, though it may not be directly relevant to Canada, and theses and dissertations from the United States and Great Britain are included if by a Canadian, and if the work deals with a Canadian topic. Author and institutional indexes.

Business

T62. "SPIS rozpraw doktorskich i magisterskich oraz prac dyplomowych, przyjętych w Wyższej Szkole Handlowej w Warszawie w latach 1912/1913-1930/1931: Index des thèses de doctorat, des thèses de magisterium et des mémoires de licence présentés à l'École des hautes études commerciales à Varsovie." <u>In</u> Warsaw. Wyższa Szkola Handlowa. <u>Rocznik</u>, 1932: 1-32.

    Lists approximately 650 theses and dissertations. In four parts: (1) dissertations, (2) theses for the magisterium, (3) theses for the period 1912/1913-1917/1918, (4) under the name of the seminar for the period 1918/1919-1930/1931. In each part the studies are listed chronologically.

_____ "1931/1932-1932/1933." In Warsaw. Wyższa Szkoła Handlowa. Rocznik 10 (1934): 1-43.

_____ "1933/1934-1935/1936." In Warsaw. Wyższa Szkoła Handlowa. Rocznik 11 (1936): 1-44.

T63. "THESES on Trust Subjects." In American Bankers Association Trust Division. The Trust Bulletin 19, no. 10 (1940): 19-25, no. 11: 19-40. ??

T64. U.S. Bureau of Foreign and Domestic Commerce. Survey of University Business Research Projects [1940-1947/1948] Washington: 1940-1949. 6 vols. Title varies.

Volumes for 1941, 1943/1944 issued in the Bureau's Economic Series.

A substantial portion of the work included is theses and dissertations. Volumes for 1940 and 1941 indicate only that the studies are being done by students. Lists for 1942-1947/1948 give degree sought and expected date of completion. Some carry descriptive note. Arranged under such subjects as accounting, economic theory, marketing, transportation. Subject, author, and institutional indexes.

T65. "ABSTRACTS of Doctoral Dissertations [1952-   ]" Journal of Finance 7 (1952)-   . Annual. Sept. issue.

Abstracts approximately ten American dissertations completed within two years prior to publication.

T66. JEHRING, John J. Theses on Profit Sharing and Allied Subjects in American Universities. Evanston, Ill.: Profit Sharing Research Foundation, 1954. 5 p. ?

T67. "DOCTORAL Dissertations Accepted [1954/1955-   ]" Journal of Business 29 (1956)-   . Annual. Jan. issue.

A subject arrangement of work completed at American

institutions.

T68. U.S. Bureau of Labor Statistics. "College Doctoral Disser-
      tations and Theses." In its Productivity: A Bibliography,
      November 1957, pt. 11, p. 143-145. By Laura H. Spatz.
      Washington: U.S. Government Printing Office, 1958.

      An alphabetical title listing of 32 unpublished
      American studies, covering the period 1950 to June
      1957.

T69. TOOTLE, Columbus E. "Doctoral Dissertations in Insurance
      and Closely Related Fields, 1940-62." Journal of Risk and
      Insurance 30 (1963): 237-244.

      An alphabetical listing of 213 dissertations. Entry
      gives institution and a reference to the source
      where citation was located.

T70. FEDERAL RESERVE BANK OF CHICAGO. Research Department.
      Abstracts of Dissertations Supported by Research Fellowships
      from Federal Reserve Bank of Chicago. Chicago: 1967.
      1 vol. (unpaged)

      Abstracts of dissertations completed between 1957
      and 1963.

Economics

General

T71. "...LIST of Doctoral Dissertations in Political Economy in
      Progress in American Universities and Colleges [Jan. 1,
      1905-Jan. 1, 1907]" In American Economic Association.
      Publications, 3rd ser., vol. 6: 737; 7: 43; 8: 42.

      First list separately printed January 1, 1904, and
      not included in the Publications.

      Dissertations listed by institution, giving probable
      completion date and candidate's previous degrees.

      Continued by:

T72. "...LIST of Doctoral Dissertations in Political Economy in Progress in American Universities and Colleges [Jan. 1, 1908-Jan. 1, 1910]" Economic Bulletin 1 (April 1908), 2 (April 1909), 3 (March 1910).

> Listed by institution, giving probable completion date and candidate's previous degrees.

> Continued by:

T73. "...LIST of Doctoral Dissertations in Political Economy in American Universities and Colleges." American Economic Review 1 (1911)- . Title varies. Annual. Vols. 10 (1920)-59 (1969) Sept. issue; vols. 60 (1970)- Dec. issue.

> Includes dissertations in progress and those completed since 1912 arranged by subject (groupings vary somewhat through the years). Recent lists separate "Degrees Conferred" from "Theses in Preparation." Entry indicates previous degrees and where taken. Publication information given until vol. 40 (1950). Beginning with vol. 56 (1966) only completed dissertations are listed and roughly half carry abstracts.

T74. "LIST of Theses in Economics and Allied Subjects in Progress in Universities and Colleges in the British Commonwealth of Nations." Economica 5 (1925)-13 (1933). Annual.

> Includes theses and dissertations mentioned in previous lists which were completed, those still in progress, and new items. Arranged by broad subjects. Entry indicates previous degrees and probable date of completion.

T75. TORONTO. University. Contributions to Canadian Economics. Toronto: The University Library, 1929, 1931-1933.

> Carries listings of Canadian and American theses and dissertations on Canadian topics. Vol. 2 (1929): 69-84 provides a classified listing of theses and dissertations for the period 1920-1929, covering such areas as agriculture, labor, banking, public finance. Vol. 2 (1929): 89-93: "List of Theses for the Degree of Doctor of Philosophy"; vol. 2 (1929): 93-97: "List of Theses for the Degree of Master of Art." Vol. 3 (1931): 53-56; 4 (1932): 50-55; 6

(1933): 62-69: "Research in Canadian Economics"
lists theses and dissertations completed and in
progress.

T76.   INSTITUT FÜR ANGEWANDTE WIRTSCHAFTSWISSENSCHAFT, Berlin.
Die wirtschaftswissenschaftlichen Hochschularbeiten. Heft
1, 1936. Berlin: Verlag für Sozialpolitik, Wirtschaft und
Statistik, P. Schmidt, 1936. 309 p.

German dissertations in progress and completed,
arranged by topics. Institutional index.

T77.   PUNJAB, Pakistan (Province). University, Lahore. A Guide
to Theses in the Economic Seminar Library. Lahore: 1941.
35 p. ??

T78.   FITZPATRICK, Paul J. "Graduate Dissertations in Economics
in Catholic Universities [1935-Sept. 1954]" Review of
Social Economics 7 (1949): 86-98; 9 (1951): 146-155; 13
(1955): 149-159.

Listings of theses and dissertations completed at
Catholic institutions arranged by institution and
subdivided by dissertations and theses. List in
vol. 7 (1949) covers 1935-June 1947 and includes
Catholic, Georgetown, Loyola, Marquette, Notre Dame,
St. John's, St. Louis, and Fordham Universities;
vol. 9 (1951) covers July 1947 to August 1950 and
adds Boston College, Detroit, and Duquesne Universities; vol. 13 (1955) covers September 1950 to September 1954 and includes Seton Hall.

T79.   MEXICO (City). Universidad Nacional. Escuela Nacional de
Economia. "Indice general de las tésis profesionales, 1934-
1950." Investigación económica (Mexico) 10 (1950): 533-541.

Lists approximately 120 items under broad subjects.

T80.   BUENOS AIRES. Universidad Nacional. Facultad de Ciencias
Económicas. Biblioteca. Tesis doctorales de la Facultad de
Ciencias Económicas, 1916-1951. Buenos Aires: Impr. de la
Universidad, 1952. 83 p.

A chronological listing of the 543 theses approved
by the Faculty. Subject index.

Continued by:

T81. BUENOS AIRES. Universidad Nacional. Facultad de Ciencias
Económicas. <u>Tesis doctorales 1965-66</u>. Buenos Aires: 1969. ?

Continued by:

T82. BUENOS AIRES. Universidad Nacional. Facultad de Ciencias
Económicas. Biblioteca. <u>Tesis doctorales aprobadas, desde
el 1º de enero hasta el 31 de diciembre de 1968;</u> [Resúmenes]
Buenos Aires: 1970. 47 p. (<u>Its</u> Serie de divulgación
bibliográfica económica, no. 43)

A classified listing of abstracts of theses accepted
by the University of Buenos Aires Faculty of Economics. Author index.

T83. "SPISOK tem dissertatsiy zashchishchennykh v [1952-1957] na
soiskanie uchenoy stepeni kandidata ekonomicheskikh nauk po
politicheskoy ekonomii, istorii ekonomicheskikh ucheniy i
istorii narodnogo khozyaistva." <u>Vestnik vysshey shkoly,</u>
1953, vyp. 8: 59-60; 1954, vyp. 3: 61-64; 1955, vyp. 8: 62-
64; 1956, vyp. 5: 62-64; 1957, vyp. 9: 94-96; 1958, vyp. 2:
96.

A listing of theses defended in the U.S.S.R. Each
year's work is under such topics as political economy, history of economic teaching, history, national
economy.

T84. BRATISLAVA. Ústredná ekonomická knižnica. Ekonomické dizertačné práce na Slovensku [1959/1960-   ] Bratislava:
Slovenské pedagogické nakl., 1961-   .

Volume for 1959/1960 edited by G. Kyrelova; 1961
edited by Boris Procházka.

Classified listing of abstracts of habilitačne,
theses, and diplomové in Slovenia. Arranged under
type of degree. Entry gives adviser.

T85. GUPTA, Girijaprasad P. <u>Economic Investigations in India;
A Bibliography of Researches in Commerce and Economics
Approved by Indian Universities. With Supplement 1962.</u>
Agra: Ram Prasad and Sons, 1961. 130 p.

Covers the period from about 1910, with an emphasis
on the post-independence era. While not all institutions in India are represented in this work, the bulk
are. Pt. 1, bibliography of subjects in which research
degrees (Ph.D., D.Phil. and D.Litt.) have been awarded,
is arranged by institution and then type of degree.
Includes a listing by broad topics. Pt. 2, research
in progress, arranged by institution, with a listing
by broad topics.

T86. "LES DIPLÔMES de géographie économique sur la Bourgogne et
la Franche-Comté." Revue de l'économie du Centre-Est 4
(1961): 74.

A chronological listing, covering 1944-1960, of
theses completed at the University of Dijon.

T87. YALE Economic Essays [1 (1961)-11 (1971)] New Haven, Conn.:
Yale University Press, 1961-1971. Semiannual.

Each number contains summaries or complete dissertations in economics completed at Yale University.

T88. RAKHLEVSKIY, Vladislav A. and G. Ushakov. Dissertatsiy po
finansam, denezhnomu obrashcheniyu, kreditu, bukhgalterskomu
uchetu i analyzu khoziaistvennoy deyatel'nosti, zashchishchennye na uchenuyu stepen' doktora i kandidata ekonomicheskikh nauk s 1939 po 1961 g.; Bibliograficheskiy ukazatel'.
Moskva: Gosfinizat, 1962. 111 p.

A classified listing of Russian theses and dissertations in the fields of finance, monetary exchange,
credit, bookkeeping, and economic analysis. Under
each part dissertations and theses are listed separately. Entry gives table of contents.

T89. SOPOT, Poland. Wyższa Szkoła Ekonomiczna. Prace doktorskie
i habilitacyjne (streszczenia) oraz Wykaz prac magisterkich
[1959/1962-   ] Sopot: 1962-   . Biennial.

In two parts: (1) abstracts of dissertations, with
separate sections for English and Russian translations, and (2) theses arranged by department.

T90. "ABSTRACTS of Doctoral Dissertations." American Economist

8, no. 1 (Summer 1964)-   . Irregular.

Selected abstracts of between 400 and 500 words.

T91.   EKONOMICKÉ dizertačné a habilitačné práce v ČSSR a diplomové
práce na Slovensku [1963/1964-   ] Bratislava: Slovenské
pedagogické nakl., 1964-   . Annual.

Lists theses and dissertations completed in Czechoslovakia and theses completed in Slovenia. Pts.
1-3 arranged by type of study taken. Pt. 4 is a
classified listing of studies for the diploma; pt.
5 lists postdoctoral studies. Subject and author
indexes.

T92.   MAI, Ludwig H. Master Theses in Economics Approved by Grad-
uate Schools in the United States, 1961-1964; An Annotated
Index. San Antonio, Tex.: St. Mary's University, Dept. of
Economics, 1964. 144 p.

Subject list of 1,348 theses based on a solicitation
to all universities and colleges in the United States
granting masters' degrees in economics. Entry gives
adviser. There is a separate listing for the University of Puerto Rico.

T93.   "TRAVAUX universitaires." Revue politique et parliamentaire,
économique, financière 66 (April 1964)-68 (March 1966).
Monthly.

Lists theses and dissertations completed in French
universities under such subjects as economics,
French economic problems, European economic problems,
public finance.

T94.   "VERZEICHNIS der erfolgreich verteidigten wirtschaftswissenschaftlichen Dissertationen [1963-   ]" Wirtschaftswissenschaft 12 (1964)-   . Title varies. Annual.

To vol. 17 (1969) includes Habilitationen.

Lists dissertations completed in the German Democratic Republic. Arranged by institution, subdivided
by department.

T95. MILIŠIĆ, Đorde. "Bibliografija doktorskih disertacija iz
oblasti ekonomskih nauka." Ekonomist (Belgrad) 1966: 515-
539.

Also appeared as Jugoslavenski institut za ekonomska
istraživanja. Radovi, 10 (1967).

A classified listing of approximately 400 dissertations completed in Yugoslavian institutions in the
period 1951-1965. Author and institutional indexes.

T96. "DISSERTATSIY zashchishchennye v Institute mirovoy ekonomikii
i mezhdunarodnykh otnoshenyy AN SSSR." In Akademiya nauk
SSSR. Institut mirovoy ekonomiki i mezhdunarodnykh
otnosheniy. Novye yavleniya v ekonomikie kapitalizma, p.
389-411. Moskva: 1967.

Annotated listing of 54 theses and dissertations
completed in 1965 and 1966.

T97. AKADEMIYA NAUK URSR, Kiev. Instytut ekonomiky. Ukazatel'
dissertatsionnykh rabot vypolnennykh i zashchishchennykh
v Institute ekonomiki AN USSR, 1946-1965 gg. Sost. E. N.
Panchenko, N. P. Boyku. Otv. redaktor A. A. Radchenko.
Kiev: Nauk. Dumka, 1967. 82 p.

A classified listing of 332 theses and dissertations
completed at the Institute. Covers such areas as
statistics, finance, economic geography. Author
index.

T98. PUERTO RICO. University. College of Social Sciences.
Department of Economics. Compendio de la tesis de maestria
presentadas ante la facultad del Departamento de Economia.
Rio Piedras: 1970. 151 p.

Lists abstracts of theses completed between 1958
and 1969 in the Department.

T99. PROCHÁZKA, Boris. Ekonomické dizertácie a habilitácie v
ČSSR. Diplomové a postgraduálne práce na Slovensku v škol-
skom roku 1970/71. 1. vyd. Bratislava: SPN, rozmn.
Západoslov. tlač., 1972-   . ?

T100. "THESES Titles for the Degrees in the United Kingdom 1971/

1972 and Michaelmas Term 1972." Economic Journal 83 (1973): 239-245.

A classified listing of theses and dissertations, including studies in such areas as economic theory and history; economic growth, development, planning, fluctuations; international economics; industrial organization; technological change; industry studies; agriculture; natural resources; welfare programming. Entry indicates availability.

Special Subjects

Econometrics

T101. "ABSTRACTS of Doctoral Dissertations in Econometrics and Mathematical Economics." American Economist 12, no. 1 (Spring 1968): 77-98; 15, no. 1 (Spring 1971): 112-144.

Fifty-three American dissertations completed between 1966 and 1970.

Growth

T102. "DOCTORAL Dissertation Abstracts in Economic Growth and Development." American Economist 15 (Fall 1971): 140-179.

Classified list of 46 abstracts of American disser- tations (though not limited to American topics) completed between 1967 and 1971, inclusive. Includes work dealing with modeling, planning, international trade, case studies, agriculture, and industry.

History

T103. BOWERS, Martha-Belle. "Theses on Latin American Economic History in the Library of the University of Chicago." Inter- American Economic Affairs 3, no. 3 (Winter 1949): 85-89.

Seventy theses and dissertations covering about 30 years. All written at the University of Chicago.

T104. "SUMMARIES of Doctoral Dissertations." Journal of Economic History 25 (1965)-   . Annual.

No listing in vol. 28 (1965).

Contains abstracts of eight to ten American dissertations completed each year.

International Economics

T105. "ABSTRACTS of Doctoral Dissertations on International Economics." American Economist 9, no. 2 (Fall 1965): 45-65.

Twenty dissertations submitted to American institutions in 1964 and 1965.

Labor Movement

T106. SELBER, Karl. "Dissertationen über Arbeiterbewegung und Sozialismus die an österreichischen Hochschulen approbiert wurden." In Milan. Istituto Giangiacomo Feltrinelli. Annali 3 (1960): 827-837.

A classified listing of 177 dissertations. Covers (1) the history and politics of the working class movement; (2) labor literature and poetry; (3) socialism, communism, and Marxism. Entry gives faculty within institution.

T107. "RECENT Unpublished Dissertations." In American Institute for Marxist Studies. Newsletter 2, no. 2 (1965)-   . Title varies. Irregular.

Lists theses and dissertations completed in American institutions.

Macroeconomics

T108. "DOCTORAL Dissertations in Macroeconomics." American Economist 13, no. 1 (Spring 1969): 143-153.

Twelve American dissertations completed between 1966 and 1968.

Microeconomics

T109. "DOCTORAL Dissertation Abstracts in Microeconomics."
American Economist 14, no. 2 (Fall 1969): 105-134.

Thirty-five American dissertations completed
between 1967 and 1969.

Monetary Theory

T110. "ABSTRACTS of Doctoral Dissertations on Monetary Theory."
American Economist 8, no. 2 (Winter 1964/1965): 63-74.

Thirteen American dissertations completed in
1963 and 1964.

Public Finance

T111. "DOCTORAL Dissertation Abstracts in Public Finance."
American Economist 14, no. 1 (Spring 1970): 110-131.

Twenty-five dissertations submitted to American
institutions between 1967 and 1969.

Soviet-Type Economics

T112. "ABSTRACTS of Doctoral Dissertations in Soviet-Type Economics."
American Economist 11, no. 1 (Spring 1967): 75-88.

Thirteen dissertations submitted to American institutions in 1965 and 1966.

Urban Economics

T113. "Doctoral Dissertation Abstracts in Urban Economics."
American Economist 16, no. 1 (Spring 1972): 166-202.

Abstracts of dissertations completed in American
institutions between 1970 and 1972.

Cooperation

T114. "DISSERTATIONEN aus dem Gebiet des Genossenschaftswesens nach der vorliegenden Jahresverzeichnissen der deutschen Hochschulschriften 1945-1951." Zeitschrift für das gesamte Genossenschaftswesen 6 (1956): 75-80.

A chronological listing of approximately 50 studies.

Continued by:

T115. "HABILITATSSCHRIFTEN und Dissertationen aus dem Gebiet des Genossenschaftswesens, 1952-1955, zusammengestellt auf Grund einer Umfrage bei Universitäten und Hochschulen der Bundesrepublic." Zeitschrift für das gesamte Genossenschaftswesen 6 (1956): 168-172.

Lists approximately 75 studies alphabetically by author under year.

T116. "DISSERTATIONEN aus dem Gebiet des Genossenschaftswesens 1945-1955 an Universitäten und Hochschulen österreichs und der Schweiz." Zeitschrift für das gesamte Genossenschaftswesen 6 (1956): 340-344.

Lists approximately 90 dissertations alphabetically by author under year.

T117. POULAT, Emile. "Soixante-dix ans d'études associationnistes; Les thèses universitaires françaises, 1885-1955." Communauté et vie coopérative; Archives internationales de sociologie de la coopération, 1957, no. 1: 176-204; no. 2: 183-215.

A classified listing of 383 French dissertations. In three parts: rural communes, urban communes, and studies dealing with cooperative efforts in particular countries. The list covers such topics as collective property, family communes, French Africa, agricultural associations, specialized cooperatives, agricultural credit. In large part represents work done in faculties of law.

T118. WARSAW. Spółdzielczy Instytut Badawczy. Ośrodek Dokumentacji Naukowej. Bibliografia prac doktorskich i magisterskich z zakresu spółdzielczości napisanych w latach 1945-

1960, w wyższych uczelniach krakowskich. Zebra**ł**a i opracowa**ł**a Felicja Kedziorkowa. Warszawa: Zak**ł**ad Wydawn. CRS,
1962. 155 p.

Classified listing of 372 theses and dissertations
on cooperation completed in institutions in the
Krakow region. Entry carries an abstract. Author
index.

T119.   Bibliografia prac doktorskich i magisterskich z
zakresu spó**ł**dzielczości przyjętych w latach 1945-1960 w
wyższych uczelniach poznanskich. Zebra**ł**a i opracowa**ł**a
Józefa Kramer. Warszawa: Zak**ł**ad Wydawn. CRS, 1963. 123 p.

A classified listing of 207 theses and dissertations
on cooperation completed in institutions in the
Poznan region. Entry gives location. Author index.

T120.   Bibliografia prac doktorskich i magisterskich z
zakresu spó**ł**dzielczości przyjętych w latach 1945-1961 w
wyższych uczelniach warszawskich. Zebrali i opracowali
Lucyna **Ł**ugowska, Krystyna Opacka, Wojciech Wrzosek.
Warszawa: Zak**ł**ad Wydawn. CRS, 1963. 191 p.

Classified listing of over 500 theses and dissertations on cooperation completed in institutions in
Warsaw. Includes such topics as agriculture, history, economics, administration, and organization.
Entry carries an abstract. Author index.

T121. FURBAY, Walter M. and Wendell M. McMillan. A Bibliography
of Dissertations and Theses on Cooperatives. Washington:
U.S. Dept. of Agriculture, Farmer Cooperative Service, 1965.
78 p. (U.S. Farmer Cooperative Service. General Report,
no. 130)

Supersedes earlier edition by Wendell M. McMillan,
issued as General Report, no. 42 (1958).

Separate lists of 167 dissertations and 419 theses,
covering the period 1913-1964. Indexed by type of
cooperative studied; aspects of cooperatives studied;
institution; geographic region referred to in title;
individual cooperatives studied; and government
agencies, farm organizations, ethnic groups, and
individuals referred to in titles.

Industrial Relations

T122. ILLINOIS. University. Institute of Labor and Industrial
Relations. University of Illinois Theses Relating to Labor
and Industrial Relations. Urbana: 1949. 12 p.

Lists approximately 200 theses and dissertations
under broad subjects, such as community studies,
labor legislation, social security and social welfare, and unemployment. Includes work completed
in all departments at the University of Illinois.
Entry gives department.

T123. INDUSTRIAL Relations Theses and Dissertations...Accepted at
...Universities [July 1, 1949/June 30, 1951-   ] V.p.:
1951-   . Annual.

Sponsored by the Committee of University Industrial
Relations Librarians.

None published for 1964-1966, 1969.

Title, editor, place of publication, and publisher
vary. Issues for 1949/1950-1957/1958 published by
California University Institute of Industrial Relations; 1958/1959 by University of Illinois, Institute of Labor and Industrial Relations; 1960/1963-
1968 by University of Wisconsin Industrial Relations
Research Institute; 1970-   by the Canada Department of Labour.

Author listing of American and Canadian research.
A separate section provides interlibrary loan and
photoreproduction information. Subject index.

Superseded in large part by:

T124. HOUKES, John M. Industrial Relations Theses and Dissertations, 1949-1969; A Cumulative Bibliography. Sponsored by
the Committee of University Industrial Relations Librarians.
Ann Arbor, Mich.: University Microfilms, 1973. 195 p.

Cumulates Item T123 and includes studies for those
years in which the annual list did not appear.

An alphabetical author listing of 7,427 studies
from approximately 40 cooperating American and

Canadian universities. Entry indicates if available
from University Microfilms. Subject index.

T125. ROSEN, Ned and Ralph E. McCoy. Doctoral Dissertations in
Labor and Industrial Relations, 1933-1953. Champaign, Ill.:
1955. 86 p. (University of Illinois. Institute of Labor
and Industrial Relations. Bibliographic Contributions, no.
5)

Alphabetical list of 1,031 dissertations completed
in American universities. Subject index.

T126. "THÈSES de maîtrise en relations industrielles, Université
Laval et Université de Montréal." Relations industrielles
21 (1966): 629-655; 23 (1968): 684-685.

The approximately 97 theses completed at the University of Laval and 150 theses completed at the
University of Montreal are listed alphabetically
by author under institution. Covers the period
1942-1968. Entry carries a descriptive note.

International Relations

T127. FAUCHILLE, Paul. Louis Renault (1843-1918) sa vie--son
oeuvre. Paris: A. Pedone, 1918. 263 p.

"Thèses de doctorat soutenues à la Faculté de droit
de Paris sous la présidence de Louis Renault": p.
235-243. Arranged chronologically for the years
1882-1918.

T128. TUFTS UNIVERSITY. Fletcher School of Law and Diplomacy.
Theses Abstracts [1947-1957] Medford, Mass.: 1947-1957.

No. 4 of 1956 not published.

Abstracts of dissertations completed in the School.

T129. BARNETT, Sidney N. "Doctoral Dissertations in American
Universities Concerning the United Nations, 1943-1961."
International Organization 16 (1962): 668-675.

A classified listing. Indicates publication infor-

mation for those printed and reference to <u>Disserta-</u>
<u>tion Abstracts</u>.

T130. EUROPEAN COMMUNITY INSTITUTE FOR UNIVERSITY STUDIES. <u>Études</u>
<u>universitaires sur l'intégration européenne. University</u>
<u>Studies on European Integration</u> [vol. 1 (1962/1963)-   ]
Brussels: 1963-   . Annual. Title varies.

Classified international listing. Under each section includes separate listings of dissertations
completed and in progress. Entry gives adviser.

Organization and Management

T131. MASSACHUSETTS INSTITUTE OF TECHNOLOGY. Library. <u>A Subject</u>
<u>List of Theses Presented by Candidates for the Degrees of</u>
<u>Bachelor of Science and Master of Science, in the Courses</u>
<u>in Business and Engineering Administration (Course XV) and</u>
<u>Economics and Social Science, at Massachusetts Institute of</u>
<u>Technology, 1917-1940</u>. Compiled by Barbara Klingenhagen.
Cambridge, Mass.: 1940. 167 p.

Includes an author index and a list of sponsored
fellows.

T132. "DISSERTATION Abstracts [1960-1969]" <u>In</u> Academy of Management. <u>Journal</u> 4 (1961)-13 (1970). Irregular.

Abstracts of completed American dissertations in
the areas of organization, management, and business.

T133. BURLINGAME, Dwight. <u>Masters' Theses Presented in the College</u>
<u>of Business Administration and the Graduate Program in</u>
<u>Hospital and Health Administration of the University of Iowa,</u>
<u>1950-1966</u>. Preliminary ed. Iowa City, Iowa: University of
Iowa Libraries, 1967. 40 p.

A subject listing of 561 studies. Author index.

T134. IMPERIAL COLLEGE OF SCIENCE AND TECHNOLOGY. Department of
Management Science. <u>Abstracts of Theses and M.Sc. Projects</u>.
London: ?

List for 1971/1972 published in 1972.

Personnel

T135. "RESEARCH in Progress and Unpublished." Public Personnel
Quarterly 2 (1941): 125-128.

A classified list of theses, dissertations, and
faculty research in public administration from 50
American institutions.

T136. EELLS, Walter C. "American Doctoral Dissertations on Personnel Problems and Procedures in Foreign Countries."
Personnel and Guidance Journal 34 (1955): 226-228.

Lists 49 dissertations, representing 15 universities, from 1922.

T137. U.S. Civil Service Commission. Library. Dissertations and
Theses Relating to Personnel Administration Accepted by
American Colleges and Universities [1955-1967/1968] Wash-
ington: 1957-1969. Annual.

A classified listing. Author index.

Political Science

T138. "DOCTORAL Dissertations in Political Science in Universities
of the United States and Canada [1910-1966]" American
Political Science Review 4 (1910)-61 (1967). Title varies.
Annual. Since vol. 44 (1950) in Sept. issue.

Has appeared annually except for vols. 9 (1915),
11 (1917)-13 (1919), 17 (1923), 18 (1924). Canadian
listings included since vol. 54 (1960), in which
those from 1951 were included. Includes dissertations in progress and those completed on the basis
of information received from graduate departments
of political science. Since vol. 45 (1951) these
have been in separate categories: (1) "Dissertations in Preparation," in which additions, changes,
and deletions are made; (2) "Dissertations Completed
since the Last Listing." Entries are arranged alphabetically by author under large subjects in each
list. Entry indicates previous degrees and institutions where taken.

Continued by:

T139. "DOCTORAL Dissertations in Political Science in Universities of the United States [1967-   ]" P. S. 1 (1968)-   . Annual.

Includes Canadian dissertations. In two parts: (1) "Dissertations-in-Preparation," subdivided into "additions," "changes," and "deletions...," which updates previous list; (2) "Dissertations Completed since Last Listing," arranged alphabetically by author under topic. Includes constitutional and administrative law, Canadian government and politics, public administration, foreign and comparative government and politics, and international organization politics and government. Entry indicates previous degress (institution and date).

T140. HORNWALL, Gert. "Gradualavhandlingar i statskunskap vid svenska universitet och högskolor under tiden 1843-1944; Bibliografi." Statsvetenskapliga föreingen i Uppsala skrifter 20 (1944): 679-701.

Also appeared as a separate.

Lists dissertations completed in Swedish institutions of higher education. Arranged chronologically under institution. Entry gives praeses.

T141. JONAS, Frank H. Bibliography on Western Politics; Selected, Annotated, with Introductory Essays. Salt Lake City, Utah: University of Utah, Institute of Government, 1958. 167 p.

Appeared as a supplement to Western Political Quarterly 11, no. 4 (1958).

A selective annotated bibliography with the emphasis on politics, rather than government or history. There is a listing for each state and under each state there is a separate section of theses and dissertations. Each state bibliography was prepared by a different editor.

T142. PACTET, Pierre. "Index de mémoires soutenues devant la Faculté de droit et des sciences économiques...pour le diplôme d'études supérieures de science politique [1957-

1962]" Revue du droit public et de la science politique en
France et à l'étranger 77 (1961): 1,149-1,156; 78 (1962):
866-872; 79 (1963): 1,096-1,102.

> Vol. 77 (1961) lists the work done at the University
> of Paris only and covers 1957-October 1, 1961; 78
> (1962) continues the listing for the University of
> Paris through 1961 and covers other institutions
> for the period 1957-1961; 79 (1963) covers all insti-
> tutions for theses completed in 1962. Entry gives
> adviser.

T143. KIDDER, Frederick E. "Puerto Rican Politics in Graduate
Studies; A Select Bibliography of Doctor's Dissertations
and Master's Theses Written at United States Universities
and Colleges Concerning the Politics and Government of
Puerto Rico Arranged Chronologically by Date of Degree."
Ciencias politicas en Puerto Rico 1 (1962): 7-11.

> Fifty-two studies completed between 1902 and 1960.

T144. FONDATION NATIONALE DES SCIENCES POLITIQUES, Paris. Travaux
inédits de science politique. Liste de thèses, mémoires et
diplômes soutenus en France de 1959 à 1962. Paris: 1963.
45 p.

> Lists 477 theses and dissertations under such topics
> as political ideas and theory, French institutions,
> administrative studies, Africa, press and opinion,
> international relations. Entry gives adviser.
> Author index.

T145. "COURS et travaux inédits de science politique [1962/1963-
]" Revue française de science politique 14 (1964)-   .
Title varies. Annual.

> Unpublished theses and dissertations submitted to
> French universities arranged under broad subjects,
> such as biography, French institutions, administra-
> tion, public opinion, political forces, elections,
> local government, international relations, African
> countries, foreign countries. Entry gives adviser.
> Author and subject index.

T146. GAUTAM, Brijendra P. Researches in Political Science in
India: A Detailed Bibliography. Kanpur: Oriental Publishing

House, 1965. 116 p.

> A bibliography of research theses for the Ph.D.,
> D.Phil., and D.Litt. completed or in progress in
> the various branches of political science in Indian
> universities. Pt. 1: research completed; pt. 2:
> research in progress. Each part is arranged by uni-
> versity and includes a topical listing.

T147. LEUTHOLD, David A., William M. Reid, and William Macauley.
California Politics and Problems, 1900-1963. Berkeley,
Calif.: University of California, Institute of Government
Studies, 1965. 64 p.

> A classified bibliography consisting in large part
> of theses and dissertations. Author and subject
> index.

T148. "CURRENT Political Research in New Zealand." _Political
Science_ 21, no. 2 (Dec. 1969)-   . Irregular.

> Published twice yearly by the Victoria University
> School of Political Science and Public Administra-
> tion.
>
> Abstracts of theses and dissertations completed or
> in progress in New Zealand. Abstracts indicate
> estimated completion date and methodology.

T149. "DOCTORAL Dissertations in Literature on Burke, 1916-1963."
Studies in Burke and His Times 10 (1969): 1,250-1,251.

> A chronological listing of 32 American, British,
> and German dissertations.

T150. CANADIAN POLITICAL SCIENCE ASSOCIATION. _Theses in Canadian
Political Studies, Completed and in Progress_. Kingston,
Ont.: Canadian Political Science Association, 1970. 71 p.

> English and French.
>
> Lists theses and dissertations completed or in
> progress at Canadian universities or on Canadian
> topics at institutions outside Canada. Designed
> to cover all work up to and including 1970. Items
> are separated into (1) completed and (2) in progress,

and classified under each part with Canadian topics
grouped separately. Author index.

_____ _____ Supplement [1971/1972-   ] Annual.

Follows same format as main work. Indicates changes
in status of items listed previously.

Public Administration and Planning

Public Administration

T151. "VERZEICHNIS von Doktordissertationen über das Post- und
Fernmeldewesen nach dem Stande vom September 1932." In
Germany. Postministerium. Archiv für Post und Telegraphie,
1932, Nr. 11, Beilage, p. 1-26.

Classified listing of 1,430 dissertations under
law, communication and industry, personal finance
and economics, and history. Entry gives publication information.

T152. CURRENT Research Projects in Public Administration, Reported
to Public Administration Service. Chicago: Public Administration Service, 1938-1943, 1947-1952. Title varies.
Annual.

None published 1944-1946; 1938-1943 issued by the
Social Science Research Council, Committee on
Public Administration.

Approximately half the items listed are theses and
dissertations in progress in American institutions.
Arranged under such subjects as housing, personnel,
planning, state finance, and taxation.

T153. TENNESSEE VALLEY AUTHORITY. Technical Library. "Unpublished
Theses and Studies." In its A Selected List of Books, Theses
and Pamphlets on TVA, p. 11-12. Compiled by Bernard L. Foy.
Knoxville, Tenn.: 1942.

An earlier edition was compiled by Ernest I. Miller
in 1940.

An alphabetical list of theses and dissertations.

T154. ROYAL INSTITUTE OF PUBLIC ADMINISTRATION. Register of Research in Political Science [1951-   ] London: 1951-   . Title varies. Annual.

Includes work for higher degrees in Great Britain and Ireland in public administration and allied fields.

T155. HARRISON, Robert W. "Unpublished Studies on Public Land Policies and Problems." Land Economics 28 (1952): 390-400.

Contains 172 studies (nearly all theses and disserta- tions) classified according to such subjects as administrative aspects, forest land policy, grazing land policy, school lands, and the law. Some of the studies cited are "in progress." Some short annotations.

T156. "A SELECTED List of Master's Theses and Doctoral Disserta- tions in Political Science and Related Fields." Philippine Journal of Public Administration 1 (1957): 74-80, 190-199, 421-441; 2 (1958): 408-414; 3 (1959): 478-482; 4 (1960): 363-366; 5 (1961): 365-368; 6 (1962): 334-337.

Lists approximately 300 theses and dissertations completed in institutions in the Philippines in the period 1915-1962. Arranged in chronological groups by date of completion and subdivided into such areas as law, political science, history, social welfare, economics, and business management.

T157. "DISSERTATIONS and Theses on Canadian Public Administration [1962-1964]" Canadian Public Administration 5 (1962): 383- 384; 6 (1963): 240-241; 8 (1964): 117-118.

Lists theses and dissertations completed or in progress in institutions in Canada, the United States, and the United Kingdom of particular relevance to Canadian public policy or administration.

T158. U.S. Bureau of Land Management. Public Land Bibliography. Washington: U.S. Government Printing Office, 1962. 106 p.

"Theses" (p. 93-106) lists 213 theses and disser- tations from the year 1880 on the topic of public land activities, programs, and legislation prior

to 1954. Some items are bachelors' theses or are
in progress.

T159. "ABSTRACTS of Master's Theses in Public Administration."
Philippine Journal of Public Administration 7 (1963)- .
Title varies. Irregular.

Abstracts of work completed at the University of
the Philippines College of Public Administration.

T160. ONTARIO. Department of Municipal Affairs. Theses Related
to Municipal Administration, Finance and Planning. 1963 ed.,
with 1964 supplement attached. Toronto: 1965. 60, 3 p.

Supersedes its Theses Relating to Community Planning
in Ontario (1961).

Contains approximately 500 theses (including bachelors') and dissertations completed or in progress in
Canadian and American universities relating to urban
history, political science, and geography. Arranged
by region, including Canada (general), the Arctic,
Quebec, and areas outside Canada but bordering on
Ontario. Under Ontario the items are subdivided by
subject.

T161. PUERTO RICO. University. School of Public Administration.
Tesis presentadas para el grado de maestro en administración
pública. Rio Piedras: 1971. 26 p.

Lists theses completed in the School between 1945
and 1970.

Planning

T162. AMERICAN SOCIETY OF PLANNING OFFICIALS. Theses Titles on
Planning. Compiled by Miriam B. Halbrecht. Chicago: 1949.
25 p. ?

T163. "ABSTRACTS of City Planning Theses." In American Institute
of Planners. Journal 26 (1960): 60-66, 135-143; 28 (1962):
35-45; 29 (1963): 55-59.

List in vol. 26 (1960) contains separate lists of

theses and dissertations completed in 1958/1959 in
American institutions. Vol. 28 (1962) includes
only theses; vol. 29 (1963) includes theses and dissertations completed since first list and through
1961.

T164. AMERICAN INSTITUTE OF PLANNERS. Abstracts of Student Theses
in City and Regional Planning. Washington: 1965. 83 p.

Theses and dissertations submitted for graduate
degrees in schools of city and regional planning.
In two parts: pt. 1, subject index of the abstracts
appearing in the American Institute of Planners
Journal, 1958-1963, with an author index; pt. 2,
U.S. and Canadian schools of city and regional
planning submitting theses, arranged by schools and
subdivided chronologically. Pt. 2 includes abstracts
of 270 theses and five dissertations submitted to
the Institute since February 1963 and covers the
period 1961-1964. Author index.

T165. CHICAGO. University. Center for Urban Studies. A Directory
of Urban and Urban Related Master Theses and Ph.D. Dissertations of the University of Chicago. Chicago: 1970. 218 p.

In two parts, (1) theses and (2) dissertations.
Under each the items are listed under such subjects
as anthropology, history, political science, psychology, economics. Subject index. Index to Chicago
area studies.

T166. RAY, William W. A Bibliography of Dissertations, Theses and
Thesis Alternatives in Planning, 1965-1970. Monticello,
Ill.: Council of Planning Librarians, 1971. 72 p. (Council
of Planning Librarians Exchange Bibliography, no. 220)

Theses from 32 institutions in the U.S. and Canada
which have graduate departments of planning. Divided into (1) dissertations, (2) theses, and (3) thesis
alternatives, and alphabetically within each section.

Continued and supplemented by:

T167. RAY, William W. and Shelly Lynch. Graduate Student Research
in Planning, Urban Design, and Urban Affairs: 1970-1972.
Monticello, Ill.: 1973. 104 p. (Council of Planning

Librarians Exchange Bibliography, no. 355)

Lists 1,269 American and Canadian dissertations, theses, and thesis alternatives completed or in progress. Includes items dated prior to 1970, if not included in previous listing. In three parts: dissertations, theses, and thesis alternatives, which are subdivided into completed and in progress.

Social Work

General

T168. AMERICAN ASSOCIATION OF SCHOOLS OF SOCIAL WORK. List of Master's and Doctor's Theses Completed 1937-38 in Member Schools of the Association. Office of the AASSW Secretary, University of Pittsburgh, Pittsburgh, Penna. Pittsburgh: 1938. 63 p. ?

Also appeared as American Association of Schools of Social Work, News Letter 4, no. 2 (1938).

T169. SOCIAL SCIENCE RESEARCH COUNCIL. Committee on Social Security. Social Security Research in Progress at Universities and Colleges [1940-1941] Washington: 1940-1941. 2 vols.

A selected listing of studies, the major portion of which are theses and dissertations, in American universities. ("Studies in Canada" are listed in the appendix.) Arranged under such subjects as unemployment compensation, relief programs, health, medical care.

T170. "INDICE clasificado de las tesis de prueba de las escuelas de servicio social Alejandro del Río, Elvira Matte de Cruchaga y de la Universidad de Chile de Santiago, Concepción, Temuco y Valparaíso." Servicio social (Santiago de Chile. Escuela de Servicio Social de la Junta de Beneficencia) 24 (Sept./Dec. 1950): 18-81.

A classified listing of theses completed between 1926 and 1949, subdivided chronologically under each subject.

_____ "Correspondiente a los años 1950-51." Servicio

<u>social</u> (Santiago de Chile. Escuela de Servicio Social de la
Junta de Beneficencia) 26 (Sept./Dec. 1952): 3-14.

T171. "DOCTORAL Dissertations in Social Work [1952/1954-   ]"
<u>Social Service Review</u> 28 (1954)-   . Annual. Sept. issue.

First list includes dissertations accepted July 1,
1952-June 30, 1954.

Includes only dissertations for degrees undertaken
in schools of social work offering doctoral programs.
In two parts: (1) "Dissertations Completed," and (2)
"Dissertations in Preparation," giving date of faculty approval of topic. Beginning with vol. 32 (1958)
the completed dissertations are abstracted.

T172. GIL, David G. <u>Doctoral Dissertations in Social Work Related
to the Field of Child Welfare</u>. Washington: U.S. Dept. of
Health, Education, and Welfare. Welfare Administration,
Children's Bureau, 1966. 21 p.

Lists 117 dissertations completed in American universities from 1920 through June 1965. Arranged
chronologically.

T173. SCHREIBER, Meyer. <u>Graduate Social Work Student Theses and
Dissertations Dealing with Mental Retardation</u>. 2d ed. New
York: Association for the Help of Retarded Children, New
York Chapter, 1966. 26 p.

A listing of 205 theses and three dissertations
resulting from a survey of the 35 American and
Canadian accredited schools with membership in the
Council of Social Work Education. Studies date
from 1930 but most were done in the 1950's and 1960's.

T174. JUDSON, Julia. <u>Home Economics Research Abstracts, 1963-
1968: Rehabilitation</u>. Washington: American Home Economics
Association, 1969. 24 p.

"Prepared for the Second Interdisciplinary Workshop,
Future Directions for Home Economics in Rehabilitation."

Contains an alphabetical author listing of abstracts
of 18 theses and dissertations supported by the U.S.
Department of Health, Education, and Welfare Social

and Rehabilitation Service; an alphabetical author
listing of abstracts of additional theses and dissertations in rehabilitation; and a listing of
theses and dissertations relating to rehabilitation
arranged under such subjects as adult programs,
child development, food and nutrition, textiles and
clothing. Author index.

T175. UNIVERSITY MICROFILMS, Ann Arbor, Mich. A Bibliography of
Doctoral Research on Crime and Law Enforcement. Ann Arbor:
1971. 70 p.

An alphabetical author listing of over 700 American
dissertations that have been published by University
Microfilms from 1938 to 1970, covering every aspect
of crime and law enforcement in the United States
and elsewhere. Entry gives reference to Dissertation
Abstracts International and the University Microfilms
order number.

T176. "SELECTED Bibliography of Unpublished Criminological Material Held in New Zealand Universities." In Victoria University of Wellington. Faculty of Law. Law Review 6 (1972):
334-336.

Lists theses and dissertations on crime and punish-
ment held at Auckland, Massey, Otago, and Victoria
Universities. Arranged by institution and subdivided
by level of study.

Individual Institutions

T177. "STUDENT Register with Titles of Theses [1938-1952]" In
Boston College. School of Social Work. Announcement 11
(1939/1940)-24 (1952/1953). Title varies. Annual. April
issue.

Entry gives previous degrees and where taken.

T178. BRITISH COLUMBIA UNIVERSITY. School of Social Work. Social
Work Research at the University of British Columbia, 1947-
1956; A Consolidated List and Analytical Classification of
Master of Social Work Theses Completed. Vancouver: 1957.
40 p.

A classified bibliography of nearly 200 theses.
Pt. 2 classifies the theses by methodology. Author
index.

T179. CHICAGO. University. School of Social Service Administra-
tion. Twenty-One Years of University Education for Social
Service, 1920-1941, with a Register of Alumni Who Received
Higher Degrees, 1920-1942, and Their Dissertation Subjects.
By Edith Abbott. Chicago: 1942. 108 p.

Altogether approximately 25 dissertations and 850
theses are listed separately.

T180. IOWA. University. School of Social Work. Bibliography of
Research Project Reports, 1951-1965. Iowa City: 1966. 23 p.

Supersedes 1962 edition.

A record of student research project reports. They
are listed by subject and by methodology.

T181. "NÓMINA y tésis de las asistentas sociales graduadas de
1950." Servicio social (Lima) 8 (Dec. 1950): 250-252.

Lists 28 theses alphabetically by author.

T182. "THESES Submitted for the Degree of Master of Social Work
[1953-1962/1963]" In Los Angeles. University of Southern
California. School of Social Work. Social Work Papers 1
(1953)-11 (1964). Los Angeles: 1953-1964. Annual.

Classified listing of theses completed in the School
of Social Work.

T183. "DISSERTATIONS Submitted for the Degree of Doctor of Social
Work [1956/1957-1962/1963]" In Los Angeles. University of
Southern California. School of Social Work. Social Work
Papers 5 (1958)-11 (1964). Los Angeles: 1958-1964. Annual.

Lists dissertations completed in the School of
Social Work.

T184. "UNIVERSITY of Southern California. School of Social Work:
Master's Theses and Doctoral Dissertations Relating to

Community Organization, 1926–1963. (Unpublished)" In Los
Angeles. University of Southern California. School of
Social Work. Social Community Organization Work; A Selected
Bibliography in a Conceptual Frame of Reference, p. 18–22.
Prepared by Arlien Johnson and the Committee on the Arlien
Johnson Collection, University of Southern California
Library. Los Angeles: 1964.

> Published as Los Angeles. University of Southern
> California. School of Social Work. Social Work
> Papers; Special Issue.

> An alphabetical author listing of approximately 50
> studies.

T185. MARÍN, Rosa C., Carmen F. Q. Vda. Rodréguez and Belén M.
Serra. Resúmenes de tesis (sometidas para optar a la
maestría en trabajo social). Año lectivo 1966–1967. Río
Piedras: Universidad de Puerto Rico, Escuela de Trabajo
Social, Facultad de Ciencias Sociales, 1968. 73 p.

> Abstracts produced by 38 students in social work
> at the University of Puerto Rico (Río Piedras)
> School of Social Work in the academic year 1966–
> 1967.

T186. PUERTO RICO. University. Graduate School of Social Work.
Lista de tesis de la Escuela Graduada de Trabajo Social.
Río Piedras: 1971. 18 p.

> Supersedes annual listings in the Revista de servicio
> social.

> Lists 163 theses completed at the School from 1945
> to 1970.

T187. "MEMORIAS de prueba para obtener el título de assistente
social de la Escuela de Servicio Social de la H. Junta de
Beneficencia de Santiago, años 1946 & 1947." Servicio
social (Santiago de Chile. Escuela de Servicio Social de
la Junta de Beneficencia), Jan.-Dec. 1947, p. 85–87.

> Approximately 40 theses arranged by year.

T188. TORONTO. University. School of Social Work. The Research
Compendium: Review and Abstracts of Graduate Research,

1942-62. Abstracts by Margaret Avison. Toronto: 1964.
276 p.

> Lists two dissertations and 410 theses submitted
> to the University of Toronto School of Social Work.
> Theses are arranged in a classified order. Author,
> agency, and subject indexes.

T189. WASHINGTON UNIVERSITY, St. Louis. George Warren Brown School
of Social Work. Summary of Research [1947-1960/1961] St.
Louis: 1948-1961. Title varies. Annual.

> Abstracts of theses and dissertations completed in
> the School.

T190. BUTLER, Alfred J. and George N. Wright. Wisconsin Rehabilitation Doctoral Dissertations; Abstracts of Research Completed for Partial Fulfillment of Requirements of the Ph.D.
in Vocational Rehabilitation at the University of Wisconsin.
Madison, Wis.: University of Wisconsin, Rehabilitation
Counseling Psychology Program, 1970. 43 p.

> Abstracts of 23 dissertations completed between
> 1964 and 1967 within the College of Education.

Sociology

General

T191. "STUDENTS' Dissertations in Sociology." American Journal of
Sociology 21 (1916)-55 (1949). Annual. July or Sept. issue.

> List in vol. 33 (1927): 118-119 supplements list
> in vol. 32 (1927): 978-986.
>
> Theses and dissertations in progress in the United
> States and Canada, including work in social work,
> divinity, and related fields if directed by a
> department of sociology. Separate lists for disser-
> tations and for theses. Entry indicates previous
> degrees (institutions and dates).

T192. "DOCTORAL Dissertations Newly Started in [1916-1964]"
American Journal of Sociology 22 (1916/1917)-71 (1965).

Title varies. Annual. Since vol. 44 (1938) in July issue.

Annually except for 1918, 1925, 1926.

Includes work in progress in sociology departments and in related areas (e.g. divinity, social work) when directed by departments of sociology. Began in 1916 as "Students' Dissertations in Sociology" and included "Masters' Theses in Progress in American Universities." The last listing of masters' degrees in progress appeared in vol. 55 (1949). Vols. 22 (1916)-68 (1961) list all in preparation; from vol. 69 (1962) only those newly started in previous year are listed. Before 1962 arrangement is alphabetical; subsequently arranged by institution. Entry includes previous degrees (institutions and dates).

Supplemented by:

T193. "HIGHER Degrees in Sociology [1936-1960]" _American Journal of Sociology_ 43 (1937)-67 (1961). Annual. Usually July issue.

Separate listings of dissertations and of theses completed in American and Canadian institutions. Entry indicates previous degrees.

Continued in part by:

T194. "DOCTOR'S Degrees in Sociology...[1937-1964]" _American Journal of Sociology_ 44 (1938)-71 (1965). Title varies. Annual. July issue.

Through vol. 67 (1961) under the title "Higher Degrees in Sociology..." consists of two lists: "Doctor's Degrees" and "Master's Degrees." Each list for degrees granted in previous year, arranged alphabetically by author. From vol. 68 (1962) lists doctors' degrees only, arranged by institution. Entry indicates previous degrees (institutions and dates).

T195. "PACIFIC Coast Research Notes: A Partial List of Research Projects Completed or in Progress." _Sociology and Social Research_ 25 (1941): 466-468; 26 (1942): 471-474.

Refers to theses in progress at the Universities of
Washington, Oregon, British Columbia, Arizona, Cali-
fornia, and Southern California and at Whittier and
Redlands Colleges.

T196. MEADOWS, Paul. "Theses on Social Movements." Social Forces
24 (1946): 408-412.

Analyzes 30 theses and dissertations in sociology
written in 17 universities.

T197. CATHOLIC UNIVERSITY OF AMERICA. Studies in Sociology. Washington: 1950-1961. 17 vols. Irregular.

Abstracts of theses and dissertations in sociology
completed at Catholic University.

T198. FISK UNIVERSITY, Nashville. Social Science Institute. The
Sociology of the South: A Bibliography and Critique of Unpublished Doctoral Dissertations and Master's Theses Written
on Aspects of the South, 1938-1948. Nashville, Tenn.: 1950.
376 p. (Its Social Science Source Documents, no. 6)

A bibliography of 223 theses from many American
universities, with 161 critical annotations on
individual items, evaluated in terms of their use-
fulness in sociological writing. Arranged by subject.
Author index.

T199. PUNJAB, Pakistan (Province). University, Lahore. Department
of Sociology. Theses Index, 1957-1967. Compiled by Muhammad
Fayyaz and Qaiyum Lodhi. Lahore: 1968. 61 p. (Its Miscellaneous Publication, no. 2)

A listing by year of the approximately 300 theses
accepted by the Sociology Department. Author and
subject indexes.

T200. LUNDAY, G. Albert. Sociology Dissertations in American Universities, 1893-1966. Commerce, Tex.: East Texas State University, 1969. 277 p.

Contains 3,993 dissertations accepted in the departments of sociology in 76 universities in the United
States. Arranged in 26 subject areas. Author index.

T201. "THESES Completed or in Progress." <u>Australian and New Zealand Journal of Sociology</u> 6 (1970)-   . Irregular.

Appears as a separate section in "News Notes."

Lists of theses and dissertations completed or in progress at Australian and New Zealand institutions. Arranged by institution and subdivided by level of degree.

T202. UNIVERSITY MICROFILMS, Ann Arbor, Mich. <u>Sex in Contemporary Society; A Catalog of Dissertations</u>. Ann Arbor: Xerox University Microfilms, 1973. 14 p.

An interdisciplinary listing of over 400 American and Canadian dissertations completed in the period 1938-1972. Arranged by broad subjects, such as sex roles and sexual identity, sex and law, religion and sex censorship, etc. Entry gives University Microfilms order number. Author index.

Special Subjects

Demography

T203. FUGUITT, Glenn V. <u>Dissertations in Demography, 1933-1963</u>. Madison, Wis.: University of Wisconsin, College of Agriculture, Dept. of Rural Sociology, 1964. 72 p.

Lists 539 American dissertations by such subjects as population theory, mortality, international migration, race and ethnic groups, occupational status, population distribution, and urbanization. Author and institutional indexes.

Immigration and Race

T204. CANADA. Department of Citizenship and Immigration. Economic and Social Research Division. <u>Citizenship, Immigration and Ethnic Groups in Canada; A Bibliography of Research. Citoyennetté, immigration et groupes ethniques au Canada; Une bibliographie de recherches. 1920-1958</u>. Ottawa: Queen's Printer, 1960. 196 p.

English and French.

Supersedes Canadian Research Branch Research Division. <u>Research on Immigrant Adjustment and Ethnic Groups; A Bibliography of Unpublished Theses, 1920-1953</u> (1955).

Subsequent supplements include theses and dissertations but consist largely of journal articles.

Includes a substantial number of Canadian and foreign theses and dissertations, arranged by subject. Author index.

T205. "STUDIES in Race and Culture [1959-1965]" <u>Phylon</u> 21 (1960)-26 (1965). Annual. Winter issue.

Includes work done in departments of anthropology, history, sociology, political science, psychology, and related fields in about 30 American institutions. In two sections: (1) "Studies Completed on Race and Culture," and (2) "Doctoral Dissertations on Race and Culture in Progress." Completed list includes both theses and dissertations, in separate lists, and gives previous degrees (institution and date).

T206. GRAYSHON, Matthew C. and V. P. Houghton. <u>Initial Bibliography of Immigration and Race</u>. Nottingham, Gt. Brit.: University of Nottingham, Institute of Education, 1966. 38 p.

Section 6, "Dissertations Abstracts U.S.A." (p. 28-30), lists 22 items for the period 1962-1964. Entry gives reference to <u>Dissertation Abstracts</u>.

T207. INSTITUTE OF RACE RELATIONS, London. <u>Register of Research on Commonwealth Immigration in Britain</u> [1st ed. (May 1966)-] London: 1966- . Annual.

None published in 1971.

Classified listings of research-in-progress, the substantial portion of which is work for advanced degrees. Includes topics such as area studies, community relations, crime, ideologies, housing, miscegenation, sociolinguistics, personality and attitudes, young people. Entry gives duration period and publication information. Author index.

Rural Sociology

T208. ANDERSON, Walfred A. <u>Bibliography of the Department of Rural Sociology, Cornell University</u>. Ithaca, N.Y.: New York (State) Agricultural Experiment Station, 1956. 50 p. (Cornell University. College of Agriculture. Dept. of Rural Sociology. Mimeograph Bulletin, no. 48)

Pt. 2: "Doctor's Dissertations" (p. 32-36); pt. 3: "Masters' Theses and Essays" (p. 36-40). Subject index.

T209. "THESES and Dissertations Completed Since July 1, 1963 [-　]" <u>Rural Sociology</u> 29 (1964)-　. Quarterly.

Appears as a section in the "News Notes..." feature.

American theses and dissertations, listed separately under university.

U. Theology and Religion

General

U1.　WEIGEL, Theodor O., firm, booksellers, Leipzig. Corpus dissertationum theologicarum sive catalogus commentationum, programmatum aliarumque scriptionum academicarum ab antiquissimo usque ad nostrum tempus editarum, ad exegeticam, dogmaticam, moralem ac reliquas disciplinas theologicas spectantium, quae in uberrima collectione Weigeliana Lipsiensi prostant. Praefatus est et indices tum locorum scripturae sacrae, tum rerum ac nominum conscripsit Otto Fiebig. Herdr. van de uitg. Leipzig: 1847. 349 p.

Reprinted 1971.

Lists 14,951 items alphabetically by author, giving institution and date. Indexes to Biblical references and to subjects and names.

U2.　MULLER, Frederik, & Co., Amsterdam. Catalogus dissertationum et orationum theologicarum defensarum et habitarum ab a. 1650 usque ad 1852 in academiis Germaniae, etc. sed praesertim Neerlandiae, quae venales prostaret apud Fredericum Muller, bibliopolam. Amsterdam: 1853. 43 p.

Lists 1,713 titles arranged by size.

Supplemented by:

U3.　_____ Supplementum Catalogi dissertationum et orationum theologicarum defensarum et habitarum ab a. 1600 usque ad 1854 in academiis Neerlandiae, Germaniae, etc. quae venales prostant apud Fredericum Muller, bibliopolam. Amsterdam: 1855. 21 p.

Lists 2,406 titles.

U4.   Catalogus plus quam 2700 dissertationum et orationum theologicarum defensarum et habitarum ab a. 1600 usque ad 1866 in academiis Neerlandiae, Germaniae, Sueciae, etc. quae venales prostant apud Fredericum Muller, bibliopolam. Amsterdam: 1867.   68 p.

An alphabetical author listing.

U5.   Catalogus dissertationum et orationum theologicarum defensarum et habitarum ab a. 1650 ad 1850 in academiis Neerlandiae, Germaniae, Sueciae, collectarum a Fred. Muller, bibliopola Amstelodamensi.   Accedunt duo indices, prior rerum, alter locorum S. Script. curante J. C. Van Slee... Amsterdam: 1868.   673 p.

An alphabetical author listing of 10,375 titles. Subject and place indexes.

U6.   BONET-MAURY, G.   "Catalogue des thèses soutenues dans les facultés de theologie de langue française."   In Encyclopédie des sciences religieuses, vol. 13, p. 235-300.   Paris: Sandoz et Fischenbacher, 1877-1882.

Separate lists of doctorate, licence, and baccalaureate degrees arranged chronologically under name of the university.   Covers the period from 1800 to 1882. Includes French language studies done at the Universities of Strasbourg, Geneva, and Lausanne.

U7.   HEEL, Dalmatius van, Father.   Theologische en philosophische theses, gedurende de 17e en 18e eeuw verdedigd in verschillende kloosters van de Nederduitsche Minderbroedersprovincie. Verzameld met voorrede, bijlagen, zaken- en personenregister. The Hague: R. K. Boek- en Kunsthandel, 1931.   210 p.

Lists approximately 750 dissertations.   Arranged chronologically under monastery.   Entry gives praeses.

U8.   "NEUE Dissertationen."   Theologische Literaturzeitung 68, Nr. 314 (1943/1944): 121-125.

A list of approximately 60 completed dissertations in theology, arranged alphabetically by author under subject headings.   Entry gives date and institution (primarily German, with some Austrian and Swiss institutions).

U9.   "REFERATE über theologische Dissertationen in Maschinen-
      schrift." Theologische Literaturzeitung 74 (1949)-   .
      Irregular.

      Abstracts of three to five recently completed German
      dissertations and Habilitationsschriften appear oc-
      casionally, currently in about six numbers per year.
      All those appearing in one volume are listed alpha-
      betically by author in that volume's index.

U10. AMERICAN THEOLOGICAL LIBRARY ASSOCIATION. A Bibliography of
      Post-Graduate Masters' Theses in Religion. Prepared by the
      Committee on a Master List of Research Studies in Religion.
      Niels H. Sonne, editor. Chicago: Distributed by American
      Library Association, 1951. 82 p.

      A classified listing of 2,682 theses for the degree
      in theology or sacred theology accepted by American
      theological seminaries. Does not include Roman Cath-
      olic or Jewish seminaries. Author index.

U11. COUNCIL ON GRADUATE STUDIES IN RELIGION. Doctoral Disserta-
      tions in the Field of Religion, 1940-1952: Their Titles,
      Location, Fields, and Short Précis of Contents. New York:
      Columbia University for the Council on Graduate Studies in
      Religion in cooperation with the National Council on Reli-
      gion in Higher Education, 1954. 194 p.

      Issued as a supplement to The Review of Religion
      18 (1954).

      An alphabetical author listing of 425 dissertations
      completed in American institutions. (An appendex
      lists approximately 150 additional items for which
      no précis was obtained.) A symbol or symbols are
      used to indicate subject or subjects of the field
      of investigation. Some publication information
      provided. Entry gives major adviser. Classified
      index serves to bring dissertations together by
      broad subjects.

      _____ Supplement [1952-   ] Brown University: n.d.
      Annual.

      Alphabetical author listings of American and Cana-
      dian dissertations. In two parts, (1) completed
      and (2) in progress.

U12. _____ _____ : <u>Dissertations in Progress</u>. N.d. 29 p.

An alphabetical author listing of approximately
350 dissertations. Entry gives adviser.

U13. "DISSERTATION Abstracts [1949-   ]" <u>Church History</u> 23, no.
4 (Dec. 1954)-   . Quarterly.

Each issue includes abstracts of dissertations
completed at American universities. Entry gives
adviser.

U14. "THESES." <u>American Jewish Archives</u> 11 (1959)-   . Annual.

Appears in "Selected Acquisitions."

Lists theses and dissertations added to the Cincinnati campus of the Hebrew University, Jewish Institute of Religion.

U15. LITTLE, Lawrence C. <u>Researches in Personality, Character</u>
<u>and Religious Education; A Bibliography of American Doctoral</u>
<u>Dissertations, 1885-1959</u>. With an index prepared by Helen-
Jean Moore. Pittsburgh: University of Pittsburgh Press,
1962. 215 p.

A first edition was published in 1960.

The 6,304 dissertations represent such fields as
personality development; character education; the
history, philosophy, psychology, and sociology of
religion; Biblical history and literature; and
religious education. Subject index.

U16. _____ <u>Toward Understanding the Church and the Clergy; Con-</u>
<u>tributions of Selected Doctoral Dissertations</u>. Pittsburgh:
University of Pittsburgh, Department of Religious Education,
1963. 218 p.

Attempts "to provide a convenient overview of selected doctoral dissertations dealing with the Church
and the ministry." "Dissertations Reviewed in the
Text": p. 214-218.

U17. SOUTHERN BAPTIST CONVENTION. Historical Commission. <u>Index</u>

of Graduate Theses in Baptist Theological Seminaries, 1894–
1962. Nashville: 1963. 182 p.

Contains 2,323 theses and dissertations completed
in U.S. Baptist theological seminaries, listed by
field of study, institution, and title. Author
and subject indexes.

Individual Institutions

U18.   BONN. Universität. Katholisch-Theologische Fakultät. Verzeichnis der Dissertationen, 1939-1952. Bonn: 1953. 98 p.

A chronological listing. Entry gives brief information about the candidate and the name of the
referent. Publication information is given as well
as abstracts for unpublished studies. Author index.

U19.   CATHOLIC UNIVERSITY OF AMERICA. Dissertations in American
Church History, 1889-1932. Washington: 1933. 27 p. (American Church History Seminar Bulletin, no. 1)

Theses and dissertations completed at Catholic
University of America. Pt. 1, "Doctoral Dissertations," is an alphabetical annotated listing; pt. 2,
"Dissertations in Manuscript," consists of theses
grouped under topics. Entry gives publication
information.

U20.   LOEHR, Gabriel M. Die theologischen Disputationen und Promotionen an der Universität Köln im ausgehenden 15. Jahrhundert. Leipzig: O. Harrassowitz, 1926. 124 p. (Quellen
und Forschungen zur Geschichte des Dominikanerordens in
Deutschland, Heft 21)   ?

U21.   MÜLLER, Wolfgang. Fünfhundert Jahre theologische Promotion
an der Universität Freiburg i. Br. Freiburg im Breisgau:
E. Albert, 1957. 180 p. (Freiburger Wissenschafts- und
Universitätsgeschichte. Beiträge, Heft 19)

Contains a chronological listing of 1,176 dissertations for the period 1470-1957 (p. 55-144).

U22.   "THEOLOGISCHE und philosophische Doktordissertationen der

Universität Freiburg (Schweiz) [1953/54-1962/63]" Freiburger Zeitschrift für Philosophie und Theologie 1 (1954)-10 (1963). Annual. 4th Heft of each vol.

Listed separately under "Theologische Fakultät" and "Philosophische Fakultät," and within those headings under published and unpublished dissertations.

U23. HEYER, Henri. Catalogue des thèses de théologie soutenues à l'Academie de Genève pendant les XVIe, XVIIe et XVIIIe siècles. Genève: Georg, 1898. 167 p. (Documents pour servir à l'histoire de l'Academie de Genève, vol. 5)

A chronological listing of 476 dissertations. Author and subject index.

Continued by:

U24. BOUVIER, Auguste. La Faculté de théologie de Genève pendant le dix-neuvième siècle. Thèses, concours, étudiants. Genève: Ramboz et Schuchardt, 1878. 95 p. (Documents pour servir à l'histoire de l'Academie de Genève, vol. 1)

Includes a chronological listing of 280 theses submitted to the Companie de pasteurs and the Faculté de theologie. Author and subject index.

U25. GAMBERT, Auguste. Recueil de la Faculté de théologie protestante de l'Université de Genève. I: Catalogue des thèses présentées à la Faculté de théologie de 1921 à 1930. Genève: Georg, 1931. 30 p.

A chronological listing of 38 studies for the baccalauréat, licence, and doctorat. Entry includes table of contents.

U26. "SUMMARIES of Doctoral Dissertations in Religion Accepted at Harvard [1960-   ]" Harvard Theological Review 54 (1961)-   . Usually Oct. issue.

Includes dissertations completed for the Th.D. awarded in the Divinity School and for the Ph.D. awarded under the Committee on Higher Degrees in the Study of Religion.

U27. "THÈSES de doctorat et mémoires de licence soutenus devant la Faculté de theologie de Lille [1954-1958/1959]" Mélanges de science religieuse 11 (1954)-16 (1959).

No list in vol. 13 (1956).

Abstracts. Entry gives adviser.

U28. LOUVAIN. Université catholique. Faculté de théologie. Le Cinquième centenaire de la Faculté de théologie de l'Université de Louvain (1432-1932). Bruges: Beyaert, 1932. 208 p.

"Liste des dissertations écrites pour l'obtention du grade de docteur (maître) en théologie": p. 193-196.

U29. MÜNSTER. Universität. Katholisch-Theologische Fakultät. Dissertationen in den Jahren [1940/1956-] Münster, Westfalen: Westfälische Vereinsdruckerei, 1956- .

First number covers 1940-1956.

A classified listing which carries abstracts of un-published dissertations. Entry gives adviser.

U30. CARRIÈRE, Gaston. "Thèses préparées aux facultés ecclésias-tiques de l'Université d'Ottawa." Revue de l'Université d'Ottawa 33 (1963): 211-234.

Theses and dissertations completed in the Faculties of Theology, Canon Law, and Philosophy from 1936 to 1961. Arranged by institute under each faculty and subdivided into work for the doctorate and for the master's degree. Entry refers to an abstract.

U31. PRINCETON THEOLOGICAL SEMINARY. Catalogue of Doctoral Dis-sertations, 1944-1960. Princeton, N.J.: 1962. 119 p.

A chronological listing of abstracts of over 100 dissertations for the Th.D. degree. Entry includes brief biographical data for the recipient and refer-ences to the author's other publications. Author and subject indexes.

U32. GAGNÉ, Armand. Répertoire des thèses de facultés ecclésias-

tiques de l'Université Laval, 1935-1960. Québec: 1960.
19 p. (His Études et recherches bibliographiques, no. 2)

Lists 129 dissertations for the doctorate arranged
as follows: (1) théologie, (2) droit canonique, and
(3) philosophie. Entry gives publication information. Author and subject index.

U33. ROME (City). Pontificia Università gregoriana. Facoltà di
storia ecclesiastica. "Elenchus dissertationum ad lauream
quae in Facultate Historiae Ecclesiasticae Pontificiae
Universitatis Gregorianae ad defensionem exhibitae sunt ab
anno 1934 usque ad annum 1958." In its Saggi storici intor-
no al papato, dei professori della Facoltà di storia ecclesiastica, p. 465-480. Roma: Pontificia Università gregoriana,
1959. (Its Miscellanea historiae pontificiae, vol. 21)

Lists 192 dissertations under the periods ancient,
medieval, recent (1400-1750), and modern history.
Entry gives publication information.

U34. ROME (City). Pontificia Università gregoriana. Secretaria.
Elenchus dissertationum ad lauream quae in Facultate Iuris
Canonici publice defensae sunt ab anno 1934 ad annum 1965.
Roma: 1965-1966. 102 p.

Lists approximately 800 dissertations. Entry gives
moderator and publication information.

U35. LOIDL, Franz. Die Dissertationen der Katholisch-Theologisch-
en Fakultät der Universität Wien. 1831-1965. Wien: Herder,
1969. 106 p. (Wiener Beitrage zur Theologie, 25)

An alphabetical author listing of accepted dissertations.

U36. NOSOWSKI, Jerzy. Skład osobowy i działalność naukowa Wydziału Teologicznego w okresie od 1. 11. 1954 do 30. 9.
1968 r. Warszawa: Akademia Teologii Katolickiej, 1969.
454 p.

Contains separate lists of the abstracts of 184
dissertations (p. 97-166) and of theses (p. 167-
436). Entry gives adviser. Classified subject
index of theses and dissertations. Author index.

Denominations

Church of the Brethren

U37. SAPPINGTON, Roger E. "Bibliography of Theses on the Church of the Brethren." Brethren Life and Thought 3 (Winter 1958): 60-70.

Also appeared as a separate.

A tentative author list of pre-doctoral theses and of dissertations written in American universities and seminaries.

Disciples of Christ

U38. DOWLING, Alfred and E. E. De Grost. Literature of the Disciples of Christ. Advance, Ind.: Hustler Print., 1933.

"Unpublished Theses Concerning the Disciples of Christ" (p. 64-68) represents an alphabetical author listing of approximately 100 bachelors' and masters' theses and dissertations completed in U.S. institutions.

U39. SPENCER, Claude E. Theses Concerning the Disciples of Christ and Related Religious Groups. Nashville, Tenn.: Disciples of Christ Historical Society, 1964. 94 p.

Supersedes the Disciples of Christ Historical Society, Theses Concerning the Disciples of Christ, edited by Claude E. Spencer (1941), and continued in Discipliana and Harbinger and Discipliana 7 (1948)-13 (1954).

An alphabetical author listing of 743 theses and dissertations, representing work done at 89 American institutions. Subject and institutional indexes.

Friends

U40. "QUAKER Research in Progress or Unpublished [1938-   ]" Quaker History 27 (1938)-   . Irregular, usually semi-annually.

Theses and dissertations were also included in "Notes and Queries" in vols. 17 (1928)-26 (1937).

Theses and dissertations, completed or in progress, make up a substantial part. Primarily American but some non-American studies. Entry gives institution and department, degree, date granted or state of research, and annotation.

U41. TOLLES, Frederick B. and Anna B. Hewitt. "Doctoral Dissertations on Quaker History Available at Swarthmore and Haverford." Friends Historical Association Bulletin 47 (1958): 45-48.

An alphabetical author listing, giving location and form in which available, institution, and date of completion.

Mennonites

U42. "MENNONITE Research in Progress." Mennonite Life 4 (1949)- . Annual. Usually April no.

Vols. 4-14 contain short narrative notes on American theses and dissertations in progress. Beginning with vol. 15, there are separate listings of theses and dissertations completed or in progress. Some studies from countries other than the United States are listed.

Continues:

U43. KRAHN, Cornelius. "Anabaptism--Mennonitism in Doctoral Dissertations." Mennonite Life 13 (1958): 83-87.

A classified bibliography of 76 dissertations completed or in progress, covering the period from about 1940. Includes some studies from institutions outside the United States. Entries give publication information.

Mormons

U44. BRIGHAM YOUNG UNIVERSITY, Provo, Utah. A Catalogue of Theses and Dissertations Concerning the Church of Jesus Christ of Latter-Day Saints, Mormonism and Utah. Provo, Utah: Brigham Young University Press, 1971. 742 p.

Compiled by the Brigham Young University College of Religious Instruction.

A classified listing of approximately 1,900 studies completed in the United States through 1969. Materials are grouped under the headings doctrine, religious education, religious history (modern), religious history (ancient), scripture, and social science-related research. List of authors and titles. Index.

Presbyterians

U45.   GILLETTE, Gerald W. "A Checklist of Doctoral Dissertations on American Presbyterian and Reformed Subjects." Journal of Presbyterian History 45 (1967): 203-221.

Lists approximately 320 dissertations under broad chronological periods, with separate lists under Jonathan Edwards, Reinhold Niebuhr, and Paul Tillich.

Special Subjects

Atheism

U46.   KONOVALOVIA, V. I. Dissertatsionnye raboty po nauchnomu ateizmu, zashchishchennye v 1964-1970 godakh. Moskva: 1972. 83 p. ?

Bible

U47.   LINDESKOG, Gösta. Svenska exegetiska disputationer under 1800-talet. Uppsala: A. B. Lundequistka, 1941. 43 p.

Also appeared as Uppsala. Universitet. Årsskrift, 1941: 7, 17.

A chronological listing of Swedish dissertations.

U48. BUSS, Martin J. <u>Old Testament Dissertations, 1928-1958</u>.
Ann Arbor, Mich.: University Microfilms, 1958. 57 p.

> Dissertations having a bearing on the Old Testament
> or on the intertestamental period, including a number
> of Near Eastern studies judged to be of interest to
> Old Testament specialists. Pt. 1: North American
> dissertations; pt. 2: dissertations written in the
> British Isles; pt. 3: other dissertations. Entries
> include reference to source of citation for addi-
> tional information.

Church and State

U49. LA NOUE, George R. <u>A Bibliography of Doctoral Dissertations
Undertaken in American and Canadian Universities, 1940-1962,
on Religion and Politics</u>. New York: National Council of the
Churches of Christ in the United States of America, 1963.
49 p.

> A classified and geographical list of 649 American
> and Canadian dissertations which contribute infor-
> mation to public policy problems in church-state
> relations. International in concern.

U50. "RECENT Doctoral Dissertations in Church and State." <u>Journal
of Church and State</u> 7 (1965)-   . Three times per year.

> Alphabetical author listings of dissertations com-
> pleted at American institutions.

Ecumenical Movement

U51. LANDIS, Benson Y. <u>Doctoral Dissertations Relevant to Ecu-
menics</u>. New York: World Council of Churches, 1965. 11 p.

> An alphabetical author listing of approximately
> 150 dissertations completed in American institutions
> since 1940. Does not include studies on missions or
> religious education. Entry gives publication infor-
> mation.

Missions

U52. PERSON, Laura. <u>Cumulative List of Doctoral Dissertations</u>
<u>and Masters' Theses in Foreign Missions and Related Subjects</u>
<u>as Reported by the Missionary Research Library in the Occa-</u>
<u>sional Bulletin 1950 to 1960</u>. New York: Missionary Research
Library, 1961. 46 p.

Two separate annotated lists of theses and dissertations (482 in all) in the fields of religion,
missionary activity, and related subjects. A few
dissertations considered to be of interest from years
prior to 1950 are included. Does not include studies
in religious education. Alphabetical by author.
Institutional and subject indexes.

Continued by:

U53. "GRADUATE Theses: Missions and Related Fields." <u>In</u> Missionary Research Library. <u>Occasional Bulletin</u> 1 (1950)-   .
Title varies. Annual. Usually Dec. issue.

Separate listings of theses and dissertations. Includes some items from institutions outside the
United States. Subject index.

Sociology of Religion

U54. "THÈSES et mémoires présentés en France touchant à la sociologie et la psychologie des religions." <u>Archives de socio-</u>
<u>logie des religions</u> 1 (1956): 159-171; 4 (1957): 158-162;
6 (1958): 149-152; 9 (1960): 155-157; 13 (1962): 139-142;
9 (1964): 153-164; 12 (1967): 149-170; 15 (1970): 123-146;
17 (1972): 175-198. Title varies. Irregular.

First list, by Émile Poulat, has title "Thèses et
mémoires présentés en France de 1940 à 1954 et
touchant à la sociologie des religions," and includes
a lengthy introduction with an analysis of the studies.

Lists theses and dissertations arranged alphabetically by author in three parts: (1) dissertations completed in state institutions, (2) dissertations completed in religious institutions, and (3) theses
completed in state institutions. Entry gives publication information.

Supplement

DD1. LIN, Che-Hwei. <u>A Preliminary Checklist of M.A. Theses and Ph.D. Dissertations Related to Asian American Studies in the UCLA Library</u>. Los Angeles: 1972. 29 p.

  Supplement (4 p.) at end: "Newly Acquired M.A. and Ph.D. Theses as of Dec. 30, 1972."

  Prepared in the University of California at Los Angeles University Research Library Bibliographers' Group.

  An alphabetical author listing of approximately 350 theses and dissertations completed in American universities.

EE1. TAYLOR, Donald W. <u>Abstracts of Selected Theses on Soil Mechanics</u>. Cambridge, Mass: 1941. 41 p. (Massachusetts Institute of Technology. Dept. of Civil and Sanitary Engineering. Publication Serial 79)

  Abstracts of nine theses completed at the Massachusetts Institute of Technology.

FF1. BAMBERGER, Stefan. <u>Studenten und Film; Eine Untersuchung an den schweizerischen Universitäten und Hochschulen</u>. Hrsg. von der Redaktion des "Filmberater," Zurich. Olten: O. Walter, 1958. 135 p.

  "Liste der an schweizerischen Hochschulen bis zum Jahre 1957 abgegebenan Dissertationen über Filmfragen" (p. 121-123) represents 18 dissertations completed since 1933, arranged chronologically.

HH1. POUND, Gomer. A Bibliography of Research in the Fine Arts Completed at Mississippi Colleges and Universities. Hatties-burg, Miss.: University of Southern Mississippi, 1965. 9 p.

Addendum (1 p.) laid in.

Lists theses completed up to 1965. Arranged under (1) art, (2) music, (3) theatre.

LL1. BRODEUR, Léo A. and Antoine Naaman. Répertoire des thèses littéraires canadiennes (janvier 1969-september 1971); Index of Canadian Literary Theses... Sherbrooke, Quebec: Centre d'étude des littératures d'expression française, 1972. 141 p. (Cahiers francophones, 2)

Continues Item L117.

A classified listing of 1,786 theses and disserta-tions on literary subjects defended or registered in Canadian universities. Works in progress are iden-tified as such.

MM1. "DISSERTATSIY po yuridicheskim naukam, zashchishchennye v 1945-1952 gg." Sovetskoe gosudarstvo i pravo, 1953, no. 7: 156-157, no. 8: 122-126; 1954, no. 1: 164-171.

Separate lists of 46 dissertations and approximately 500 theses completed in the U.S.S.R. Arranged under such subjects as the theory of the state and law, history of the state and law, state law, and admin-istrative law.

PP1. "DISSERTATSIY zashchishchennye sotrudnikami Instituta fiziologii im I. P. Pavlova AN SSSR za period [Dekabr' 1950-Dekabr' 1957]" In Akademiya nauk SSSR. Institut fiziologii im I. P. Pavlova. Vklyuchitel'no trudy 2 (1953)-9 (1959). Irregular.

Separate lists of 38 dissertations and 166 theses defended at the Institute. The items are numbered consecutively.

SS1. DARGENT, J. L. Bibliographie des thèses et mémoires geogra-phiques belges. Supplement, 1959-1965. Bruxelles: Commis-sion belge de bibliographie, 1966. 64 p. (Bibliographia belgica, 92)

Lists 188 theses for the Licence and doctorate arranged by institution, including some not included
in second edition (Item S76). Entry indicates type
of degree and publication information. Index.

UU1. SCHULENBERG, W. Dissertations Submitted to the Faculties of
Dutch Universities, 1946-1960; A Supplement to...The Present
Position of Dutch Theology, by W. C. van Unnik. Richmond,
Va.: 1961. 17 p.

Issued as a supplement to the Union Theological
Seminary in Virginia Second Annual Bibliographical
Lecture.

A chronological listing of approximately 140
dissertations.

Index of Institutions

A

Aachen. Technische Hochschule
E69

Aberdeen University P16

Aix-en-Provence. Université
J72

Akademiya nauk Azerbaydzhanskoy
SSR, Baku P61

Akademiya nauk SSSR.
Gel'mintologicheskaya labora-
toriya S46
Institut etnografii T44
Institut fiziologii im I. P.
Pavlova PP1
Institut geologii i razrabot-
ki goriuchikh iskopaemyk
E101
Institut mirovoy ekonomiki i
mezhdunarodnykh otnosheniy
T96
Institut vostokovedeniya C11
Matematicheskii institut S125

Akademiya nauk URSR, Kiev.
Instytut ekonomiky T97
Instytut mekhaniky E112

Alberta. University C65
Faculty of Education G70

Algiers. Université B1

Alma-Atinskiy meditsinskiy
institut P62, P63

Antwerp. Institut universitaire
de territoires d'outre-mer C12

Astrakhanskiy gosudarstvennyy
meditsinskiy institut P64

Azerbaydzhanskiy meditsinskiy
institut P65

B

Banaras Hindu University G71,
S50

Basel. Universität H16, P67

Belfast. Queen's University
C138

Berlin. Freie Universität.
Theaterwissenschaftliche Institut H78

Berlin. Universität L55
Medizinische Fakultät P68

Bern. Universität. Medizinische
Fakultät P69

Bonn. Universität.
Katholisch-Theologische Fakul-
tät U18
Mathematisch-Naturwissenschaft-
liche Fakultät S25
Medizinische Fakultät P70
Rechts- und Staatswissenschaft-
liche Fakultät M22

Index of Institutions

Bordeaux. Université. Faculté de médecine et de pharmacie P71

Boston College. School of Social Work T177

Boston University G336, G337
Graduate School of Education G259

British Columbia. University E129
School of Social Work T178

Brünn. Vysoka škola zemědělská a lesnická. Fakulta veterinární P151

Budapest. Magyar Közgazdaságtudományi Egyetem. Központi Könyvtár T13

Buenos Aires. Universidad Nacional.
Facultad de Ciencias Económicas T80-T82
Facultad de Ciencias Exactas, Fisicas y Naturales S26
Facultad de Ciencias Médicas P72

C

Cairo. Jāmi'at al-Qāhirah. Kullīyat al'Ulūm S27

Cairo. Jāmi'at 'Ayn Shams. Kullīyat al-Tarbiyah G72

California. University C30, C89, G73, G74, G76, T46
College of Engineering E70
College of Engineering. Division of Mechanical Engineering E111
School of Education G75, G77
University at Los Angeles. School of Engineering and Applied Science E71

Cambridge University. Faculty of History J24

Catholic University of America G78, N28, T197, U19
Dept. of Education G79
School of Nursing P130

Chapingo, Mexico. Escuela Nacional de Agricultura E17

Cheng chih ta hsüeh, Mu-cha, Formosa. She hui k'o hsüeh tzu liao chung hsin J47

Chicago. University C73, F1, F2, G345, N7, S28
Dept. of Education G81, G82
Graduate Library School N29
School of Social Service Administration T179

Chile. Universidad, Santiago.
Escuela de Ingeniería Forestal E130
Facultad de Ciencias Juridicas y Sociales T19

Cincinnati. University. Teachers College G83

Clark University, Worcester, Mass. R15, S73

Clermont-Ferrand, France. Université. Faculté mixte de médecine et de pharmacie P73

College royal de chirurgie, Lyons P96

Colombia. Universidad, Bogotá.
Facultad de Agronomía, Medellín E19, E20
Facultad de Agronomía del Valle, Palmira E21
Facultad de Agronomía e Instituto Forestal E45
Facultad de Medicina P51, P74

Colorado. Northern Colorado
University SEE Northern
Colorado University

Colorado. State University,
Fort Collins. Dept. of Civil
Engineering E72

Columbia University C71, F23,
L102, S107, S141
Dept. of English and Compara-
tive Literature L8
Dept. of Industrial Engineer-
ing and Management Educa-
tion E110
Dept. of Zoology S138
Faculty of Political Science
T20
Russian Institute C111
School of Library Service N30
Teachers College G85-G89,
G176

Concepción, Chile. Universidad.
Escuela de Agronomía E47

Copenhagen. Universitet B22,
B23

Córdoba, Argentine Republic.
Universidad Nacional. Facultad de Odontológia P124

Cornell University J104
College of Agriculture. Dept.
of Rural Sociology T208

Costa Rica. Universidad Nacional, San José B20
Facultad de Agronomía E22

D

Dayton, Ohio. University.
School of Education G90

Delft. Technische Hoogeschool
E73

Denver. University G91

Dijon. Université T86

Dnepropetrovskiy meditsinskiy
institut P76

Donets'kyy derzhavnyy medychnyy
instytut P75

Dorpat. Universitet. Medicin-
ische Fakultät P77

Dublin. University College G92

E

East Africa, University of A27

École du Louvre, Paris H23, H24,
H26, H27

École des chartes, Paris H22,
J33, M23

Edinburgh. University P78, P79

F

Fisk University, Nashville G181

Florida. State University, Tallahassee G95
Library School N31

Florida. University, Gaines-
ville.
College of Education G96
School of Forestry E131

Frankfurt am Main. Universität.
Medizinische Fakultät P80
Wirtschafts- und Sozialwissen-
schaftliche Fakultät T21

Franklin and Marshall College
D26

Freiburg. Universität U21
Medizinische Fakultät P81

Freiburg (Schweiz). Universität
U22

Index of Institutions

G

Geneva. Université U23
  Faculté de droit M24, M25
  Faculté de théologie U24
  Faculté de théologie protestante U25

George Peabody College for Teachers, Nashville G93, G94, G398

George Washington University G242

Georgia. University. College of Education G391

Gettysburg, Pa. Theological Seminary of the United Lutheran Church in America D25

Giessen. Universität.
  Institut für Landswirtschaftliche Betriebslehre. Abteilung für Wirtschaftsberatung E33
  Juristische Fakultät M26

Glasgow. University S29

Göttingen. Universität. Mathematisch-Naturwissenschaftliche Fakultät S30

Gor'kovskiy gosudarstvennyy meditsinskiy institut P82

Graz. Universität J63

Griefswald. Universität. Medizinische Fakultät P83

Guatemala (City). Universidad de San Carlos.
  Escuela de Biblioteconomía B43
  Facultad de Ciencias Jurídicas y Sociales M27
  Facultad de Humanidadaes B44

H

Haifa. Technion. Israel Institute of Technology E74

Halle. Universität M28

Hanover. Technische Universität E75

Harvard University C85, L53, L54, L94, L100, U26
  Dept. of Classics L54

Hebrew University, Jerusalem.
  Faculty of Agriculture E28
  Hadassah School of Medicine P86

Heidelberg. Universität. Medizinische Fakultät P84

Houston. University.
  College of Education G97
  Dept. of Psychology G97

Howard University C31

I

Idaho. University. College of Mines E117

Illinois. Northern Illinois University, DeKalb G303
  College of Education G98

Illinois. University G270, T122
  College of Education G99
  College of Engineering E76
  College of Physical Education G271
  Dept. of Geology S108

Imperial College of Tropical Agriculture (Trinidad and Tobago) E24, E54

Indian Institute of Science, Bangalore S31

New School for Social Research, New York. Graduate Faculty of Political and Social Sciences T24

New York. City College. School of Education G124

New York State College of Forestry, Syracuse University E137, E138

New York University.
Dept. of Business Education G228
Institute of Fine Arts H18-H21
School of Education G125, G126, G229

Newark, N.J. College of Engineering E82

North Carolina. State University, Raleigh E59

North Carolina. University.
Dept. of Physics S132
Institute of Statistics S126
School of Library Science N35

North Dakota. University.
College of Education N37

Northern Colorado University G84

Northwestern University.
Dental School, Chicago P127
School of Education G127
School of Music H43
Technological Institute E83

Notre Dame University. Dept. of Education G128

O

Oberlin College E95, E96

Ohio. State University, Columbus D23, G129, J31, S47
Dept. of German L69

Ohio. State University, Kent.
School of Library Science N38

Oklahoma. State University, Stillwater G130, G239
College of Engineering E84

Oklahoma. University C56, G131, G132

Oslo. University R3

Ottawa. Université J32, U30

P

Panama (City). Universidad B65, D49

Paris. École de médecine P107, P108

Paris. École des chartes SEE École des chartes, Paris

Paris. École du Louvre SEE École du Louvre, Paris

Paris. Université H91, J35, L111, T45
École de pharmacie P141-P143
Faculté de droit et des sciences économiques M30, T127
Faculté de droit et des sciences économiques. Centre de documentation africaine C8
Faculté de lettres et sciences humaines L9, L56
Faculté des sciences S37

Pennsylvania. State University.
College of Engineering E85
School of Education G133

Index of Institutions

Santo Domingo. Universidad
B25, B26, P144

São Paulo, Brazil (City).
Universidade.
Escola Superior de Agricultura
"Luiz Quieroz," Piracicaba
E35
Faculdade de Odontologia P128

Saratovskiy meditsinskiy institut P112

Semmelweis Orvostudományi
Egyetem P145

Sheffield. University C68

Singapore. University J34

Sopot, Poland. Wyższa Szkoła
Ekonomiczna T89

South Carolina. University C60

South Dakota. University.
College of Education G143

Springfield College, Springfield, Mass. G264

Stanford University S39
School of Mineral Sciences
E119

Stockholm. Tekniska högskolan
E88
Universitet. Wenner-Grens
institut för experimentell
biologi, fisiologisk kemi
och ämnesomattningsforsk-
ning S40

Strasbourg. Université.
Faculté de médecine P113,
P114
Faculté des lettres L107-L109

Stuttgart. Technische Hochschule E89

Sydney. University. Dept. of
Architectural Science E97

Syracuse University C76

Szeged, Hungary. Orvostudományi
Egyetem P146

T

Tartu. Ülikool.
Raamatukogu B95
Teaduslik Raamatukogu P115

Temple University, Philadelphia.
Teachers College G136, G137

Texas. University C148, G144,
J36, J111
College of Education G145
Dept. of Geology S111
Dept. of History J110

Texas A & M University, College
Station. Dept. of Agricul-
tural Economics and Sociology
E44

Toronto. Queens University
G146

Toronto. University.
School of Social Work T188
Ontario College of Education
G146

Toruń, Poland. Universytet.
Wydział Biologi i Nauk o
Ziemi S48

Toulouse. Université M31

Tübingen. Universität. Medizinische Fakultät P116

Tufts University. Fletcher
School of Law and Diplomacy
T128

Tulane University C53

Index of Names and Titles

A

Index of Names and Titles

Index of Names and Titles

Chalaupka, Christl H76

Chalifoux, Jean-Pierre N34

Chambers, J. Richard G337

Chapingo, México. Escuela Nacional de Agricultura E18
Biblioteca Central E17

Chapman, T. E24

Charles, Dorothy N29

Chatham, James R. L126

Chavernac, P. P131

Chavis, John J96

Cheek, Emory E60

Chemical and Engineering News S57

Chemical Engineering Progress E99

Chemické listy S64

Chemie-Ingenieur Technik E100

Chemistry in Canada S56

Cheng chih ta hsüeh, Mu-cha, Formosa. She hui k'o hsüeh tzu liao chung hsin J47

Chevalley, Sylvie H77

Cheydleur, Raymond D. F27

Chicago. University S28
Center for Urban Studies T165
Committee on Communication F1, F2
Dept. of Education G81, G82
Far Eastern Library C73
Graduate Library School N29
School of Social Service Administration T179

Childers, Barbara S. S120

Chile. Universidad, Santiago.
Escuela de Ingeniería Forestal E130
Facultad de Ciencias Jurídicas y Sociales. Anales M16, T1, T19
Instituto de Geografía. Informaciones geográficas S95

Chimia S61

China Institute in America. Bulletin D36

China Quarterly C95

Chinese Culture D39

Chinese Culture Quarterly D40

Chiswick, Jeanne H. C64

Chronic, Byron J. S97, S98

Chronic, Halka S97, S98

Chung yang t'u shu kuan, T'ai-pei B29

Church History U13

Ciencias politicas en Puerto Rico T143

Cincinnati. University. Teachers College G83

Civil War History J40

Clark, Charles T. T57

Clark University, Worcester, Mass. Library R15

Clarke, George T. T42

Clements, H. M. G121

Index of Names and Titles

Index of Names and Titles

Fizika v shkole G368

Flasche, Hans L106, Q5

Fleischhack, Curt E5

Flemion, Philip F. C142

Flint, Richard W. P161

Florén Lozano, Luis B25, P144

Florentino, Alberto S. L91

Flores, Raúl H. B72

Florida.
  State University, Tallahassee.
    Library School N31
  University, Gainesville C141
    College of Education G96
    School of Forestry E131
    School of Inter-American
      Studies C142

Fock, Gustav, firm, booksellers,
  Leipzig B37, C110, L51

Focus on Dance H30

Foerster, Norman L32

Folk Dance Guide H32

Fondation nationale des sciences
  politiques, Paris T144

Fontaine de Resbecq, Adolphe
  C. T. M3

Forest Science E125

Forestry Chronicle E127

Forschung und Beratung E4

Forschungsgesellschaft für
  Agrarpolitik und Agrarsoziologie E6, E7, E10

Forstarchiv E126

Fort Hays Kansas State College.
  Language and Literature
  Series L20

Foster, Richard A. G318

Foy, Bernard L. T153

Fränkel, Gottlob H. F. P8

France. Direction des bibliothèques de France B31

Franke, Lydia G65

Frankfurt am Main. Universität.
  Medizinische Fakultät P80
  Wirtschafts- und Sozialwis-
  senschaftliche Fakultät
  T21

Frantsuzskiy ezhegodnik J69

Franzmeyer, Fritz F14-F18

Frarey, Carlyle J. N12

Fraser, J. Keith S90

Freeman, Max H. G237

Freiburger Zeitschrift für Philosophie und Theologie U22

French Review L114

Frickl, Jobst P. H45

Friends Historical Association
  Bulletin U41

Fronius, Stefan E108

Frost, S. E., Jr. G12

Fürer-Haimendorf, Elizabeth
  von T50

Fuguitt, Glenn V. T203

Furbay, Walter M. T121

G

Gaffney, Theresa W. G258

Gagné, Armand U32

Gallaudet College, Washington,
D.C. Library P158, P160

Gambert, Auguste U25

Gammeltoft, S. A. R2

Gammerman, A. F. S49

Gardner, Murray F. E102

Garlick, Peter C. C31

Garmon, Gerald M. L153, L154

Garnier, Gabriel P142

Garszczyńska, Bożena S48

Gasparyan, Aschot M. P117

Gauri, K. B. E13

Gautam, Brijendra P. T146

Gazette des beaux arts A17,
H11, H18, H22, H26, H27

Gentzsch, Gerhard E114

Geographischer Jahresbericht
aus Österreich S71, S72

Geological Society of America.
Special Paper S101

George Peabody College for
Teachers, Nashville G13, G93,
G94, G398

Geoscience Abstracts S99

Geoscience Information Society
S101

Gerig, John L. L99-L102

Germain, Alexandre C. P102

Germany.
Postministerium. Archiv für
Post und Telegraphie T151
Reichsforschungsstelle Land-
wirtschaftliches Market-
wesen E1

Gero, John S. E97

Gesamtverzeichnis österreichischer Dissertationen B4, D5

Getchell, Charles M. L140

Ghana. University. Balmi
Library C36

Ghana Library Board B42

Giefer, Gerald J. S136

Giessen. Universität.
Institut für Landwertschaft-
liche Betriebslehre E23
Juristische Fakultät M26

Gifted Child Quarterly G261

Gil, David G. T172

Gillette, Gerald W. U45

Gillis, Frank H56

Ginn, R. M. S113

Glasgow. University S29

Gloss, G. M. G284

Glozman, O. S. P89

Index of Names and Titles

H

Hackett, Roger C. G298

Hahn, A. P108

Haifa. Technion, Israel. Institute of Technology E74

Halbrecht, Miriam B. T162

Hall, James H. G249

Hall, John C68

Hamer, Clifford E. H92

Hamilton, Thomas T., Jr. G99

Hampel, Margaret G318

Han'guk Yŏn'gu Tosŏgwan, Seoul B77

Hankin, Robert G382

Hanover. Technische Universität E75

Hanusch, Gerhard C102

Harbinger and Discipliana U39

Harding, Walter R. L161

Harris, Michael H. N21

Harrison, Robert W. T155

Hart, Donn V. C76

Hartley, Kenneth R. H57

Hartman, Howard L. E116

Harvard Studies in Classical Philology L53, L54

Harvard Theological Review U26

Harvard University. East Asian Studies at Harvard University C85

Harvey, C. C. G373

Hassinger, Herbert C126

Hassinger, Hugo C126

Hatto, Arthur T. L12

Hayashi, Teksumaro L160

Hayes Memorial Library C45

Haynes, Benjamin R. G232

Headlee, William H. P87

Heckman, Lee Ann G54

Hedrick, Basil C. C142

Heel, Dalmatius van U7

Heffter, Johann K. P1

Heidelberg. Universität. Medizinische Fakultät P84

Henley, Elton F. L165

Henrion, Roger M40

Hergenroeder, Stanley G302

Hernández de Caldas, Angela E19

Herrera, Carmen D. de B65

Herrera, E. E24, E54

Herrfahrdt, Heinrich T9

Herrick, Mary D. C14

Hewes, Leslie S69

Jerusalem. Hebrew University.
Faculty of Agriculture E28
Hadassah School of Medicine
P86

Jewish Education G187-G190

Jewish Journal of Sociology
G190

Jinnah Postgraduate Medical
Center. Basic Medical Sciences Division P88

Joblin, Elgie E. M. D1

Johnson, Albert E. H71

Johnson, Arlien T184

Johnson, Harvey L. L122

Johnson, J. W. E111

Johnson, Melvin E. G405

Johnson, Wendell P166

Johnston, George P. P79

Jonas, Frank H. T141

Jonas, Klaus W. L150

Jones, John A. D2

Jones, Lawrence J. L41

Joos, Elisabeth G68

Jordan, Dale G236

Josephson, Aksel G. S. A11

Journal for Research in Mathematics Education G367

Journal for Social Research SEE
Tydskrif vir Maatskaplike
Navorsing

Journal of Agricultural Economics SEE American Journal of
Agricultural Economics

Journal of American Studies C50

Journal of Asian Studies C84

Journal of Broadcasting F29,
F31-F34

Journal of Business T67

Journal of Business Education
G229-G231

Journal of Canadian Fiction
L46, L118

Journal of Chemical Education
S53

Journal of Church and State U50

Journal of Creative Behavior
G262

Journal of College Student
Personnel G254

Journal of Communication L146,
P163

Journal of Developmental Reading SEE Journal of Reading

Journal of Economic History
T103

Journal of Education G336, G337

Journal of Education for Librarianship N22

Journal of Educational Data
Processing E107

Journal of Educational Psychology R13

K

Kansas.
  State University of Agriculture
    and Applied Science E52
  Engineering Experiment
    Station E79
  University G105
    Bulletin of Education G105
    School of Education G106

Kansas Association of Teachers
  of History and Related Fields
  J92

Kansas Teacher G14

Kantor, Harry C141

Kappert, Petra C10

Karmeniemi, Kaija B28

Karrow, Paul F. S112

Karynbaev, Sibagatulla R. P63

Kaul, Jagan N. T7

Kazanskiy gosudarstvennyy meditsinskiy institut. Trudy
  P90

Kędziorkowa, Felicja T118

Kelly, L. A. T61

Kentucky. University. College
  of Education G107, G108

Kentucky Foreign Language
  Quarterly L162

Kentucky Historical Society
  Register B106

Kentucky Library Association.
  College and Reference Section
  B106

Kerr, M. M. P161

Kharkov. Universytet. Matematychnyi viddi. Zapiski S127

Khimiya v shkole G361

Khirurgiia P59

Kholdzhuraev, Khabibullo K. J86

Kholodil'naya tekhnika i tekh-
  nologiya E121, E122

Khorunov, R. KH. G365

Kidder, Frederick E. C142-C144,
  C155, J108, T143

Kidery, Marianne H9

Kiel. Universität. Medizinische Fakultät P91

Kieslich, Günter F24

Kim, Yung-Min C163

Kincheloe, H. Karen G184

Kindermann, Heinz H81

King, James H. G384

Kinzl, Hans S82

Kirby, Harold G236

Kirkby, Edward A. S115

Kirsch, Guido D16, D17

Kishinevskiy gosudarstvennyy
  meditsinskiy institut P92

Klain, J. M. H72

Klement, Alfred von H38

Klinck, Carl F. L44, L46

Klingenhagen, Barbara T131

Index of Names and Titles

Lester, Robert M. B103

<u>Letzeburger Land</u> S24

Leutenegger, Ralph R. P165, P166

Leuthold, David A. T147

Levene, J. R. P133

Ley, Ralph L75

<u>Leyte-Samar Studies</u> G63

Li, Tze-Chung D38

Lian The C88

<u>Library Literature</u> N3

<u>Library Quarterly</u> N1, N4, N30

Liddell, Duncan P16

Lidén, Johan H. A2

Liège. Université. Bibliothèque A25

Lietuvos TSR Mokslų akademija, Vilna. Centrinė biblioteka P32

Lieutaud, Victor D31

Lima. Universidad de San Marcos.
  Facultad de Derecho y Ciencias Políticas M29
  Facultad de Medicina Veterinaria P148

<u>Limba Romînă</u> L96

Lin, Che-Hwei DD1

Linder, Kerstin H46

Linders, John E88

Lindeskog, Gösta U47

Lindsay, Kenneth C. H10

Lingenfelter, Mary R. G311

Linguistic Society of America.
  <u>Bulletin</u> L88

<u>Linguistica Antverpiensia</u> L89

<u>Linguistics</u> L85

<u>Literatura v shkole</u> L134

<u>Litopys knyh</u> B98

Little Lawrence C. G209, G352, U15, L16

Litto, Frederic M. H80

Litton, Maurice L. G299

Litvinova, E. V. P33

<u>Livres et auteurs quebeçois</u> L116

Loague, Nehume G211, G212

Lockhart, A. H29

Lodhi, Qaiym T199

Lodz, Poland. Museum Archeologiczne i Etnograficzne L67

Loeb, Fritz P12, P13

Loehr, Gabriel M. U20

Logan, Ida-Marie C. J113

Loidl, Franz U35

London. University.
  Institute of Advanced Legal Studies M14, M15

London. University.
Institute of Education. Education Libraries Bulletin SEE Education Libraries Bulletin
Institute of Germanic Studies C123, C124
Institute of Historical Research J5, J44 Bulletin J4, J27
Institute of Latin American Studies C146
School of Librarianship and Archives N32

Longstreet, Wilma G342

Los Angeles. University of Southern California.
Library. Committee on the Arlien Johnson Collection T184
School of Social Work T184 Social Work Papers T182, T183

Louisiana. State University and Agricultural and Mechanical College. Bureau of Educational Materials and Research G111

Louisiana Library Association. Bulletin C52

Louvain.
Convent of Discalced Carmelites D41
Université catholique. Faculté de théologie U28

Low, Jesse B. S146

Lozano Rivera, Uriel N33

Lozinskaya, L. A. E112

Ludwicki, Henryk P139

Lücke, Peter R. J20

Lufer, Margarete G59

Ługowska, Lucyna T120

Lukenbill, Willis B. L21

Lum, William W. D4

Lumbard, Emily C. S136

Lunday, G. Albert T200

Lunquest, C. Howard G238

Lunze, Joachim E10

Luso-Brazilian Review C4, C5

Lvov. Universytet. Naukovi zapysky S32

Lyda, Mary L. G29

Lynch, Shelly T167

Lyons. Université. Faculté mixte de médecine et de pharmacie P97

M

Maatschappij der Nederlandsche Letterkunde, Leiden. Commissie van Geschied- en Oudheidkunde J80

Macauley, William T147

McCann, James A. S137

McClusky, Frederick D. G222

McCoy, Ralph E. T125

McCredie, Andrew D. H62

McGill Journal of Education G155

McGlasson, Maurice A. G380

Index of Names and Titles

Michigan.
  College of Mining and Technology, Houghton. Library E118
  State University, East Lansing. Bureau of Business and Economic Research T58
  University.
    Bureau of Educational Reference and Research G115
    Center for Japanese Studies C91
    Geology Dept. S110
    School of Dentistry. Dental Library P125
    School of Education. Bulletin G116
    School of Natural Resources S33

Michigan History J95

Microfilm Abstracts A17

Micropaleontology S44

Mikhail, E. H. H83

Milan. Istituto Giangiacomo Feltrinelli. Annali T106

Milatz, Alfred J73

Milišić, Đorde T95

Military Affairs J39, J42

Miller, Arthur H. L155

Miller, Ernest I. T153

Millet, Allan R. J42, J43

Minas Geraes, Brazil. Universidade Federal. Faculdade de Odontologia. Biblioteca P122

Mineralogicheskiy sbornik S18

Minkel, Clarence W. S94

Minnesota. University.
  College of Education G120
    Committee on Educational Research G294
  Graduate School. Mayo Foundation for Medical Education and Research P100

Miranda P., Jorge T53

Mirzoyan, G. G. P65

Miscellanea Musicologica; Adelaide Studies in Musicology H62

Misra, Panchanand J48

Missionary Research Library. Occasional Bulletin U53

Missouri. University G201
  College of Education G121

Missouri Historical Review J100

Mitchell, Ronald W. G371

Modern Humanities Research Association C121

Modern Language Association. Publications L11
  Conference on Research Opportunities in Renaissance Drama H85

Modern Language Journal L16, L80

Molstad, John G223

Monatshefte L69-L71, L77

Monroe, Walter S. G1, G2

Music Teachers National Association H64

Musica Disciplina H39

Die Musikforschung H40, H50

Musyka H51, H58

Myers, John H. T33

Myerson, Joel L155

N

N.T.A. (Newfoundland Teachers Association) *Journal* G160

Naaman, Antoine L117, L118, LL1

Nancy. Université P140

Nantes. Université. Bibliothèque P106

Narang, H. L. G164

National Art Education Association. Information Studies Committee G217

National Association for Business Teacher Training Education. *Bulletin* G233, G241

National Association for Research in Science Teaching G360
Committee on Research in Science Teaching G369

National Association of Deans of Women. *Journal* G193

National Association of Directors of Physical Education for College Women. Committee for Research G266

National Association of Marketing Teachers. Committee on Research Projects T35

National Association of Secondary School Principals. *Bulletin* G195, G197, G373, G374, G378

National Business Education Quarterly G234, G236, G244-G246

National Catholic Education Association. *Bulletin* G186

National Conference of Christians and Jews G350

National Council of Educational Research and Training G60, G61

National Council of the Churches of Christ of the United States of America. Bureau of Research and Survey G347

National Council on Religion in Higher Education U11

National Federation for Educational Research in England and Wales G25

National Institute of Economic and Social Research T4

National Library of Nigeria B64

National Psychological Research Council for the Blind P154

National Recreation and Park Association G291

National Rehabilitation Association G249

Index of Names and Titles

<u>Prepodavanie istorii v shkole</u>
G381

Pretorius, D. A. S102

Price, Warren C. F11

Prilutskiy, David N. E120-E122

Princeton Theological Seminary
U31

<u>Problemy osobo opasnykh
infektsiy</u> P119

Procházka, Boris T84, T99

Proehl, Friedrich-Karl B40

<u>The Professional Geographer</u> S70

<u>Progress of Medieval and Renais-
sance Studies in the United
States and Canada Bulletin</u> L7

<u>Provence historique</u> J72

<u>Psychological Abstracts</u> R6

<u>Public Personnel Quarterly</u> T135

<u>Publizistik</u> F4, F24, F30

Puerto Rico. University.
  College of Social Sciences.
    Dept. of Economics T98
  Graduate School of Social Work
    T186
  Institute of Caribbean Studies.
    <u>Caribbean Bibliographic
    Series</u> C151
  School of Public Administra-
    tion T161

Punjab, Pakistan (Province).
  University, Lahore T77
    Dept. of Sociology T199
    Institute of Education and
      Research G139

Purdue University. Engineering
  Experiment Station E86

Purdy, G. Flint N6

Q

Qassim, Nazar M. D44

<u>Quadrivio</u> C140

<u>Quaker History</u> U40

Quandt, Ivan J. G346

<u>Quarterly Review of Historical
Studies</u> (Calcutta) J16

Québec (City). Université
  Laval. Centre de documentation B17, S21

R

<u>R.M.A. Research Chronicle</u> H48

Raat, William D. J79

Radchenko, A. A. T97

Rafaj, Emil E106

Ragatz, Lowell J2

Rahe, Harves G246-G248

Rahn, Douglas J. H67

Rakhlevskiy, Vladislav A. M19,
  T88

Ranchi Agricultural College E34

Rasulov, M. YA. P34, P35

Raus, Lidia B71

Rauschning, Dietrich M39

Raveneau, Jean S92

Index of Names and Titles

Revue de l'Université d'Ottawa
L115, U30

Revue de littérature comparée
L61, L62

Revue des études italiennes C139

Revue des études latines L56

Revue des sciences philosophique
et théologique B33

Revue du droit public et de la
science politique en France
et à l'étranger T142

Revue du nord J71

Revue française de science
politique T145

Revue française de sociologie
T11

Revue historique J6

Revue historique du droit
français et étranger M18,
M23, M31

Revue politique et parliamentaire, économique, financière
T93

Reykjavík. Landsbókas-afnith.
Árbók C136

Rhode Island College, Providence
G140, G141

Ricker, Karl L., firm, bookseller, St. Petersburg P11

Ringius, C. E88

Robertson, James I., Jr. J40

Robinson, Anthony M. B74

Rocznik Toruński S48

Rodgers, Margaret D. J81

Rodrigues Guimarães, Pedro P66

Rodriguez, Carmen F. Q. Vda.
T185

Rodiquíz, Amelia E20

Röhrich, Lutz L64

Roepka, Kurt D16

Rogers, M. H. C33

Rohloff, Hans-Joachim G65

Rohracher, H. R7

Rojek, Hans J. H79

Rolfe, W. D. Ian S105

Romanic Review L60, L99–L102

Romantisches Jahrbuch L104,
L105

Rombach, M. A. C118

Rome (City). Pontificia Università gregoriana SEE
Pontificia Università
gregoriana, Rome

Rosen, Ned T125

Rosenberg, Ralph P. L60

Rosval, Sergei J. D27

Roueche, John E. G304

Rousset, Jean P96

Roxas, Aurora R. T25

Royal College of Surgeons of
London. Library P10

Royal Geographical Society. New Geographical Literature and Maps S79

Royal Institute of Public Administration T154

Rubin, Selma F. C142

Ruiz-Fornells, Enrique L126

Ruka, Mary L. C62

Runden, Charity E. G221

Rural Sociology T209

Russell, H. K. L82

Russia (1923- U.S.S.R.)
Upravlenie prepodavaniya obshchestvennykh nauk J82
Ministerstvo putey soobshcheniya. TSentral'naya nauchno-tekhnicheskaya biblioteka E141

Russkiy fol'klor L66

Rut, N. A. G406

The Rutherford B. Hayes-Lucy Webb Hayes Foundation, Fremont, Ohio C45

Rutz, Walter M32

Ruys, D. C118

S

Sabine, Julia C54

Sackett, Everett B. G194

Sackett, S. J. L20

Sadilova, N. M. P29

Safety Education G354

St. John College, Cleveland, Ohio G142

Salamanca. Universidad. Facultad de Filosofía y Letras. Catedra Miguel de Unamuno. Cuadernos de la Catedra Miguel de Unamuno L163

Salgado, Cristobal T26

Samlaren L19

San Salvador. Universidad Nacional. Biblioteca Central B72

Sanchez, George I. G168

Sander, Willy E123

Sandoval Guerrero, Margarita E15

Santo Domingo. Universidad. Anales B25, P144

São Paulo, Brazil (City). Universidade.
Escola Superior de Agricultura "Luiz Quieroz," Piracicaba E35
Faculdade de Odontologia. Seccão de Documentacão Odontologia P128

Sapin, M. R. P46

Sappington, Roger E. U37

Saratovskiy meditsinskiy institut P112

SarDesai, Bhanu D. C90

SarDesai, D. R. C90

Saskatchewan Bulletin G162

Sassouni, Viken P121

Index of Names and Titles

Index of Names and Titles

Strasbourg médical P114

Stratman, Carl J. H75, H84, H87, H94

Strong, Merle E. G403, G404

Strunk, William O. H35

Stuart, Merrill M. S86

Stucki, Curtis W. C79

Studia germanica gandensia L76

Studies in Burke and His Times T149

Studies in Music (Australia) H61

Studies in Philology L31

Studies in Philosophy and Education G53

Stumper, Robert S24

Stutsman, Ellen B106

Stuttgart. Technische Hochschule E89

Sudebno-meditsinskaya ekspertiza P50

Suë, P. P107

Sukhwal, B. L. S87

Summers, Edward G. G332-G335, G340-G342, G358, G363, G366, G370, G371

Summers, Robert E. F32

Suprun, M. N. P94

Sushkevich, A. K. S127

Suydam, Marilyn N. G367

Suzuki, Peter T. C161

Sveikatos apsauga P31

Svensk tandläkare tidskrift P123

Svensk tidskrift för musikforskning H46

Svenskt musikhistoriskt archiv. Bulletin H68

Swanson, Charles E. F22, F23

Swedish Journal of Economics T59

Swift, Catherine G. B63

Swift, Fletcher H. G75

Swindler, William F. F10

Symposium on the Languages and Literatures of Spanish America and Brazil, University of Texas, 1956. Proceedings L122

Syracuse University C76

T

Tagorov, R. SH. J87

Tarasova, L. A. E112

Tarbox, George E. S121

Tartu. Ülikool B95
  Teaduslik Raamatukogu P115

Tashjian, Nouvart G126

Tashkend.
  Institut inzhenerov zheleznodorozhnogo transporta Sbornik trudov G365
  Universitet. Fundamental'naya biblioteka B99

Index of Names and Titles

Vierteljahrshefte für Zeitgeschichte C129

Vietti, Edward G245

Viewpoints G346

Virginia. Dept. of Education
G39

Virginia Magazine of History and
Biography J114

Viridarskii, M. S. B99

Vishnyakov, I. M. G51

Vochele, Jaroslav C74

Vogelsang, Thilo J73

Volkov, S. S. L95

Voprosy filosofii Q3

Voprosy geografii C114, S77

Voprosy istorii J9, J10

Voprosy istorii estestvoznaniya
i tekhniki S22

Voprosy nachertatel'noi geometrii
i. inzh. grafiki G365

Voprosy onkologii P33

Voprosy virusologii P43

Vrachebnoe delo P28

W

Wageningen. Landbouwhogeschool
SEE Landbouwhogeschool,
Wageningen

Wagner-Rieger, Renate H15

Wahlberg, Carl G. B81

Waitová, Miloslava F37, G279

Walk, George E. G136

Walker, George H., Jr. D34,
D35

Walsh, Edward J. Q7

Walters, John E129

Walther, Christoph F. B6

Walther, Karl E61

Ward, Clarence E95, E96

Ward, Dederick C. S99-S101

Warsaw.
Spółdzielczy Instytut Badawczy. Ośrodek Dokumentacji
Naukowej T118-T120
Szkola Główna Gospodarstwa
Wiejskiego E40
Wyższa Szkoła Handlowa.
Rocznik T62

Washington, Alethea G178

Washington (State).
Dept. of Commerce and Economic
Development. Business and
Economic Research Division
T60
State University, Pullman.
Dept. of Education.
Research Studies G147

Washington University, St. Louis.
George Warren Brown School of
Social Work T189

Wathelet-Willem, Jeanne L97

Wattel, Pierre C12

Wawryznek, Utta Q5

Weaver, J. Fred G367

578

Index of Names and Titles

Wohlrab-Weinzette, Hertha J64

Wood, W. Donald T61

Woodress, James L40

Woodward, Frances J67

Wool Bureau, Inc., New York E53

Worthington, Richard A. G323

Woźniewski, Zbigniew P56

Wright, George N. T190

Wright, Grace S. G41

Wrzosek, Wojciech T120

Wu, Eugene C94

Wundt, Wilhelm R1

Wydallis, Elizabeth A. S47

Wylie, Enid B2

Wylie, Margery B. C53

Wyman, Roger E. C63

Y

YIVO Annual of Jewish Social Science D19

YAkobson, M. B96

Yale Economic Essays T87

Yale University.
  Graduate School S52
  School of Forestry E140

Yang, Ki P. D45

YAsemtsik, F. C. E50

Yearbook of Anthropology T47

Yearbook of School Law G198

Year's Work in Modern Language Studies L84

Yeshiva University. Bernard Revel Graduate School L78

Yoder, Don D22

Yoder, Ray A. E124, E125

Yost, Charles P. G356

Yüan, T'ung-Li D37, D39, D40

Z

Zalai, Károly P145, P146

Zamkova, Zinaida N. P103

Zamyatin, V. P. P93

Zavala Cordero, Jaime M27

Zdravookhranenie Kazakhstana P89

Zeitschrift für Anglistik und Amerikanistik C40-C43, C47

Zeitschrift für das gesamte Genossenschaftswesen T114-T116

Zeitschrift für die Geschichte der Juden in Deutschland D16

Zeitschrift für Pädagogik (Berlin) G46

Zeitschrift für Slawistik J84, L130

Zeitschrift für Tuberkulose P22

Zeitschrift für Völkerrecht M36, M37

Zeitungswissenschaft F15-F18

Subject Index

A

Accounting T27-T34

Acting SEE Theatre

Administration SEE Management

Administrative law SEE Law, Administrative

Advertising and marketing T35-T43

Aeronautics E144

Africa C6, C12-C38
 Central C12
 East C33, C34
 Economic conditions C20
 Education G69, G148, G149
 Geology S102
 History J44
 Literature L22
 Social sciences C20
 West C36

Aged P152

Agriculture E1-E60, S43
 Economic aspects E6, E7, E10, E41-E44
 Engineering E32, E45-E51
 History E51
 Study and teaching G213-G216, G395
 Tropics E24, E54

Alaska C59

Alberta - Education G156

Algeria (In) B1

American Indians SEE Indians of North America

American literature SEE U.S. - Literature

Anatomy P11, P17, P46, P118, S1

Anglo-American literature L23-L50

Anglo-American studies C39-C64

Anglo-Saxon language L26, L49

Anglo-Saxon literature L12, L26, L49

Animal husbandry E13, E15, E52-E55

Anthropology D2, T22, T44-T55

Antibiotics P45, P54

Arab countries SEE Middle East

Arabs as authors D30

Child development SEE Family
relations - Child development

Child psychology SEE Psychology, Child

Child study K16, R9, R10

Child welfare T172

Childbirth P4

Children
Care and hygiene P27
Growth R9

Children's literature L21

Chile (In) B18, B19

Chile
Geography S95
Literature L123

China C94-C96
Education C93
History J47
Social conditions C93

Chinese as authors D36-D40

Chinese in America C94

Chinese in Canada D11

Christian literature, Early
L59

Church U16
Education G183, G184
History U13
Music H57

Church and education SEE
Education, Religious

Church and state U49, U50

Church of the Brethren U37

City planning SEE Planning

Civil engineering E72, E81,
S98

Classical antiquities J1, L52-
L54, L56-L59

Classical languages SEE Greek
language, Latin language

Classical literature L56-L59

Classical studies L51-L59

Clemens, Samuel L. L148

Clergy U16

Clothing SEE Textiles and
clothing

Collective settlements T117

College students G252-G254

Colleges and universities -
Faculty G203, G299

Colombia C157

Commerce SEE Business

Communes SEE Collective
settlements

Communication E142, F1-F3,
F12, F26, K11

Communication and mass media
F1-F36, G221

Communism T106, T107
Russia B88, J82, J83

Community life T184

Comparative literature SEE
Literature, Comparative

Religion G352, R15, T191, T192,
  Sociology of U54

Religious education SEE Education, Religious

Renaissance - Literature SEE
  Literature, Renaissance

Retail trade T39, T43

Rice E57

Roman law SEE Law, Roman

Romance languages and literature
  G319, L93, L99-L128

Romania (In) B71, D46

Romanians as authors D46

Roosevelt, Franklin D. J89

Ruanda-Urundi C12

Rural life SEE Farm life

Rural sociology SEE Sociology,
  Rural

Russia SEE U.S.S.R.

Russian literature SEE
  U.S.S.R. - Literature

Russians in Canada D27

S

Saar C130

Safety education SEE Education,
  Safety

St. Louis J101

Sales management T38

El Salvador (In) B72

Sanitary engineering E81

Saskatchewan - Education G162

Scandinavia C123

Scandinavian languages L12

School assembly programs SEE
  Education - School assembly
  programs

Schools, Rural SEE Education,
  Rural

Science A20, A21, A23, B5,
  E65, S1-S148
  History S22, S23
  Study and teaching G357-
    G359

Science and mathematics -
  Study and teaching G357-G371

Scotland - Geology S105

Secretarial education SEE
  Education, Secretarial

Sex T202

Shakespeare, William L156,
  L157

Shaw, George Bernard L158

Shorthand G248

Singapore (In) B73

Skin - Diseases P40, P41

Slavic and East European languages and literature
  L129-L134

Slavic and U.S.S.R. History
  J82-J88

Social movements T196

V

Vega Carpio, Lope Felix de L164

Venereal diseases P40, P41, P83

Veterans - Education G214

Veterinary medicine E15, E17, E31, E32, P9, P22, P97, P108, P147-P151

Vienna J64

Virginia J114

Vocabulary studies G392-G394

W

Wales C67

Washington (State) - Geology S118

Water S98

Water resources S134-S137

The West SEE U.S. - The West

West Indies SEE Caribbean

Westphalia C131-C133

Wildlife - Conservation S139, S140, S144-S147

Wind instruments H44

Wine and winemaking T51

Wisconsin C62-C64

Women - Education G193

Women as authors D47, D49, G192, G349, G362, L16, L27, S15

Wool E53

Wordsworth, William L165

World War, 1939-1945 J89

Worms S46

Wyoming - Geology S118

Y

Yorkshire, England C68

Yugoslavia (In) B109-B111

Z

Zionism C160

Zoology E55, S13, S46, S138-S148